THAT NOBLE
MAGNIFICENT JOURNEY

From Palmyra to the Great Salt Lake

Shell B. Abegglen

authorHOUSE®

AuthorHouse™
1663 Liberty Drive
Bloomington, IN 47403
www.authorhouse.com
Phone: 833-262-8899

Published by AuthorHouse 08/29/2022

ISBN: 978-1-6655-6969-9 (sc)
ISBN: 978-1-6655-6968-2 (e)

Print information available on the last page.

Any people depicted in stock imagery provided by Getty Images are models, and such images are being used for illustrative purposes only.
Certain stock imagery © Getty Images.

Scripture quotations marked KJV are from the Holy Bible, King James Version (Authorized Version). First published in 1611. Quoted from the KJV Classic Reference Bible, Copyright © 1983 by The Zondervan Corporation.

This book is printed on acid-free paper.

Because of the dynamic nature of the Internet, any web addresses or links contained in this book may have changed since publication and may no longer be valid. The views expressed in this work are solely those of the author and do not necessarily reflect the views of the publisher, and the publisher hereby disclaims any responsibility for them.

Contents

Author's Note

The story of Joseph Smith is a most remarkable story, and to SEVENTEEN MILLION PEOPLE, it is one of the most important stories since the birth, life, and the atonement of Jesus Christ. The boy Joseph's first vision and the establishment of the new church that would become "The Church Of Jesus Christ of Latter Day Saints" is a sacred event for millions of Church members scattered around the entire world. The early history of the Church of Jesus Christ of Latter Day Saints and the life of Joseph Smith are inextricably intertwined in a fateful and historic series of events. This is a fascinating story of visions, angels, gold bibles, exotic ancient records, forgotten civilizations, merciless discrimination, sham trials, and the unjustified persecution and oppression of a religiously devout and innocent people.

Joseph Smith and his faithful followers were persecuted for 16 years, unremittingly from 1830 to 1846, and were compelled to leave one beautifully settled community after another as they were violently forced into leaving behind their well-kept homes and their valuable property without any compensation whatsoever. They were hounded, persecuted, and driven out of upper state New York, Kirtland Ohio, Western Missouri, and Nauvoo Illinois, and then finally, virtually out of the Union itself. These unjustifiable expulsions were brought about through the many concerted efforts of callous and very violent vigilantes, intolerant self-righteous religious hypocrites, anti-Mormon news papers, misinformed and biased politicians, merciless state militias, and marauding mobs who used threats, vandalism, beatings, rape, arson, and sometimes, even cold-blooded murder to drive the Mormons from their own homes.

At no time was there ever any kind of recompenses for their property losses, or the many injustices, and the persecutions that had been perpetrated upon a just and honorable people. Ironically enough, in America where the "Bill of Rights" was inspired and written to protect the basic principles of freedom of speech and religion for all its citizens, the Mormons have been the only American citizens in the history of the United States that have ever had an "extermination order" executed against them by an elected state government official specifically because of their religious faith. For whatever reason, it took another 138 years for the authorities in Missouri to officially recognize the justice in rescinding the infamous "extermination order," which was finally withdrawn in 1976.

In this free nation, which was originally sought out by the pilgrims for the very purpose of having a "Free Land" where the right to "Religious Freedom" was a priority, it seems like a significant lax in justice for any group of individuals to deliberately persecute any other group of American citizens solely because of their religious faith. It is simply contradictory to the basic dream and principle of living in America where all its citizens can enjoy freedom of speech and religion. The faithful members of The Church Of Jesus Christ of Latter Day Saints who have never had any desires other than to live their religion and raise their families in peace, and who have never had any kind of inclination or desire to mistreat anyone else, have found this historical unjustified persecution and blind unfounded prejudice an unexplained mystery.

*   *   *

Chapter One

———✦～◦℮ᴛᴏᴏᴛ℮◦～✦———

THE IMPETUS

* * *

One thousand eight hundred and twenty years after Christ had walked the streets of Palestine, a young farm boy in America's upper state New York walked into the woods near his home to pray. Having been inspired by some provocative words from his mother's Bible, he was prompted to make supplication to the divine being when he read in James 1:5 that "If any of you lack wisdom, let him ask of God." So he did just that, and when he came out of those woods, his life and world would forever be profoundly changed. And so would the future lives of more than 17,000,000 people around the world after hearing the Joseph Smith story, and being inspired by what Joseph had heard and seen in that sacred grove as it was introduced to him by God in those idyllic woods of New York State. This then was the very beginning of the restoration of "The Church of Jesus Christ of Latter Day Saints."

During the growing up years of Joseph Smith in the early 1800's, there was a very energetic religious revival making its way throughout New England, particularly in upper state New York. The area was so inundated with religious revivals that it was dubbed the "burnt-over" district. Joseph himself described the overly zealous religious debates as being a "tumult of opinions." The heated arguments were everywhere as each religion attempted to disprove the tenets of one religion while extolling the virtues of their own.

In Joseph's own family, four of them had joined with the Presbyterians, while the rest of the family including Joseph had not made up their minds. In his thinking, the answer to the far-reaching question of what church to join was much too important to leave it up to any heated debates or dispirited arguing, and so that's when Joseph decided to make that fated walk into the woods to find out for himself just which church among them all was the true church of Christ.

And so it was right there in that quite serene grove of trees as he knelt in humble prayer that he was suddenly without warning completely seized upon by an overpowering dark force, which rendered him without physical strength and left him unable to speak. Just when he thought he would surely succumb to an inevitable death by some suffocating and fiendish dark evil force, he desperately pleaded with God to save him from what seemed to be certain destruction.

Almost immediately, there was a wondrous and mitigating relief from the hold of this dark power as a pillar of light manifested itself over his head and two personages so bright and glorious that their description defied all words appeared before him. One of them spoke saying, "This is My Beloved Son. Hear Him."

When Joseph was finally able to compose himself, he asked the question that had brought him to the woods in the first place, which was which church should he join? To his surprise, the voice of the one that had been called "The Son" said that he should join none of them; because "They draw near to Me with their lips, but their hearts are far from Me." Along with this surprising answer and among other things related to the boy, the personage added that "all the creeds were an abomination" and their proponents are corrupt in their beliefs. The personage also declared; "They teach for doctrines the commandments of men, having a form of Godliness, but in reality they deny the power thereof." Joseph was simply amazed by this declaration and later wrote; "for at this time it had never entered into my heart that all were wrong." - 1a

After this surprising revelation, the divine being who was called "The

Son" once again commanded Joseph to join none of the churches. Then without the aid of any melodious trumpets or the accompaniment of heavenly angels making their celestial announcements, the two divine beings, "The Son" and "The Father" disappeared in an exceedingly bright light up through a conduit into the heavens.

This holy and extraordinary appearance as it was presented before the eyes of Joseph Smith that morning had unveiled to him two divine and completely separate heavenly beings. This would be an entirely new concept for the majority of Christian Church goers; a whole new perception for them to absorb; that is that God and His Son really were two separate individuals. For the bigger part of Christian world, this divine disclosure would be an entirely new understanding as it pertains to the nature of the Godhead.

There is no uncertainty about the fact that the young boy Joseph was more than just astonished by the appearance of the duel beings, and he was completely overwhelmed by the celestial exquisiteness of their glory as they revealed themselves enveloped in that brilliant supernal light. He was even further amazed by the fact that they actually spoke to him. "The Lord opened the heavens upon me and I saw the Lord and he spake unto me saying Joseph my son thy sins are forgiven thee. And my soul was filled with love and for many days I could rejoice with great joy and the Lord was with me." – 1b

To top it all off, he was awestruck by the reality that they had left him with nothing less than an extraordinary and most important message, which was not only a truly unexpected revelation to him, but most certainly would be to the rest of the Christian world. This mind-blowing, revelatory experience at the time left the young boy Joseph weak, flat on his back, and unable to move as he was completely sapped of his strength.

When he had recovered his vitality and energy, he returned home to a worried mother who asked him what was wrong? He replied that he was well, but he had learned for himself that "Presbyterianism is not true." His mother and father believed and supported him fully from the first. Even though his own family fully trusted his word and knew he wouldn't lie about such a thing, it was certainly not so with the vast majority of the rest of the community who were not only cynical, but treated him with an air of haughty disdain. This then would be the beginning of a life of much opposition, great turmoil, and relentless persecution. Never the less, on the positive side, his life would otherwise be highlighted with many exalting and unprecedented glorious events, which included more than one holy manifestation of heavenly beings accompanied by many divine revelations.

The seesaw of "miracles and malice" in the events of Joseph Smith's life would all be experienced in a comparatively quick succession of dramatic occurrences as they took place in the short life span of the Prophet. Never the less, he had been favored as the one and the only "pure young man chosen by the Lord to restore His true Church." It would certainly be difficult for anyone to think of a greater call that has been bestowed upon any man since the Father sent His own Son down to retrieve the World.

Joseph's vision in the woods was more than extraordinary by anyone's standards, but to a fourteen-year-old boy it was nearly incomprehensible. He felt compelled to relate what he had seen and heard to the members of his own family, but he mistakenly thought that surely the local Methodist preacher would be very excited and most interested in hearing about such a remarkable event. However, in a very disappointing response, the preacher dismissed the boy's wondrous and remarkable experience saying that "It was all of the Devil, that there were no such things as visions in these days; that all such things had ceased with the apostles, and there would never be any more of them." - 1c

The young Joseph was quite disappointed in the preacher's reaction to his amazing experience. Yet he knew what he had seen. He knew the Gods in the Woods had really spoken to him. And he knew they had commanded him to not join any church on the earth at the time, for all these churches had been corrupted before the Lord.

The dismissive preacher was not the only one to shrug off the boy's vision as mere fantasy, nor who would come to manifest expressions and attitudes of malice towards young Joseph when they heard of his celestial experience. As the story made its way around the community, the local preachers unjustly incited bitter persecution among their own followers towards the young boy. Joseph was totally dumfounded that he could be the subject of so much controversy. How could a fourteen-year-old farm boy draw so much attention, and even more shockingly, cause such bitter resentment and hostility from the most prominent religious leaders in his community? He really thought that they would have and should have been more excited than anyone to learn more about this marvelous unprecedented spiritual event. The remarkable story of Joseph Smith's miracle and his vision would come to spawn a great deal of ill will and persecution towards him and his supporters the rest of his mortal life.

During his growing up years, Joseph had acquired an overall comparative standard of formal education approximately equal to a fifth grade level, but he had no other formal education. Joseph wrote in 1832, "we were deprived of the bennifit of an education suffice it to say I was mearly instructid in reading writing and the ground rules of Arithmatic which constuted my whole literary acquirements." – 2

His opportunity for education had been somewhat limited by the necessity to help his father on the farm, which called for a sacrifice of his formal education, and so instead of bookwork, he most often spent considerable time working on his father's newly acquired property outside of Palmyra near the village of Manchester in upper state New York. Palmyra was situated along the banks of the Erie Canal, which had been under an ambitious construction project until its opening in 1825. The area had provided much needed work for the locals during the hard times and was bustling with activity. Thus Palmyra with its lively docks and trading center was the busiest little town with any significant commerce in the entire area. - 3

The Smith family had moved from Sharon Vermont, the place where Joseph had been born in 1805, to the flourishing Palmyra area when he was ten years old. And so it was that Joseph knew hardly anything about the world outside of those family farms in Vermont and Palmyra at this juncture of his life. The facts surrounding his meager education and his very limited exposure to the world outside of those farming communities is a thing of substantial importance as it is extraordinarily relevant to the mystery of his unbelievable accomplishments. For what he was about to bring forth to the world would not only require a brilliant mind with extraordinary literary skills, but a high degree of knowledge of obscure facts surrounding exotic cultures, unconventional languages, and far-off civilizations; knowledge that was simply not known to ordinary men in America at that time, not even to college professors. So just how does an unlearned farm boy acquire such a great volume of exotic knowledge and then put it all together into a comprehensive written work of more than

500 pages in a period of less than sixty working days, all the while being subjected to relentless duress from his persecutors? Just how is that possible?

It would take no less than true divine intervention, intervention that came by way of a magnificent angelic being sent from God Himself. It was this angel who would place in the hands of the boy Joseph a "sacred book written on Gold Plates." These sacred Gold Plates had been buried under the earth for over fourteen hundred years. They contained the words of a number of ancient authors who had engraved their history and their wisdom on to thin leaves of gold and inscribed into metal books during those ancient times of their own antiquated civilizations. These entirely civilized cultures had originally come from the Middle East and then had risen up their cities on the American Continents. Their writings would cover a time period of most of a millennium that extended from 600 B.C. to 400 A.D.

And so one must ask; just how was it possible that this marvelous, mysterious, authenticated, and very significant book of ancient religious writings could possibly become known to some obscure farm boy in the state of New York in America in the 1800's? And then after many centuries of being buried in the dust, how did it all come about that these ancient records would be placed in the hands of a seemingly average and ordinary young man during what was considered at that time, to be the modern world of the nineteenth century? How was it all possible? - 4

*   *   *

1a. See JS—H 1:10, 18; Jessee, pp. 198, 200.

1b. See Papers of Joseph Smith 1:6-7).

1c. See "JOSEPH SMITH-HISTORY" History of the Church Vol. 1 Chapters 1-5

2. See Encyclopedia of Mormonism – Vol. 3 Joseph Smith

3. See Economic History of the United States by Fite and Reese – p. 165

4. See JOSEPH SMITH AND THE BOOK OF MORMON, Encyclopedia Mormonism, Vol. 1

*   *   *

Chapter Two

THREE YEARS LATER

*   *   *

The mistreatment and persecution of the young boy Joseph Smith continued for reasons that he didn't completely understand. He thought of himself as not really being any different from any of the other boys in the community. Therefore given his jovial nature and his desire to fit in with his friends, he frequently "displayed the weakness of youth," and what he came to perceive as being the shortcomings of human nature. Later he bemoaned the fact that this desire to be one of the boys among his group of friends had led him "into divers temptations, offensive in the sight of God." He then qualified this admission of guilt by saying that; "In making this confession, no one need suppose me guilty of any great or malignant sins. A disposition to commit such was never in my nature."

Though he had not committed any great sins, his carefree teenage behavior was bothering his conscience. Never the less, even though his sins were considerably less than loathsome, Joseph did have some misgivings about his own levity and his dubious associations with the local "jovial" crowd and this led him to feel a certain amount of guilt in not having the proper behavior for one that had been called of God as he had been. - 1

Some three years later after Joseph had experienced that marvelous and unprecedented appearance of the dual Divine Beings of the Godhead in the sacred grove, he was given the privilege of having another and most remarkable vision at the age of seventeen. On the evening of the 21st of September 1823, after saying his bedtime prayers and asking sincerely for forgiveness for his sins, he prayerfully requested some kind of a sign from the Lord that he might know his current standing with God.

It was at this time that he would experience another divine manifestation in the form of a resurrected celestial being appearing before him. This heavenly being revealed himself to the young boy unannounced and certainly most unexpectedly. Thus it was that the "Angel Moroni" appeared to him in his very own bedroom while he was in the very act of calling upon God in sincere prayer that night. In a hallowed display of unexpected divine communication there came into his room a bright light, a light that continued to increase in its brightness until the room seemed to him brighter than at noonday. So it was that with little warning, the divine being appeared at his bedside; an angel standing in the air no less, for his feet did not touch the floor. The divine being wore a loose robe of exquisite and intense whiteness, and Joseph commented that he didn't think that anything earthly could be made to look so "exceedingly white and brilliant." The personage seemed to have had no other clothing on other than the loose robe, and so it appeared as though even his very countenance was glorious and bright with a light of all its own. Naturally Joseph felt a certain amount of trepidation and was understandably uneasy at first, but he soon realized that this particular being was not appearing before him to cause him harm, but to bring him a specific message.

The divine personage called the boy by his name, Joseph, and then said that his own name was Moroni, and that he had been sent from "the presence of God" to convey a divine message. He told the boy that God had a work for him to do and because of this work Joseph's name would be known "for good and evil among all nations, kindreds, and tongues" and among all people.

The angel then revealed to Joseph that there was a book deposited in a nearby hill, which was written upon "gold plates," and this historic record not only contained an account and history of the ancient inhabitants of this continent, but a "fullness of the Everlasting Gospel." He further elaborated saying that these "gold plates" of antiquity were accompanied by "two stones in silver bows, and these stones, fastened to a breastplate, constituted what is called the Urim and Thummim." These items had been deposited anciently along with the plates made of gold and then buried by Moroni himself many centuries ago. Joseph was then shown a vision of the exact place where the plates were deposited in a nearby hill in a vision so clear that he was able to easily recognize the very place when he later would see it.

It is a most interesting thing to note, that this same type of "seer's" apparatus described here by Joseph Smith called the Urim and Thummim; the term meaning "Lights and Perfections," is also mentioned prominently in conjunction with Old Testament scripture. One can find mention of this same unusual apparatus in four of the five books of Moses, namely Exodus, Leviticus, Numbers, and Deuteronomy. Found in these sacred books of the Jewish Torah, as well as being mentioned in the Holy Bible, these "seers stones and the breast plate" seemed to have been used exclusively by Aaron and Levi in the tabernacle of the congregation. These same seer stones are also referred to as well in 1st Samuel 28:6, the 2nd chapter of Ezra verse 63, and Nehemiah, chapter 7:65. The possession and use of these sacred stones by the prophets comprised the "seers" of ancient times. God himself had now prepared these very same sacred implements of translation for the express purpose of enabling Joseph Smith to translate this ancient record. This historical record on gold Plates had been written long ago by a number of ancient prophets as they had recorded and engraved their sacred writings on gold leaves for future generations and their own posterity. - 2

As Moroni continued with his message to the young Joseph, the angel proceeded to quote certain relevant scriptures from the Old Testament, which included quotes from Malachi, Isaiah, and Joel. As soon as the divine being had delivered his amazing and very significant message, he left the room. Joseph described his dramatic exit as such, "a conduit opened right up into heaven, and he ascended till he entirely disappeared," leaving the room dark as before.

As Joseph lay there in his bed trying to get his mind around all that had just happened, he was most surprised to see the very same heavenly messenger shortly reappear at his bedside once again, and repeat the very same message without variation from the previous visit. The Angel Moroni then added that great judgments were coming upon the earth, which would include "great desolations by famine, sword, and pestilence." After making this grave warning, the divine being once again disappeared into the heavens leaving Joseph in the dark overwhelmed by all that he had heard and seen.

While he was trying to process and comprehend all that he had just witnessed, much to Joseph's surprise, the very same angel appeared for the third time and repeated everything that he had previously said, but this time the grave warnings were to Joseph himself who was still dazed from what he had heard. Moroni warned him that every conceivable ploy would be used to take the "Gold Plates' from his possession. However, the angel strongly emphasized that Joseph must not allow this to ever happen. He also strongly advised Joseph to be especially guarded against the weaknesses of his own frailties of human nature, such as selfishness, greed, and the desire that he might become famous. He was counseled to be very diligent in avoiding these temptations and any desires that might entice him to sell the plates of gold for his own gain. Finally, the Angel sternly admonished Joseph that he must have no other motive in obtaining the plates other than to glorify God and to build God's Kingdom; otherwise he would never be allowed to possess the "Gold Plates."

After this divine personage had disappeared for the third time, Joseph felt totally drained of his energy and was quite surprised when he heard the cock crow and realized his encounter with the divine being had taken the entire night. In spite of his great fatigue, he knew he must arise and start the workday with his father. Although he was totally exhausted, he attempted to do his work as usual, but his father perceived very quickly that something was wrong with his son and so told him to go to the house and rest. As he was attempting to cross the wooden fence out of the field, he collapsed and became unconscious right up until the moment he was awakened by the voice of the very same angel that had kept him up all night. Once again, the angelic messenger called Joseph by name and related for the fourth time everything that he had said the evening before. He then instructed young Joseph to go to his father in the field and tell him of the whole of these events.

Joseph Smith Senior was a man of faith and with some sensitivity to spiritual things, and therefore totally believed his son. He then declared to his son Joseph that what he had experienced was of God and so Joseph should now obey the divine messenger's commands and that he should proceed as he had been instructed to do by the angel to go to the place where the plates were hidden. And thus Joseph did obey his father and did follow the angel's instructions and proceeded to the designated hill.

In the Palmyra area and close to the nearby village of Manchester, there was a very long and high tear dropped shaped hill. Geologists call this type of a hill a drumlin. It was of considerable size and had been created during the Ice Age by a prehistoric ancient glacier. This particular hill was where the "gold plates" had previously been hidden by an ancient prophet. The locals knew it as "Pliney Sexton's Hill" and Joseph immediately recognized it from his earlier vision. He soon found the exact spot where he discovered that at the top of the hill there was a large flat stone, which seemed to be covering and protecting some kind of a stone box. After obtaining some type of a lever, and then removing the dirt from around the edges of the flat stone, Joseph was soon able to lift up the heavy flat rock at which time he discovered to his amazement inside the bigger stone box, two smaller long stones laying crosswise inside the box. The stones were holding up the precious gold plates, the breastplate, and the Urim and Thummim, all placed neatly in the stone box just as the angel had previously described them. As Joseph attempted to take the plates out of the anciently crafted stone box in which they lay, the Angel Moroni appeared before him and said rather firmly, that the time had not yet arrived for him to take possession of them. Instead, Joseph was instructed to return to this very spot each year at the same time and same place to receive divine direction and instruction.

And so Joseph obeyed the Angel Moroni and did just that returning each year to receive additional sacred instruction, and in the process, he acquired a great deal of knowledge from this unusual heavenly messenger and divine teacher. As the four years came and went by somewhat quickly, the Angel Moroni instructed the prophet Joseph Smith on many different occasions right through the succeeding next four years. "The messenger did not limit his instruction solely to these annual meetings, but made contact with Joseph on numerous occasions (Peterson, pp. 119-20). "In all, the angel Moroni visited Joseph Smith at least twenty times," to teach and instruct him. – 3

Meanwhile Joseph looked forward with much anticipation to the time when he would finally be able to receive the plates and take them into his own possession. During the intervening period, he was preoccupied by the considerable labor that needed be done on his father's farm in that never-ending endeavor to provide a living for the Smith family and provide for their basic livelihood. Yet as Joseph worked on the farm, he often dreamt of the day when he would get the plates.

As an interesting side note, it should be pointed out that although the vast majority of LDS people call the hill where Joseph retrieved the plates in New York, "the Hill Cumorah," Joseph himself never used that particular name for the hill where he received the gold plates. The first known use was by Oliver Cowdery in 1830 when he referred to the plate's location as being at "Cumorah," while he was preaching to the Delaware Indians. By 1835 the term "Cumorah," as used to designate the name of the hill where the plates were uncovered, seems to have been in common use among most of the Church's members.

Joseph Smith himself only used the name "Cumorah" once in his writings, and it was twelve years after the Book of Mormon was published and the Doctrine & Covenants was given to the Church members. The statement is found in D&C 128:20, which says, "And again what do we hear? Glad tidings from Cumorah! Moroni an angel from heaven, declaring the fulfillment of the prophets…"

In attempting to analyze this particularly provocative phrase, one is tempted to ask, just, which Cumorah was Joseph referring to? Was he speaking of the local hill in nearby Palmyra New York or was he referring to the legendary Hill Cumorah in the Book of Mormon, or are they both in reality the same hill?

In spite of these very puzzling questions, it seems significant that Joseph never did correct any of his associates for using the term "Cumorah" in referring to the hill near Manchester where the plates were unearthed. Possibly because he thought it was as an appropriate name as any for this historical and most important hill in the Manchester New York area.

Many Book of Mormon scholars have analyzed the details described in the description of the "Hill Cumorah" in the Book of Mormon and have come up with a dozen different characteristics and geographical conditions that the New York "Hill Cumorah" should have if it were the exact same hill as described in Book of Mormon. However, the hill in New York meets very few of those requirements, such as being "near the first landing site of the people of Mulek (Alma 22:30), which was just north of the land Bountiful and a narrow neck of land (Alma 22:32) between the east sea and a west sea." It should also have an extensive west coast compared to its east coast, should be in an area with many fountains and abundant rivers, and it should have an implied thick jungle like wildernesses in a climate without snow. There is also a noticeable lack of an abundance of weapon artifacts in the New York area, especially that of the type of artifacts that would have indicated that this was the place where tens of thousands of warriors had died at this massive battle site in the last great war of the Book of Mormon. In addition to that, there is also significant lack of evidence that would indicate that this is the place where there had been numerous past volcanic eruptions with many violent upheavals in the area as was described in the details of chapter 8 of 3rd Nephi.

Yet in this intriguing debate, there are also many who are just as adamant in their arguments that insist the Book of Mormon's Hill Cumorah was and is in New York in the northeastern section of North America. As proof, they cite a great deal of archeological evidence found among the very prolific constructions of the "Mound Builders" that are scattered all over a number of the eastern states. There are scientifically dated artifacts here that have been found in many of these prehistoric and mysterious mounds that appear to be authentic in their cultural styling and have been dated as being in the right time period. They just simply can't be explained away by saying they are fake evidence planted by fraudulent historians and fake hoax perpetrators.

There is one particular artifact that arouses much wonder and inquisitiveness, even defying an ordinary explanation. It consists of a clay tablet engraved with an intaglio figure that has been designated in an ancient language as being Moses. Surrounding the outside border of the tablet and the figure, and also written in an ancient language, are the Ten Commandments. This would be a very unusual artifact for any known tribes of Native Americans to create. So did an antiquated people who were familiar with the Bible create it? Is it really possible that during the Book of Mormon time, a period of more than 1000 years, the peoples of the Book of Mormon gradually migrated from Central America to North America?

At the present time there is simply not any conclusive or absolutely confirmed evidence that would show an indisputable single location for the Hill Cumorah as it is described in the Book of Mormon. However, since the Book of Mormon itself clearly names within its pages two totally different cities called Jerusalem, as well as two totally separate locations named Bountiful, it seems very much within the realm of possibility that there could also have been two totally different Hill Cumorahs in two totally different geographical locations. We may never know for sure in this lifetime. - 4

Please note this dictionary entry in the official Encyclopedia of Mormonism:

"Cumorah* (1) A hill in which the Book of Mormon prophet Mormon concealed sacred records before the annihilation of his people;'

"(2) The hill in New York State, near the town of Palmyra, where Joseph Smith unearthed the gold plates from which he translated the Book of Mormon."

*   *   *

Note the two completely separate entries indicating that the two definitions are two separate hills. This is not proof that the two places are two separate hills in two separate geographical locations, but it certainly leaves the possibility. Interested Book of Mormon researchers, laymen, and scholars using textual clues from the book itself have formulated over sixty possible geographies for the Book of Mormon Lands. In regards to the endeavor to actually pinning down the Book of Mormon's geography, President Joseph F. Smith declared that the "Lord had not yet revealed it," which more or less puts to rest the idea of any actual and conclusive facts about the book's geography. John A. Widtsoe, an Apostle, said, "All such studies are legitimate, but the conclusions drawn from them, though they may be correct, must at the best be held as intelligent conjectures." In the early days of the Church, the most common opinion among Church members and their leaders was that Book of Mormon lands encompassed all of North and South America.

*   *   *

1. See LDS Scriptures "Pearl of Great Price" - Joseph Smith History 1:28

2. See Mark E. Petersen, Improvement Era, June 1957, p.432

3. See LDS Scriptures "Pearl of Great Price" - Joseph Smith History 1:29-54 Also see Moroni, Visitations of. Encyclopedia of Mormonism, Vol.4, VISIONS OF JOSEPH SMITH

4. See http://www.jefflindsay.com/BMEvidences.shtml

*   *   *

Chapter Three

THE GOLD PLATES

*　　*　　*

It is no secret that Joseph Smith's parents were poor farmers with limited financial means, and so Joseph and his older brother Hyrum sometimes hired out as day laborers to earn extra money for the family finances. The going rate in Joseph Smith's time was a paltry wage of twenty-five cents per day plus meals. The entire family worked hard at what ever they needed to do to support the overall welfare of the Smith family. Joseph's oldest brother, Alvin had begun construction on a larger house for the Smith family. Unfortunately though, before he could finish it, he succumbed to a serious illness and sadly passed away at age 25 from what was believed to have been an overdose of medication that had been prescribed for his stomach ailment. This particular tragedy was not only a devastating and a very distressing emotional loss to the Smith family, but in addition there was the collateral effect of a loss of manpower in providing for the family's income, which further imposed a general financial hardship on the whole family.

It was now up to Joseph and Hyrum to supplement the family income as much as they could by hiring out as farm laborers. Sometimes Joseph and Hyrum were able to find work near the farm and return home at night. At other times, because of the excessive distance from home, they were required to stay overnight at their place of hire. In that case, they usually slept in some farmer's barn worn completely out after a long hard day in their attempt to earn a little extra money to keep the family going financially.

In 1825, Joseph hired out to an old gentleman by the name of Josiah Stoal, who lived in Chenango County, New York. Mr. Stoal had come across some information that had led him to believe that the early Spanish explorers had left an old abandoned silver mine in nearby Harmony Pennsylvania just over the state line. After finding the digging to be a little too much strain on an old man, Mr. Stoal hired Joseph along with some other "hired hands" to come and help him dig for the Spanish mine. Laboring hard for over a month at this unsuccessful venture, Joseph the other men finally convinced the old gentleman that it was a useless endeavor.

Even though Joseph had been no more than just one of the hired hands, the rumors and label of old Joe Smith being nothing more than a "greedy treasure hunter" who had dug up some kind of an old "Gold Bible" in New York, now seemed to be even more justified by the story of his digging for Spanish treasure in Pennsylvania. And so the "money digger" stories continued to make the rounds helping to further vilify his reputation. This led to Joseph's many critics labeling him as nothing less than a charlatan, a "fortune hunter;" and a con man who was only interested in silver, gold, and buried treasures, and having little sincere interests in any kind of a legitimate religion.

While Joseph was working in Harmony for Mr. Stoal, he boarded with the family of Isaac Hale, who just happened to have an attractive dark haired, intelligent, and charming daughter by the name of Emma. As fate would have it, Joseph and Emma were married a year and a half later on the 18th of January of 1827. However, after becoming increasingly aware of Joseph's disreputable reputation, Emma's own father and mother were not exactly happy about this union, and so Joseph and Emma necessarily moved out of the uncomfortable situation. Joseph then quit his job working for Mr. Stoal, and he and Emma moved back to the Smith family farm in upper state New York to help Joseph's aging father.

The four years from the time that he had first been shown the ancient book until he was allowed to take possession of the gold plates seemed to have passed rather quickly. And now the time had finally come for him to receive the plates into his own hands. So it came to pass that some eight months after his marriage to Emma, on the appointed date of September 22 1827, Joseph and Emma together rode by horse and wagon to the bottom of the Hill Cumorah.

While Emma waited patiently at the bottom of the hill, Joseph ascended the steep elevation to meet with the Angel Moroni as he had been hitherto instructed to do in order to retrieve the sacred and anciently buried records. And so just as he had anticipated, the Angel Moroni did make his appearance before the young Joseph and he did deliver the "Gold plates" into Joseph's hands giving him strict instructions to protect the plates at all cost. These Plates were now in Joseph's charge and were his most sacred responsibility and he must take every precaution to keep them safe until the time that the Angel Moroni would again call for them.

Joseph soon learned why the angel had been so stringent in his warning to protect the plates at all cost. Somewhat ironically, even though the entire community was convinced that Joseph's "Cock and Bull" story was completely delusional and nothing more than a fantasy, there were still more than just a few unscrupulous treasure hunting thieves who were absolutely determined to get "Old Joe's Gold Bible." Joseph commented that; "The most strenuous exertions were used to get them from me. Every stratagem that could be invented was resorted to for that purpose."

After receiving the plates, and feeling just a bit uneasy about walking around with the very valuable gold book, Joseph hid it in the woods near the hill in a rotted log, which he had hollowed out with his pocketknife to make a receptacle in which to hide them for the time being. Later on when he went to retrieve them, "He was going home in broad daylight, with the plates, wrapped in his linen frock, under his arm." He was still nearly three miles from home, when three devious and greedy thieves attacked him.

"On the way, as he was jumping over a log, a man sprang up from behind it and gave him a heavy blow with a gun. Joseph turned around and knocked him down, then ran at the top of his speed. About half a mile farther he was attacked again in the same manner as before; he knocked this man down in like manner as the former and ran on again; and before he reached home he was assaulted the third time." - Elder G. Smith

This dramatic description of the attacks comes from Eldred G. Smith, Conference Report, October 1967, p.84. After struggling with those three attackers, he was barely able to get away by using the heavy plates in the bag as a club. It was only through his youthful athleticism along with some divine help that he was able to escape.

At various times Joseph had been forced to hide the plates in all sorts of places, including a dead tree, another time under the fireplace hearth, and still another time in a barrel of beans. At one point, the greedy thieves even ransacked the Smith family workshop tearing up every thing, even the floorboards, as they proceeded to meticulously search the entire shop for those gold plates that the rest of the community had already declared to be no more than a fantasy of Joseph's imagination. Yet the thieves were undeterred by the public opinion of it all just being a fairy tale, and so the greedy searchers continued enthusiastically in their quest to acquire the so-called imaginary "Book of Gold."

Greed seems to be a great motivator of human beings and it turned out to be enough incentive for nearly a dozen covetous and unscrupulous men to completely ignore the public perception that the "Gold Bible" was nothing more than "Old Joe Smith's imagination." It was declared by many skeptics that the only angels "Old Joe" ever saw were in his delusional mind. Never the less, the would-be thieves persisted in seeking the imaginary "Gold Plates" as they continued to ignore all the fantastical wild tales of "visions, fantasy, and of imaginary angels handing out gold bibles." In spite of all the mocking cynical gossip, the searchers resumed to contrive every possible strategy that they could think of to obtain "Old Joe Smith's Gold Bible."

The irony of it was that even though the treasure hunters were all convinced that Joseph Smith was nothing more than a dreamer, a fraud, and a complete charlatan who lived in a fantasy world, they somehow didn't see any kind of contradiction or hypocrisy in their own actions as they themselves continued to use their illogical reasoning along with their best efforts to steal "old Joe's" fantasy gold bible. If it was all nothing more than a mere fairy tale as they thought, why did they attempt to justify their own plans of larceny by claiming they had just as much right to have that "Gold Bible" as "Old Joe Smith" did?

Even to this day, there are still many critics of Joseph Smith that remain very skeptical of the idea that there ever was any "Gold Bible." The critics say it's just highly improbable that anybody would ever actually find any legitimate ancient historical records that had been put together with metal rings and holding together metal plates inscribed with antiquated writings on gold leaves that had been buried under ground. They also insist that it would be highly implausible that any kind of genuine records would ever actually be buried in some stone box under dirt in such an unlikely manner as Joseph had described, rather than being kept in the much safer confines of a palace treasury or the antiquated archives of some ancient hidden city.

Apparently these cynics and skeptics have not kept up to date in the latest archeological discoveries, which have revealed the actual findings of several sets of anciently buried books made of precious metal plates held together with rings and containing genuinely inscribed ancient characters carved into the real leaves of gold, silver, and or brass. What? That sounds just like Joseph's description of the Gold Plates. And furthermore, these authentic ancient records which have been discovered in modern times, have been kept safe from the elements and from greedy men in the exact same manner as Joseph Smith had described in the details of his gold plates; which was that of being buried in an anciently crafted stone box that had been kept under ground.

In one of these recent discoveries, there is a set of plates that provides a very prominent example of an excellent comparison to what Joseph Smith had described concerning his own discovery. These particular plates were discovered by archeologists under the ancient stones of the palace of the Chaldean monarch, Sargon, and contain exotic characters that are inscribed on gold leaves, as well as others on thin silver leaves of metal. And they too had been placed in a stone box carefully buried for safe keeping beneath the ground many centuries ago, just as Joseph Smith had described in the circumstances of the ancient records that he had in his possession.

Another very significant example and of like comparison was discovered in the Middle Eastern country of Iran. These metal plates were found to belong to the great King Darius dating back to 518 B.C. The beautifully engraved plates were discovered to be of gold and of silver and inscribed and stored in the same basic manner as the gold plates that Joseph Smith had previously described under very similar conditions to his acquired buried records. One might ask, so just how were these records preserved? They too, like the Book of Mormon plates had been placed in a carefully handcrafted box of stone and then buried underground during ancient times.

So as it all turns out, Joseph Smith's Gold Bible story was not nearly as far-fetched as some skeptics had portrayed it to be. In fact in all reality, Joseph Smith's account is very much consistent with the handling and storage of many different ancient records, which have been discovered by a number of legitimate archeologists in modern times. – 1a

Mean time in the Palmyra area, the skeptics and tormentors of Joseph Smith became increasingly belligerent and aggressive in their harassment, even to the point of confronting Joseph and Emma on the streets of Palmyra and harshly ridiculing them. The persecution towards Joseph and his family became so severe and so intolerable that Joseph and Emma had to leave Manchester and move back to Susquehanna County in Pennsylvania.

In the interim, there was a local and well-respected wealthy farmer in Palmyra, by the name of Martin Harris, who had become quite fascinated with the Joseph Smith story. When he became aware of Joseph and Emma's problematic situation, he felt compassion for the beleaguered couple and generously gave them $50.00 to aid them in their move back with Emma's family. If $50.00 doesn't seem like very much money, one must remember that many men at that time were doing a hard days labor for a mere 25 cents a day.

Even though Emma's father had never been happy with her choice of a spouse, he apparently had enough compassion for his own daughter to let them move back into his home, and so it was that the couple moved back to live with the Hale family in Harmony. This is the place where Joseph began his first efforts to translate the characters on the gold plates and it was Emma Smith herself who would become the Prophet's first scribe.

Emma recalled sometime later that as Joseph dictated each sentence to her word for word, he was able to correct her scribal errors when necessary even though he could not even see what she had already written down. Although Joseph never did show Emma the actual plates because he had been instructed by Moroni to show them to no one, curiosity overcame her one-day and she reached down and felt of them, "tracing their outline and shape," as they lay on the table under a linen cloth. She said they; "... would rustle with a metallic sound when the edges were moved by the thumb, as one does sometimes thumb the edges of a book..." Emma's personal descriptive statement describing her experience in the handling of the plates comes from the "Testimony of Sister Emma." -1b

In the meantime, Martin Harris had become totally intrigued by Joseph's work, and so he proceeded to travel to Pennsylvania in order to confer with Joseph. After offering his services to help the Prophet translate, he subsequently became Joseph's scribe. Being nearly obsessed and completely captivated by Joseph's work, he eventually felt compelled by his curiosity to make a trip to the big city carrying with him a copy of some of the ancient characters along with part of Joseph's translation to have the work examined by a genuine language expert. He felt compelled to have it all authenticated for his own peace of mind, and to hopefully alleviate his wife's skepticism and that of his family.

Thus acquiring a copy of the ancient characters and Joseph's translation of the same, Martin Harris traveled to New York City to meet with professor Charles Anton, a well-known expert in ancient languages. The professor not only enthusiastically stated that the characters were legitimate Egyptian, Chaldaid, Assyriac, and Arabic, but said that the translation was more correct than he had ever seen. After giving Martin Harris a certificate of authenticity, the professor then asked where Mr. Harris had acquired them. When Martin told him the truth, the professor said there was no such thing now days as the ministering of angels and he then abruptly requested that the certificate be given back to him, which he promptly tore up. He then strongly suggested that Martin Harris bring the plates to him and he would personally translate them. Martin replied that some parts of the plates were sealed and he was forbidden to bring them to anyone. The professor responded by saying, "I cannot read a sealed book."

Little did Professor Anthon know that with this very statement, he was fulfilling a prophecy written in the book of Isaiah almost word for word nearly three millennia ago. It is a most remarkable thought for one to realize that 2600 years before this Martin Harris incident ever occurred, the Prophet Isaiah prophesied that a book would be delivered to one who was learned and the learned one would reply that he could not read a sealed book.

Isaiah 29:11 *"And the vision of all is become unto you as the words of a book that is sealed, which men deliver to one that is learned, saying, Read this, I pray thee: and he saith, I cannot; for it is sealed:"* - These prophetic words written nearly three millennia ago can still be read today in the King James Version of the Holy Bible.

Despite the fact that Martin Harris had been somewhat disappointed by the reaction of Professor Anthon in that the professor had rescinded the validation of the translation, this was not the end of Martin's quest in New York City. Although very disappointed by Professor Anthon's response, Brother Harris proceeded to seek out an alternate expert and he took the characters and translation to another professor by the name of Dr. Mitchell who verified everything that professor Anthon had concluded about the characters and their translation. All in all, in the mind of Martin Harris, the trip to New York City had all been a worthwhile trip in that he had actually had the authenticity of the engraved characters and the accuracy of the translation verified by two different experts to the complete satisfaction of his own mind. – 2

Unfortunately, and not too long after the trip to New York, it would come to pass that Martin would thereafter unintentionally loose 116 pages of the Book of Mormon. Martin had emotionally besieged Joseph and begged him into letting the manuscript from the translation be taken and shown to his wife Lucy and other family members so that he himself might convince them that it wasn't all just a big hoax. Even though the Lord said no to that request three times, Martin continued to plead and Joseph continued to ask on behalf of Martin Harris and so the Lord decided to teach Joseph and Martin a lesson and finally granted the request. Consequently, 116 pages of the irreplaceable transcript were lost.

Martin's wife Lucy had become very bitter and angry when Joseph declined to personally show her the "Gold Plates" and so her thoughts turned to revenge. And so it would be Martin's own very skeptical and unsupportive wife Lucy who would get the blame for allegedly having burnt the 116 pages in their own stove. Other reports say she stole the 116 pages and quietly hid them until another time when she planned to bring them forth in order to shame and blacken the reputation of the Prophet. So in the end whose ever plan it was to use the missing manuscript to discredit Joseph found their plan completely foiled as the Lord commanded Joseph to not retranslate those 116 pages.

In consequence of the loss, Martin would not only loose his privilege to be a scribe for the Prophet Joseph, but would experience in addition, the devastating and inconsolable feeling that he had lost his own soul. If all that wasn't bad enough, Martin's relentless begging had also caused the Prophet too to also loose favor with the Lord and so the Prophet Joseph temporarily lost his privileges to translate. This incident resulted in a valuable lesson for the Prophet and Martin Harris. - 3

However, luckily due to divine design, the information on those pages from the Book of Lehi that appeared to have been lost forever actually had a literal backup written by Lehi's son Nephi in his own writings. In the Book of Mormon when Nephi and Jacob quote their father Lehi, they seem to be quoting from the Book of Lehi and from his lost words found in the 116 pages. So it seems that the first eight chapters of 1 Nephi and possibly some other parts that were written on the small plates appear to be based on the original record of Father Lehi, and it covers the same basic information thought to have been lost by Martin Harris. What a lucky and amazing coincidence or was it just coincidence, or was it more likely all just a part of a master insurance plan? So it appears that these ancient authors really did inspirationally duplicate that information for a future backup, all by divine design in case these important writings might be lost some day, or it sure does seem like that is the case.

Meanwhile, there was a schoolteacher staying with the family of Joseph Smith Senior, who had been teaching the Smith children in return for his board and room. He listened with great interest to the incredible story of their son Joseph and the coming forth of the Book of Mormon. This schoolteacher by the name of Oliver Cowdery became so intrigued with the story of the plates that he decided to make a special trip to Harmony Pennsylvania to see for himself what this incredible story was really all about. It was just before Oliver left for Harmony to check out the story of Joseph and his "Gold Bible" that he happened to meet a young man in Palmyra who was on a business trip from the "Fingers Lake" region of Fayette, New York.

In a very short time, the two men became good friends and that led

Oliver to relate the story of Joseph Smith to the very much-interested David Whitmer. He happened to mention to Whitmer that he himself was now in the process of preparing to go to Harmony to find out for himself the truth of the Joseph Smith story. Intrigued by the fascinating account, David Whitmer then invited Oliver to come and stay at the Whitmer home in Fayette, as Oliver would be passing through that part of the country on his way to Pennsylvania. Subsequently after Oliver's visit to the household of the very welcoming family of the Whitmers, the entire family became so enamored with the story of Joseph Smith that all of them had a real desire to be personally involved in some way with the Prophet's work. Their great interest, enthusiasm, and their willingness to serve would bring about the circumstances where the Whitmer family would come to play a major role in the bringing forth of the Book of Mormon and the eventual establishment of the new church.

Oliver Cowdery arrived in Harmony Pennsylvania the first week of April 1829. Two days later, he found himself "scribing" for The Prophet as Joseph translated the mysterious inscriptions on the gold plates. Just a month later, on May 15th, 1829, Joseph and Oliver went into the woods to pray and inquire about some references made in regards to baptism in the translations. In the very act of praying, a most remarkable event occurred as they had a divine messenger appear before them enveloped in an aura of bright light. The messenger said he was called "John The Baptist," and he was here under the direction and authority of the Apostles Peter, James, and John to confer upon Joseph and Oliver the Aaronic priesthood, which would give them the power and the authority to baptize each other "by immersion for the remission of sins." He thus laid his hands upon them saying;

"Upon you my fellow servants, in the name of Messiah, I confer the Priesthood of Aaron, which holds the keys of the ministering of angels, and of the gospel of repentance, and of baptism by immersion for the remission of sins; and this shall never be taken again from the earth until the sons of Levi do offer again an offering unto the Lord in righteousness." - 4

Thus as they were commanded to do, they baptized each other. And even though John had already conferred the Aaronic Priesthood upon them, he then commanded them to lay their hands upon each other's heads respectively and ordain each other to the Aaronic Priesthood. John the

Baptist also said and added that in a very short time thereafter, the Apostles Peter, James, and John would soon come to ordain the two of them to the higher Melchizedek Priesthood, where in Joseph would become the First Elder of the Church and Oliver would be the Second.

After their baptism, Joseph and Oliver's minds were enlightened to a whole new understanding of the scriptures, which they had previously found to be somewhat confusing and a bit of a mystery to them. But now the scriptures had become plain to them and the true interpretations were revealed to their minds. They were also further enlightened and able to prophesy of things concerning the growth of the new church that was about to be established.

Interestingly enough, on their way back to the house, they overheard Joseph's brother, Samuel, engaged in secret prayer. Joseph commented to Oliver that it seemed obvious that Samuel was ready to be baptized. Oliver agreed, and after speaking to Samuel about being baptized, Oliver and Samuel went into the water and Samuel Smith was baptized, and would soon become the very first missionary of "The Church of Jesus Christ."

In the interim, a renewed spirit of persecution had become prevalent in the area surrounding the Hale Family's residence. However, Joseph's father-in-law had now become sympathetic and he was consequently taking up the defense for Joseph, Emma, and Oliver. Thus he made great efforts to keep the persecution at bay, while Joseph continued his work to translate from the gold plates. The Hale family had went out of their way to be good hosts and accommodate Joseph, Emma, and Oliver, even though the local persecution had continued relentlessly, which was putting a mounting pressure upon the family. In his high regard and gratefulness for the Hale family, the Prophet was becoming more and more concerned for their safety and welfare.

Finally Joseph felt it necessary to impose on Oliver's friendship with the Whitmer family in Fayette, and so he asked Oliver to contact them to see if he, Emma, and Oliver could stay at their home for a while so that Joseph and Oliver could continue translating. After receiving Oliver's letter of inquiry regarding the need for board and room for him and the Smiths while Joseph translated, the Whitmer family agreed without hesitation and sent their son David with a wagon to retrieve the three refugees from Harmony.

However, in Fayette the Whitmer cabin was rather small and was already sheltering a somewhat large Whitmer family, so now taking in three more boarders would be a significant sacrifice, especially for Mary Whitmer who had to maintain the house, the cooking, and the cleaning for all of them. The Whitmer men were kept busy with farming, and Emma Smith was still not feeling well enough to be of much help to Mary. Never the less, Mary Whitmer carried on with her many tasks and continued to labor faithfully taking care of her added burdens the best she could.

Mary Whitmer's faith and steadfastness in the carrying out the extra duties placed up on her, and the reward that she would receive for such faithfulness are of a special note and pose a most interesting story. She had unselfishly accepted the many physical burdens that were placed upon her shoulders as she took care of her own large family in addition to caring for Joseph, Emma, and Oliver while the Prophet was translating in her home. As a divine reward for her faithfulness, she would personally be shown the "Gold Plates" by the Angel Moroni in a most remarkable manifestation. Oddly enough, Moroni appeared to her in her own yard as an ordinary gray haired old man carrying a knapsack containing the scared plates. It is thought that Moroni appeared to Mary Whitmer in this ordinary form of a common man so as not to shock or frighten her. This very special and unusual appearance by Moroni to Mary Whitmer was for the purpose of inspiring and strengthening her while she was under the great stress of the many added burdens that she felt obliged to endure. Her son David Whitmer verified the truth of the miraculous incident as found in the following references.

"The extra burdens were not easy on Peter and Mary Whitmer, who were hosting the Smiths and Oliver Cowdery in their home. Their son, David, said that this added burden greatly increased the anxiety of his mother. She did not complain, but she felt overwhelmed. David later related what happened one day as his mother went to the barn to milk the cows."

"She was met out near the yard by the same old man [seen earlier by David] (judging by her description of him) who said to her: 'You have been very faithful and diligent in your labors, but you are tired because of the increase of your toil; it is proper therefore that you should receive a witness that your faith may be strengthened.' Thereupon he showed her the plates." - 5

Mary Whitmer became the only woman to ever see the actual gold plates, although there were at least four other women who testified to having seen the outline of them under their cloth cover. Many people found Mary Whitmer's story to be fantastically far-fetched. Yet her grandson John C. Whitmer testified that she was able to describe the gold plates in detail, even before any other Whitmer members of her family or any of the other eight Witnesses had seen them. Mary Whitmer had given her first descriptions of the plates to her relatives nearly a month before any of the three witnesses or the eight witnesses had ever witnessed the Plates. How was she able to do this if she hadn't seen them first hand and before the other witnesses? Other relatives also testified that she had related to them the story and they found the retelling to be consistent in its details. Naturally, this miraculous event greatly strengthened Mary Whitmer's testimony and her resolve to continue in her support of Joseph Smith and the important work he was engaged in.

Due to the Whitmer family's great faith, loyalty, and the strong support that they gave to Joseph, this family would eventually come to play a major role in the Joseph Smith story, as they would soon become faithful witnesses and avid supporters of the Prophet. Their strong testimonies of his divine work were most reassuring to the Prophet, and he very much appreciated their moral support as well as their most generous material support. The entire Whitmer family would eventually become very much involved in the establishment of the new church. Several of the Whitmer family members, which included Christian, Jacob, Peter, and John, would play the most important role of becoming four of the very significant eight witnesses to the gold plates. Their names are listed in the front pages of the Book of Mormon along with the four other witnesses where they too did testify of seeing the "Gold Plates" first hand.

Their son David Whitmer not only became one of the special "Three Witnesses" of the Book of Mormon, but a major player in the establishment of the Church of Jesus Christ. Finally, it was the home of father Peter Whitmer that would be the very place that the new church would be first organized, the very place where the Church of Jesus Christ would be officially established and restored to the Earth once again. And most significantly, it would be the first time the True Church of Christ would be on the earth since the time of the Great Apostasy. – 6

*   *   *

1a. See Mark E. Petersen, Improvement Era, June 1957, p.432

1b. See "Testimony of Sister Emma" Saints Herald, Oct. 1 1879 p.290.

2. See Joseph Smith – History 1:65

3. See Sec. 3 Heading of the Doctrine and Covenants, and Encyclopedia Of Mormonism- Manuscript, Lost 116 Pages

4. See Joseph Smith History 1:69

5. See "Church History In The Fulness Of Times" Student Manual, (2003), 52–66 - See also Peterson, pp. 114, 116

6. See LDS Scriptures "Pearl of Great Price" - Joseph Smith History 1:55 -75

*   *   *

Chapter Four

THE NEW CHURCH OF CHRIST BEGINS

*   *   *

A month after Joseph, Emma, and Oliver Cowdery arrived at the Whitmer family home; Joseph completed his translation of the Book of Mormon. He had been aided by the invaluable assistance of Oliver Cowdery his scribe, the very much appreciated day-to-day material substance and moral support of the Whitmer family, the support of Emma, and of course the help of the Lord. Not too long after he had completed the translation, Joseph received a revelation revealing that the truth of the Lord's work would be established in the mouths of three witnesses whom the Lord Himself would choose. On hearing this, Martin Harris entreated Joseph incessantly to let him have the privilege of being one of the witnesses. A short time later, it was revealed to the Prophet by the Lord, that Oliver Cowdery, David Whitmer, and Martin Harris would be the three special witnesses to the Book of Mormon, providing that Martin would humble himself and repent fully.

Not too long after receiving the revelation naming the three witnesses, Joseph went into the woods accompanied by the three especially chosen men near the Whitmer family home to pray for guidance. At this time Joseph received a special revelation on behalf of Oliver Cowdery, David Whitmer, and Martin Harris in June of 1829, just previous to their seeing the plates.

"Behold, I say unto you, that you must rely upon my word, which if you do with full purpose of heart, you shall have a view of the plates, and also the breastplate, the sword of Laban, the Urim and Thummim, which were given to the brother of Jared upon the mount, when he talked with the Lord face to face, and the miraculous directors which were given to Lehi while in the wilderness, on the borders of the Red Sea. And it is by your faith that you shall obtain a view of them, even by that faith which was had by the prophets of old. And after that you have obtained faith, and have seen them with your eyes, you shall testify of them, by the power of God;" – 1

A short time later they entered the woods and while they were thus praying in humble supplication, they experienced some thing of a delay in receiving any answer to their prayers, where upon Martin Harris withdrew himself from the others as he was feeling some doubts in regards to his own personal worthiness. Following Martin's departure from the group, it was then that a most remarkable manifestation did materialize in a most dramatic way. There before their very eyes the Angel Moroni made a celestial appearance from the heavens and thus did divinely display the actual "Gold Plates" before Joseph and the two witnesses. In addition, the two witnesses were shown the Urim and Thumin, the breastplate, the sword of Laban, and Lehi's Liahona, also called the director ball. They were understandably filled with wonder and awe.

At this point, the Prophet left the other two brethren where they were, and went to seek out Martin Harris who he soon found already engaged in fervent prayer. Joseph reverently joined Martin in his praying. While the two were in the act of making their oblations and their sincere requests before their God, the Angel Moroni again appeared and thus revealed the gold plates to the two prayerful men. It was at this point that Martin Harris "rejoiced exceedingly," as he too was filled with wonder and awe.

Following this unveiling of the scared objects before the three witnesses, they were commanded to "bear record" that they actually had seen an angel who had shown them the "Gold Plates" with mysterious engravings upon those plates, and that it had all come through the power of God and not of man. The three special witnesses would later have their powerful words of testimony printed in the front pages of the published Book of Mormon saying in part; "And we declare with words of soberness, that an angel of God came down from Heaven and brought and laid before our eyes, that we beheld and saw the plates, and the engravings thereon; and we know that it is by the grace of God the Father, and our Lord Jesus Christ, that we beheld and bear record that these things are true." – See the Introduction to the Book of Mormon.

Soon after this extraordinary event took place, Joseph was then allowed to show the "Gold Plates" to eight more witnesses wherein he did let these eight witnesses also handle the plates. Each one then incredulously reached out and "hefted" the plates and solemnly turned the individual gold "leaves" of the sacred plates and they did examine very closely the engravings of "curious workmanship" that were written upon the plates. And so it was that Joseph did let each of them touch and feel of the ancient engravings carved upon the gold leaves so they could also testify to the reality and authenticity of the "Plates." They too would record their sacred testimonies in the front pages of the Book of Mormon saying in part; "BE IT KNOWN unto all nations, kindreds, tongues, and people, unto whom this work shall come; that Joseph Smith, Jun., the translator of this work, has shown unto us the plates of which hath been spoken, which have the appearance of gold; and as many of the leaves as the said Smith has translated we did handle with our hands; and we also saw the engravings thereon, all of which has the appearance of ancient work, and of curious workmanship." The complete testimonies of the three witnesses and the eight witnesses can be found in the Introduction to the Book of Mormon.

And so as it happened, out of the eight witnesses, four of them belonged to the Whitmer family, three to the Smith family, and the eighth was Hiram Page, a son-in-law to the Whitmers. These eight witnesses along with the three special witnesses, Oliver Cowdery, David Whitmer, and Martin Harris, when added to the witness of the Prophet Joseph Smith himself, comes to a sum total of an even dozen individuals who saw and actually handled the "Gold Plates." And so it was that each of these twelve good and honest men solemnly testified to the reality of the "Gold Plates." Under any ordinarily circumstances, the testimonies of twelve honest men witnessing to anything would be enough to convince any court in the land of the truth of any proposition presented before it. However, in this incredible and seemingly implausible case, it simply wasn't enough for the great many doubting skeptics of the world. Many people outside the Church still continued to question the actual existence of the Gold Plates, even after what for all intended purposes was the verified and undisputed testimony of twelve reputable men, and so the non-believers continued to remain skeptical. Even to this very day, there are still a great many people who doubt the Gold Plates ever existed despite these dozen powerful testimonies given by these twelve very sincere and honest men.

So after the twelve witnesses had all verified the existence of the Gold plates, which was one of the first steps of the restoration, just what would be the next important step in bringing forth the Book of Mormon? Next on this very important agenda would be to put those divine words of the book before the world and place the book into hands of the common man so that all who believed the sacred words might be enlightened to the true gospel. However, when it all came right down to the practical reality of dealing with the logistics and coming to terms with the actual publishing of multiple copies of the Book of Mormon, things turned out to be a little more complicated than Joseph and his supporters had expected.

First of all, there was a considerable amount of work in just extrapolating the translated words from off the "Gold Plates," and then composing them into a readable English manuscript in a clear and legible form that a professional printer could read accurately. Second, there was the substantial task of securing funding for the publication of the book. Third would be the searching out of a willing letterpress printer who would commit to actually do the work of the printing. Finally, there was the chore of making all the arrangements for the monumental undertaking of printing thousands of copies and distributing them to ordinary people who were actually willing to read the book.

So as Joseph and his supporters faced up to the very real world of the existing logistics holding up the work of publishing the Book of Mormon, they came across another frustrating hurdle that would become more than just another annoying bump in the road. That would be the invariable and unpredictable fickleness of human beings in general and the public's capricious perception of what the Book of Mormon was really about, and the convincing of the skeptics of its important message. This ungrounded and foolish cynicism would further complicate the serious task at hand and create a totally unfounded prejudice against the book with the full intentions of stopping its publication all together. Joseph and his supporters found that the bitter cynicism, the irrational skepticism, and the prejudices of a negative public not only caused things to not go quite as smoothly as Joseph would have hoped, but in some cases would actually delay the printing. At times the human factor seemed like the most impeding and exacerbating obstacle of all preventing the publication of the Book of Mormon. The majority of the local citizens in the area were dead set against the "evil book" and were totally against it even being published at all, even though they absolutely had no idea of what was in it. And so it was that these obstructers made their unfounded criticisms loudly known to all that would listen to them, and this would eventually come to a situation where it would halt the printing process itself.

At the beginning of the project, the financing for the publishing of the Book of Mormon was seemingly a serious obstacle in and of itself. Just where were they going to acquire the considerable funds for the printing of the Book? The printer wasn't even going to start on the project until he had some kind of assurance that he would be paid in full for his work. Fortunately for Joseph and his supporters, it would be the semi-wealthy farmer Martin Harris who would step up to the task, and who would be inspired to mortgage his farm to get the necessary funds for the printer. And so it came to pass that the first few pages of the Book of Mormon were finally printed out in August of 1829.

Unfortunately, there were other problems even after the printing of the Book of Mormon had already begun. One such problem was that the good citizens of Palmyra decided to hold a special meeting in which they would all solemnly pledge among themselves to not buy or read this book of "The Devil," even though they still had no idea what was in it. Upon hearing of this development among town's people, the printer brought the printing of the Book of Mormon to a dead halt. Consequently, Joseph found it necessary to come all the way up from Harmony Pennsylvania to get the situation straightened out so that the printing could resume and get back on track.

Accompanied by Martin Harris, Joseph went to the printer to reassure and convince Mr. Grandin that they would personally guarantee that he would be paid in full for every single thing he printed, and they eventually persuaded him to get back on task because they truly needed the printing to resume as soon as possible. Mr. Grandin consequently agreed to continue the printing of the Book of Mormon after Martin Harris agreed to mortgage some of his farm for $3,000 as a security. Subsequently, the first complete edition of 5,000 copies of the Book of Mormon were finally printed by Egbert B. Grandin at Palmyra New York for the cost of $3,000 in March of 1830. That was just eight months after the printing was originally begun.

Nearly a month later and only a short time after the book had been published, the special spirit of the Book of Mormon converted a number of people and the excited founders of the new church proceeded to go forward and officially organize the Church of Jesus Christ on April 6, 1830. This very significant event took place at the home of Peter Whitmer Sr. in Fayette, upper state New York, in the "Fingers Lake" region of Seneca County. There on that significant and historic day, and in accordance with the laws of the State of New York, six members made up the original membership of the Church, which included Joseph Smith, Oliver Cowdery, Hyrum Smith, Samuel H. Smith, Peter Whitmer Jr., and David Whitmer. The Lord's Church had now been officially established and restored to the earth with much more enlightenment to come in due time.

At the time of the official organization, the sacrament was passed, and those who had previously been baptized were confirmed. In addition, four new members were baptized, which included Joseph's own father and mother. It is unclear as to whether Martin Harris and Porter Rockwell were also baptized on this exact day or very shortly thereafter. The Prophet recorded it as such; "Several persons who had attended the above meeting, became convinced of the truth and came forward shortly after, and were received into the Church; among the rest, my own father and mother were baptized, to my great joy and consolation; and about the same time, Martin Harris and Orrin Porter Rockwell." – 2

On this very special day, the members of the new church sustained Joseph Smith as the first Elder of the Church and Oliver Cowdery as the second Elder, just as John the Baptist had previously stated that they would be at the time he conferred the Aaronic Priesthood upon them. Joseph then ordained Oliver Cowdery to the office of an Elder by the laying on of hands, and Oliver did the same for Joseph. At this point, Joseph and Oliver then laid their hands upon those previously baptized members so that they could receive the gift of the Holy Ghost, and then be confirmed as members of the Church of Jesus Christ.

Note that the name of the Church used at that time was a bit shorter than today's title. The original Church of Jesus Christ was not officially entitled with the complete name of the Church of Jesus Christ of Latter Day Saints until eight years after its establishment when Joseph Smith received the edict by revelation on April 26th 1838. – 3

It is important to note that at some juncture of time between the receiving of the Aaronic Priesthood through John the Baptist and the actual establishment of the Church by the authority of the Melchizedek Priesthood, the higher Priesthood had to have been restored to Joseph and Oliver so that they could ordain each other as the official Elders of the Church. Unfortunately, the details of the account of them receiving the higher Melchizedek Priesthood are a bit sketchier than the details surrounding the restoration of the Aaronic priesthood. In point of fact, there is not even a specific date or an exact location given for this very important event concerning the Melchizedek Priesthood. Never the less, there is confirmed information that Joseph and Oliver actually did receive the Melchizedek Priesthood at the hands of Christ's ancient apostles, Peter, James and John.

It was several years after the Church was already established that the Prophet gave the general location where he and Oliver had received the higher priesthood and where the ordination had taken place under the hands of the ancient apostles Peter, James, and John. Joseph revealed the general local during an address to the Saints written in 1842: "Again what do we hear? ... The voice of Peter, James, and John, in the wilderness between Harmony, Susquehanna county, and Colesville, Broome county, on the Susquehanna river, declaring themselves as possessing the keys of the kingdom of the dispensation of the fullness of times." – 4

So now that there is a solid clue through the Prophet Joseph Smith as to where the approximate location of the restoration of the Melchizedek Priesthood took place, that being on the Susquehanna River; what was the date? Even though there is no exact date given for the ordination of

Joseph and Oliver to the Melchizedek Priesthood, it had to have occurred some time within a specific eleven-month window; that is sometime between the 15th of May 1829 when they received the Aaronic Priesthood from John the Baptist and before April 6th the next year when they first organized the Church under the authority of the Melchizedek Priesthood in 1830.

The important part of all this is that after receiving their ordinations to the Aaronic Priesthood by John the Baptist, Joseph and Oliver had the higher Priesthood bestowed upon them by Christ's Apostles, Peter, James and John and before the Church was officially organized. Subsequently Joseph and Oliver became the first Elders of the Church as had been specified by John the Baptist and they did properly establish the Church of Jesus Christ under the appropriate Melchizedek Priesthood authority.

Though this all may sound a bit redundant, it is a very important matter to solidly establish that Joseph and Oliver were unequivocally authorized to act in the name of God to organize and preside over God's restored Church here on Earth when they became the presiding Elders of the Church of Jesus Christ and thus they did do it with the absolute and proper priesthood keys and the complete authority to do so. When all of the aforementioned sacred priesthood events are connected and taken together as a complete chain of events, it is very clear that the Church of Jesus Christ of Latter Day Saints was fully established and restored to the earth under the proper and full priesthood authority of God until Christ comes in person to rein over His Church again. - 5

* * *

1. See History of the Church, Vol.1, Ch.6, p.53

2. History of the Church, Vol.1, Ch.8, p.79 – See also History of the Church, Vol.1, p.76, Footnotes & p169

3. See the heading in the LDS Scriptures of D&C Section 21 and D&C Section 115:3-4

4. - See D & C Sec. 128:20

5. See Joseph Fielding Smith, Gospel Doctrine, p.194

*   *   *

Chapter Five

JOSEPH'S ARRESTS AND OTHER DIVERSIONS

* * *

After finishing up with the pressing items of organizing the Church in Fayette New York, Joseph and Emma returned to live at Harmony Pennsylvania for the time being. Nearby and some thirty miles to the north of Harmony across the Pennsylvanian New York border there was a village called Colesville, which was where a gentleman by the name of Joseph Knight Sr. lived as a neighbor to Joseph's former employer, Josiah Stoal. This area of New York State was popularly known as the Colesville-South Bainbridge region, and unfortunately, it was soon to become another hotbed of anti-Mormon sentiment.

Back when Joseph was working for Mr. Stoal, he had on different occasions worked also for Josiah's neighbor, Joseph Knight. By happenstance one afternoon, he had told these two neighbors there in Colesville, the story of his miraculous visions. Somewhat surprisingly, both men believed Joseph's absolutely incredible story, accepted these unbelievable tales of miraculous occurrences as being fact, and as a consequence both men became extremely interested in the work and the calling of the Prophet Joseph Smith.

A couple of months after the Church's organization, the entire family of Joseph Knight Sr. became so enthused about the new church that they were very desirous to be baptized as soon as possible. Unfortunately things did not go as smoothly as they would have liked in their humble quest to become members of the Church of Jesus Christ. Due to the hostility of their so-called good neighbors and friends, who were not exactly in harmony with the Knight family's choice of beliefs, the Knights were frequently harassed and mocked for their new faith. In fact, their neighbors showed nothing but contempt for the Knight family and their new religion. Consequently their fine neighbors did more than just spew out a few derisive epithets to show their disapproval and disrespect. With no regard for the Knight's constitutional rights to worship as they pleased, the hostile neighbors spitefully and violently tore out a dam that had been built for the express purpose of performing the anticipated baptisms. If that wasn't bad enough, they continued to show their loathsome disapproval of the Knight's beliefs by shouting out loud insults at the family and at their family friends as the Knights tried to hold a Sabbath service that was being conducted at the their home.

Undeterred by all the harassment and the ruined dam, the family with the help of the Prophet Joseph Smith and their supporters rebuilt the dam by moonlight as they worked through the night. And so they proceeded with the baptisms unopposed in the quiet hours of the next early morning as this special event was smiled upon by the inspiring light of a beautiful sunrise.

Due to Emma's delicate condition earlier in the spring, she had not been baptized at the time that the Church was first organized and so she had waited until now to be baptized at the time of these June baptisms, which were being held especially for the Knight family and a few of their friends. Appropriately enough, Emma Smith was the first one to be baptized on this special occasion.

The much-desired confirmations to complete the baptisms were necessarily postponed until the next day to avoid further harassment from their "ever so compassionate" neighbors. Later on as they were proceeding to conduct the formal Church business of taking care of those confirmations at the Knight home, there was an unexpected knock at the front door. It turned out to be a Constable Wilson from Chenango County who said he was arresting Joseph Smith and taking him to South Bainbridge to stand trial for disorderly conduct and for inciting discord in the community and causing the whole country to be in an "uproar."

Even though Joseph didn't quite understand the reason for the charges, he went along peaceably. Somewhere along the line and somewhat surprisingly, he must have impressed this particular lawman with his manner and poise, for the sheriff soon confessed that there was a mob of angry men waiting to ambush them about a mile down the road from the Knight home. This villainous welcoming party of very hostile and agitated men had it in their minds to beat Old Joe Smith "with in an inch of his life." The constable then strongly advised Joseph to get a good grip on his seat and to hang on for dear life because he was going to bust right through "the likes of that mob." He thus determinedly forged on with a wild and furious ride right through the middle of those shouting angry men and left them far behind in a dusted fury of anger and in a state of nothing less than very disappointed outrage. - 1

Constable Wilson, being an honorable man and sworn to follow his duty, then delivered Joseph safely to trial in South Bainbridge. To say that this trial was a trumped up circus of "damnable lies" is an understatement. Joseph was accused of stealing Josiah Stoal's horse. However, Josiah testified that he had a promissory note from Joseph to pay for the horse and he completely trusted Joseph's word. Joseph was also accused of acting inappropriately with Josiah's daughters. Both girls denied any such occurrences. Joseph was accused of extorting a yoke of oxen from a local farmer by claiming to have received a revelation that he was to have the oxen for himself. The farmer testified that Joseph bought the oxen as any other man would. Other low life witnesses were brought in to testify of things that were so absurd that even the prosecuting attorney was embarrassed by such a series of ridiculous and very obvious lies. Then finally, the defense lawyer for the accused prophet produced several well-respected and credible character witnesses to testify on Joseph's behalf, which persuaded Justice Chamberlain to quickly dismiss all charges.

However, the spontaneous celebration by Joseph's friends and supporters was short lived. Before they were even able to leave the court room, a large burly and very hard looking man stepped forward shoving a piece of paper under Joseph's nose saying something to the effect of; "Mr. Smith, I am Constable Boyd and I have a writ to take you to Colesville for trial on charges of disturbing the peace."

As they arrived in Colesville for the next trial, Sheriff Boyd stopped at a tavern for a beer, and then very unprofessionally let the riffraff and other drunks mock and even spit upon the Prophet. The trial itself was even less credible than the previous trial. The testimonies were embarrassingly contradictory. Many of the witnesses were forced to admit that their testimonies were merely "hear say" and that they had only heard the unflattering stories about Joseph from other people. This made these half-baked but enthusiastic liars look extremely foolish and therefore they lacked any credibility in the eyes of the court. To the reasonable and fair-minded judge, the trial proved to be a complete sham and waste of everybody's time, and so once again, all charges were dismissed.

Meanwhile, towards the end of the proceedings and to Joseph's complete astonishment, the burly Constable Boyd came and sat down beside Joseph. He then quietly stated that he felt foolish in having been taken in by some of the terrible lies that had been said about Joseph and he now realized that they were nothing more than ridiculous fabrications. He discretely apologized and asked for Joseph's forgiveness and then declared firmly in a louder more determined voice that he would see to Joseph's safety despite the angry mobs that were waiting for them outside. True to his word, Constable Boyd did accompany Joseph and his friends safely out of town, and he faithfully delivered Joseph from yet another mob that had been waiting for them with hot tar and feathers at the side of the road. After another wild ride through the night, they finally arrived safe and sound just at dawn at the home of Joseph's sister-in-law.

The persistent annoyance of being personally harassed almost daily, along with the general worry of a constant malicious persecution of the new church by the many religious bigots was certainly more than enough aggravation to disrupt the Prophet's life and distract him from his duties.

However, added to all this and perhaps even more of a distress to the Prophet Joseph was the unpleasant reality of also having to deal with the occasional disappointment coming from a few of the already baptized members within the Church itself. Sadly some of these troublesome headaches were perpetrated by some of the Church's most upstanding and ostensibly loyal members. As there is with any organization of any size, there sometimes arise difficulties with some of the insiders who have gone off on their own tangent and with a different agenda. They just aren't quite in tune with the true spirit of the program and the overall intended purposes of the organization. Such was the case with Brother Hiram Page.

Hiram Page, one of the eight witnesses to the Book of Mormon and a son-in-law to the Whitmers, presented something of a quandary in a highly unusual case to deal with, and consequently caused a certain amount of stress for the Prophet. Hiram had at some point in the past studied Folk Medicine and Folk superstitions and so when he somehow ran across an unusual and intriguing unique flat stone, he started wearing it around his neck on a chain and began claiming it had special powers. His in-laws kept asking him to use the magic amulet to look into the future of the Church with the aid of the peculiar stone. And so it was that he began receiving revelations through this mysterious rock and thus began actually making prophecies by its means as related to the entire future of the newly established church. Not only did he delude several naive Church members concerning the power of the stone, but also in addition, he had even taken in Oliver Cowdery with the seemingly amazing and mysterious powers of this particular rock. This shocking circumstance was quite surprising in that Oliver had been at the Prophet's side when they had seen visions, angels, and the actual Gold Plates, and he would soon be chosen to be the first counselor to the Prophet in the First Presidency of the Church. So how is it possible that even Oliver Cowdery could be duped by what appeared to be some type of black magic? The clever and deceiving dark forces are not to be toyed with or underestimated!

Through inspiration the Prophet Joseph Smith then perceived that there was something askew about the whole matter concerning the mysterious rock and the questionable prophecies about the future of the Church. After going to the Lord for help with the very perplexing matter, Joseph received a revelation that was directed at his own counselor, Oliver Cowdery. This revelatory disclosure established just who it is that is actually authorized to receive revelation for the entire Church. The revelation, which is found in the 28th section of the Doctrine and Covenants, proclaims that Joseph Smith is the only one who holds the keys to the mysteries and revelations and the only one on the earth at that time who is appointed by God to receive revelation for the whole Church as it comes directly from the Lord.

The revelation went on to further direct Oliver Cowdery to approach Hiram Page, take him aside, and tell him that without question the dubious revelations he had been receiving from the stone were not of the Lord, but instead of a dark and deceiving power. Therefore it would be well advised for Hiram Page to accept the fact that revelation concerning the whole Church only comes through one man, and that man is the one who holds the authority and the keys given to him by God, not some magic stone. After Oliver spoke sincerely and firmly to Hiram, Hiram consequently was set straight as to who had the authority to receive revelations for the Church. Soon after that, Hiram was touched by the spirit of the Holy Ghost and thus dutifully complied without further argument and furthermore, he denied the stone had any sort of power. He apparently received no more revelations from this mysterious stone. – 2

In the mean time, while Oliver Cowdery was staying in Harmony with Joseph and Emma, he received a call by revelation though the Prophet Joseph to serve a mission to the Lamanite people in Missouri and Ohio where he would be accompanied by Peter Whitmer and Parley P. Pratt. During the interim of Oliver's absence, John Whitmer was designated to take over for Brother Cowdery as Joseph's scribe while the Prophet continued with his translating work. Later on, a new convert by the name of Sidney Rigdon, would be called by revelation to become the chosen scribe for the Prophet as the Prophet continued his work on the translation of the Bible. – 3

Back during these early days of the Church, a young Campbellite preacher by the name of Parley P. Pratt, who at the time had never heard of Joseph Smith, journeyed to New York to begin preaching his Campbellite beliefs. By mere happenstance when Parley P. Pratt was sent forth by his mentor Sidney Rigdon to preach the religion of the Campbellites in New York State, he was introduced to the Book of Mormon by happenstance. Somewhat surprisingly, he was introduced to the book by a Baptist Deacon named Hamblin as they were traveling together on the Erie Canal. Parley soon became infatuated with this new book. He slept little and ate even less while he read the Book of Mormon from cover to cover; he avoided as much interruption as possible and became more and more impressed with it. And so it came to pass that he ended up traveling to Palmyra New York to find out more about its origins from the Smith family, being that he was completely intrigued by the impressive book. At the Smith family home, Hyrum Smith, the Prophet Joseph's own brother, offered to accompany Parley to Fayette to meet with Oliver Cowdery, the Prophet's scribe. It was while he was there that Parley was converted and baptized by Oliver Cowdery and then was ordained as an Elder. He would later have the opportunity to meet the Prophet Joseph Smith himself in Fayette, and he was subsequently called on a mission to the Lamanites in Ohio.

During the fall of 1830, while on their missions, Parley P. Pratt, Ziba Peterson, Oliver Cowdery, and Peter Whitmer visited Mr. Sidney Rigdon at his home near Kirtland Ohio. Sidney had been Parley P. Pratt's highly respected and admired mentor in the Campbellite ministry and so Parley was anxious to introduce Sidney to the Book of Mormon and to this new wondrous religion of Christ. At the time, Sidney Rigdon was the chief Campbellite leader in Ohio.

Presenting Sidney with a bound volume of the Book of Mormon, Parley then with great enthusiasm and sincerity stated to Sidney it was a "Revelation from God." Sidney shortly after that not only accepted this statement to be a genuine truth, but also became quickly converted by Parley's strong testimony and the powerful spirit that comes from the Book of Mormon itself. So it would come to pass that shortly after Parley introduced the Book of Mormon to Sidney Rigdon, he was converted, and so it was that Sidney would soon have his own future changed most dramatically.

In what many would consider as an unprecedented accomplishment, Sidney then persuaded a large portion of his Campbellite followers to come into the new Church of Jesus Christ with him. By December of the year 1830, Sidney had traveled to Fayette to meet with the Prophet Joseph and was soon called by revelation to be Joseph's personal scribe. – 4

While all these positive things were happening in the Church of December 1830, the opposition side of the coin was just beginning to present some of its own very ominous developments. The persecution in New York State and Harmony Pennsylvania had nearly reached a point of being very nearly intolerable. Consequently the Lord spoke to Joseph and gave a commandment for His church to proceed to Ohio: "Behold, I say unto you that it is not expedient in me that ye should translate any more until ye shall go to the Ohio, and this because of the enemy and for your sakes. And again a commandment I give unto the church, that it is expedient in me that they should assemble together at the Ohio, against the time that my servant Oliver Cowdery shall return unto them." - 5

During the cold of winter of 1831 and in the latter part of January, Joseph records that he and Emma, along with Sidney Rigdon and Edward Partridge left New York State to travel all the way to Kirtland Ohio. They finally arrived unannounced and totally unexpected at the store of Newel K. Whitney around the first of February after a long wintery journey. – 6

The unexpected arrival of Joseph at the Whitney store makes for an interesting tale. On arrival Joseph jumped down from the horse drawn sleigh, looked up at the sign on the store and briskly walked up the steps and into the store. He immediately stepped across the room holding out his hand and loudly declared; "Newel K. Whitney, thou art the man."

Mr. Whitney being caught off guard and somewhat at a loss for words indicated that he was apologetic for not knowing to whom he was speaking. Joseph replied matter-of-factly; "I am Joseph the Prophet. You have prayed me here. Now what do you want of me?" Somewhat in shock; Newel asked in disbelief; "You're Joseph Smith?'

Joseph replied that he was, and that he and his wife had just arrived from New York after a long and cold journey. He then asked Mr. Whitney, "Did you not pray for me to come?"

Mr. Whitney replied that yes, he and his wife had been praying for someone to bring them a true faith, but how did Joseph know this? In an incredible and somewhat shocking answer, Joseph explained that he had actually seen Newel and his wife in a vision where they were down on their knees humbly praying at the side of their bed, which Mr. Whitney then verified to Joseph as something that had actually taken place. Mr. Whitney was more than dumbfounded by this revelation of Joseph seeing him and his wife praying, for at the time of this vision, Joseph was still residing in New York and had never even seen or heard of Newel K. Whitney. But

Joseph now recognized Newel the instant that he saw him. At some length and after more fascinating conversation, Newel Whitney insisted that Joseph and Emma should stay at his home just across the street. Joseph's other traveling companions, Sidney Rigdon and Edward Partridge, had made alternative arrangements at the homes of nearby relatives where they could stay for their lodging.

Brother Whitney and his wife were very accommodating to the Prophet and Emma, taking them into their home and then, even turning over the upper part of the store for Joseph's use. The Whitneys would soon become loyal and faithful followers of Joseph Smith and would support and take care of the needs of Joseph and Emma for the next year and a half. Joseph recorded in his own words; "My wife and I lived in the family of Brother Whitney several weeks, and received every kindness and attention which could be expected, and especially from Sister Whitney." - 7

Not only did the Whitneys provide board and room for Joseph and Emma, but also in addition to all the rest of their generosity, they even turned over the upper part of the Whitney store to Joseph for a temporary headquarters for the Church and also provided for a translation and revelation room. Another portion of the upstairs was turned over to the Prophet to be used as a schoolroom. It was this very schoolroom that would become "The School of the Prophets." By revelation through the Prophet they would "teach one another the doctrine of the kingdom" and be "instructed more perfectly in theory, principle, in doctrine, in the law of the gospel, in all things that pertain unto the kingdom of God."

The first session of "The School of the Prophets" began in January of 1833 with fourteen high priests and elders. Through the Prophet Joseph, one of the first revelations that came out of this school was the "Word of Wisdom," which was given to these men specifically due to their very unappetizing and unhealthy personal habits such as smoking, chewing, and the spitting of disgusting splats of chewing tobacco on the floor. Emma's repugnance of having to clean up after these men inspired the Prophet to ask of the Lord concerning the matter. The "Word of Wisdom" thus was given to Joseph Smith at that time and was later extended to the general body of the Church.

Subsequent Prophets declared that it was not just a temporal commandment involving a very beneficial health code, but it had even more important spiritual implications that dealt with the purity of the soul and ones inner desire to have an unblemished spirit as well as a cleansed body. In addition, obeying the "Word of Wisdom" demonstrates to the Lord one's desire to be an obedient servant who wishes to live by His commandments. – 8

So it came to pass that with the new directive from the Lord to move to Ohio firmly held in their minds, large groups of Saints from New York State began to gather at the docks on the Erie Canal and board the canal boats, even as they were being relentlessly persecuted by the religious bigots nearly daily. From there they would travel to the terminal in the city of Buffalo on the shores of Lake Erie, board the steamboats, and continue on sailing west to the port at Fairfield Ohio where they would finish their journey overland to Kirtland.

It was in one of those particular groups of Saints from New York State, that the Prophet's own mother, Lucy Mack Smith, was chosen to lead a group from the Waterloo-Fayette area all the way to Fairfield Ohio by way of wagons, canal boat, and steamship. Although Lucy Mack Smith was less than five feet tall, she had a very commanding presence and did not hesitate to use her powerful personality, experience, and confidence to lead and direct her group as necessary and to guide them by her wisdom and no nonsense thinking. Thus she was able to maintain their trust in her leadership.

When Mother Smith's group finally arrived in Buffalo, they were very disappointed to find out that Buffalo Harbor was closed due to a gigantic ice jam caused by the spring thaw and the relentless and very stiff winds of the Great Lakes jamming huge chunks of ice into the harbor. This resulted in hundreds of stranded passengers, some of whom had been waiting for as long as two weeks, taking up all available room and board in the harbor town. However, Lucy, by her usual no-nonsense resourcefulness, was able to make arrangements with a particular ship's captain to board her people onboard his steamer and she was even able to get him to agree to let them wait out their time while they were camped on the deck of his boat.

Even though these generous arrangements had already been made for them, many of Lucy's highly discouraged followers still wanted to give it all up and go home, and they were quite seriously discussing the idea of returning to the Waterloo-Fingers Lake region. However, Lucy became very insistent that they were not going to give up, but instead, they were all going to carry on just as originally planned, if only by the strength of their faith. She furthermore stated and rather firmly too, that they were all just going to have to stop murmuring, buck up, and persevere through their trials by their prayers and their trust in the Lord. Thus with her forceful confident attitude and irresistible persuasiveness, she was able to shame them into dropping to their knees right there on the steamer's deck, and so they submitted to her unassailable faith. Thus they began praying and asking for forgiveness for their murmuring and for their lack of faith.

It was at that moment that a miracle happened. While they were all in the very act of humbly praying, they heard a very loud rumbling and some distinctive cracking sounds coming from out of the ice jam. As the humbled Saints turned and looked around, they watched a giant crack in the ice wall open wider and wider before their very eyes. The astute Captain without hesitation shouted to his men to "Heave Ho" and ordered them to quickly get the steamer underway. And so in a miraculous turn of events, the steamer was able to slip through the very narrow ice canyon just barely by inches and by no less than a bone fide miracle. For as soon as they had passed through the narrow canyon of jammed up ice, the huge icy gates began cracking loudly and rumbling menacingly as the giant ice gate itself once again began to slowly close up tight right behind the steamer and just as the escaping Paddle Wheeler scarcely reached the freedom of the open water and freeing the Saints to continue their journey. – 9

The other Mormon travelers were not so lucky and that group under the direction of Thomas Marsh, along with the other Colesville group under the leadership of Newel Knight, would have to wait for another day to sail on to the harbor at Fairport Ohio. When Mother Smith's group had first arrived in Buffalo, the other Mormon leaders had strongly advised them to not reveal their religious affiliations so as to not be treated with any bias in obtaining room and board. There may be no actual connection between the lack of success by the other Mormon groups in trying to leave Buffalo and their reluctance to exhibit their faith in front of the non-Mormon crowds in Buffalo for fear of being ridiculed, but yet, there they were still stuck in Buffalo. In contrast, when Mother Smith's meek, humble, and submissive group got down on their knees in front of the entire crowd of onlookers at the wharf and ever so humbly invoked the powers of the Good Lord, they had their prayers answered right on the spot, even as they were praying. And so it was that their solemn request was answered in a very dramatic and miraculous fashion when they chose to acquiesce to the strong admonitions of Lucy Mack Smith and show their faith in sincere prayer. The Prophet Joseph Smith's mother was a truly amazing woman with an extremely strong faith and she seemed to exemplify remarkable leadership abilities.

*　　*　　*

1. See History of the Church 1:86-88 and also HC 1:88-89

2. See section 28 of the D & C

3. See the heading of D&C 35, D&C 32:1-2, and also Teachings of the prophet Joseph Smith, notes p.10

4. See the Life of Sidney Rigdon, by his son, John W. Rigdon (Ms p. 18): See also History of the Church, Vol.1, Ch.11, p.121 & 122

5. See History of the Church, Vol.1, Ch.12, p.139

6. See History of the Church, Vol.1, Ch.13, p.145

7. See History of the Church, Vol.1, Ch.13, p.145

8. See D&C 88:74-80 & Sec. 89 also History of the Church 1:322-324

9. See "History of Joseph Smith by His Mother" – pp 195-197

*　　*　　*

Chapter Six

STARTING NEW IN KIRTLAND

*   *   *

When the Prophet Joseph Smith was given the commandment that the main body of the church was to move to Ohio, the predominant membership of the church at the time was largely coming out of upper state New York. Most of those new members who were following the Prophet Joseph Smith were coming out of the areas of Manchester, Fayette, the Fingers Lake region, and the Colesville-South Bainbridge district. These early Saints, as previously mentioned, found that the best and most practical route to Ohio was to make their way to the north end of state, board the canal boats, and then from there, traverse the Erie Canal to the harbor in Buffalo where they would board the steamships and sail west across Lake Erie to the port at Fairport Ohio. After reaching the harbor at Fairport, their final mode of travel was either by horse and wagon, or on foot as they made the last twelve miles south to their final destination to the small but fast growing community of Kirtland Ohio.

Kirtland wasn't exactly a thriving metropolis at the time, and so by necessity many new cabins had to be built in haste to provide the Saints and their families with housing or some type of shelter for how ever long they might stay. In the year 1831, when the Latter-day Saints were gathering in Ohio, they were a poor people who now found themselves in crowded sparse conditions as they attempted to survive in extremely humble circumstances after leaving their former comfortable homes and moving to a newly developing community with few earthly belongings. From any standpoint of worldly possessions, they were destitute of riches; yet they were united in their common faith, in a positive hope for the future, and by a solid trust in the Prophet Joseph Smith. Furthermore, they were an energetic people with a solid work ethic, and within a short period of just five years, they built beautiful homes for themselves, created a pleasant peaceful community, and constructed a magnificent temple at the considerable cost of $75,000. - 1

There are still many people who don't realize that for seven years the events happening in the Kirtland period in Church history were taking place in parallel with the events happening in Missouri during that very turbulent epoch of the Church's history. In fact, at the June conference of 1831 held in Kirtland, less than six months after Joseph had newly arrived in Ohio, the Prophet received a revelation that the very next conference of the Church would be held in the land of Missouri. The Prophet Joseph would make many trips between these two Church centers between 1831 and 1838. While the arrangements for the trip to Missouri were being made, more than two-dozen new missionaries were called for missionary service at this same June conference. Additionally, Joseph and Sidney Rigdon were commanded by the Lord to journey to the land of Missouri on the Lord's errand, and were to be accompanied by Edward Partridge and Martin Harris. - 2

And so the Prophet Joseph Smith and his companions started their trek to Missouri on the 19th of June 1831 and finally arrived in Independence Missouri during the middle of July. There was one report that said Joseph Smith himself walked all the way from St. Louis to Independence, a distance of about 300 miles. – 3

By August and a month after arriving in Missouri, the Prophet held a sacrament meeting and baptized two new members into the church. Soon after, he felt a need to return to Kirtland. On the trip home, the Prophet and his companions had a frightening experience that could have been very dangerous. The Prophet wrote:

"On the 9th, in company with ten Elders, I left Independence landing for Kirtland." On their way back home as they traveled by canoes, the traveling elders experienced an unusual, perhaps even a frightening occurrence on the river. The heading of D&C Sec. 61 describes it best. "On the return trip to Kirtland the Prophet and ten elders had traveled down the Missouri River in canoes. On the third day of the journey many dangers were experienced. Elder William W. Phelps in a daylight vision, saw the destroyer riding in power upon the face of the waters." – This Revelation through the Prophet Joseph Smith took place on the banks of the Missouri River August 12, 1831, near McIlwaines's Bend. Through it the Saints learned of following decree as it came concerning Elder William Phelps' daylight vision of the destroyer upon the Missouri River.

"For I, the Lord, have decreed in mine anger many destructions upon the waters; yea, and especially upon these waters .... Behold, I, the Lord, in the beginning blessed the waters; but in the last days, by the mouth of my servant John, I cursed the waters. Wherefore, the days will come that no flesh shall be safe upon the waters." (D&C 61:4-5, 14-15.)

Through this revelation the Lord revealed to the Prophet the calamities and disasters of the end times and also, "the perils to be wrought upon the waters in the last days by the destroyer." Never the less, this decree is not meant to discourage or forbid today's modern day Saints from traveling by waterways in these times; it was only meant to warn those Elders at the time with a word of caution during that particular situation, and perhaps as a future warning to be delivered in the last days for that particular prophecy period.

Meanwhile back in Kirtland, there were certain members of the Thompson branch who had originally come from the Colesville New York area, who were now embroiled in a major controversy concerning private property. The dispute was spawned by the disappointing choices of certain new members who had reneged on honoring their consecration covenants. During the course of this exasperating incident that was happening in Kirtland in the year of 1831, a former member of the "Shakers" religion, Brother Leman Copley accepted the Gospel in part, but yet had retained some unproductive ideological baggage from his previous religion. He unfortunately was having a difficult time giving up some of his "Shaker" beliefs.

Among the strange beliefs was a belief that Christ's "Second Coming" had already happened and Christ had already appeared again on earth in the form of a woman by the name of "Ann Lee." Mother Ann had had a vision in England where upon she took the position of being the Shaker leader. Due to much unwarranted persecution she then immigrated to America and started a new following in New York. Supposedly this "Ann Lee" could heal the afflicted by the mere touch of her hand. Though she had passed away more than 45 years before Leman Copley even had joined the Shakers, she still maintained a strong following in the New York area.

In addition to this "Second Coming" fallacy being perpetrated by the Shakers and their mysterious woman Savior, the "Shakers" also did not believe in the eating of meat, especially pork, baptism by immersion, nor did they believe in the holiness of marriage believing that celibacy was of a higher order than marriage. They also avoided socializing outside of their own reclusive communities.

Parley P. Pratt described in some detail the Shaker's odd behaviors: "Some very strange spiritual operations were manifested, which were disgusting rather than edifying, some persons would seem to swoon away and make unseemly gestures, and be drawn or disfigured in their countenances. Others would fall into ecstasies and be drawn into contortions cramp, fits etc. Others would seem to have visions and revelations which were not edifying and which were not congenial to the doctrine and spirit of the Gospel." - Parley P. Pratt

Parley and his fellow brethren found any attempt at trying to change these distorted beliefs to be an extremely offensive affront to the Shaker's pride. Therefore they were very unreceptive to any suggestions or changes, and in general, stubborn and resistant to any corrections. Thus trying to change their minds was a wasted effort bound in futility.

In a response to a request from Bishop Edward Partridge, the Prophet sought after and received a revelation concerning a number of delicate matters concerning their religion, along with a caution regarding some of the erroneous Shaker beliefs. He subsequently sent Leman Copley, Sidney Rigdon, and Parley P. Pratt to the Shaker community near Cleveland to correct their beliefs with the aid of a copy of his revelation. Never the less, and not too surprisingly, the "Shakers" completely rejected the salient points that would correct their errors as stated in Joseph's revelation, and consequently, they did so without even considering the corrections as having any sort of validity, not in the least.

Previous to this particular incident, the Lord had actually made a promise to Leman Copley, which said that if he would be obedient; "and by so doing I will bless him, otherwise he shall not prosper." However, for whatever personal reasons, Leman Coley broke his own covenant to the Church leaders to consecrate his large farm to the LDS Church under the law of consecration, and as a consequence of reneging on his covenant, brother Leman Copley most certainly did not prosper. Later on, after another regrettable incident where he testified against the Prophet in a lawsuit, he eventually humbled himself and asked for Joseph's forgiveness and asked to be reinstated into the Church.

Brother Copley's broken covenant of consecration became one of the major factors in the failing of the "law of consecration" in the Ohio area at that time. Another prominent player in that controversy over concentration of property was Brother Ezra Thayre who was also involved in the property turmoil. Even though the Lord Himself in D&C Sec. 56 told Ezra to repent of his pride, his selfishness, and his ignoring the commandment concerning the place where he lived, he subsequently failed the Lord and sorely disappointed his fellow brethren in the Church. The Lord told Ezra if he would "repent of his pride and of his selfishness and obey the former commandment, he still could be appointed to go to Missouri, otherwise he, "shall be cut off out of my church, saith the Lord God of Hosts." He was subsequently cut off.

These particular incidents involving property consecration caused a significant amount of strife and stress to come into the branch at Thompson Ohio and resulted in a great deal of hardship for the Church members from the Coleville New York area who had been led to believe that they would have property to settle on in Ohio. Brother Newel Knight was the Coleville leader and became highly discouraged and very disappointed in the way things had turned out for his little flock. They had all been very much counting on and were looking forward to settling upon this donated land at Thompson. And now, they were being forced to look for an alternative plan to meet their immediate needs, and so the Prophet's advice was sought. In a response to the touchy situation, Joseph received a revelation that directed Brother Newell Knight to lead his Coleville flock to the land of Missouri. "And thus you shall take your journey into the regions westward, unto the land of Missouri, unto the borders of the Lamanites." – 4

So the Coleville members journeyed to Missouri and arrived in Independence during the same week of August as the Prophet's arrival. They then established a settlement in the Kaw Township of Jackson county Missouri where they acquired property, built homes, and practiced obedience to the Lord in following His specific commandments. In the distant future, this same area would later become known as Kansas City, Missouri. Meantime, they did prosper in light of their obedience, or at least they did for a while, until the mobs forced them to move once again.

During the meantime and in the summer of 1831, a conference was held for all Saints who had gathered in Missouri. At the conference certain special assignments were made. Edward Partridge was made a bishop; Sidney Gilbert was called to be a financial agent, and W. W. Phelps was assigned to be a printer and editor of their local newspaper with Oliver Cowdery as his assistant printer and editor. Soon after Joseph Smith had returned to Kirtland, Bishop Partridge as he had been directed, began buying up real estate for the Saints for their new inheritances.

Although Joseph had received a revelation on his arrival in Missouri, which declared that Independence would be the center of the new Zion and would be the New Jerusalem where the temple would be built, he also had it revealed to him that both Independence Missouri and Kirtland Ohio would continue to be built up for the establishment of the Church and to provide homes for the Saints in both places. As a result, Joseph would keep the road quite warm between Missouri and Kirtland as he made several trips back and forth in the following years.

From the moment Emma Hale Smith married Joseph Smith, any idea of having a permanent home of their own was no more than a dream in the distant future. Between taking care of the needs of the newly organized church, the trips between Missouri and Kirtland, and the dogged harassment that seemed to follow them everywhere they went, there was simply no chance to settle down and stay in any one place for any length of time. Joseph and his family would be driven out of three different states before they would finally find a home in Illinois where they initially built that first cabin on the old homestead. Later on they would build a much bigger and roomier home that they called the Mansion House there in Nauvoo. Even so, that too would turn out to be only temporary.

Meanwhile, after returning to Ohio from Missouri in September of 1831, Joseph held another conference in Kirtland. This gathering turned out to be a life-changing event for one particular couple living in Hiram Ohio, located just south of Kirtland. The couple had developed a great curiosity about the new church and had made plans to attend this particular "Mormon" conference. And so it was that John and Elsa Johnson with their considerable curiosity about the Mormon people and their faith, decided to look into it a bit further. Their own two sons, Lyman and Luke Johnson, had roused their parent's interest when the two brothers announced that they had already joined in with the Saints. Lyman and Luke then urged their parents to attend this particular conference in Kirtland so they would be able to further investigate for themselves and see just what the excitement was all about. After attending this conference and being duly impressed by the Prophet, John and Elsa Johnson further heard that they might possibly have a chance to meet the Prophet Joseph Smith in person, and so they excitedly went to visit with him at the Newell K. Whitney home where Joseph and Emma had been staying through the good graces of the Whitneys.

This good woman, Elsa Johnson, had been suffering severely from a lame arm for many years. Since this affliction had hindered her housework and made all her other activities very difficult, she became extremely interested when the subject of priesthood blessings was brought up during the conversation at the Whitney home. She thus became intensely attentive to what was said and was becoming absorbed in the idea that these healing powers of the priesthood could even possibly cure her own affliction. So she asked about the possibility. After further visiting with her, the Prophet asked her if she truly believed she could be healed by the power of the priesthood. Upon hearing the affirmative answer, he prayed for her and gave her a priesthood blessing that she would be made whole. Miraculously Elsa's arm was healed immediately and she was able to lift it even above her head having full use of it straightaway. Her joy was beyond words and she was certainly more than grateful for this miracle.

One of the witnesses to the Elsa Johnson blessing and healing was Philo Dibble, a new convert who had just been baptized by Parley P. Pratt in Kirtland. His own account of the Elsa Johnson miracle is quite interesting. "There was a woman living in the town of Hiram, forty miles from Kirtland, who had a crooked arm, which she had not been able to use for a long period. She persuaded her husband, whose name was John Johnson, to take her to Kirtland to get her arm healed. ...Joseph asked her if she believed the Lord was able to make him an instrument in healing her arm. She said she believed the Lord was able to heal her arm....he met her at Brother [Newel K.] Whitney's house. There were eight persons present, one a Methodist preacher, and one a doctor. Joseph took her [Elsa Johnson] by the hand, prayed in silence a moment, pronounced her arm whole, in the name of Jesus Christ, and turned and left the room. The preacher asked her if her arm was whole, and she straightened it out and replied: 'It is as good as the other.' The question was then asked if it would remain whole. Joseph hearing this answered and said: 'It is as good as the other, and as liable to accident as the other.' On invitation of Father [John] Johnson, of Hiram, Joseph removed his family to the Johnson home, to translate the New Testament. This was in the year 1831." - 5

Elsa and her Husband being very grateful desired to prove the genuine extent of their gratitude by turning over their own home to the Prophet Joseph, along with Emma and Sidney Rigdon, so Joseph could continue his work. It was there in the Johnson home in Hiram Ohio that Joseph and Sidney would continue the important work of translating and correcting passages in the Holy Bible.

As it all turned out, Hiram Ohio was where the Prophet would receive a dozen and a half revelations over the course of the next six months; sixteen of them are found in today's Doctrine and Covenants. In addition to these revelations, Joseph and Sidney would also have the privilege of receiving a number of visions at Hiram Ohio. Meanwhile, they further found time to conduct several conferences in that area where they were able carry out the important actions that were decided at these very conferences. One such action was to send Oliver Cowdery to Missouri to have the revelations of the Doctrine & Covenants published, and during that same time period, they carried out another objective of formally organizing the first presidency of the Church. In the fulfillment of that particular goal, Joseph chose as his counselors Sidney Rigdon and Frederick G. Williams, and thus those two were set apart for these important callings.

Besides the other work that they were involved in at Hiram, Joseph and Sidney Rigdon had been compiling revelations from the Lord in what they called "The Book of Commandments." Regrettably, even as they worked on these important spiritual undertakings, the ugliness of persecution shoved its impudent face into their lives once again. This time, it was in the very disappointing circumstance of having some former members of the Church turn into vile traitorous apostates and attempt to do serious harm to the Prophet. Somehow these men had been filled with hate and were holding on to ridiculous and silly unjustified grievances against Joseph. And now these disgusting malcontents proceeded to perpetrate their hate in the form of direct acts of physical violence against the Prophet and Sidney Rigdon.

One night while the Prophet Joseph and his family slept at the John Johnson home, a dozen "mobbers" broke into the Johnson house, grabbed Joseph and proceeded to drag him outside in the cold winter air for a violent beating and to be tarred and feathered. In the process of this attack, the evil-intentioned men left the door of the house wide open resulting in the cold night air exasperating the sickly condition of one of Joseph and Emma's adopted twin babies who passed away shortly thereafter. Emma was so traumatized by the unnecessary peril to the baby and the unwarranted violence against her husband, that she was physically and emotionally unable to even attend to Joseph's wounds, and so it was left to some of his friends to take care of him in his bruised and tarred condition.

In addition to all this, the "Mobbers" broke into Sidney Rigdon's home as well, and dragged him outside by his heels across the frozen ground while violently beating him, and then proceeded to tar and feather him just as they had the Prophet. To add insult to injury, the very next day, one of the leaders of these apostates had the audacity to show his hypocritical face in church. He was Simonds Ryder who was holding on to an unwarranted animosity against the Prophet and was nursing nothing more than a silly and ridiculous grievance against Joseph for simply misspelling his name on a paper that would have been his own mission call. One can reasonably assume that he didn't go on that mission, but more than likely was making a much different choice of life's chosen paths, maybe towards the fringes of hell.

The fact that Ryder even showed up in Church the next day showed his blatant hypocrisy and his irreverence for righteousness, as well as his lack of remorse for his sins against the Prophet. The vindictive Simonds Ryder must have been quite shocked and very disappointed when he attended church that next morning and looked up to see the badly bruised but undeterred Prophet Joseph Smith cheerfully preaching his normal Sunday sermon. At this point, the Prophet as responsible, dutiful, and revered leader proceeded to baptize three new members into the Church. – 6

"The works, designs, and purposes of God cannot be frustrated. Neither can they come to naught....Remember, remember that it is not the work of God that is frustrated, but the works of men." - Joseph Smith

*   *   *

1. See Alma Sonne, Conference Report, October 1958, p.25

2. See D&C 52:2-3

3. See Hugh B. Brown, Conference Report, April 1967, p.80

4. See D&C 54:8 & sec. 56:7, See heading to D&C Sec. 49 & Sec. 54

5. See Philo Dibble autobiography, in Faith Prom Classics (1968), p.79

6. See History of the Church 1:215-216 and 261-265

*   *   *

Chapter Seven

TROUBLED TIMES IN MISSOURI

*   *   *

Missouri at the beginning of the nineteenth century could have been a fascinating anthropological study for researchers studying human behavior or certainly an intriguing experiment for the curious minds and observation by sociologists. With the juxtaposition of two diametrically opposed cultures attempting to cohabit under the same sky, it was inevitable that these two very different and incompatible ideologies were bound to collide. It seems to have been one of those unavoidable situations that was bound to degenerate into distrust, biased judgments, extreme harassment, and even violent hate crimes perpetrated against an innocent people. In the final stages, it resulted in Governor Boggs issuing his infamous "Extermination Order" that was carried out by the state's militias who were assisted by the unrestrained severe persecution of the Saints by hateful vigilante mobs. It all resulted in the very bigoted and determined removal of a singled out religious group culminating in the

Saints unjust forced expulsion from Missouri and the elimination of entire Mormon population from that state.

At the time the Mormons first arrived in the state, Missouri was located at the edge of what was then called "Indian country." The land required tough hardened men accompanied by rough, ruddy women to survive in such an environment. The whole of the state suffered from a noticeably blatant lack of civilization with most of the inhabitants giving very little deference to any laws. Many of these unsavory and "rough shod" residents had left eastern civilization to get away from the more restrictive rules of society and a few were even on the run to escape possible prosecution by the law. And they were now crude and raw in their manners, indulging in various forms of debauchery, drinking hard liquor, smoking, spitting, swearing, brawling, amusing themselves with fast loose women, and in general, they were quick on the trigger and ill mannered with little considerations for the rights of any outsiders or any one else's point of view.

Most often they lived in rustic small cabins or in the hovel of a crude sod hut surviving on the merest of basics to sustain life. However, for the most part, these roughshod souls found this to be a perfectly satisfactory life in as much as it met their basic needs for a place to sleep, eat, and to stay dry during inclement weather as they sat around the fire content with a jug of whiskey enjoying the warmth and comfort of their rustic cabins. The majority of the Missourians were living in a state of squalid poverty and so the greater part of these unsophisticated settlers were certainly not in any kind of a financial position to afford the ownership of slaves, never the less; they adamantly supported the practice of slavery.

On the other hand, the Mormon people had immigrated mostly from England, Canada, and the northeastern part of the United States and came from a background where they were ideologically opposed to the whole idea of slavery. This caused the old Missourians to have great concern about the possibility of being out voted politically on any issues of slavery.

Back in 1820 with the help of the somewhat shaky and the hard fought Missouri Compromise, which dealt with the very touchy issue of slavery, the politicians had let Maine come into the Union as a free state and Missouri into the Union as a slave state, the 24th state of the America Union. As part of the compromise, slavery was prohibited from then on in territories north of Missouri's southern border except in the state of Missouri. However, even ten years later, the slavery issue would be a major sore spot between the Mormons and the Missourians, as would their opposing political views on just who had the right to vote in the new state of Missouri.

For the most part even their basic cultural differences were point of a grating irritation to the Missourians and they showed a noticeable disdain for the Mormons. The Mormon "new comers" arriving in Missouri presented a striking contrast to the established existing culture of the unsophisticated old Missourian settlers. In an obvious cultural conflict with the homespun unpolished ways of the Missourians, the Mormon settlers were just a little more cultured in their life style, certainly more literate in reading and writing, generally better educated, neater in their appearance, and they most definitely enjoyed a more refined idea of entertainment as opposed to the rowdy drunken brawls enjoyed by the Missourians. By and in large, the Saints were a more industrious people exhibiting outwardly their desire for nicer homes, nicer yards, and having well kept manicured property, as well as exhibiting better-planned communities.

Somehow, this dramatic contrast between the roughshod Missourian lifestyle and what the Missourians considered as the "uppity" culture of the Mormons, was something of an irritation to the unrefined old settlers and they expressed their annoyance towards the more genteel Mormons with vulgar mocking disdain and often times, just out right belligerent and degrading epithets. For the most part, the Mormons tried to ignore the unremitting insults.

The Saints wasted no time in making themselves at home in their new habitation, planning, building, and settling down into what they hoped would be a more permanent community. As mentioned before, on arriving in Jackson county Missouri on the twentieth of July 1831, the Prophet Joseph held a conference and received a revelation, which in part declared: "Behold, the place which is now called Independence is the center place; and a spot for the temple is lying westward, upon a lot which is not far from the courthouse." In addition, this same revelation gave instructions for purchasing specific plots of land, where as Sidney Rigdon and Edward Partridge were assigned to receive moneys and to act as land agents assigning inheritances. Furthermore, Sidney Gilbert was given an assignment to establish a church store, while William Phelps and Oliver Cowdery were directed to set up and operate a printing office and printing press for the Church. – 1

On the second day of August 1831, a dozen newly arrived Saints, who symbolically represented the twelve tribes of Israel, laid a log on top of a cornerstone that had already been put in placed by Oliver Cowdery. This was considered to be the symbol of the new "Zion City." The very next day they laid a cornerstone for the temple some half-mile west of the courthouse in Independence as designated in the Revelation. Being the sort of industrious people that they were, the new comers immediately set to acquiring land, building cabins, cultivating the soil, sowing crops, and settling in to their new life.

A short year later there were nearly four hundred new Mormon settlers in the Independence area, and by November of 1832 over 800 Saints had arrived. All this growth caused some serious concerns among the old Missourian settlers regarding the very frightening and definitely unwanted possibility of a major shift of political power in their new state. They themselves saw the situation to be nothing less than a serious threat to their very way of life. – 2

It didn't take very long before there were many rumors spreading quickly through the local communities about the Mormons trying to completely take over the county with the intentions of confiscating Missourian property for their "Mormon inheritance." In addition to this, there were rumors that the Mormons were going to supposedly bring in Negroes from the North to corrupt the thinking of the black slaves that were already in Missouri and give them crazy ideas like being freed from their owners and masters. Some of the local Missourians claimed that they had actually heard these unsettling rumors from the Mormon settlers themselves, which in some cases of exaggerated local gossip may have even been true, but it was certainly not backed up by any official agenda of the Mormon leadership.

Back in Kirtland Ohio, in April of 1832, Joseph Smith received a revelation that he, Sidney Rigdon, Newel Whitney, and Jesse Gause should journey to Missouri to encourage and teach the Saints there in Jackson County. Thus they proceeded to Missouri. After spending a month in the Independence area "bucking up" and teaching gospel principles to the local

Church members that were now settled in Missouri, they soon departed and returned to Kirtland.

Meanwhile, the Missourians were exhibiting increasing contempt for the Mormon settlers. By the spring of 1832, minor acts of violence against the Mormons were common, such as throwing stones at what they considered to be the Mormon intruders, shooting at Mormon houses, destroying haystacks, and other comparatively minor harassments. Soon though, there were more serious acts of violence being perpetrated in an attempt to drive the Mormons completely out of Missouri. The Saints made feeble attempts to defend themselves, but this only infuriated the Missourians.

Ironically, some of the worst Mormon haters were actually the local Christian Ministers, such as the infamous Reverend Pixley and the Reverend McCoy. These two so-called Reverends along with a number of other hypocritical Shepherds for Jesus, who should have been representing Jesus Christ in spreading love and good will to their neighbors, had actually become the instigating leaders of this hatred and persecution. And so it was that they led many of the marauding mobsters on their violent raids against the hated Mormons.

The increasingly volatile situation finally came to a boil on July twentieth of 1833, when over four hundred Missourian citizens, including some county officials and law enforcement officers, all met in Independence Missouri to put end to what they perceived as the Mormon encroachment on their homeland. Confronting the Mormon leaders in Independence, the mob leaders then very curtly informed W.W. Phelps, Bishop Edward Partridge, and Sidney Gilbert along with any other Mormons listening to them, that they were all going to have to just shut down their businesses and remove themselves and their families from the whole area and get completely out of Independence. When the Mormon Church leaders asked for a three-month period to comply, they were roughly told, "You have fifteen minutes."

The mob then quickly moved on to brother Phelps' printing office and home and ruthlessly threw his family out into the street including an infant, and then they proceeded to violently destroy the printing office and the press. They also attempted to ruin what they could of the Book of Commandments that brother Phelps and Oliver Cowdery were in the process of printing. Sidney Gilbert's Church store was next on their agenda, but Sidney immediately closed the store down and saved it from the enraged mob's destruction. The unsuspecting Bishop Partridge was not forgotten by the raging angry mobs. After being dragged from his home, he was taken to the public square near the courthouse and tarred and feathered. Other Church members also received a similar painful and humiliating treatment.

In an interesting side note, Mr. Lilburn Boggs, the Lieutenant Governor of Missouri, was said to have been present on that particular day in Independence watching this totally unjustified attack on the Saints and the infringement of their citizens' rights. It was assumed that his lack of making any kind of critical comments that might express his condemnation of these deeds of violence against the Mormons appeared to show that Mr. Boggs approved of these heinous acts against the Mormons despite its unlawfulness and injustice. – 3

While W.W. Phelps' printing office and press were being destroyed, fifteen-year-old Mary Elizabeth Rollins and her sister watched in horror as the angry men devastated everything they could get their hands on at the printing office. When the girls saw the mob throwing out the loose sheets of the Book of Commandments and collecting them in a pile to burn, Mary Elizabeth felt a compelling duty to save what she knew was God's word on those unbound sheets, which the frenzied mob was about to destroy. Even though the girls were trembling in nearly uncontrollable fear, Mary was able to persuade her sister to aid her in this reckless but very courageous deed of running out into the street and gathering into their arms as many of the loose sheets as they could carry.

One of the men from the angry mob spotted the two girls and shouted at them to stop, but they ran behind a building and out into a cornfield to save the Book of Commandments. A number of the infuriated "mobbers" chased after them as the two girls ran for their lives. About thirty yards into the cornfield, the girls laid down flat on the ground between the narrow cornrows and began to pray fervently to their Heavenly Father as they clutched on to the precious papers.

The frustrated men started to systematically search in a criss-cross pattern to find the two little brats that had stolen their fun, but they eventually gave up when they were simply unable to determine if the two brave little girls were even still in the cornfield. The good Lord surely did answer the prayers of the two courageous sisters that were just lying there seemingly invisible to the bad men, ever so still as they prayed, even as they stared at the boots of the enraged mobsters who were diligently searching for them. Even though these angry mobbers had been very determined to find these two little brats, the girls seemed to be miraculously invisible to them, and so the trusting girls were saved from harm by their strong simple faith. – 4

Three days later a group of five hundred armed men accosted some Church members, threatened their homes, and even lashed some of the Mormon men with their cruel whips. Under this kind of pressure, the Mormon leaders agreed to evacuate half their population by the end of the year and the rest by spring. The Saints had appealed to lawyers, law officers, government officials, and even the Governor, all to no avail. They were simply told there was no protection available to their people through any existing official channels or law enforcement as this particular matter appeared to be nothing more than just a local dispute. And then without actually saying it, they insinuated that there was especially no help for any Mormons.

Meanwhile, the Saints were not vacating the premises fast enough for the Missourian ruffians, and so these mob minded men decided to give them a little more incentive to get out of the state just a little bit quicker. On Halloween night, the mobs attacked the Whitmer settlement on the Big Blue River, destroyed several homes and they whip lashed several Mormon men. They also attacked homes near Independence as well as homes and stores right in the town. During one of these attacks, a young Missourian boy was somehow shot in the thigh. When the news spread among the mobs about the young Missourian boy being shot, the Mormon war was on in earnest.

Two days later, a mob of forty ruffians were harassing innocent Mormon women and children near the Big Blue River when a group of thirty Mormon men, only about half armed, arrived to see the plight of the helpless victims and the sight of the barbaric treatment being perpetrated on these innocent Saints. Almost immediately, a violent fray began with many shots being fired by both sides. As a result two Missourians were killed, while several on both sides of the skirmish were wounded. The

Missourians were now infuriated far beyond any possibility of a reasonable non-violent compromise that would provide a way for the Mormons to leave the state peaceably.

On the very next day, November 5th, the Jackson County Militia under the command of Colonel Thomas Pitcher was activated under the authority of the State. He then demanded that the Mormons give up all the Mormon men who had been involved in the skirmish at the Big Blue River and also give up all their weapons immediately. Lyman Wight, a veteran of 1812 war, spoke on behalf of the Mormons saying that they would give up their weapons providing that the Militiamen would also give up their weapons. Colonel Pitcher seemed to agree amicably, but in reality he had no intention of disarming his own men. After the trusting Saints turned over their weapons consisting of a variety of forty-nine guns to the custody of Pitcher, the Colonel unethically reneged on his agreement. Then he took his well-armed Militia and proceeded to go house to house among the Mormons threatening and harassing everyone they ran across, and demanded that all Mormons regardless of their circumstance must immediately get out of Jackson County Missouri or else pay the dire consequences.

The unarmed Saints now had little choice in what to do and so they fled. Some were fired upon or were captured by the Militia and then unmercifully and cruelly whipped. Some 190 women and children were driven across the prairie without food or water, while another 150 were pelted by rain, sleet, and cold in their attempt to reach the banks of the Missouri to cross by the ferry and get out of Jackson County to the safety of Clay county. Soon there were more than 1200 frightened men, women, and children pacing up and down the banks of the Missouri River waiting for their turn to cross the wide and muddy river aboard the sanctuary ferry. They were all hoping to reach the refuge of the other bank before they were further abused, whipped, or even killed. – 5

Mary Elizabeth Rollins, the brave little girl who had saved the Book of Commandments at the W.W. Phelps printing office, now found herself and her family without any money, along with two other families, all of them stranded on the banks of the Missouri without enough cash to pay for the ferry to cross the river. They were becoming increasingly nervous as they anxiously waited to get across to the safety of the other bank, for they didn't know when the mobs might show up at any time to subject them to further harassment and cruelty.

Mary Elizabeth described the situation in her own autobiography: "Some of our brethren were tied to trees and whipped until the blood ran down their bodies. After enduring all manner of grievances we were driven from the county. While we were camped on the banks of the Missouri River waiting to be ferried over, they found there was not money enough to take all over. One or two families must be left behind, and the fear was that if left, they would be killed."

While they were waiting on the banks of the Missouri, one of the brethren suggested to Mary Elizabeth that there was a possibility that the ferry operator might just accept "a big old catfish" in payment for her fare. So the energetic and positive thinking Mary Elizabeth put out some baited fishing lines with one end tied to a tree and the other hooked and baited end tossed out into the muddy waters. Then she got on her knees and proceeded without hesitation to faithfully pray for a big fish. The next morning, Mary Elizabeth not only got her big fish, but a genuine bona fide miracle for a bonus. When Brother Higbee offered to help her gut and clean the huge two-foot long catfish, the two friends unexplainably found three bright shiny silver half-dollars hidden inside the entrails of the fish. It just so happened that that was the exact amount of fare needed for the three stranded families to cross the river, including Mary Elizabeth's family. This incredible miracle of Mary Elizabeth's brought about through her sincere prayer and her actions of faith enabled all three families to pass over the river to other side as they looked to the safety and peace of a new home in Clay County. – 6

While the Saints in Missouri were being driven like cattle from Jackson County, Joseph the Prophet was still residing in Kirtland Ohio, having last been in Missouri in April of 1832. Since then, many of the Saints had moved to Missouri without any consultation or the proper authorization from the church to do so, and then decidedly ignored the law of consecration, as well as engaged in petty arguments and bitter criticisms among their other indiscretions. And so as one looks deeper into the situation, many of the Saints at this time were not generally obedient to what the Lord had in mind for his Saints that were settling in Missouri.

The Prophet's unhappiness with their disobedience resulted in him sending an explicit and straightforward letter to the Saints of Missouri. The Messenger and Advocate published it. And according to John Whitmer's history, the quotes from the letter of chastisement were signed by Joseph Smith, Jun., Sidney Rigdon, Frederick G. Williams, W. W. Phelps and John Whitmer.

The opening paragraph declared that; "The High Priests, Teachers, Priests, and Deacons, or in other words, all the officers in the land of Missouri, belonging to the Church, are more or less in transgression, because they have not enjoyed the Spirit of God sufficiently to be able to comprehend their duties respecting themselves and the welfare of Zion; thereby having been left to act in a manner that is detrimental to the interest, and also a hindrance to the redemption of Zion. Now if they will be wise, they will humble themselves in a peculiar manner that God may open the eyes of their understanding....It will be clearly manifested what the design and purposes of the Almighty are with regard to them, and the children of Zion, that they should let the High Council, which is appointed of God and ordained for that purpose, make and regulate all the affairs of Zion, and that it is the will of God that his children should stand still and see the salvation of redemption." - 7

After the Saints in Missouri had received this justified rebuke from the Prophet, many of these guilty, chastised, prideful, and somewhat unhappy Church leaders there in Independence felt quite offended. Consequently they became extremely critical of their own Church leaders in Kirtland, including going so far as perpetrating the rash act of actually denouncing the letter and severely criticizing the Prophet. This very disappointing and unwarranted faultfinding against the Prophet Joseph Smith found among some of the Missourian Saints included some surprisingly prominent brethren, even men who hitherto were of high standing. Somewhat astonishingly, two of those formerly very faithful brethren just happened to be two of the special witnesses to the Book of Mormon, Oliver Cowdery and David Whitmer. Needless to say, this was extremely disappointing to the Prophet.

When Joseph Smith was made aware of some of these letters of criticism, the Prophet warned them all that the seeds of apostasy would ripen in Zion and they would all eventually be placed under the strong hand of the judgment of God. Later on, when the Prophet heard about the

Saints being so violently driven from Jackson County, he commented that the disobedience of some had resulted in the affliction of all. – 8

*   *   *

1. See D&C sec. 57:1-14

2. See James E. Talmage, Articles of Faith, p.515, Footnotes

3. See History of the Church 1:372-400

4. See "Church History in the Fulness of Times" pp. 133-134

5. See History of the Church 1:426-436 and Autobiography of Parley P. Pratt p.82

6. See "Mary Elizabeth Rollins Lightner" p. 197

7. See History of the Church vol. 2 p 229 Footnotes

8. See History of the Church 1:454

*   *   *

Chapter Eight

THE ENIGMA OF ZION'S CAMP

*   *   *

The harassment and forced expulsion of the Saints by the Missourian mobs in Jackson County continued until every last Mormon was eradicated from the county. Meanwhile, in February of 1834, after hearing of the many injustices in Jackson County, the Prophet received a revelation concerning the very troubling situation. This revelation instructed the Prophet Joseph Smith to lead an expedition to Missouri to defend and give help to the Saints and attempt to aid them in their problems. The expedition would be called Zion's Camp and it would have the mission and purpose of protecting the Saints in Independence, to restore their homes and businesses, and defend their property in the state of Missouri. – 1

There have been a number of people who have thought that Zion's camp mission was an ill-conceived fiasco and in all reality was nothing short of a complete failure. Considering the narrow vision of these skeptics, they completely missed the bigger picture in regards to the overall value of this expedition, an expedition that was commanded by the Lord for His purposes.

It seems as though nothing so completely reveals the true nature of human character, as does a long arduous trek filled with hardship, disappointment, and discouragement. When ordinary human beings are thrown into difficult and trying situations, the good, the bad, and the ugly in them seems to rise to the surface exposing their true nature and revealing their actual inner character. Most certainly, Zion's Camp did bring out the worst and the best in the men that participated in its exhaustive trials and grueling hardships on their way to Missouri.

Joseph Smith's many critics declared Zion's Camp to be a miserable failure of a fallen prophet who had completely lost sight of the true desires of the Lord, and therefore had perpetrated an unnecessary and very dangerous trial on the men who blindly followed him in this misguided adventure. The enemies of the Prophet saw it as nothing less than an egotistical selfish attempt to elevate his own public image or even worse, something that Joseph had concocted from his delusional mind.

However, there were wiser and more faithful men who were more in tune with the right spirit and thus were able to see the bigger picture. It just may have been that the Lord's main purpose in commanding the Zion's Camp expedition was in all reality for the purposes of teaching, training, weeding out the weak, and to create strong leaders to oversee and strengthen His church. The list of prominent and strong leaders that came out of the Zion's Camp ordeal reads like a who's who of the greatest leaders of the Church. That list includes such great leaders as Brigham Young, Heber C. Kimball, Wilford Woodruff, Orson Pratt, Parley P. Pratt, Orson Hyde, George A. Smith, Lyman Wight, and more. Many of them would continue on serving in the Church to become apostles, counselors in the First Presidency, and even more significantly, at least three of them would one day become Prophets and be called as Presidents of the Church.

When Brigham Young, who had himself endured the hardships of the Zion's Camp trek, was confronted by an accusation that the whole trip was a big waste, he had somewhat of a disarming comeback. "Well," said the scoffer, "what did you gain on this useless journey to Missouri with Joseph Smith?"

"All we went for," promptly replied Brigham Young. "I would not exchange the experience gained in that expedition for all the wealth of Geauga County," referring to the county in which the inhabitants of Kirtland lived. - 2

In as much as it was the Lord Himself that had commanded the expedition of Zion's Camp to Missouri, the Prophet Joseph Smith was not about to disobey or ignore it. However, the necessity of leaving Kirtland at that particular time was somewhat inconvenient for the Prophet to say the least. One of the very real concerns on his mind at the time was that he was continually needed at the Kirtland temple site advising, approving, and directing its construction and design. In addition to this worry, he was also very concerned about the Church being right in the middle of a financial crisis with several of its creditors. And to top it all off, there was the added worry of an exasperating lawsuit filed against the Church being perpetrated by an apostate who was trying to take Church owned property.

Although these matters were of importance and needed to be taken care of, if Joseph himself didn't actually lead the expedition to Missouri, it would probably fall flat on its face and never get off the ground. It was going to be difficult enough, even with the Prophet taking the lead, to persuade volunteers to leave their homes and businesses and go on a long arduous and trying journey where they might be involved in a violent armed conflict. And there were many of the Kirtland Saints who felt that the whole affair in Missouri was actually none of their business anyway.

Of course, Joseph did have one positive thing going for him. He knew the Lord "giveth no commandment unto the children of men, save he shall prepare a way for them that they may accomplish the thing which he commandeth them," just as the Prophet Nephi had proclaimed in the Book of Mormon. He knew the Lord would come through for him and "prepare a way" for him to carry out the commandment to go to Missouri. All he had to do was ask and it would be given to him just as Nephi had said. And so it came to past that in response to Joseph's prayerful petitions, the Lord did lay out the best solutions for the most effective answers to Joseph's humble prayers.

First off, the Lord let the Prophet Joseph know that if he was diligent and humble and prayerful, the Lord would soften the hearts of the Church's creditors and He would send a means by which the Church's debts could be paid in full. See (D&C 104:80)

The Lord also inspired the Prophet as to how he could solve the problem of the temple's building supervision, just simply by assigning the very capable Oliver Cowdery and Sidney Rigdon to oversee and direct the temple construction while he was gone. Finally, the Lord answered the third concern simply through the law of the land and its legal system, which then carried out the just workings of the law. The courts themselves took care of the lawsuit worries as they ruled against Philastus Hurlburt who experienced an utter failure in his attempt to take over the Church's property.

Now that all three of Joseph's original concerns were alleviated and solved through the divine help of the Lord, the Prophet was in a position to carry out the Lord's commandment to go to Missouri. However, Joseph's next big hurtle was to be able to persuade a small army of his brethren to drop everything personal and make that long hard journey with him to Missouri. After a long month spent on the road traveling some 550 miles through Ohio, Pennsylvania, and New York, Joseph finally recruited over a hundred men who were willing to go to the rescue in Missouri. The little army would eventually grow to over two hundred faithful men. They left Kirtland on the fifth of May 1834 on what was to be the beginning of a 2,000-mile trek over the next three months, and it would be a learning experience of a lifetime for those who rubbed shoulders daily with the Prophet and bowed before the Lord each night. – 3

The expedition's schedule was rigorous as the men arose at the sound of a trumpet at 4:00 A.M., had prayer and breakfast, and then trekked an average of about 27 miles per day, and in the process, wore many a blister on many a foot. The 130 men were split up into "platoons" of about twelve men each, which was directed and overseen by a captain over each group, but of course, all of them remained under the ultimate leadership of Joseph the Prophet. Joseph even allowed a few of the men to bring along their wives and their children to help with the cooking and laundry.

Unfortunately, and as one might expect in such a large group, not every single member of the expedition was completely in tune, or feeling that "esprit de corps" like they should have. There were a few who just did not show a genuine interest in the general well being of their fellow members nor did they seem to have a serious desire to contribute to and carry out the purposes of the expedition.

There was one particular man in the group, one Sylvester Smith, who seemed to become agitated about something or other almost daily and he became very quarrelsome with the other men of Zion's Camp. Joseph felt compelled to warn the company that unless they maintained a good spirit within the camp, they would be plagued with misfortunes. His warning of "You will know it before you leave this place," most regrettably came to pass.

That very night one of the most devastating trials of the trip arose when all of their horses foundered. This was a very serious situation where the hooves of the horses became inflamed within the sensitive tissues inside the hoof, which rendered them crippled and unable to continue on with the journey. It goes without saying that all the horses were desperately needed to pull the twenty wagons, and so this brought the expedition to a dead halt rendering the entire expedition incapable of carrying on any further. When Joseph learned of the fate of the horses and realized why it was happening, he told the men that all of those "who would humble themselves before the Lord, should know that the hand of God was in this misfortune, and their horses should be restored to health immediately."

After the men humbled themselves and prayed, they were rewarded. By noon the same day the horses had recovered and were up on their feet and ready to continue the journey, with one exception, and that was Sylvester Smith's horse. The poor thing became very ill and promptly died. Perhaps it was just a coincidence that Sylvester's horse was the only one that succumbed to the affliction. Never the less, it is a fact of this existence, that sooner or later in life, one will receive a just and proper reward for whatever good or whatever bad one does in the course of living their life.

Shortly thereafter, following Joseph's warning to avoid contention in the camp, the camp was faced with an array of lesser but very exasperating trials ranging from fear of milk sickness to some minor mishaps while they were crossing the mighty Mississippi river. One of the unexpected trials came from dealing with the locals. Most surprisingly, a strong anti-Mormon sentiment from the area's residents seemed to pop out of the clear blue. Some of the local inhabitants had even sent spies into the Mormon camp to ascertain just who this company was, where had it come from, and just what business did they have even being in the area? For the most part, although the nosey inquiries and assorted disparagements were annoying, they did little harm and did not hinder the expedition.

Meanwhile as they continued their travel through the Illinois area, the men of Zion's camp became quite intrigued when they discovered a large hill topped with ancient altars. These altars and other ancient constructions had been left behind by the famed "Mound Builders." In one of the mounds they discovered a skeleton of an ancient warrior that appeared to have been killed by an arrow. Joseph's explanation of just who the warrior was amazed the men of the expedition.

Elder Heber C. Kimball who was with the camp on that occasion recorded the incident in his journal: "While on our way we felt anxious to know who the person was who had been killed by that arrow. It was made known to Joseph that he had been an officer who fell in battle, in the last destruction among the Lamanites, and his name was Zelph." - 4a

In another fascinating incident, the company was somewhat endangered by a very nerve-racking encounter with a large number of rattlesnakes coming into the camp. Though the snakes presented a very real possibility of being a danger to the men, the Prophet who had a deep respect for all life, somehow persuaded his men to not kill the snakes, but instead, asked the men to carefully carry the rattlesnakes out away from the camp and turn them loose to live another day.

As the expedition wore on, the spirit of dissension started to spread among some of the men, mostly stirred up by Sylvester Smith. He hated Joseph's pet bulldog and even threatened to kill it, which Joseph uncharacteristically responded to Sylvester with a threat of his own. He turned to Sylvester and said, "If you kill that dog, I'll whip you." Sylvester was sorely offended by the threat and accused Joseph of having unfairly singled him out to be picked on and harassed. He continued to spread his disruptive dissension among the others and became more and more obstinate and so he "pretty much disagreed" most churlishly with every decision Joseph made. The fact was that in reality, he was opposed to the whole idea of Joseph's leadership in any form. He continued to severely criticize the Prophet's abilities to make any wise decisions what so ever and so attempted to orchestrate dissension among the ranks.

Even after the members of Zion's Camp had returned to Kirtland, Sylvester was so obsessed with creating difficulties for the Prophet that he had the audacity to make criticizing statements and accusations against Joseph back home. As one of the High Councilors in Kirtland, he accused President Joseph Smith with criminal conduct during their journey to and from Missouri. The High Council seeing through Sylvester's unfounded vitriol, apathetically ignored most of his criticisms and so he eventually gave up his disrespectful accusations against the Prophet. At a later date, and for whatever reason, he became penitent and finally did apologize for his false accusations and his disruptive conduct. - 4b

Sylvester Smith was by far the worst thorn in Joseph's side, but there were others who also tried the Prophet's patience during the Zion's trek. Some of the men were lazy; others irresponsibly fell asleep on guard duty, many seemed to complain unceasingly about the inconveniences of the trek, others acted more like a bunch of children dragging their feet when ever they were asked to follow up on their assignments.

At one point, Joseph became quite upset with Martin Harris and was compelled to rebuff him for attempting to arrogantly show his fellow travelers that he could handle poisonous serpents without being harmed through the power of his priesthood. Joseph recorded the incident as such; "Martin Harris having boasted to the brethren that he could handle snakes with perfect safety, while fooling with a black snake with his bare feet, he received a bite on his left foot." - 5

In response to the irresponsible incident, Joseph reminded Martin and the other brethren listening to him that the Lord would protect them from this kind of harm when necessary, but would not protect them from their own foolish stupidity. They were warned to never put the Lord to the test where they were deliberately provoking an unnecessary demonstration of His power, especially when it came from out of a selfish desire to bolster one's own vanity. This most certainly would not be a very wise thing to do. Apparently Martin did recover from the bite and thus became a wiser servant to the Lord and his fellow travelers.

The rebellious spirit in the camp continued to spread until Joseph warned them once again that they must repent of this bad spirit or he would not be able to stop what ever would come next in the form of the Lord's chastisement through His powerful hand. Just before Zion's camp crossed the Mississippi into Missouri, the Prophet stood on a wagon wheel and told the entire encampment that they were going to suffer a severe scourge due to the spirit of rebellion and the contentious air among the camp members.

The Lord revealed to the Prophet on the Fishing River of Missouri in June of 1834 the following: "And my people must needs be chastened until they learn obedience, if it must needs be, by the things which they suffer." See (D&C 105:6.) Three weeks later a deadly cholera epidemic broke out amongst them, not only devastating Zion's camp itself with fourteen members of the camp dying from the affliction, but even affecting some of the local members of the Church living in the area, and most regrettably, resulting in several untimely deaths.

As they continued on their journey to Missouri and drew nearer to Jackson County, there arose rumors of a large group of Missourians that were headed their way. This scuttlebutt stirred up a contentious debate among the men over what would be the safest place for their next campsite. In consequence, about twenty of the so-called faithful Saints rejected the Prophet's leadership and in a spirit of mutiny, chose to follow Lyman Wight and Sylvester Smith to an alternate camping site in the woods as opposed to the site the Prophet had chosen on the prairie. A few hours later, and after some thoughtful soul searching by Lyman Wight, he and the other dissenters humbly rejoined Joseph's camp. The unrepentant Sylvester Smith, however, retained his fractious and rebellious attitude. – 6

Just as Zion's Camp approached Liberty Missouri, five well-armed Missourian ruffians approached the camp to ask with an air of contempt, if this was the mighty Mormon army they had been hearing so much about. Lyman Wight and Joseph spoke to them with politeness but firmness. The ruffians mocked them and caste detestable threats upon the whole camp saying, "They would all see Hell before morning." They then left abruptly while shouting something about a large group of Missourians being on their way to wipe out the Mormons once and for all.

After the ruffians left, the Mormon army settled into near chaos and much disarray as wild speculation tore the unity of the group completely apart. After some somewhat calming and realistic reasoning, Joseph was able to quite them down and calmly told them that they were on the Lord's errand and the Lord would protect them. He then powerfully proclaimed; "Brethren, stand still and see the salvation of God." - 7

Then suddenly they heard the thunder of hooves coming from off the river bottom near the Big Fishing River. Thirty or forty Missourians riding hard and fast appeared to be heading directly towards the camp, and almost certainly with the idea in their heads of wiping out the Mormons. Pandemonium broke out in Zion's camp as the men attempted to quickly arm themselves and prepare for the inevitable attack.

And then it happened; without any forewarning at all, the Lord showed the power in His mighty hand. Out of a clear sky, a huge black ominous cloud appeared out of nowhere, and only moments later a deluge of torrential rain and hail accompanied by deafening thunder and blinding strikes of lightning from God Himself wracked the eerie scene. The Mormon men quickly found shelter in an old abandoned Baptist church. The Prophet Joseph came inside all wet while shaking the rain off his hat, and then proclaimed that the hand of God was in this storm. Joseph Smith's description of the scene is intriguing:

"When these five men were in our camp, swearing vengeance, the wind, thunder, and rising cloud indicated an approaching storm, and in a short time after they left the rain and hail began to fall. The storm was tremendous; wind and rain, hail and thunder met them in great wrath, and soon softened their direful courage, and frustrated all their designs to kill Joe Smith and his army." - 8

The Missourians on that day were not as lucky as the Mormons in finding shelter as the devastating storm caught them by complete surprise. It pelted them unmercifully stopping them dead in their tracks, and so their unwarranted attack on the Mormon army was quickly forgotten as they attempted to dodge the stinging hail and the deadly lightning bolts while scrambling for their very survival. In addition, the now churning muddy river was filled with dangerous trees and broken limbs like a conveyer belt of giant clubs that would make it a suicide mission to cross over the river in any further attempts to attack the hated Mormons. And so it was that the malevolent intentions of the Mormon hating Missourians were brought to a dramatic end, completely thwarted by the divine intervention of a deluge from the hand of God.

When the men of Zion's Camp finally timidly came out of the old church, they suddenly realized that they had miraculously been spared from the worst of the storm. It appeared that the area around the church had hardly been touched while every thing else had been unmercifully pelted with an unusually destructive hailstorm. Again Joseph describes what happened.

"Many of my little band sheltered in an old meetinghouse through this night, and in the morning the water in Big Fishing river was about forty feet deep, where, the previous evening, it was no more than to our ankles, and our enemies swore that the water rose thirty feet in thirty minutes in the Little Fishing river. They reported that one of their men was killed by lightning, and that another had his hand torn off by his horse drawing his hand between the logs of a corn crib while he was holding him on the inside. They declared that if that was the way God fought for the Mormons, they might as well go about their business." – 9

After the storm Joseph described another scene: "We drove five miles on to the prairie where we could procure food for ourselves and horses,... While camped here on Saturday the 21st, Colonel Sconce, with two other leading men from Ray county, came to see us, desiring to know what our intentions were; 'for,' said he, 'I see that there is an Almighty power that protects this people, for I started from Richmond, Ray county, with a company of armed men, having a fixed determination to destroy you, but was kept back by the storm, and was not able to reach you.' ..."

Joseph made his response: "Addressing them, I gave a relation of the sufferings of the Saints in Jackson county, and also our persecutions generally, and what we had suffered by our enemies for our religion; and that we had come one thousand miles to assist our brethren, to bring them clothing, etc., and to reinstate them upon their own lands; and that we had no intention to molest or injure any people, but only to administer to the wants of our afflicted friends; and that the evil reports circulated about us were false, and got up by our enemies to procure our destruction. When I had closed a lengthy speech, the spirit of which melted them into compassion, they arose and offered me their hands, and said they would use their influence to allay the excitement which everywhere prevailed against us;..." - 10

The weak-spined and biased Governor Dunklin of Missouri refused to uphold the laws of the land that were already put in place by the Nation's forefathers to protect all of the citizens of this Nation, as well as the citizens of his own state, which technically should have included the Saints and their property just like everyone else. The Governor subsequently announced very unsympathetically and with a brazen attitude some strong and chilling advice to all the Mormons in Missouri; "Sell your property and just get completely out of Jackson County for your own safety."

It was very soon after this insensitive and unsympathetic advice, that the Prophet Joseph received divine revelation from the Lord on the banks of the Fishing River on the 22nd of June 1834. He forthwith ordered General Lyman Wight to discharge all of the men of the Zion's Camp Company immediately. A short time later, the Prophet himself made it official and disbanded Zion's Camp permanently giving its members leave to return to their homes. Zion's Camp and its seemingly failed mission had come to a sudden and inglorious end. – 11

Many critics have been quick in their attempt to point out the folly of Zion's Camp and the waste of time of its seemingly failed mission, and have called it a great-misguided and unnecessary useless endeavor. These opinionated and narrow-minded personal judgments reveal the limited view of the critics who have completely missed the point in their understanding of the Lord's real purposes. The Prophet Joseph Smith saw much more in the value of Zion's Camp, such as an incalculable value in its treasure of leadership training and the weeding out of unreliable men, which it turned out to be.

Even though Oliver Cowdery himself had missed out being in on the Zion's Camp trek, after hearing the various reports of the expedition, contemplating those events, and making his own personal assessments, he more or less attempted to sum up the Zion's Camp expedition in his own opinionated editorial in "the Evening and Morning Star." His overall assessment was less than stellar as it follows:

"Had the members of Zion's camp been more faithful, less contentious, more united; had the saints in the eastern branches had more faith, faith to send up to Zion more men and more money with which to strengthen the hands of the saints on the land of Zion, the history of Zion's camp might have been different: for with a larger force they would doubtless have been able to hold their lauds against the mob, ...thus it is: what men and great movements might attain to is often defeated, sometimes by the actions of enemies, sometimes by the lack of devotion and faith and energy on the part of those into whose hands great enterprises are committed. While God's general purposes will never ultimately be defeated by man, ... the history of this first march of Zion's camp; and the redemption of Zion has been left to other hands, and to other times. But that its redemption will come no one doubts who believes in the firm decrees of God." - 12

The Prophet Joseph Smith and the Lord had no such reservations. Brother Joseph in the meantime had already received a revelation concerning the brethren of Zion's Camp, and in this divine disclosure, the Lord said he had accepted the offering of sacrifice by the brethren of Zion's Camp, even as he accepted that of the Prophet Abraham and therefore He had a great blessing laid up in store for them. Their sacrifice was not wasted.

*   *   *

1. See D&C 103:24-40

2. See History of the Church, Vol.2, Introduction, p.23

3. See History of The Church 2:40 and 2:63-101

4a. See Joseph Fielding Smith Jr., Doctrines of Salvation, Vol.3, p.239

4b. See History of the Church, Vol. 2, Ch.10, p.142

5. See History of the Church Vol. 2 Chap. 7 Zion's Camp in Missouri

6. History of the Church 2:63-101 and Church History in the Fullness of Times pp.141-151

7. See History of the Church Vol. 2, p.102-106, also Gerald Lund's "The Work and the Glory", vol. 2 p.430

8. See History of the Church Vol. 2, Ch. 2, and see History of the Church, Vol.2, Ch.7, p.105

9. See History of the Church 2:102-106 and History of the Church, Vol.2, Ch.7, p.105

10. See History of the Church, Vol.2, Ch.7, p.105

11. See section heading to D&C 105:7-10 and also History of the Church 2:108- 111

12. See History of the Church, Vol.2, p.126, Footnotes

*   *   *

Chapter Nine

THE GLORY DAYS OF KIRTLAND

*   *   *

It would be well to be reminded that the inspired search for the priesthood brethren, who would be chosen to become the first Twelve Apostles in this dispensation, actually began in June of 1829 nearly ten months before the Church was even organized in April of 1830. At that time the Lord through revelation emphasized to Oliver Cowdery and David Whitmer that their calling was the same as that of the Apostle Paul's and then He gave them a commandment to "search out the twelve."

"And now, behold, I give unto you, Oliver Cowdery, and also unto David Whitmer, that you shall search out the Twelve, who shall have the desires of which I have spoken;" - D&C 18:37

At the particular time this revelation was given, Martin Harris unfortunately had once again found himself out of favor with the Lord by wavering in his faith and therefore had been excluded at this point in time. And so it was that the other two brethren, Brother Cowdery and Brother

Whitmer, were told by word of the Lord that they would be guided and inspired in making these most important choices in the search for the twelve apostles. The Lord declared in D&C 18:38, "And by their desires and their works you shall know them."

Six years after those particular words of the Lord had been spoken, and not too long after the trials and hardships of Zion's Camp, the inspired selection of the Twelve Apostles all came together. In February of 1835, eight months after their return from Missouri and after Zion's Camp had been disbanded; the Prophet held a special meeting in Kirtland and invited all those who had participated in the Zion's expedition to meet with him. He told them that God had not designed the trials and suffering that they had all endured on that trek simply for nothing. He then with help from two of the three witnesses proceeded to name and call Twelve Apostles out of that group of men. Under the supervision of the Prophet and by the capable hands of Oliver Cowdery and David Whitmer, who had been previously instructed by the Lord to do this, twelve brethren were ordained to the apostleship, and they were given "the power to heal the sick, cast out devils, raise the dead, give sight to the blind, have power to remove mountains," and it was declared that angels would minister unto them and all things should be subject to them through the name of Jesus Christ.

It is still somewhat unclear as to just how much participation Martin Harris had in the selections of the Twelve Apostles. The fact that Oliver Cowdery, Brother Whitmer, and the Prophet Joseph Smith made the inspired choices for the Twelve Apostles very soon after their return from Missouri has been well established, but Martin Harris' actual role in the selections is a bit sketchy. The following notes from Elder Kimball seem to say Martin Harris may have possibly been involved in some way, but offer little clarification in exactly what way.

The writings of Heber C. Kimball in the published extracts of his journal, give his view of the matter. After listing the names of the Twelve men chosen, Elder Kimball writes: "After having expressed our feeling on this occasion, we were severally called into the stand, and there received our ordinations, under the hands of Oliver Cowdery, David Whitmer, and Martin Harris." So here he named Martin Harris as being a part of the ordinations.

"While these statements make it very clear that the Prophet Joseph did not join with the Three Witnesses in ordaining the Apostles--except in the way of confirming the ordination they received from the Witnesses, as described by Elder Kimball--the minutes of the meeting held February 21st, at which Parley P. Pratt was ordained, state that he was 'ordained one of the Twelve by President Joseph Smith, Jun., David Whitmer, and Oliver Cowdery.' Martin Harris must have been absent, and the Prophet evidently joined Oliver Cowdery and David Whitmer on that occasion because of the absence of Harris; but whether or not the Prophet was mouth on that occasion does not appear in the minutes or in Elder Pratt's autobiography." – 1a

Nine of these Twelve Apostles had endured the trials of Zion's Camp and had been well initiated and prepared for their new callings having survived the many taxing tests of perseverance, obedience, and enduring the ordeal of facing the Church's most violent enemies. They had passed their trials of leadership and as such, now appeared before the Lord well tested and ready and willing to accept their callings and thus fittingly prepared for their challenging leadership positions through the trials of adversity that they had endured during the Zion's Camp trek.

Two weeks later, the Prophet was inspired to organize the First Quorum of the seventy and every one of those brethren had also been with him on the Zion's Camp expedition. Some time later, the Prophet would reflect in deep thought on those men who had died during the Zion's camp expedition, and would say that if he himself received no more of a mansion as bright as theirs, he would "ask no more." -1b

And so it was at this time that the first apostles in this dispensation were finally called to fill the important positions of the first Quorum of the Twelve Apostles. These especially chosen twelve men were Lyman Johnson, Luke Johnson, Brigham Young, Heber C. Kimball, Orson Hyde, David W. Patten, William E. McLellin, John F. Boynton, Orson Pratt, William Smith, Thomas B. Marsh, and Parley P. Pratt.

Ironically, even though these Twelve Apostles had been chosen by what one would assume as inspiration and for their potential to be faithful and righteous servants in the building up of God's Kingdom, at least half of these especially called brethren would neither fulfill their potential as apostles of the Lord nor would they remain faithful to the Prophet or steadfast in the Church. And so in a very disappointing and sad turn of events, several of these especially chosen men would regrettably not only apostatize from the Lord's Church, but they would manifest the utmost disloyalty to the Prophet Joseph Smith and would eventually leave the Church with much bitterness. Some of them would even attempt to do as much damage to the Church as possible. This very disappointing and particular list of shamed brethren, shame brought upon themselves by their disloyal apostate actions, would include the following men: the two brothers, Luke and Lyman Johnson, William E. McLellin, John F. Boynton, the Prophets own brother, William Smith, and most regrettably, the President of the Twelve, Thomas B. Marsh.

Considering the fact that their initial callings were assumed to have been inspired by the Lord, it was extremely disappointing that they had now absolutely failed in their callings as apostles. Their sacred calls were subsequently blighted by their own actions of a disappointing betrayal to the Prophet and the Lord. One has to seriously wonder why God didn't inspire the Prophet Joseph Smith in the beginning and let him know ahead of time as to their fatal flaws before they were chosen. It would have been nice to have been able to avoid the embarrassment and strife that was created by calling these disappointing dissenters. If Joseph had been made aware of their serious shortcomings before they were ever called to these high positions, certainly better choices could have been made.

But on the other hand, looking at the bigger picture, one must consider the fact that only the Lord can see the entire picture of free choice, moral agency, and redemption, which allows the basic principle of the Lord's plan of salvation to apply to all men. No matter how lowly or high their station, all men have the universal entitlement of having the all-inclusive free agency to make bad choices and what may seem to be really stupid mistakes. This privilege even goes for men of high position from which a great deal is expected, however very disappointing their choices may be to the Lord and His prophets. Of course, we must not forget that Satan was probably involved up to his neck in these bad choices and thus can be given a lot of the credit for influencing these disappointing choices and their dismaying outcomes where these men were concerned.

However, on the more positive side of things, the rest of the Twelve Apostles who were called to these high callings, except for David W. Patten who was martyred, would go on to singularly distinguish themselves by their works, their loyalty, and their extreme faithfulness in carrying out their duties. And through their praiseworthy steadfastness and faith, they would press on to become some of the greatest and most honored leaders in the Church, including that of becoming faithful Apostles and even highly respected members of the First Presidency.

Meanwhile, back in Kirtland the Prophet's thoughts and energy turned to the monumental project of building a temple to the Lord. In December of 1832, the first temple erected in this dispensation was commanded by the Lord to be built on a specified location in Kirtland Ohio where the Lord said that His house would be built upon this spot, "even a house of prayer, a house of fasting, a house of faith, a house of learning, a house of glory, a house of order, a house of God." – 2.

It should be remembered that the Saints at this time were still comparatively few in numbers and very poor in worldly possessions, and hardly in any position to build such an expensive edifice. Never the less, they were asked by their Prophet and the Lord to make great sacrifices, persevere through their poverty, and employ their best efforts to erect a magnificent temple in the name of the Lord, one which would be worthy of his name. And so it came to be, that more than three years later the Kirtland temple was finally completed and dedicated on the 27th day of March 1836.

The very special events surrounding the dedication of the Kirtland Temple went beyond just being the most impressive beautiful temple dedication ever conducted. This awe-inspiring occasion was glorified by the most unusual and the holiest of spiritual manifestations like no other time in all of Church history. The events of that day were so resplendent, so magnificently inspiring, and so exalting that it is difficult for many people even today to believe that they actually did occur. Yet there were dozens of eyewitnesses who actually saw and experienced these miraculous events. Not all of those present saw everything that was going on at the time of this glorious occasion, but there were a great many Saints who were granted the privilege of observing manifestations of spirits, seeing glorious angels, experiencing visions, and a few who prophesied and spoke in tongues. The house of the Lord was filled with heavenly beings that were seen by most of the congregation, and a few Saints even claimed that they had the privilege of seeing a vision of the Savior.

The spirit of prophecy came upon a number of the leading priesthood brethren, just as it had done some 2000 years ago on the day of Pentecost as described in the second chapter of Acts. And just as those ancient proceedings were presided over by the holy priesthood authority of the Apostle Peter on the Day of Pentecost, the Prophet Joseph Smith presided in authority here at the Kirtland temple with a similar priesthood power. On this special occasion, the Prophet Joseph Smith gave a very specific prayer of dedication that was given to him by revelation as it is found today word for word in section 109 of the Doctrine and Covenants.

The Prophet described these magnificent and miraculous proceedings by saying, "when a noise was heard like the sound of a rushing mighty wind, which filled the Temple, and all the congregation simultaneously arose, being moved upon by an invisible power; many began to speak in tongues and prophesy; others saw glorious visions; and I beheld the Temple was filled with angels, which fact I declared to the congregation. The people of the neighborhood came running together (hearing an unusual sound within, and seeing a bright light like a pillar of fire resting upon the Temple), and were astonished at what was taking place." - 3

And so by the means of these holy manifestations, it was clearly made known to the Prophet and to the Kirtland Saints that the Lord had truly accepted this sacred edifice as His house, as was evidenced by the many demonstrations of his divine spirit being present. Thus the Kirtland Temple had now become undeniably the house of the Lord and it now had the distinction of being the very first temple to be erected in modern times; "for not since the days of ancient Israel had a Temple been erected among God's chosen people to honor the Holiness of the Lord." – 4

Even before the temple at Kirtland was finished and while it was still under construction, it was put into limited use. As soon as provisions would allow, there were sections of the temple that were used for class instruction as well as for other auxiliary purposes. In fact, as early as January 1836, which was more than two months before the temple dedication, the first of the preliminary or partial endowments were performed in the Kirtland temple. The Lord had already instructed the Prophet Joseph Smith in this particular preliminary ordinance while the Prophet was still camped on the Fishing River in Missouri during the Zion's Camp trek, and it was there that the Prophet was commanded to bring this holy ordinance to the Saints. See D&C 105:33

Never the less, the Kirtland temple was never built to be a full service temple, but instead was only intended to be a preparatory temple. In fact there was no provisions made in this temple for the salvation of the dead and there was no baptismal font, and no full endowments were done for the dead. "An endowment, such as was necessary at the time, was given in part but this was not as complete as the endowment would be later revealed," and as it would come to be in the full service temples.

Therefore not all of the temple ordinances were given to the Prophet at this time. Later on, what ever the Kirtland Temple may have lacked in ordinance completion, the Nauvoo Temple would be constructed according to a more perfected pattern to provide for the completion and performance of all the sacred ordinances as was later shown to the Prophet Joseph Smith. – 5.

Most regrettably, just as the Temple of Solomon was defiled and polluted in ancient times back in the days of old Jerusalem, the Kirtland Temple would also be polluted and defiled. Sadly, this desecration would come about through the bitterness and animus of the Church's own apostate members who had been disguised in sheep's clothing up until this time and were then found surreptitiously strewn among the Church's own members. Consequently, through the apostate's evil efforts and unholy defilement, the Kirtland Temple would necessarily cease to be a sanctuary to the Holiness of the Lord, and therefore today it is no longer extant as a sacred temple even though it still exists as a physical building in Kirtland Ohio.

However, one must understand that even if it had never been defiled, the Kirtland Temple was never designed to be used with all the necessary essential ordinances that are performed in the Church's modern temples today. Even though the ordinance of the washing of the feet, and the preliminary or partial endowments were performed within its walls, it simply was not dedicated to be a full service temple. Never the less, the Kirtland Temple did serve a vital purpose as a very important structure during its short season of existence as a holy edifice. And thus it had been especially dedicated to achieve its particular mission and fulfill the Lord's special intended purposes for that particular time, place, and season, and however short the time must have seemed, the Kirtland Temple did fulfill its important mission.

The truth of that very significant statement is evidenced by a most glorious event that happened shortly after the 1836 March dedication of the Kirtland Temple. A few days later, on the very special day of April 3rd 1836, an event of an exalting spiritual affirmation came from the Lord. The Savior Jesus Christ, Moses, Elias, and Elijah appeared to Joseph Smith and Oliver Cowdery at the Kirtland Temple on that day. At this time the divine messengers restored the absolutely invaluable keys of the restoration of the true gospel of Jesus Christ. This most important momentous occasion would be the sublime and outstanding final event to cap off Kirtland's glory days. – 6

The prophet introduced this special event by saying; "In the afternoon, I assisted the other Presidents in distributing the Lord's Supper to the Church, receiving it from the Twelve, whose privilege it was to officiate at the sacred desk this day. After having performed this service to my brethren, I retired to the pulpit, the veils being dropped, and bowed myself, with Oliver Cowdery, in solemn and silent prayer. After rising from prayer, the following vision was opened to both of us." – 7

The vision is thus detailed in some very captivating and inspirational passages by the Prophet in D&C 110, verses 1-16, that describe this magnificent event and the holy manifestations that Joseph and Oliver experienced in the Kirtland Temple on that special day of April in 1836. This pivotal event is highlighted by the divine appearance of Moses, Elias, and Elijah restoring some of the most important keys of the Gospel in an unprecedented occurrence. One can barely absorb or even imagine the sublime glory and the extraordinary importance of this awe-inspiring event as one reads the following verses.

*   *   *

D&C 110:1 "THE veil was taken from our minds, and the eyes of our understanding were opened."

2 "We saw the Lord standing upon the breastwork of the pulpit, before us; and under his feet was a paved work of pure gold, in color like amber."

3 "His eyes were as a flame of fire; the hair of his head was white like the pure snow; his countenance shone above the brightness of the sun; and his voice was as the sound of the rushing of great waters, even the voice of Jehovah, saying:"

4 "I am the first and the last; I am he who liveth, I am he who was slain; I am your advocate with the Father."

Then following up in the next important section, verses 11 through 16 of the Doctrine and Covenants, it continues on to declare:

D&C 110:11 "After this vision closed, the heavens were again opened unto us; and Moses appeared before us, and committed unto us the keys of the gathering of Israel from the four parts of the earth, and the leading of the ten tribes from the land of the north."

12 "After this, Elias appeared, and committed the dispensation of the gospel of Abraham, saying that in us and our seed all generations after us should be blessed."

13 "After this vision had closed, another great and glorious vision burst upon us; for Elijah the prophet, who was taken to heaven without tasting death, stood before us, and said:"

14 "Behold, the time has fully come, which was spoken of by the mouth of Malachi--testifying that he Elijah should be sent, before the great and dreadful day of the Lord come-"

15 "To turn the hearts of the fathers to the children, and the children to the fathers, lest the whole earth be smitten with a curse-"

16 "Therefore, the keys of this dispensation are committed into your hands; and by this ye may know that the great and dreadful day of the Lord is near, even at the doors."

*   *   *

And so it was that on April 3rd 1836 in the Temple at Kirtland Ohio that the Lord unquestionably proclaimed His acceptance, His intentions, His promises, and His expectations, and most clearly expounded His covenant and warning to the Prophet Joseph and the Saints saying:

D&C 110:7 "For behold, I have accepted this house, and my name shall be here; and I will manifest myself to my people in mercy in this house."

D&C 110:8 "Yea, I will appear unto my servants, and speak unto them with mine own voice, if my people will keep my commandments, and do not pollute this holy house." Amen.

*   *   *

1a. See Times and Seasons, vol. vi, p. 868

1b. See History of the Church 2:181n.

2. See Joseph Fielding Smith Jr., Doctrines of Salvation, Vol.2, p.239 - p.240

3. See History of the Church, vol. 2, p. 428.

4. See Joseph Fielding Smith Jr., Doctrines of Salvation, Vol.2, p.240 - p.243

5. See Joseph Fielding Smith Jr., Doctrines of Salvation, Vol.2, p.240

6. See LeGrand Richards, A Marvelous Work and a Wonder, Ch.13, p.167

7. See also heading to D&C section 110

*   *   *

Chapter Ten

DARK SHADOWS OVER KIRTLAND

*   *   *

Although there were many active and worthy Saints well qualified to be Church leaders living in Missouri during this epoch period of Church history, it was in Kirtland that the most significant positions of church leadership existed. It was there that the de facto center of Church government in Ohio was organized and it dominated the leadership through January of 1838. Kirtland was where it was all happening. In just a six year period, the Church in Kirtland went through extensive membership growth, established an extended and enhanced organizational structure, instituted the development of important religious doctrine, published the Doctrine and Covenants as scripture, and fostered a truly perceptible increase in the spiritual growth of its Church members. Much of that spiritual growth in the Church could be attributed to the wonderfully selfless atmosphere throughout the Kirtland community during the construction of the Kirtland temple where the unselfish volunteer work became a big part of the positive community feeling. This favorable "esprit de corps" was made even stronger and glorified even further by the divine experiences and sublime manifestations that were witnessed on that momentous occasion of the temple dedication. Then to top it off, the appearance of the ancient prophets in the Kirtland temple who restored the important keys of the Gospel, only added further spiritual ambience to the atmosphere in Kirtland.

The supernal manifestations that were witnessed in the Kirtland temple were unquestionably some of the most astounding spiritual events of the nineteenth century. And they are quite possibly some of the most amazing and divine occurrences that have ever taken place within the walls of any temple in the history of the Church of Jesus Christ of Latter Day Saints. These astounding spiritual manifestations in their impressiveness, rank just below the first vision and the advent of the Angel Moroni.

However, it seems terribly ironic that even after all those wondrous and magnificent happenings that surrounded the dedication of the Kirtland temple, the beautiful spiritual atmosphere would soon flee most unexpectedly and rather quickly from the city of Kirtland. It would all seem to just crumble and fall apart with little warning and deteriorate into nothing less than a spiritual and secular wasteland in an unbelievably short time. Like the winter wind stirring the fall leaves and blowing them away, the previously good spirit in Kirtland would seemingly be blown away and then scattered under the strong gusts of fault-finding, the degenerating faith in the leaders, criticism, dissension, apostasy, and most regrettably, an utter loss of faith in the Prophet Joseph Smith. Sadly, the next few years in Kirtland would go down as some of the blackest days in all of Church history and those dark inauspicious days would foreshadow the beginning of the end for the season of the Saints in Kirtland Ohio.

In 1834 the Lord ordered a new precept and decree in the Church. It is found in D&C 104:48, where this principle is revealed and says; "After you are organized, you shall be called the United Order of the Stake of Zion, the City of Kirtland. And your brethren, after they are organized, shall be called the United Order of the City of Zion."

What the Lord required of men living under this United Order, was that every man who belonged to the Church of the "living God" should take all the goods that he might receive above what was necessary for the support of his own family, and put the extra in the Lord's storehouse for the benefit of others who were less fortunate. However, due to the weaknesses of human nature and the fact that most people just simply want to keep most of what they earn, the Lord decided to changed the edict to better suit the all too human shortcomings of His children. The Lord changed the order on April 10th, 1834 after He found that the United Order wasn't being lived like He had intended.

D&C 104:49 "And they shall be organized in their own names, and in their own name; and they shall do their business in their own name, and in their own names;" D&C 104:53 "Therefore, you are dissolved as a united order with your brethren…"

And so the Church High Council met and in April 1834, "On the 10th, had a council of the United Order, in which it was agreed that the Order should be dissolved, and each one have his stewardship set off to him." The Church Council of Kirtland then took it upon themselves to see to the proper functioning of the "mercantile and printing businesses" in the city. – 1a

The rescinding of the United Order would be only the beginning of the unfortunate unveiling of the different weaknesses found among the Church's members. Their greed, their critical nature, and their egregious disloyalty, and a few other indiscretions would come to plague the city of Kirtland. This moral frailty would soon overtake the Saints in that city and result in much grief and disappointment and in what seemed to be a baffling paradoxical change in the moral, ethical, and spiritual direction of Kirtland. Within just months after that special temple dedication, things began to break down in the spiritual unity of the citizenry in Kirtland due to the lack of faith and steadfastness among the members of the Church. As it turned out there were a number of reasons for this unfortunate transformation into a very divided community and the extremely disappointing break up of the Church's brotherhood.

By 1837 more than 13,000 converts in America and Canada had joined the Church, and a great many of them were settling in Kirtland. Most of this increase came about through the dedicated efforts of the Church's missionaries carrying out the work of the Lord. However, with these kinds of numbers coming into the Church, there was bound to be a few problems with some of the new comers bringing along with them their all too human faults, their trivial issues over minor concerns, their over-sensitivity to offenses, and their ideological baggage from their former religions, as well as their petty backbiting and incessant complaining and criticisms of their new Church leaders. All of these little annoyances created more than just a few situations of unwelcome discord in the overall unity of the Church and the community.

Most certainly, many of the new members should have been more thoroughly converted before they were ever rushed into baptism. This might have alleviated many of the problems that would come later with some of these converts who eventually became dissenting, disgruntled, unfaithful members, and decidedly troublesome critics of the Prophet and the Church. Some of these malcontents, unfortunately, would soon stand out as the most influential and the most hateful of all the apostates, and in some cases, the worst enemies of the Prophet.

One prominent apostate, a "Doctor" Philastus Hurlburt, had filed a suit against the Church, and became a bitter anti- "Mormon" and a dedicated enemy of the Prophet Joseph Smith. In the Prophet's description, he was not a physician, as the title "Doctor" indicated, but because he was the seventh son in his family, he supposedly possessed supernatural qualities that would make him a doctor according to an old folklore superstition. Sidney Rigdon wrote in 1839, that he "was never a physician at any time, nor anything else but a base ruffian. He was the seventh son and his parents called him 'Doctor.'" After he made a weak and unsuccessful attempt to actually get into the practice of medicine, he next eagerly sought position in the Church after having come from a Methodist background. Failing to get an important calling in the Church, he then became determined to marry into the "first families," of Kirtland. Unfortunately, he was soon found to be a very immoral man.

In 1834 "A conference of High Priests convened in the translating room in Kirtland. The first case presented was that of "Doctor" Philastus Hurlburt, who was accused of un-Christian conduct with women, while on a mission to the east. On investigation it was decided that his commission be taken from him, and that he be no longer a member of the Church of Christ." All this was written and recorded according to the minutes of the High Priests council and he left the Church in great bitterness and would later attempt to take away Church property in what turned out to be an unsuccessful lawsuit.

In a few instances of conversion, even when some people had been truly converted, they dared not join the church due to peer pressure and anti-Mormon sentiment coming from their families, friends, and even their local ministers. Parley P. Pratt reported that on his mission to Canada, that even though a blind widow women was miraculously healed and had her eye sight restored through the laying on of hands by the missionary brethren, she dared not be baptized due to the pressuring intimidation from the anti-Mormon Methodist Society that had been taking care of her while she was blind. And so sadly, she was never baptized.

Anti-Mormon sentiment seemed to spread through out North East America and Canada faster than the measles, and was often evident before the missionaries could even introduce themselves into a new area and make their unsuccessful attempts to dispel the many distorted ideas and the false and shameful degrading rumors. The Mormon missionaries were rudely turned away and sometimes even physically accosted and often severely persecuted for their beliefs to the point that some of the missionaries began to doubt the very the worth of their missionary work, or any real need for their hopeless ill-fated missions.

If things seemed bad out in the mission field, things were even worse in the city of Kirtland. Alas, it wasn't too long after those spiritual highlights at the Kirtland Temple dedication that Satan renewed an all out attack on the new church resulting in the apostasy of some of the most prominent men in the Church. This most regrettable decline in the overall spiritual unity of the Saints was brought about through an atmosphere of extreme criticism mostly aimed at Joseph Smith with some collateral animus directed at a few of his closest supporters within the leadership. In this atmosphere of contention, there appeared to pop up out of nowhere the pettiest and most illogical criticisms over the most minor offenses. And in addition, there seemed to be among some of the members an alarming and even a crippling loss of faith in the Prophet, not only in him, but even in the very authenticity of the Church itself.

This devastating development of a loss of faith in Joseph Smith as a Prophet spread like a disease even affecting the people's confidence in the other prominent leaders in the Church. Found lurking in this heavy atmosphere of criticism were unjustified personal attacks on some of the other leaders and an unexplained bitterness towards them and even their families. In addition to this, there were even some totally unwarranted acts of persecution towards the ordinary rank and file faithful members of the Church who attempted to continue their support for the Church leaders. Naturally this unwarranted scourge of faultfinding and criticism became exceedingly fertile ground for doubt and apostasy to quickly grow in the Church. Furthermore and somewhat surprisingly, there seemed to be a subtle but a perceptive disenfranchisement even from their very basic Christian beliefs; such as "love thy neighbor" and "do unto others as you would have them do to you." This certainly didn't help the fellowshipping efforts among the non-members in the community and regrettably it undeniably hindered the spreading of the gospel in the Kirtland area.

The situation seemed to become graver by the day, but that wasn't the worst of it. Something even more sinister was lurking just over the horizon to finally and completely fracture the spiritual unity of the Church. And this new scourge was going to add even more fuel to this already volatile atmosphere of intense discord. This very destructive entity, which would cast the darkest of shadows over Kirtland, was a glaring preoccupation with money matters and the worry and speculation that comes with obsessing over ones monetary ruin.

There seemed to come over the Saints a pervasive, crippling, anxiety surrounding money matters, financial doubts, a mistrust of everyone, and a perceptive increase in the insidious human weakness called greed. And it would soon put a devastating curse upon the harmony and unity of the entire Church and under its malevolent influence; it would very nearly destroy the new religion. During those early days of the Church, the instability of the financial situation in Kirtland evolved and developed into an evil scourge upon the entire community and a grave affliction upon the feeling of brotherhood in the Church. So the already contentious atmosphere in Kirtland quickly deteriorated into an atmosphere of such contention that it almost felt like it could be cut with a knife.

And so as it all turned out, the rapidly growing doubts surrounding the Saint's financial situation and the resulting turmoil became the proverbial last straw that broke up the peace, unity, and happiness of the Saints in Ohio. The badly shambled structure of finances in Kirtland brought about an economic uncertainty that was hugely destructive and brought anarchy not only to the Church but also to the entire area. The consequences were complete bedlam in the finances of the community at Kirtland and a destructive mess in the Church's own monetary structure resulting in a very divided hostile community. It is only a true manifestation of the Lord's intercession that the Church was even able survive the Kirtland years and the devastating economic fiasco that plagued it.

This instability and disorder of the financial times in Kirtland was brought about by a number of causes that would create great unrest in the Church. First of all, many of the converts who did join the church and who showed up in Ohio, were dirt poor with no means of support, and therefore they drew heavily on Church charity adding to the Church's increasing debts. Second, the flimsy unbacked credit was rampant through out the different communities causing unprecedented inflation and created undue pressure on people's finances and a feeling of frightening economic uncertainty in Kirtland.

Third, the Church's real estate and building acquisitions had added considerable debt to its financial obligations. Even as one recognizes the importance of the Kirtland Temple and the great blessings that came from it, it never the less had left the Church in serious debt reaching upwards of more than $13,000 worth. Furthermore, the Saints owed another $6,000 on Church land purchased in Missouri, all of which put the Church itself in a situation of serious financial jeopardy. Last of all, it didn't help the situation any when the entire rest of the country found itself in the middle of a nation wide financial panic during the year of 1837. It was most certainly seriously bad timing for the Church's finances to be in shambles.

Whether the financial solutions that the Church leaders came up with were inspired or not, is much too complicated of a subject for any uninformed and uninspired critics to make a fair judgment. At that particular time, the best idea that the Prophet Joseph Smith could come up with was to create a Church owned bank in Kirtland that would issue loans and currency and hopefully stabilize the local economy. There were many in the Church who thought this hair-brained idea of starting a bank lacked any kind of inspiration from the Lord, and they regarded Joseph's solution as having come from Joseph the man, and not Joseph the inspired Prophet. Joseph didn't help things any nor did he inspire a lot of confidence when he told one particular couple; "A prophet is a prophet only when he is acting as such." Many doubters took this to mean he hadn't been under any kind of inspiration when he had been dealing with the Church's finances. He recorded the particularly provocative quote in his diary.

Meanwhile, there came to Joseph's attention an idea for a quick financial band-aid. A new member of the Church by the name of Brother Burgess had told the Prophet that he had grown up in Salem Massachusetts and he knew of a house in Salem where in the past there had been a large buried treasure in the cellar, although he admitted that it had been many years ago since he had been there. The Prophet suggested that it was worth looking into, especially since they were going to New York anyway on business to speak with some creditors, and Salem would not be all that far out of their way.

Joseph's and Brother Burgess' buried treasure idea met with a very quarrelsome debate in a meeting held in the temple; so much so that the Prophet had to remind them all of how the Lord had chastened them during Zion's camp when they quarreled. It was after this meeting that Martin Harris, John Boynton, Luke and Lyman Johnson, and Joseph's personal secretary, Warren Parrish, all met together to secretly discuss and criticize the Prophet's "nutty ideas" and to seriously question his leadership. This backyard sedition and disloyalty would eventually and unfortunately lead to the misdeeds of apostasy for every last one of these particular men.

In August of 1836, Joseph Smith along with his brother Hyrum, Sidney Rigdon, and Oliver Cowdery traveled from Ohio to Salem Massachusetts where they met up with Brother Burgess. In a very disappointing let down, Brother Burgess couldn't even remember where the exact house was that supposedly contained the buried treasure. Although the meeting with Brother Burgess was discouragingly unsuccessful and a grave disappointment to the group from Kirtland, they did proceed to transact some items of Church business, plus they were able to do some missionary work among the locals.

Though they came up empty handed where the buried treasure was concerned, the Prophet received a revelation in Salem saying; "I have much treasure in this city for you...", referring to the new members coming from the missionary seeds they planted, which would eventually bare fruit. Five years later, Erastus Snow on a Church mission to Salem was able to baptize 120 new members, their conversion being spawned by the previous missionary efforts, which brought to pass the Lord's promise that many people would come to the Church out of Salem in due time. The Lord also promised; "Concern not yourselves about your debts, for I will give you power to pay them." - D&C 111:5 and -1b

With the buried treasure idea not panning out so very well, the Church leaders were compelled to come back to the solution of starting a Church owned bank. Joseph and the others were very hopeful and envisioned their bank as "serving the important purpose of providing credit and a circulating medium of exchange to the growing community." If all went as planned, the Church would soon work its way out of debt and in addition, would aid the entire community in getting on its financial feet.

Unfortunately and in a case of very bad timing, there was a national economic depression across the entire country, and so the State of Ohio was not granting bank charters to anyone. Never the less, there were several public banks in Ohio during this period who proceeded to operate without a charter. Therefore the Church leaders, following the lead of the other banks and acting out of a bit of desperation, decided to go ahead anyway and form "The Kirtland Safety Society Anti-Banking Company" to provide banking services for the Church members and to hopefully solve the Church's financial problems.

Even though the operation of the Church's bank was technically not approved by the state of Ohio, many of the Saints went ahead and placed their faith in the new bank and went along with the Prophet and so they deposited their own money to help get the bank started and operating. Among these investors acting in blind faith, was the Prophet Joseph Smith himself who put in his own personal financial investment. Soon after that, the bank was issuing its own currency. By November of 1837 the new bank had put into circulation a substantial amount of paper money. Meanwhile the bank accumulated $100,000 in unresolved debt resulting in quickly depreciating bank notes, a great deal of customer doubt, and the possibility of financial chaos for the Bank. It was inevitable the financial uncertainty and the increasing widespread economic problems across the country would cause the Bank to struggle to keep a healthy financial balance and consequently the depositors began to loose their confidence in the Bank's ability to stay solvent. When the depositors panicked and finally made a run on the Bank, the Church's "Kirtland Safety Society Bank" was bankrupted and became defunct in its operation and its printed money became worthless. Ironically today a single bill from the "Kirtland Safety Society Anti-banking Company" goes for as much as $13,000 among collectors.

In May of that year, the bigger banks in New York ceased to make any cash transactions pertaining to any cash business to prevent a run on the banks. Other banks soon followed and the panic was on. The Church's Bank was only one of many banks that was forced to close its doors during those unsettled times. Although there was more than one reason for the big nation wide bank crash, President Andrew Jackson is given credit for the financial mess because he stopped funding the National Bank in order to curb the elitists big bankers and their power over the common citizen. Somehow this caused out of control inflation and the crisis exploded. In fact, during the nation wide panic of 1837, 800 banks closed their doors and the new nation experienced its first major financial crash, and the Church was caught up in the middle of it all. – 2

By 1837 there had come into the Church all types and classes of men and women with various loyalties, opinions, and their own biased thinking, and they certainly did exhibit varying degrees of faith and testimony. And so now came the time for all of them to have their faith, loyalty, and testimonies tried and tested by a major financial crisis.

As it turned out, the fiasco and failure of the Kirtland bank was like an ill wind that selectively sifted the chaff from out of the wheat. Sadly and in very disappointing turn of events, many of the most prominent leaders in the Church did not past this rigorous test of faith and loyalty, and so they were effectively sifted from out of the "good wheat," meaning out of the loyal and faithful members among the Saints.

Yes, sometimes the good Lord does let bad things happen to good people when it is for the sake of a bigger need, even if it seems to harm the faithful as much as the unfaithful. Thus the non-discriminating affliction does test the strength of all testimonies and sifts out the weakest ones that are not sincere in following the faith. "Therefore, they must needs be chastened and tried, even as Abraham, who was commanded to offer up his only son." – See D&C 102:4

Human beings are cursed with many weaknesses of the flesh, which can and do effect their overall spiritual well being. High on Satan's list of useful tools is persuading human beings to focus on their worldly wealth and to distract their attention from being guided by the spirit. Any time the concern over money is brought into the bigger picture, a preoccupation with personal finances can do strange things to people's thinking and can detour their thoughts and actions in a most negative manner, which often puts a great strain on their faith and loyalty. As it turned out, a great many of the Saints directly blamed Joseph Smith for their personal financial losses and consequently, they simply lost their faith in him as an inspired prophet.

Brigham Young was not one of them, and he would stand out as a major supporter of the Prophet Joseph Smith. Brigham's father had fought under George Washington during the Revolutionary War, and then in 1804, his father moved the rest of his family along with his young son Brigham to Western New York. Joseph Smith Senior would also move his own family to this same area soon after. Brigham spent most of his early years working on his own father's farm, attended very little schooling, and later would work as a painter, glazier, and eventually as a master carpenter and furniture maker. Little did he know how much his future would be affected by this new religion that was destined to dominate his life.

It was the Prophet Joseph's own brother, Samuel Smith, one of the Church's very first missionaries, who introduced Brigham's Father and the rest of that family to the Book of Mormon. The young Brigham was only luke warm about the new church at first. After two more years of careful study and being cautiously mindful and thorough in his investigation of the Church, Brigham Young finally received his testimony and was soon baptized in 1832. It wasn't long until he subsequently became an avid supporter of the Prophet Joseph Smith.

More than five years later, in a gathering in the upper room of the temple, the heated debate became so contentious that Brigham Young had to stand up and adamantly defend and declare Joseph as a true prophet, even as the others in the meeting wanted to replace him outright with David Whitmer. Brigham told them that they might rail and slander Joseph as much as they pleased, but they could not destroy the appointment of the Prophet of God, but "You can cut off your own authority. You can cut the thread that binds you to the Prophet, and you can sink yourselves to hell, if you choose."

He then pointed out that in the end, it was God's confidence in Joseph that mattered and not what they thought or what their opinions were of Joseph, and therefore, they could not destroy the Prophet, but in seeking to destroy Joseph, they would end up only in destroying themselves, which sadly came true. Brigham's gallant and well-put defense on behalf of the Prophet was not well received and certainly not accepted with any kind of a favorable attitude by the angry dissenters. – 3

Despite all the hateful opposition towards the Prophet and the derogatory rhetoric that his worst critics used to convince others that he was a fallen prophet, Joseph Smith remained as the Prophet of the Church until his death. He would go on to receive from the Lord twenty more visions in the next seven years before his martyrdom. Never the less, the financial failure of the Kirtland bank caused untold damage to the faith of a great many of the Saints and even caused doubt and disillusionment among some of Joseph's closest associates.

In a monumental turn of events, all three of the special witnesses, Oliver Cowdery, David Whitmer, and Martin Harris, all of who had actually saw the Angel Moroni with their own eyes and witnessed the reality of the Gold Plates, turned their backs on the Prophet in the aftermath of the Kirtland bank failure. However and very significantly, it must be noted that not one of the three ever denied their testimonies of the divine dawning of the Book of Mormon or what they had actually witnessed concerning its origins. Their individual stories and the consequences of their actions are outlined a little later in this chapter.

There were also other prominent Saints who had previously been faithful members of the Church that also seemed to completely lose a hold on their faith. Frederick G. Williams, Luke S. Johnson, Lyman E. Johnson, John Boynton, the Prophet's personal secretary, Warren Parrish, and even Parley P. Pratt, all became bitter enemies of the Prophet after the Kirtland bank debacle. They blamed the Prophet wholly for the financial fiasco and they just seemed to ignore all the factors of the many economic variables that were simply not under the Prophet's control.

One such minor detail that they all seemed to have forgotten, was that there was a nation wide economic crisis, which had bankrupted a great many banks all across the country, not just the Church's Bank. In addition to this important overlooked and very substantial detail, there was another very pertinent fact that greatly contributed to the Kirtland bank's failure. Many of the Saints and the non-members who had borrowed money from the Church Bank, defaulted on paying their loans back causing the Bank to become insolvent and unable to continue its business.

To top it all off, the spirit of speculation was feeding a disastrous inflation of prices. Everywhere in Kirtland there was rampant money speculation, bank speculation, land speculation, speculation in buying and selling city lots, all propagated by the greed of people trying to make a quick buck on the back of their neighbors. It appeared as though, that throughout Kirtland in 1837, the Saints had completely lost their heads, their good sense, their sense of fair play, and even their very ability to reason. It was no less than the spirit of worldly greed that swept over their hearts and minds during this very disappointing and most regrettable juncture in Church history.

There was one more little pertinent item contributing to this financial fiasco of the Kirtland Bank that the apostates were not talking about publicly. It was the criminal act of the apostate Warren Parrish himself. He had formerly been Joseph's secretary and scribe, and also a clerk and cashier at the bank, which made his breech of trust and acts of embezzlement even more heinous. He personally had contributed significantly to the institution's failure when he surreptitiously embezzled $20,000 from the Kirtland Bank. He then straightaway became a blatant severe critic of Joseph Smith as well as a disgusting lying hypocrite that viciously disparaged the Prophet, and he eventually became one of the Prophet's most bitter enemies.

Another very bitter and vengeful enemy of the Prophet was an unscrupulous Mormon hater by the name of Grandison Newell. Using one of his acquaintances as a shill, he persuaded this collaborator Samuel D. Rounds to swear out a complaint against Joseph Smith Jr. and Sidney Rigdon for fraudulent banking and issuing unauthorized bank notes. On October 24th, 1837, the Prophet and Sydney Rigdon were both charged with perpetrating fraud and doing unauthorized banking. Both brethren were fined a $1,000 each. More than twenty years after the Prophet had left Kirtland, Newell's lawyers sought restitution through probate proceedings and were awarded the Property of the Kirtland Temple. It eventually ended up in the ownership of the RLDS Church. It is a true miracle that the Prophet and the Church ever survived the bleak days of the Kirtland bank fiasco. - 4a

Taking everything into consideration, there was a long list of contributing factors that crippled the Kirtland bank, which were beyond the Prophet's control, and thus contributed to its failure causing the bank to suspend business and close its doors. The critics never acknowledged or seemed to even care that the Prophet himself had lost his own substantial investment too. Yet Joseph's detractors ignored these things and were not deterred from blaming it all on to the Prophet. As a consequence, they virtually forced Joseph by their bitter accusations, their extreme criticism, their hateful epithets, and their threats to take his very life, to react to this opposition in self-defense and thus discreetly take a leave of absence and to go to Missouri for a brief period of time.

The Prophet wrote; "I returned to Kirtland on or about the 10th of December. During my absence in Missouri, Warren Parrish, John F. Boynton, Luke S. Johnson, Joseph Coe, and some others united together for the overthrow of the Church. Soon after my return this dissenting band openly and publicly renounced the Church of Christ of Latter-day Saints and claimed themselves to be the old standard, calling themselves the Church of Christ, excluding the word 'Saints,' and set me at naught, and the whole Church, denouncing us as heretics, not considering that the Saints shall possess the kingdom according to the Prophet Daniel." – 4 b

One would be thinking wrong to think that the entire Church leadership was critical of the Prophet and that he didn't have any supporters other than Brigham Young at this time. As this entry from the Church High council indicates, there were others that still supported the Prophet and were very critical of Joseph's apostate enemies.

"We, the undersigned, feeling ourselves aggrieved with the conduct of Presidents David Whitmer and Frederick G. Williams, and also with Elders Lyman E. Johnson, Parley P. Pratt, and Warren Parrish, believing that their course for some time past has been injurious to the Church of God, in which they are high officers, we therefore desire that the High Council should be assembled, and we should have an investigation of their behavior, believing it to be unworthy of their high calling--all of which we respectfully submit." – 5

Three of the named men in that statement, David Whitmer, Lyman Johnson, and Warren Parrish, would eventually be excommunicated. Only Frederick G. Williams and Parley P. Pratt would humble themselves enough to return to the Church in good standing. The scourge of apostasy caused untold damage to the testimonies of even the previously active and faithful Saints. Sadly and most regrettably, these apostates were not satisfied with just walking away from the Church and going on with their own lives. They seemed to have an irrepressible compulsion to completely destroy Joseph Smith in his entirety from his head to his toe and a strong desire to relegate his church to a state of ashes and ruins. In their extreme hatred they lost complete sight of the fact that it was Christ's Church, not Joseph's.

In a rather odd occurrence that was being promoted among some of the apostates, Lyman Johnson and Warren Parrish had ran across a young girl who supposedly had some type of a magical black stone that gave her special powers to see the future and make her own prophesies. She proclaimed that Joseph Smith was most definitely a fallen prophet and therefore he must necessarily be replaced by David Whitmer. Her particular designation of David Whitmer to become the new prophet would seem to be somewhat suspect as it just so happened that she was residing at David Whitmer's home at the time. What is truly amazing, is that David Whitmer, who had been chosen by God to be a witness of the Gold Plates, who had seen the Angel Moroni, and who had been a trusted companion and an assistant to the Prophet, could himself be so easily duped by a young girl practicing sorcery. How could this possibly happen to Brother Whitmer? It is not known what the girl's particular motives were or who had instigated them, but it would be a reasonable assumption to believe it was not of a divine source, but most likely a dark maleficent power.

The young girl was able to convince the apostates that the time for real action was now critical and things couldn't wait any longer. How much influence the girl's urging may have had on their actions and how much simply came from their own hatred is not known, but they certainly didn't need much persuasion to conspire against the Prophet.

Thereafter, the apostates continued to escalate their opposition to the Prophet Joseph to the furthest degree and met often in various places to discuss the very real reality of deposing the Prophet from his high office. In what most people would call a sacrilege or even a desecration of the temple, the apostates often met inside the holy Temple itself to criticize the Prophet Joseph Smith when he was absent.

On one occasion, when there was a public assembly in the Temple and Joseph was gone, over a dozen of the apostates showed up armed with knives and pistols and attempted to intimidate Joseph's supporters and the rest of the congregation as they took over the Aaronic Priesthood Pulpits. The dissidents were led by the sinister Warren Parrish who was backed up by the brazenness of Lyman Johnson and John Boynton, both of whom were armed with weapons and perpetrated ominous glaring stares intended to warn the congregation to not oppose them.

Due to Joseph's absence at this meeting, his own father Joseph Smith Senior was conducting this particular assembly. When he turned the time over to Zebedee Coltrin of the Quorum of the Seventy to speak, the apostates loudly and belligerently interrupted the speaker pretending to take offense to Brother Coltrin's use of the word apostasy. He had merely said that apostasy itself was "eating at the very foundations of the Church." They took personal offense to this and accused him of directly looking at them when he said it, and so everybody knew it was them that he was talking about, and that it was obvious that he was insinuating that they were the apostate perpetrators that were eating away at the foundation of the Church, which they were.

Responding to their brazen interruptions, Father Smith stood and reminded Warren Parrish that Brother Coltrin had the floor and should not be interrupted. Parrish and the others combatively demanded to be heard and things escalated quickly from there. However, Father Smith remained firm and refused to be intimidated by the belligerents. Then suddenly without warning, the very angry Warren Parrish ran down the aisle to the pulpit, grabbed Father Smith by the lapels of his coat, and began shaking him and shouting into his face. Meanwhile, Parrish's armed backers brandished their pistols and waved them around in the general direction of the congregation shouting warnings that no one should interfere with Parrish's "discussion" with Father Smith.

When William Smith, a big strong angry young man, saw his own father being attacked, he was infuriated and charged down the aisle like a wild bull towards Warren Parrish, picked him up off his feet in a vise-like bear hug and started towards the door to forcefully and rather roughly throw him out into the street. Just at that moment, somebody yelled; "POLICE!" The city police officers quickly entered the building to disperse the rowdy gathering and to place the situation back under control. Consequently, the congregation was finally quieted down and ceased to panic, while the militant and cowardly apostates made a sneaky escape to plot further dark deeds against Joseph the Prophet. – 6

There were a select few of the apostates that would later come to their senses and repent of their disloyalty. Elder Parley P. Pratt was one such lost sheep that would return to the fold. Even though he had been the very missionary who had originally converted Elder John Taylor to the Church while in Canada, Elder Pratt at this point had temporarily lost his way, and here was Brother Taylor's opportunity to repay him for his previous kindness and fellowship. And so now it was John Taylor's turn to sway Parley with his words of faith and a sincere testimony that would cause Parley to rethink his entire actions, then come to his senses and think seriously about his own testimony and the personal anguish he felt in separating from the Prophet Joseph and the Church. Consequently Parley finally did humble himself and fully repented of his disloyalty to the Prophet.

Parley wrote; "after I had returned from Canada, there were jarrings and discords in the Church at Kirtland, and many fell away and became enemies and apostates. ... And at one time, I also was overcome by the same spirit in a great measure, and it seemed as if the very powers of darkness which war against the Saints were let loose upon me. But the Lord knew my faith, my zeal, my integrity of purpose, and He gave me the victory. I went to Brother Joseph Smith in tears, and, with a broken heart and contrite spirit, confessed wherein I had erred in spirit, murmured, or done or said amiss. He frankly forgave me, prayed for me and blessed me..." – 7

It was back in his missionary days back in Canada that Parley P. Pratt's missionary efforts sewed the seeds for the British mission. "Several of the saints in Canada were English, who still had friends and family in England," explained Parley P. Pratt. "Letters had been sent to them with information regarding the rise of the Church, and of its wondrous principles. Several of the Canadian Elders felt a desire to go on a mission to their friends in England. At length, Joseph Fielding, Isaac Russell, John Goodson and John Snider, of the Canadian Elders, were selected for a mission to England. Elders Heber C. Kimball and Orson Hyde, of the Quorum of the Twelve, were selected to go at the head of the mission, and Elder Willard Richards was appointed to accompany them."

Thus it was inevitable that many good men, women, and families would come into the Church from the English mission, and some of them would soon become prominent leaders. Many of these happy missionary events and their beneficial results to the Church were initiated by Parley P. Pratt's original missionary efforts. – 8

Meanwhile, one of the worst and most dangerous groups of dissenters in Kirtland was now challenging the Prophet Joseph Smith's authority and they were determined in their desire to do him real physical harm. The group called themselves the "Church of Christ" and they were led by the obnoxious and deplorable Warren Parrish. Parrish had already been accused of embezzling funds from the Church's Kirtland Safety Society Bank and consequently he had been excommunicated. Soon after this, he alleged that Joseph Smith had fallen from his divine calling to be the head of the Church, and then Parrish himself claimed that he was the one that had the authority to lead the Church now, although no one could explain exactly how he pulled that particular rabbit out of his hat. He even went so far as to put his own personal curse on the Prophet, and he fully believed that Joseph's subsequent but very temporary illness was the result of that curse.

Surprisingly and in a very disappointing turn of events, Warren Parrish was able to gain the support of three of the members of the Quorum of the Twelve Apostles. Later on, when the entirety of the group of the Twelve Apostles was presented one by one for a sustaining vote, these three apostles were not sustained. Luke S. Johnson, Lyman E. Johnson, and John F. Boynton were rejected and disfellowshipped. The very corrupt Warren Parrish's false and denigrating propaganda had pulled away these three brethren as well as some members of the Seventies. Unfortunately, they were not the only ones who would soon become disaffected from the

Prophet during the economic crisis in Kirtland. The apostates were even able to poison the mind of Parley P. Pratt's own brother, Orson Pratt, but only for a short time. Thankfully, this nefarious and dysfunctional apostate group would eventually brake up and in the end would predictably and essentially self-destruct. – 9

Perhaps the most disappointing of all the disaffections in the mind of the Prophet was those of the men who he had loved and personally trusted beyond question, the three witnesses. Between December of 1837 and April of 1838, all three of "The Three Witnesses" left the Church and completely turned their backs on the Prophet Joseph Smith. They took this most astonishing and unexpected step even though they had been especially chosen by God to be His special witnesses to the Gold Plates and the Angel Moroni. And even though they had seen these miraculous occurrences with their own eyes in the presence of the Prophet Joseph Smith, they still fell away and into apostasy. It is somewhat mind boggling to think that after all they had witnessed, that they could actually turn their backs on this honest friend and a Prophet of God. Never the less, it seems as though when Satan is able to persuade men to place their priorities on the things of the world, it is all too easy to sway their thinking and so greed and pride becomes one of the best and most powerful tools that Satan has. And thus it would be that all three of the special witnesses would find serious fault with the Prophet over the Kirtland Bank failure and would consequently reject him.

Surprisingly enough to most people, it was Joseph's very own right-hand man, Oliver Cowdery, who became one of the first to be detoured spiritually and found himself in serious conflict with the Prophet's thinking and management. Thus he vehemently disagreed with Joseph on economic and political issues, even after being especially privileged to have witnessed several actual visions in company with the Prophet Joseph Smith. He would later uncharacteristically turn his back on the Prophet and selfishly pursue after his own personal financial independence to put money in his own pocket, which was counter to the cooperative spirit of the financial system that was essential to the society of Zion, which the Prophet had envisioned.

Oliver's Church trial had been tied to the trials and excommunications of Oliver's two brothers-in-law, John Whitmer, and David Whitmer, their trials having been conducted at the same time. The Church court presented five charges against Oliver. They were inactivity in the Church, accusing the Prophet of adultery, and three charges of beginning a law practice and seeking to collect debts after the Kirtland bank failure. After his excommunication, Oliver returned to Ohio and continued his law study and began a practice in Kirtland. In 1840 he moved to Tiffin, Ohio, where he became a prominent civic leader and an active Democrat.

It should be significantly noted that never at any time did Oliver Cowdery succumb to the considerable pressure placed on him to deny his Book of Mormon testimony. His own letters indicated that he was personally very hurt at the Church's rejection of him, but yet he remained a deep believer as his words showed when Oliver rejoined the Church. On his return, he did not seek office or leadership in the Church, but only desired rebaptism and fellowship. In the end, "he publicly declared that he had seen and handled the Book of Mormon plates, and that he was present with Joseph Smith on the occasions when 'holy angels' restored the two priesthoods." – 10

David Whitmer too was initially a very faithful supporter of the Prophet and also had witnessed many divine events in the company of the Prophet. His rebellion and rejection of Joseph greatly saddened the Prophet. And nearly as painful to Joseph was his great disappointment in having the rest of the Whitmer family also abandon him. Despite their former unwavering support, their great generosity in material support in the beginning days, and standing out as some of the first and most faithful members of the new Church, the Whitmer family now had completely turned on the Prophet. By 1838, David Whitmer and all the rest of his family had disavowed Joseph and the Church, all due to their complete disillusionment brought about during the financial chaos in Kirtland.

David Whitmer was a proud, stubborn man, and he was still agitated and hurt over the controversy concerning his leadership in Missouri when he was disposed from a local area Stake Presidency. The Prophet's revelation in 1830, which is found in D&C 30:2, warned Elder Whitmer, "Your mind has been on the things of the earth more than on the things of me, your Maker, and the ministry whereunto you have been called; and you have not given heed unto my Spirit, and to those who were set over you, but have been persuaded by those whom I have not commanded."

Five main charges were brought against David at the disciplinary council that excommunicated him on April 13, 1838. The following charges were made against Whitmer in the case against him as it came before the High Council at Far West that was assembled for that purpose. "First--For not observing the Word of Wisdom. Second--For unchristian-like conduct in neglecting to attend meetings, in uniting with and possessing the same spirit as the dissenters. Third--In writing letters to the dissenters in Kirtland unfavorable to the cause, and to the character of Joseph Smith, Jun. Fourth--In neglecting the duties of his calling, and separating himself from the Church, while he had a name among us. Fifth--For signing himself President of the Church of Christ in an insulting letter to the High Council after he had been cut off from the Presidency."

It was then officially recorded by the council; "After reading the above charges, together with a letter sent to the President of said Council, the Council held that the charges were sustained, and consequently considered David Whitmer to no longer be a member of the Church of Latter-day Saints." However, there are other unverified accounts that say he withdrew his name from the Church records just before he was excommunicated and immediately after he heard that charges were going to be brought against him at the time of Oliver Cowdery's excommunication.

After leaving the Church, he moved to Richmond Missouri to open a livery stable, which he ran until 1888. Although he was the only one of the "Three Witnesses" to never come back into the Church, David Whitmer repeated once more just before his death, for the local news paper, "I have never at any time denied that testimony or any part thereof, which has so long since been published with that Book, as one of the three witnesses. Those who know me best, well know that I have always adhered to that testimony." - 11

The third of the three witnesses, Martin Harris, was one of the most avid of Joseph Smith's personal supporters in the early days of the Church, and his loyalty and unselfish service were exemplary with his willingness to serve and donate his invaluable financial contributions, which made possible the printing of the Book of Mormon itself. He had truly been an important part of the new church's future during those early days. Never the less, in 1837 during the unfolding of the regrettable and intense financial conflicts within the Church, Martin lost his faith in the Prophet. He also found himself in a strong personality conflict with Sidney Rigdon, which was causing some unhealthy squabbles among the Church leadership.

He absolutely refused to support the Kirtland Safety Society Bank that was sponsored by the Church. With his keen business sense, Martin Harris was in complete defiance to the bank's continued issuing of paper money, all of which was being done in spite of Martin's best business advice and reasoning, which he had conveyed to the Church leaders. Martin Harris was finally released from the high council in September of that year and was excommunicated during the last week of December of 1837. After a trip to England to promote the Book of Mormon, he returned to Kirtland to become a self-appointed caretaker and guide to the Kirtland temple.

Although there are some that say that Martin Harris was never excommunicated officially, he never the less accepted the previous action as was evident when he asked to be re-baptized on November 7, 1842. In 1869, Brigham Young, and many other Latter-day Saints helped him financially to make the journey to Utah. He was still comparatively active at age eighty-seven and arrived by train in Salt Lake City on August 30, 1870. "He accepted rebaptism as evidence of his reaffirmation of faith on September 17, 1870, and at Brigham Young's invitation, he publicly testified of the Book of Mormon." The accuracy of Martin's Church records, and that of his excommunications, and his re-baptisms are a matter of some vagueness and possible error as they are found recorded in his personal and Church history, apparently due to unclear record keeping and poor recollections.

Martin's wife Caroline and their children had previously moved to Utah fourteen years earlier in 1856. He lived out the end of his life in Clarkston Utah where he died in July of 1875. The powerful story of Martin Harris' life and testimony have been presented in the past in an entertaining and stirring theatrical presentation at the Martin Harris Pageant held in Clarkston Utah. – 12

Meanwhile, the situation in Kirtland continued to worsen until the apostates became absolutely determined to dispose of the Prophet Joseph Smith by whatever means of artifice or chicanery that they could possibly contrive, even violence if that's what it took. In one 1837 meeting, the villainous Warren Parrish proposed that the priesthood body who was present at the time should summarily remove the Prophet and replace him immediately with David Whitmer. In that meeting, Brigham Young as a senior apostle confronted the apostates and bore strong testimony through the power of the Holy Ghost that Joseph was a true prophet. Brigham's testimony so infuriated Warren Parrish and the other apostates that they literally threatened Brigham's life and he was forced to flee that very night to the state of Indiana to avoid harm. And so as it happened, Brigham Young subsequently journeyed back east to Dublin Indiana on December 22, 1837 to be taken in by relatives.

Satan's cunning influence completely overtook the evil-minded apostates and thus they conspired and made finalized plans to assassinate both the Prophet and Sidney Rigdon henceforth. However the apostate Luke Johnson just couldn't bring himself to go along with actual murder of Joseph and so he secretly warned the Prophet of what the plotters had in mind for him.

Even after having been warned, Joseph was unable to get out of town before the apostate assassins were able to surround the house where he was visiting. By happen stance; there was a coffin in the cellar of the house. Using some cleverness and ingenuity of their own, Joseph's friends nailed him inside the coffin and then proceeded to solemnly carry the "unknown deceased" right out through the middle of the menacing and devilish mob with safety and without any interference.

Joining Brigham Young in Indiana, Joseph left on January 13th of 1838, and sent for his family shortly thereafter. Emma and the children joined the Prophet there along with Sidney Rigdon and his family. All of them ended up staying in Dublin for a brief period of time. There in Indiana, they found themselves short of the funds necessary to travel to their ultimate destination in Missouri, but a certain Brother Thomlinson, who had just sold his farm, generously gave Joseph $300.00 to make the long trip to the Mormon settlements in Missouri. – 13a

In January of 1838, the Prophet Joseph Smith, Sidney Rigdon, and several other Church leaders began their relocation and moved their families to western Missouri and then arrived in Far West two months later on March 14th of 1838. Joseph wrote of their experience traveling to Far West.

"The weather was extremely cold, we were obliged to secrete ourselves in our wagons, sometimes, to elude the grasp of our pursuers, who continued their pursuit of us more than two hundred miles from Kirtland, armed with pistols and guns, seeking our lives." And then he continued; "I parted with Brother Rigdon at Dublin, and traveling different routes we met at Terre Haute, where, after resting, we separated again, and I pursued my journey, crossing the Mississippi river at Quincy, Illinois." – 13b

After seeing the majority of the Church leaders leave Kirtland, there was a mass exodus by the rest of the Saints who then headed for the state of Missouri. They mostly left in small groups of a four or five dozen at a time, however, there was one large group of 500 Saints who were dubbed as the Kirtland Camp, which left in mass. By the time summer rolled around, most of the Saints had left Kirtland for good, never to return, and so the days of the Church at Kirtland were now gone for good and those bleak dark days in Kirtland became notorious for being the darkest days in the entire history of the Church.

It came to pass that the faithful Saints followed their church leaders west in hopes of finding some kind of a new Utopia. They had sincere aspirations of moving their families to what they thought would be a safe place and a new life in Caldwell County Missouri. As Brigham Young moved his own family out of Dublin Indiana and arrived in Caldwell County several weeks thereafter, he and his family were also in hopes of a new and brighter future. – 14

*   *   *

1a. See History of the Church Volume 2 Chapter 4

1b. See Church History in the Fullness of Time pp. 170-171- See also the heading at sec. 111 of the Doctrine and Covenants

2. See Encyclopedia of Latter-Day Saint History p. 622 – Also Church History in the Fullness of Times pp. 171-173

3. See Manuscript History of Brigham Young pp 15 &16

4 a. See The Kirtland Safety Society Anti-Banking Company www.byu. studies.byu.edu and Also see Wikipedia.com – Joseph Smith and The Criminal Justice System

4 b. See History of the Church, Vol.2, Ch.36, p.528

5. See History of the Church, Vol.2, Ch.34, p.484

6. See History of Joseph Smith by His Mother – p. 241 – Also Joseph Smith's Kirtland: Eyewitness Accounts - Karl Anderson p. 220-221

7. See Autobiography of Parley P. Pratt, pp. 183-184.

8. See Autobiography of Parley P. Pratt, p. 183

9. See Encyclopedia of Mormonism, Vol.3, SCHISMATIC GROUPS Also Comprehensive History of the Church HC 1:403-407

10. See Encyclopedia of Mormonism, Vol 1, COWDERY, OLIVER

11. See History of the Church, Vol.3, Ch.2, p. 18-19 and Encyclopedia of Mormonism, Vol.4, WHITMER, DAVID

12. See Encyclopedia of Mormonism, Vol.2, HARRIS, MARTIN

13a. See History of the Church, Volume 3, Chapter 1 "The Prophet Joseph's Departure from Kirtland And Arrival in Missouri"

13b. History of the Church, Vol.3, Ch.1, p.2 and 3

14. See Encyclopedia of Mormonism, Vol.2, HISTORY OF THE CHURCH, and also "The Heavens Resound: A History of the Latter Day Saints in Ohio" pp. 342-343 - Desert Book Co. Salt Lake City 1983

*   *   *

Chapter Eleven

INCREASING DISTRESS IN MISSOURI

*   *   *

With the hasty exodus of the most prominent church leaders from Kirtland, the faithful left the city in droves heading for Missouri to follow the lead of their Prophet. And so it came to pass that during the bright spring days of March 1838, Joseph Smith soon found himself comfortably settled among his own people in the Mormon pioneer village of Far West in Caldwell County of northwestern Missouri. Joseph and the other new comers to Missouri all had high hopes of finally finding peace here in Caldwell County. Needless to say, those local Saints who had been recently ran out of Jackson County on the other side of the Missouri river, were also entertaining high hopes of having escaped the barbaric treatment and the merciless harassments that they had previously suffered in Independence.

A month later on April 26th, Joseph received a revelation instructing the Saints to gather in Far West, with the Lord proclaiming, "...it is my will that the city of Far West should be built up speedily by the gathering of my saints," and moreover, "… I command you to build a house unto me,…"

In addition to these specifically stated commandments, in another part of that revelation the Lord would make a special declaration. It was to be a significant change in the name of His Church and He would now give to the Saints a noteworthy appendage to the Church's title. The Prophet received the word from the Lord that the Church of Jesus Christ at this time would now be officially renamed as the revelation declared; "For thus shall my church be called in the last days, even The Church of Jesus Christ of Latter Day Saints, scattered abroad in all the world."

So this comprehensive revelation given at that time, called for the move to Far West, the building of a new temple, declared a new appendage to the Church's name, and then finished up with a very clear reaffirmation of the Prophet Joseph Smith's true and validated calling. "For behold, I will be with him and I will sanctify him before the people; for unto him have I given the keys of this kingdom and ministry, even so. Amen." – See D&C 115:3-10, and 17-19.

Although the Saints were now beginning a new era in the Church with a strong hope for peace in their lives there in Caldwell County, they soon would find their hopes were for naught for in a very short time their optimistic expectations were once again dashed upon the rocks of blatant bigotry, abusive language, and even threats. As a quickly developing atmosphere of resentment and unexplained hostility towards the Saints once again showed its ugly face, the very biased and inhospitable old Missourian settlers soon made it clear that Mormons were not welcome here either. And so this brought back all too quickly those painful memories of being forcefully driven out of Jackson County and Ohio. With the new incidents of name calling and even harassment, the hoped for reprieve from persecution was discouragingly short and of course, very disheartening. And so it all became just one more failed dream of serenity that had been built upon a real hope for peace and now seemed to disappear rather quickly like mere gossamer fading away in the pale moonlight.

Alas, there was just one simple fact that seemed to completely escape the understanding of the peace loving Saints; that was the fact that the two widely differing life-styles of the Mormons and the Missourians were just simply incompatible. And as far as any non-violent peaceful cohabitation with the Missourians was concerned, it was nothing more than hopeless hoping, and seemingly just one more unattainable longing for that elusive peace and tranquility that they so much desired. Therefore, it was only a matter of time before vehement hatred and aggressive conflicts between the two cultures came about and sooner or later, it was inevitable that there would be violence.

The fledgling city of Far West in Caldwell County rapidly grew into a western metropolis as new arrivals came into the city almost daily. The overflow of newcomers quickly spread into Daviess County and into the smaller settlement of Adam-ondi-Ahman, also known as Di-Ahman. It was Brother Lyman Wight that had been the one to originally start the settlement at Adam-ondi-Ahman back in the early days and the site of his farm was first known as "Spring Hill."

The Prophet Joseph had by inspiration designated this particular location, "Spring Hill," as being a very special place. During a visit made by the Prophet Joseph Smith to Brother Wight's farm and somewhere near Wight's ferry, the Prophet received a revelation saying that, "this is the place where Adam shall come to visit his people, or the Ancient of Days shall sit, as spoken of by Daniel the Prophet." - See the heading and verse at D&C 116:1 and Dan. 7:9-14

There is a very interesting excerpt found in the LDS GOSPEL LIBRARY- MORMON DOCTRINE - ADAM-ONDI-AHMAN that is worth noting. It concerns Brother Wight's Spring Hill and says: "On May 19, 1838, Joseph Smith and a number of his associates stood on the remainder of the pile of stones at a place called Spring Hill, Daviess County, Missouri. There the Prophet taught them that Adam again would visit in the Valley of Adam-ondi-Ahman, holding a great council as a prelude to the great and dreadful day of the Lord. At this council, all who have held keys of authority will give an accounting of their stewardship to Adam. Christ will then come, receive back the keys, and thus take one of the final steps preparatory to reigning personally upon the earth." (Dan. 7:9-14; Teachings, p. 157.) Today this same site is still designated as a Mormon historical site with some road maps labeling it as a "Mormon shrine."

By June of 1838, the population of Mormon settlers in the Di-Ahman settlement had grown so much that it prompted the Prophet to organize the Di-Ahman stake. However, this onslaught of new un-checked population growth in the area was very alarming to the indigenous population and caused some serious concerns in the minds of the old Missourian settl1ers. This concern would eventually evolve into an unwarranted paranoia and soon after developed into some very volatile situations. These smaller conflicts of interest would shortly thereafter escalate and eventually be marked by physical violence.

Added to the difficulties of the Mormon population growing so briskly that it was putting the old Missourians on edge and at odds with the newcomers, there unexpectedly arose some significant problems within the Church membership itself. Unfortunately, the seemingly diminutive initial criticisms of Church leaders quickly grew into a larger and more serious problem of dissension eventually causing a type of mutiny against the leadership of the Church. Naturally, this all would have a very detrimental effect on the unity of the entire Mormon community in Far West. Possibly, the most disheartening development of all was that much of this dissension was starting to come from some of the most prominent and previously faithful members in the Church. Most sadly, these disharmonious dissenters now included three of the twelve apostles, which were Elder William McLellin and the two apostle brothers, Luke and Lyman Johnson. Perhaps even more disappointing than that to the Prophet, was the disaffection of two of the "Three Witnesses," Oliver Cowdery and David Whitmer who were now living there in Missouri. The two were beginning to, and somewhat surprisingly, coming to the point of outwardly expressing their strong opinions and disagreements with the Prophet that were verging on not just mere disagreement, but actual defiance of the Prophet's directives. The dismaying particulars and reasons for the defections of all three of the original "Three Witnesses" have already been detailed in the previous chapter.

Added to the very bitter disappointment of loosing three members of the twelve Apostles as well as two of the "Three Witnesses" was a further disappointing disaffection. It was the unfortunate rebellion of another couple of prominent Church leaders, W. W. Phelps, and John Whitmer. When President David Whitmer was deposed as the local Stake President, his two counselors W. W. Phelps, and John Whitmer in the Missouri Stake Presidency were also excommunicated at the same time. All of these above named men were eventually excluded officially from the Church for stirring up trouble within the community of the Saints at Far West and for purposely attempting to do damage to the Church and instigating turmoil and doubt among the new members that were just coming into Far West.

These very unhappy and lamentable developments, caused by the rebellious defectors, provoked Sidney Rigdon to give a scathing sermon from the pulpit that clearly let these malcontents know that they were no longer welcome in Far West. The speech given in June of 1838 became famously known as "The Salt Sermon" as it was based on the scripture from Matthew 5:13 where Jesus said that when salt loses it savor, "it is thenceforth good for nothing, but to be cast out, and to be trodden under the foot of men." – 1

The Salt Sermon had its desired effect and within a few days the dissenters took their families moved to another county. It should be noted that even though W.W. Phelps and Frederick G. Williams were a part of this group of malcontents in the beginning, they were able to happily reconcile with Church leaders and in the end, they returned to the Church in good standing.

In the meantime, the Missourian old timers were less than tolerant of anything the Mormons did, but there were a few particular incidents that created some real friction. Most certainly, Sidney Rigdon did not help matters when he gave a fiery speech on the fourth of July 1838 standing in front of the Liberty pole in Far West. In the style of his Campbellite preacher days, Sidney laid out a long list of grievances that the Mormons had suffered from their abusers. And then in loud defiance he said, "We will bear it no more!" Among other things in his long oratory, he said that the Church members would never be the aggressors nor would they ever infringe on anyone else's rights, but they were going to defend their own rights until the last drop of blood of their enemies was spilt, either that or "they will have to exterminate us."

The Mormon crowd applauded his words enthusiastically, but when the speech in its letterform was published in the Missourian newspapers, the old Missourians were nothing less than infuriated. Only a few days later the liberty pole in Far West was destroyed by a lightning strike that burned it into nothing less than an ugly blackened stick. Soon after, there was gossip around the community speculating that this shocking dazzling display of nature's power was possibly just portending the bleak future of Far West.

It was inevitable that all the negative discourse with its inflammatory rhetoric would be like throwing a torch into dry weeds and therefore would invariably result in a flare up of violence between the two clashing cultures. As history has come to prove so many times, a good fertile place to start any conflict can be found most often in the volatile contentious rhetoric of politics.

1838 was an election year and the local elections were being held in Gallatin, the Daviess county seat. Although neither of two men who were running for state representative for Daviess County were Mormons, they were considerably different in their attitude and feelings towards the local Mormons. The one candidate was well known to be fair-minded and honest and thus fair with the Saints, while the other was widely known as a Mormon hater and reported to have come to Davies County from out of the Missouri militia. The Mormon hating candidate, titled himself as Colonel William Peniston, and he was absolutely determined that his supporters were not going to be outvoted in this election, no matter how many Mormons showed up to vote.

On Election Day, a courageous group of a dozen Saints from Di-Ahman went to Gallatin to vote. The Mormon hating candidate stood at door of the saloon where the voting was to be held, and he was very effectively stirring up a drunken crowd with insults and false accusations against the Mormons. Peniston then very boldly and belligerently proceeded to tell the Mormon men they were not allowed to vote in this town, "no more so than any 'Negro' would be."

When the Mormons insisted that it was their right to vote and then tried to step around the men blocking their way, drunken bullies led by the hulky and very nasty Dick Welding began throwing punches and swinging clubs. However, one of the Mormon boys, John Butler, who was also a large and a very strong bull of a man wasn't particularly happy with the way that his friends were being assaulted. He spotted a nearby woodpile, chose his weapon, and consequently stepped into the fray with unbridled determination and fury. While brandishing a two foot long oak club, he proceeded to wade through the drunken mob like a scythe through ready to harvest wheat. Many men on both sides of the fracas were injured, bloodied, and lying scattered upon the ground leaving the entire scene looking like a battlefield. The now battle bruised Mormons made a hasty retreat without voting, sadly limped home, and left behind an injured bloody and angry enemy determined to exact their revenge in the very near future. – 2

After the wild fracas in Gallatin, there arose many rumors among the Saints of an armed mob from Daviess County that was coming to D-Ahman to take care of the Mormons once and for all, and to get bloody retribution for their injured pride. Some of the Mormon men that had been involved in the Gallatin brawl took the precaution of taking their families down on the river bottom to hide out, while others formed up a small militia with the aim of protecting their families and property.

However, the wild rumors of the vengeful mob coming to wipe out the Mormons never actually materialized. Never the less, the partisan rhetoric of the anti-Mormon local newspapers continued to promote the false narrative of the Mormons having attacked the innocent peaceful voters in Gallatin. These very distorted and inaccurate rumors made their way to the Governor's office. A letter was quickly sent out from the adjutant general's office to General Atchison of the Missouri Militia to prepare 400 men to put down the recent raids by the Indians and to take care of the unwarranted civil disturbances by the unruly Mormons. Similar letters all signed by Governor Boggs were sent to seven other generals of the militia, which effectively alerted and brought together a very large army of over three thousand men of the Missouri State Militia to protect the Missourian settlers from the Indians and put down any kind of rioting among the out of control Mormons.

Fortunately, not all of the generals in the Missouri Militia were anti-Mormon. Two such men were not only generals but also lawyers who were fair and friendly towards the Church. Alexander Dolniphan proved to be such a good friend to Joseph Smith, that the Prophet later named one of his own sons after Alexander. The other friend was David Atchison, who was the senior commander in the northern Missouri militia, and he made a promise to protect the Saints from any unwarranted attacks by the violent mobs.

So when the Prophet was arrested along with his companion Lyman Wight, Joseph asked both of these fine legal men to represent him and Brother Wight as their legal counsel in their defense against the court charges that were filed against the two brethren by William Peniston. The vile and completely dishonest Peniston was making the most ridiculous accusations regarding the Daviess county voting incident, even accusing Joseph and Brother Lyman of being the ones instigating the vicious attack upon the innocent voters.

Judge King, no friend of the Mormons, presided over the hearing and ruled that Joseph and Lyman Wight should be held over for the circuit court and only released on a $500.00 bond. Despite the fact that many witnesses testified before the judge that the Prophet Joseph and Lyman Wight weren't even present at Gallatin, and not withstanding that even the judge himself was mostly convinced that the prisoners were more than likely not guilty, he still jailed the two Mormon leaders anyway. If there can be any defense of the judge's decision, it might have been that he was attempting to avoid further mob violence and uncontrolled rioting by acting quickly to appease the very anti-Mormon and potentially violent crowd by holding over the two innocent men in jail.

The rumors that the Mormons were in an all out armed rebellion were spreading everywhere, including all the way to Governor Boggs' office. The situation in western Missouri then quickly deteriorated into acts of revenge that included cattle rustling, Mormon livestock being shot, animals run off, and haystacks being set on fire, all unwarranted and perpetrated by the roving Missourian mobs.

General Parks was then sent to check into the situation and to report back to the Governor. General Parks and General Atchison both concurred and reported to Governor Boggs that after looking into the situation, that they found the Mormons showed no disposition to resist the laws nor did they show any form of hostile intentions. Strangely enough there has never been found any record that Governor Boggs showed any reaction in any way to these positive reports about the Mormons. Many people think this was an indication of his biased lack of interest in wanting to know the truth about the so-called Mormon uprising. – 3

In October of 1838, as many as 150 old Missourian settlers disgruntled by the large influx of Mormons, rode into the small town of DeWitt

Missouri, about 70 miles south of Far West, and brazenly demanded that the Mormons pickup and leave their homes and farms within ten days or be killed. The Mormon leader of the Saints in DeWitt was George Hinkle who refused to leave DeWitt and subsequently sent for help from the Governor, which never came. In a matter of days, an unauthorized contingent of the Missouri militia joined the mob and surrounded DeWitt putting the entire town under siege. As the situation continued to deteriorate and the cold weather began to move in, a man named Brother Caldwell volunteered to ride to Jefferson City and take a written request directly to the Governor for help. Three days later, he retuned with a final message for the Mormons. The brief message said that the quarrel was nothing more than a local dispute and hence not under the authority of the Governor, and therefore the old settlers and the Mormons would all just have to work out their differences and resolve the matter among themselves.

In an act of desperation, the citizens of DeWitt took the next last-ditch step and sent a messenger to the head of the Church, Joseph Smith the Prophet. He subsequently agreed to return to DeWitt with the messenger. Joseph slipped into the city under siege by night, assessed the situation, and decided that the almost certain loss of lives was just not worth any very costly gains in defending the settlement. A few days later, based on Joseph's advice, about seventy some wagons loaded up, abandoned DeWitt, and headed for Far West. They were harassed by gunfire even as they were leaving.

With many of the outlying settlements such as DeWitt coming in to Far West for refuge, the Church leaders were having a difficult time even accommodating the ones already there. And so it became really overwhelming to add another 500 more refugee Saints from the Kirtland Camp who were just arriving after a long arduous journey from the abandoned city of Kirtland back in Ohio. It was like adding more drowning passengers to an already overfull lifeboat. This all spawned a very problematic situation where more than 6,000 people in Far West were trying to survive in circumstances that had become greatly aggravated by crowded conditions, sparse supplies, and very few accommodations for the newcomers.

Through inspiration, Joseph proceeded to organize a group of especially assigned Church members who were divided into specialized aide groups to handle the needs of the needy, and provide whatever necessities were required for the destitute. It was most certainly a big help in alleviating the wretched and desperate conditions among some of the Saints in Far West at the time.

It goes without saying that under these trying circumstances, any personal feuds among the Church members would not be helpful and certainly not conducive to the overall morale and unity of the community. Unfortunately, what was to become known as the "milk strippings" feud would not only end up completely dividing the Far West community, but in the final outcome, it would result in the very regrettable situation of the excommunication of the Chief Apostle of the Twelve and his wife, all due to a petty human weakness known as stubborn pride.

Thomas B. Marsh, the President of The Twelve, had a wife who was less than honest with her neighbor, that being Sister Harris. The two had made an agreement to combine the milk from their cows to make cheese from the cream skimmed off the milk. However, Sister Harris discovered that Sister Marsh had been holding back the richest part of the milk, called "the strippings," for her own personal use. When confronted by Sister Harris, Sister Marsh denied that she had done any such thing, which resulted in Sister Harris taking the matter before the priesthood quorum. The quorum decided that Sister Marsh should make restitution to Sister Harris, but Sister Marsh was stubbornly defiant, and she continued to be very haughty, aggressively obstinate, and rebelliously disobedient even when confronted by her Bishop, the High Council, the First Presidency, and eventually, even the Prophet.

The situation escalated into a great division of the Saints in the Far West community with some people taking the side of Sister Marsh because she was the wife of the Senior Apostle, while others took the side of Sister Harris because she was backed by the High Counsel and the Prophet. Naturally, all of this turmoil resulted in a great deal of unnecessary contention and a very regrettable serious division in the unity of the Mormon community at Far West.

Even though Thomas B. Marsh was the highly respected President of The Twelve Apostles and the one who should have been setting an example for supporting the priesthood leadership, he never the less felt a strong-minded obligation to side with his stubborn uncompromising wife.

Therefore he set himself up against the decisions of the priesthood quorum, a bishop's court, the High Counsel, and the First Presidency, as well as the Prophet Joseph's personal decision.

As a result of their stubborn pride, Marsh and his wife left the Church in defiance. Marsh subsequently traveled to Richmond Missouri to make an affidavit before Judge Henry Jacobs falsely testifying against Joseph Smith and the Church, which resulted in the stirring up of even more hostility and hatred towards the Saints. This all was playing right into the hands of the Mormon haters who were just looking for any reason to instigate further violence, more hate, and further division among the settlers at Far West.

Some historians say that Thomas B. Mash's dissension went far deeper than his wife's feud. It was reported that even before the "milk strippings" incident, he was already siding with Orson Hyde and some other dissenters in Missouri as they cast very criticizing aspersions upon the Prophet Joseph Smith. The following in part is his testimony before the Judge:

AFFIDAVIT OF THOMAS B. MARSH:

"They have among them a company, considered true Mormons, called the Danites, who have taken an oath to support the heads of the Church in all things that they say or do, whether right or wrong... On Saturday last, I am informed by the Mormons, that they had a meeting at Far West at which they appointed a company of twelve, by the name of the Destruction Company, for the purpose of burning and destroying, and that if the people of Buncombe came to do mischief upon the people of Caldwell, and committed depredations upon the Mormons, they were to burn Buncombe; and if the people of Clay and Ray made any movement against them, this destroying company were to burn Liberty and Richmond. The plan of said Smith, the Prophet, is to take this state; and he professes to his people to intend taking the United States, and ultimately the whole world." - 4

Thomas B. Marsh's pride and vengeful actions led him into spreading many lies against the Church leaders resulting in his regrettable apostasy and a very inauspicious outcome for his own future. Ultimately, it led to his and his wife's complete separation from the Church and the Prophet Joseph Smith. They were soon excommunicated in March of 1839. Some years later, Elder John Taylor ran across Marsh in Nebraska, and described him as "a broken-down man." The dejected Marsh asked Brother Taylor about the affairs of the Church, expressed his own feeling of what "a wretched position" he had put himself in, and wondered how the people of the Church would feel about him coming back?

Then after 18 long years of disenfranchisement from the Church, he finally came around to a more repentant attitude towards the Church leaders and the Church. Much of his newly contrite attitude was brought on by the loss of his wife, followed by the loss of most of his worldly possessions, along with a bleak and very depressing feeling of dejection and isolation from society. Afflicted by these trials, he eventually became penitent and was re-baptized in July of 1857, but would never again hold a church position or the high respect of the people that he once served. At one meeting after his reinstatement into the Church, he declared to the congregation; "If any of you want to see the effects of apostasy, look upon me." One has to wonder then, if he finally in the end did come to realize how destructive stubborn pride can be, and if he found the truth in the age-old warning; "Pride goeth before destruction, and an haughty spirit before a fall." – Prov. 16:18

In an overall view and while entertaining an open-minded assessment, the Saints in Missouri at this time were simply not living up to the harmonious and obedient standards set by the Lord and thus they were not protected from their enemies. The following excerpt from the "Gospel Doctrine'" manual is very telling concerning the situation. "And because the Saints have free access to the Holy Spirit, and may walk within his light and fellowship and possess the intelligence which he is able to impart, a stricter harmony among the Saints may be insisted upon than in any other organization of men whatsoever. For the same reason, lack of harmony may be more severely censured and persistent opposition and rebellion more justly denounced and swiftly punished." - 5

This excerpt would insinuate that the Saints in the late 1830's living in Missouri were simply not worthy of the Lord's protection and His blessings due to their disharmony, a great deal of contention, and much bickering amongst themselves. Many of them displayed an obvious rebellion and dissension against their Church leaders, and a few even showed a blatant disrespect for the Prophet, even defiance. They simply were not worthy of God's blessings, and so their chastisement as one might expect was severe.

On October 13th 1838, Joseph received a communication from his friend, General Alexander Doniphan, saying that 800-armed men were headed for a violent showdown with the Mormons living in Di-Ahman. With this ominous situation hanging on the horizon, the General then officially authorized Joseph Smith to activate and organize a Mormon Militia for their own defense; a militia that would be established under the authority of a fully commissioned officer of the Missouri State Militia, who just happened to be a member of the Church, one Colonel George M. Hinkle.

So with this new directive in place, the Mormons had received an official authorization to fight back against the increasing abuse and harassment coming from their enemies and to defend themselves against this possible devastating attack. And so it came to pass that the calamitous sequence of historical events that were about to take place were all now set into motion by the juxtaposition of these fatalistic events. The scene was now set for the concluding stages of the inglorious last days of Far West and the end of the Saints living in Missouri. – 6

*   *   *

1. See also Encyclopedia of Mormonism, Vol.2, MISSOURI CONFLICT

2. See History of the Church 3:55-58, Church History in the Fullness of Times – p.194

3. See History of the Church 3:67-68, 84-85

4. See John Taylor, The Gospel Kingdom, p.186

5. See GOSPEL DOCTRINE CHAPTER 8, Joseph Fielding Smith, p.131 THE CHURCH AND THE MAN HARMONY

6. See History of the Church 3:161

*   *   *

Chapter Twelve

THE FINAL DAYS
OF FAR WEST

*   *   *

The Saints were feeling somewhat relieved to hear that they would now have a viable means of defending themselves from the violent mobs through the protection of their very own officially armed militia. Their new defensive force was led by a fully commissioned officer of the Missouri State Militia who was. charged with the responsibility of defending them from the harassment of the merciless raiders by whatever means necessary. The newly commissioned Mormon Commander, Colonel George M. Hinkle, responded to his new assignment soon after he was appointed, and thus assembled his troops and headed out to secure the lives, property, and homes of the Saints in Di-Ahman from the anticipated Missourian raiders.

However, the wild rumors of the large Mormon army coming to defend Di-Ahman spread quickly and caused any would be ruthless raiders to think twice about their nefarious intentions. Consequently the vigilante raiders under the diabolical leadership of the vile and malicious Reverend

Sashiel Woods and the ruthless Cornelius Gilliam soon abandoned their plans of their intended blitzkrieg against Di-Ahman and so headed for easier pickings.

So instead of attacking Di-Ahman, the malicious band of Mormon-haters proceeded to burn and pillage the easier targets of the outlying Mormon homesteads as well as many of the smaller settlements. When General Parks of the Missouri Militia heard the reports of the unauthorized raiding of the small Mormon settlements, he then directed the other Mormon military commander, Lyman Wight, to get his men ready for active military duty and ordered them to proceed forth to curb and in effect put down the pillaging and burning by deadly force if necessary.

In addition to these two defensive Mormon militias companies under the command of Colonel Hinkle and Commander Lyman Wight, Joseph Smith organized a third company of armed men similar to a group that might resemble a National Guard Company of today, which he called the "Companies of The Armies of Israel." Their duties were not only to protect the Saints from harassment and persecution, but also to help provide any humanitarian needs for the Saints and to contribute the necessary emergency services that were required for the many destitute new refugees.

Most regrettably, despite all the good intentions of the civil Army of Israel, there was a most insidiously closeted traitor among the troops of the "Armies of Israel." He was a deceitful self-serving and evil-minded man by the name of Doctor Sampson Avard. This Dr. Avard had his own ulterior motives for being affiliated with "The Armies of Israel" and his true agenda was eventually revealed, which was; "to form a secret combination by which he might rise as a mighty conqueror, at the expense and the overthrow of the Church. This he tried to accomplish by his smooth, flattering, and winning speeches, which he frequently made to his associates." - 1a

Thus it was that the fiendish Sam Avard was conspiring with his cohorts to eventually take over the leadership of the Church and use the religious organization itself for his own selfish purposes. This was only one of many villainess plans on his agenda, as he insidiously worked his way into the confidence of his weak-willed supporters who thought the same way he did about the hated Missourians. And so it was that he was able to surreptitiously organize a secret society from among Joseph's National Guard group to take revenge upon and kill all Missourians. This evil, insidious, and unscrupulous band of thugs would soon become known as the violent raiders of the infamous "Danites," being named after a warlike tribe of ancient Israel. They preferred to be called the "Destroying Angels."

They touted themselves as a fraternity of patriotic avenging warriors whose aim was to avenge the wrongs against the Mormon people and fight against the Missourian "mobacrats." However, they soon revealed that they had little interest in any real justice, but were more interested in violent bloody revenge. They perpetrated their extreme violence on all Missourian settlers without any regard for whom was actually guilty of the raiding against the Mormons. And so it didn't matter which of their victims were innocent or which were culpable; they would all be branded without exception as the hated Missourians that must be exterminated. Thus the Danites became greatly feared by the local population. Being that they were utterly steeped in their own depraved form of what they called justice, the Danites came to foster a detestable inventory of oaths, secret signs, and death threats, and proceeded to mercilessly perpetrate brutality and revenge on any and all Missourian civilians that they ran across during their violent raids.

After Dr. Sam Avard was finally and ultimately kicked out the Church by the Mormon leadership, the vindictive commander completely turned traitorous to Joseph Smith and the Saints and treacherously conspired with the anti-Mormon Missourians in an attempt to completely destroy the Church. In his blatant acts of revenge against the Church, he proceeded to testify to a profusion of outrageous vile lies against his former Mormon leaders. During this perpetration of his despicable lies before Missourian authorities, it was really quite amazing as to how he was able to use his skills of deceit to cleverly transfer the biggest share of the blame for his own horrendous deeds from off his own back and on to the backs of the Church leaders. Church History records this interesting excerpt:

"About this time Sampson Avard was found by the mob secreted in the hazel brush some miles from Far West, and brought into camp, where he and they were 'hail fellows well met;' for Avard told them that Daniteism was an order of the Church, and by his lying tried to make the Church a scape-goat for his sins." – 1b

His lies and double-crossing deceptions were taken in with relish and were welcomed by the Missourian authorities. However, among the Saints, he was despised and forthwith excommunicated from the Church, but not before he did considerable damage to the reputation of Joseph Smith and to the good name and stature of the Church in general in the minds of the citizens of Missouri.

As might be expected, after the Mormons had been given authority to mount their own defenses to resist the violence of the mobs through their own-armed militias, things were bound to escalate into a full-blown shooting war. On October 25th 1838, a group of about sixty armed Mormon Militiamen under the leadership of Captain David W. Patten, who was at the time acting as the current president of the Twelve, set out on a mission to rescue three Mormon prisoners that they had been ordered to retrieve by Judge Higbee of Caldwell county.

Previous to the judge's order, there had been a vigilante group of Missourian ruffians led by Captain Samuel Bogart that had violently taken three Mormon men as hostages and had threatened to execute them without a trial. On this particular day, while the Mormon troops were searching for the hostages and marching towards the Crooked River, they were suddenly without any warning attacked. One of the Mormon troops was shot dead in his tracks from a vigilante ambush that was well hidden in the bushes. Captain Patten immediately ordered a charge down the hill towards the river and the skirmish was soon in pitch battle in a fully armed and a very deadly conflict. The battle turned out to be short and bloody. Although their assigned mission was successful at the "Battle of Crooked River," in that it retrieved the Mormon hostages, it resulted in regrettable casualties on both sides. The most lamentable casualty was the fatal injuries of Captain David Patten. Also among the deaths were two more Mormon troops, and in addition, one dead vigilante, and six other men who were badly wounded. Some time before this incident, Captain David Patten had once prayed that he might become a martyr for his Savior. His prayer was answered on that day, as he became the first apostolic martyr of this dispensation. – 2

The news of the "Battle at Crooked River," which was also called "The Bogart Battle" after it's vigilante leader, spread like wildfire throughout the state as the incident was being portrayed as absolute proof that the Mormons were in open rebellion against the state of Missouri. Two days later, on October 27th 1838, Governor Boggs of the State of Missouri issued an executive order, commonly known as "the Extermination Order," in which it flatly stated; "the Mormons must be treated as enemies, and must be exterminated or driven from the State if necessary for public peace." Yes it was the infamous Governor Lilburn W. Boggs of Missouri that perpetrated this outrageous directive and order, which was nothing less than an egregious breach of civil rights under the U.S. Constitution. This above detestable order, which called for the out right extermination of Mormons, has been taken directly from Governor Boggs words in his own letter to General John B. Clark that is found in the "Document Containing the Correspondence, Orders, & C., p 61."

This abominable and unlawful executive order not only activated the entire State of Missouri's Militias against the Mormons, but it effectively, if not intentionally, gave license to every vigilante in Missouri to do what ever they willed against any and all Mormons. It brought on wholesale burning, looting, destruction of animals and property, flogging of Mormon men, vile assaults on Mormon women, and an absolute and unrelenting determination to drive the Saints from the State of Missouri by any and all means.

On hearing of this order, the Prophet strongly advised all the Saints in the area including those outlying settlements to come into safer ground. He made a specific invitation accompanied by a strong warning to the leader of the settlement at Haun's Mill to bring his people in to a safer place. Unfortunately this vital warning went unheeded.

Jacob Haun was a German immigrant who was one of the first of the settlers to come into the northwest area of Missouri. He established a gristmill on Shoal Creek in 1836, which soon grew into a small Mormon settlement. Even though Joseph Smith had strongly advised Brother Haun to move his settlers into a safer area, Brother Haun remained stubborn citing an officially agreed upon treaty between the Haun's Mill settlement and Colonel Jennings of Livingston County. Brother Haun insisted that they were going to be just fine and perfectly safe under the signed agreement. Unfortunately, the treaty gave the Saints of the small settlement a false sense of security, as they apparently did not understand that the hate driven violent mobs cared very little or virtually nothing at all for any treaties made with any Mormons.

So during this time when the greater part of the Missouri Militias were already gathering for a planned siege at Far West, there took place in another location by Missourian "Mobacrats" one of the most violent, merciless, and unconscionable crimes that was ever perpetrated upon the Mormon people. The violent murders that took place there at the settlement of Haun's Mill were unjustifiable and inexcusable, and the most egregious of any attacks on innocent civilians ever perpetrated by the Missourians upon the Mormons and it was most definitely a massacre by any measure or definition. - 3a

On the afternoon of October 30th, 1838, a large group of 240 Mormon-hating Missourian vigilantes rode into the Haun's Mill settlement yelling like wild banshees that sent men, women, and children into a panic. The vigilantes were dressed as wild Indians in feathers and war paint and were led by an evil man called Nehemiah Comstock. Among the other innocent men and boys that were shot dead on that day, the mob shot down an old man known as Father McBride. "An old man after the massacre was partially over, threw himself into their hands and begged for quarter, when he was instantly shot down; that not killing him, they took an old corn cutter and literally mangled him to pieces. A lad of ten years of age, after being shot down, also begged to be spared, when one of the mob placed the muzzle of his gun to the boy's head and blew out his brains." -3b

Nearby, a dozen Mormon men ran to take cover inside the blacksmith shop that was made of heavy logs. Unfortunately the logs had not been chinked and there were large spaces between the logs, 2 to 3 inch gaps of space, which allowed the raiders to fire their guns through the cracks and systematically shoot and murder every last soul inside the shop.

It has been estimated that the ruthless men fired over 1600 rounds of ammunition at approximately thirty Mormons, including men, women, and children, killing at least eighteen of them, and wounding over a dozen including at least one woman and a nine year old boy. After the massacre was over, the mob proceeded to pillage the houses, wagons, and tents of bedding and clothing, and then drove off the horses and wagons leaving the widows and orphans wanting for the necessities of life. If all that wasn't loathsome enough, they stripped the clothing from off the bodies of the dead. It was one of the most heinous of crimes and the most infamous day of persecution that has ever been recorded in the history of the Saints. - 4

At the end of October, as the Generals of the Missouri Militias dutifully responded to the Governor's extermination order, they formed up and gathered for war. Under the orders of General John B. Clark, General Samuel D. Lucas, General Atchison, and General Doniphan along with General Graham and General Wilson of the Missouri Militias, the wide spread gathering of troops under the state's best militia commanders mustered near Far West with a combined force of more than 2,500 soldiers. The large army formed up only sixteen miles from the city and made their preparations to engage the Far West settlement in heavy battle.

The next morning, on the 31st of October 1838, General Lucas received a message from the Mormon commander, Colonel Hinkle, who was asking for a meeting to see if there could be some sort of a compromise or any sort of a peaceful settlement in an attempt to avoid bloodshed. The two Commanders and their staffs met under a white flag near a designated point outside Far West at which time, General Lucas gave Colonel Hinkle his conditions for a peaceful settlement:

They were "First--To give up their Church's leaders to be tried and punished."

"Second--To make an appropriation of their property of all who have taken up arms, to pay their debts, and indemnify for damages done by them."

"Third--That the balance of the Mormons should leave the State to be protected by the militia, while being permitted to remain under protection until further orders were received from the commander-in-chief."

"Fourth--To give up all the arms of every description, to be receipted for." – 5

*   *   *

It was then that General Lucas most unsympathetically gave Colonel Hinkle one hour to comply with the agreement, or Far West would be attacked and would then suffer the devastating consequences. Although the Mormon leader Colonel Hinkle has been called a traitor, one must understand that his decision was made under great duress as he was confronted with a short time table and a very real fear for his greatly outnumbered men, and then the had added worry of having the ultimate responsibility for the lives of a great number of civilians in the Far West community. Hinkle was unable to see any hope in going up against such an overwhelming force with only 800 men, and therefore he reluctantly agreed to the terms. If this decision can be defended because of the overwhelming odds against his own smaller defenses, his personal actions involving the misleading of the Church leaders and betraying them cannot be so easily justified. There are even some unsubstantiated reports that say Colonel Hinkle accepted a substantial bribe, maybe as much as $750, to betray the Church leaders.

At 9:AM the next morning, the entire Missouri Militia took up their assigned positions with General Wilson's brigade forming the west line, General Doniphan on the east line, and General Graham and General Parks at the south line, complemented by an artillery company and a cannon in the center. They left the north side of the reception square open for the formal Mormon surrender. Under these conditions, the Missourian Generals accepted the weapons of the Mormon army and took into their custody the promised Church leaders as prisoners.

This group of unwitting Mormon prisoners consisted of Joseph Smith Jun., Sidney Rigdon, Lyman Wight, Parley P. Pratt, and Joseph's secretary, George W. Robinson, all of whom were delivered in compliance with the surrender terms agreed to between General Lucas and the Mormon Colonel Hinkle. However, Joseph and the other Church leaders reported later that they had been misled by Colonel Hinkle into thinking that they were only going to meet with General Lucas to discuss the terms of a peaceful settlement, merely to have a "consultation," but certainly not to be taken into custody and become General Lucas' prisoners as they were to find out too late.

General Lucas then made his report; "The 'Mormon' army, reduced to about six hundred men by desertion and otherwise, under their commander, Colonel Hinkle marched out of their town through the space into our square, formed a hollow square, and grounded their arms. Colonel Hinkle then rode forward and delivered up to me his sword and pistols." - 6

General Lucas in his cautious vigilance kept all the men of the disarmed Mormon militia under guard while he sent most of the rest of his army into the settlement of Far West to search for further weapons. With most of the Mormon men being held prisoner, the undisciplined and greedy searchers took this order as a license to loot, pillage, abuse the Mormon women, and ransack every last cabin in Far West. There appeared to be no orders of any kind from the higher up leadership to curb in any way this depraved behavior.

"After depriving (the Mormons) of their arms the mob continued to hunt the brethren like wild beasts, and shoot several, ravished the women, and killed one near the city. No Saint was permitted to go in or out of the city; and meantime the Saints lived on parched corn. The brethren at Far West were ordered by General Clark to form a line, when the names of fifty-six present were called and made prisoners to await their trial for something they knew not what. They were kept under a close guard." - 7

Heber C. Kimball wrote that the Church brethren were forced to sign over all their land at the point of a bayonet with the rationalized excuse that the confiscation of Mormon property was perfectly justified to defray the cost of fighting the Mormon war. The wicked routinely justify their immoral and malevolent behavior with lame excuses.

General Clark addressed the Saints at Far West saying in part; "Another article yet remains for you to comply with, and that is, that you leave the state forthwith; and whatever may be your feelings concerning this, or whatever your innocence, it is nothing to me; General Lucas, who is equal in authority with me, has made this treaty with you--I approve of it--I should have done the same had I been here--I am therefore determined to see it fulfilled. The character of this state has suffered almost beyond redemption, from the character, conduct and influence that you have exerted, and we deem it an act of justice to restore her character to its former standing among the states, by every proper means." – 8

On the following day, the betrayed Church leaders were given a brief time to say their good-byes to their families. They were placed under the careful guard of a militia, which were in reality no more than the vigilantes styled to look like "serious soldiers."

Hyrum Smith, the Prophet's older brother, had been ill and so wasn't included in the original prisoners that were taken earlier that morning, but then later on in what seemed to be an act of betrayal, Colonel Hinkle led armed guards to Hyrum's home and arrested him. It was then at his home in Far West at the point of a bayonet, accompanied by vulgar oaths and curses, that Hyrum was ordered to make his last farewell to his wife as they told him that his "doom was sealed" and brazenly added that he would never see her again. Others were also told the same concerning their families. Even under these dire circumstances of having to relinquish their property by force, having their women being abused, and their men killed, the Saints attempted to keep up their spirits by rejoicing and praising the Lord right in the face of their abusers. Seeing this sight, Judge Cameron commented; "See them laugh and kick up their heels. They are whipped, but not conquered." - 9

In an impetuous civil tribunal ordered by General Lucas on November 1st, the Church leaders were summarily tried and sentenced to be shot the following morning. When the compassionate and considerably more fair minded General Doniphan received the order from General Lucas that the prisoners were to be executed, he personally judged it to be nothing short of murder and wrote a message to General Lucas stating that he refused to obey the order. The following excerpts are the actual statements that have been taken from copies of the original exchange of letters between General Lucas and General Doniphan:

Brigadier-General Doniphan: "SIR:--You will take Joseph Smith and the other prisoners into the public square of Far West, and shoot them at 9 o'clock tomorrow morning." SAMUEL D. LUCAS 'Major-General Commanding.

However, General Doniphan, in the righteous indignation of his own conscience, promptly replied to his impetuous superior with this message:

"It is cold-blooded murder. I will not obey your order. My brigade shall march for Liberty tomorrow morning, at 8 o'clock; and if you execute these men, I will hold you responsible before an earthly tribunal, so help me God." W. W. DONIPHAN, 'Brigadier-General - 10

It was at the army camp on Goose Creek that the Mormon prisoners were being held for a summary execution. General Doniphan being compelled by his own moral integrity, and who had now set himself up perfectly well for a court marshal, walked over and spoke to Joseph Smith saying that he refused to be a part of what he considered murder, and so he was going to order his brigade to leave the camp as an act of protest.

This brave act by General Doniphan, which could have easily resulted in his court-martial and being dismissed from the army for refusing to obey an order, appeared to have literally saved Joseph and his companion's lives that morning. General Lucas responded to General Doniphan's protest and insubordination with an uncharacteristically change of heart, and then unexpectedly ordered Joseph Smith to be taken to Jackson County instead and be tried there and executed. The custody of the Mormon prisoners was then turned over to General Wilson of Jackson County.

Later while Joseph and the other church prisoners were being taken and loaded into a wagon, five vigilantes brazenly shoved their way through the ranks of the soldiers that were guarding the prisoners, yelling "Kill them," at which point they fired all five of their pistols directly at "old Joe Smith's head." They fully intended to assassinate him just as he was getting into the wagon. Incredibly every one of the pistols misfired. Three of the five pistols flashed in the pan without setting off the main charge, while the other two pistols only clicked harmlessly. Though it was not unusual for any flintlock pistol to occasionally misfire, it was a true miracle that not a single one out of the five weapons ignited the main charge in any of the pistols. Therefore and most remarkably, there were no projectiles fired from any of the five flintlocks, which left the Prophet Joseph Smith miraculously unharmed.

Reacting quickly to the assassination attempt, General Wilson immediately ordered the failed assassins arrested and put into chains. As the wagon hauling the church leaders lurched ahead, Joseph proceeded to quietly comfort his companions. Parley P. Pratt related the incident: "As we arose and commenced our march on the morning of the 3rd of November, Joseph Smith spoke to me and the other prisoners, in a low, but cheerful and confidential tone; said he: 'Be of good cheer, brethren; the word of the Lord has come to me last night that our lives are to be given us, and that whatever we may suffer during this captivity, the Lord has promised that not one of our lives shall be taken.'" - 11

In response to a sincere and humble request from the Prophet, General Wilson allowed the Church leaders to go and say their good-byes to their families and obtain any necessities for the journey. He faced stiff objections from General Lucas who thought General Wilson was being much too accommodating to the Mormons.

Amazingly enough, the impetuous General Lucas never reprimanded General Doniphan for his insubordination and refusing to obey an order. Years later, the Saints recognizing the brave act of General Doniphan in saving the Prophet's life, greeted him in the streets of Salt Lake City as a hero in 1873. Saving Joseph's life was not his only good deed in helping out the Prophet. In addition, General Doniphan had also acted as Joseph Smith's lawyer in front of Judge King at Richmond. He was a true friend to the Prophet Joseph Smith.

Among his other gestures of good will towards the Saints, General Doniphan had also been involved in giving the Mormon people the aid of his political clout. Before the siege at Far West, General Doniphan had passed a bill in the state legislature to set aside Caldwell County and to specifically designate it for Mormon settlement. Due to no fault of his own, the large Mormon population just kept coming and eventually spilled over into Daviess, Carroll, Ray, Livingston, Clinton, and Chariton counties, which incited a wide spread Mormon phobia among the Missourians. This large influx of Mormons inevitably gave rise to a situation where old settlers had an overwhelming fear that the Mormon were completely taking over their state, even though the Mormons had no intentions of stepping on anyone's toes, or running anyone else out, nor did they have in mind to do any harm to their neighbors. The Missourians were especially afraid the huge numbers among the Saints would eventually lead to an overpowering vote to eliminate slavery in Missouri.

Never the less, this fear of being over run by the Mormons escalated into a war between the two incompatible cultures. Eventually, it led to the mandatory exodus of the Mormon people, which was then officially carried out under the uncompromising decree of the "Extermination Order" set forth by the very biased Missourian Governor Lilburn Boggs. There was certainly no mercy for any Mormons to be found anywhere in Missouri in the 1830's.

Looking back some 180 years and trying figure out just how a different less abusive more peaceful outcome could have been orchestrated, it is still very difficult even today to see how any kind of an arrangement could have been put in place to facilitate the peace and have them all living together in harmony. Under the aggravating circumstances at the time, it was just unrealistic that any kind of a harmonious, workable agreement could have been established for them to live side by side in peace, considering their opposing views on slavery, the dispute over voting rights, the uncompromising and belligerent attitude of the Missourians towards the Mormon religion, and their vast dissimilarities in culture and lifestyle.

Meanwhile, at Far West, a large crowd of Saints gathered to say their farewells to their Church leaders at the time of their arrest, along with a sizable crowd of curious onlookers who wanted to leer at the notable Mormon prisoners. Besides friends and family of Joseph's and his companions, there were many there to just simply play their part as spectators and hecklers. Some of them even yelled insults at the Prophet's own mother as she pushed her way through the soldiers. The prisoners were not allowed out of the tightly covered canvas prison wagon. However, Lucy Mack Smith was able to put her hand under the canvas and say her goodbyes to Joseph and Hyrum, her two beloved sons. At the time, she thought it would be the last time that she would ever see them, and they too thought the same, as they knew they were being hauled off to Independence Missouri to be executed. – 12

Five days after the fall of Far West, General Clark and his men showed up again. This time he ordered every young man among the Saints between ages of eighteen and fifty-five to step forward and be accessed for their involvement and accountability in regards to the Mormon war. General Clark was aided in making these guilty assessments by some traitorous Mormon apostates who seemed only too happy to point out the prominent priesthood leaders, and thus fifty-six of the Church leaders at Far West were taken into custody to be hauled off to Richmond Missouri for trial.

Fortunately, two of the most prominent leaders of the Church were overlooked. Brigham Young, the most senior apostle, lived 3 or 4 miles outside of Far West and so he was luckily missed in the roundup. Heber C. Kimball, second in seniority among the apostles, had just returned from his mission in England and so he too was overlooked. Because of the blessed and lucky circumstance of these brethren being overlooked, providence had seen to it that General Clark's aim to completely eradicate any leadership from among the Saints had decidedly failed. – 13

Speaking to all the Mormon men whose names did not show up on the prisoners list, General Clark ordered them to return to their families and provide for them until such time that they would duly carry out and honor the agreement of the exodus and promptly make their arrangements to leave the state of Missouri. Meanwhile, all the other brethren whose names were indelibly written on the list, and who had definitely been identified by the treachery of the apostate turncoats, were made captive and taken into custody. They then were ordered by the authorities in charge to be imprisoned until their trial, at which time it was fully expected that they would receive a harsh punishment, presumably even execution for their crimes against the state of Missouri.

Even though the original order from the commanding militia leader had been to take Joseph and the other prisoners to Independence for trial and execution, General Cark made a request to the Governor asking him to let the prisoners be tried in Richmond where the well-known Mormon hater, Judge King, could see to their sure and ultimate punishment. When the request was granted, Colonel Sterling Price took charge of the prisoners with a contingent of seventy-four guards, who to nobody's surprise, were found to be less than humane in their treatment of the Mormon prisoners.

When it came time to camp for the night, the guards imprisoned the Mormon leaders in an old abandoned farmhouse until morning. The prisoners were padlocked together with chains and required to eat with their bare hands. They were forced to listen to the most intolerable vile speech and lewd vulgar bragging concerning what the Missourian men had done to the Mormon women; "...they recounted to each other their deeds of rapine, murder, robbery, etc., which they had committed among the "Mormons" while at Far West and vicinity. They even boasted of defiling by force the wives, their daughters and virgins, and of shooting or dashing out the brains of men, women and children." This vivid and unsettling account related here regarding the Saints' treatment, was reported by Elder Parley P. Pratt as he related it in History Of the Church vol 3.

When the Prophet Joseph Smith could simply take no more of the vile talk, he abruptly arose in his rattling chains and loudly exclaimed; "SILENCE, ye fiends of the infernal pit. In the name of Jesus Christ I rebuke you, and command you to be still; I will not live another minute and hear such language. Cease such talk, or you or I die THIS INSTANT!"

The instantly humbled guards were cowered into complete silence; very nearly trembling, and they dared not utter another vile word. Parley P. Pratt later commented on the incident saying; "I have seen the ministers of justice, clothed in magisterial robes, and criminals arraigned before them, while life was suspended on a breath, in the courts of England; I have witnessed a Congress in solemn session to give laws to nations; I have tried to conceive of kings, of royal courts, of thrones and crowns;

and of emperors assembled to decide the fate of kingdoms; but dignity and majesty have I seen but once, as it stood in chains, at midnight in a dungeon, in an obscure village in Missouri." - 14

On November 13th 1838, the prisoners from Far West found themselves facing a judge well known as an avid Mormon hater. Judge Austin King's sham trial in Richmond was intended to go exactly in the manner that he desired it to go, even if he had to threaten witnesses to say what he wanted them to say. One of the witnesses had to literally flee for his life because he was not complying with the contrived accusations against the Mormons.

In the ultimate sanctimonious act of pure hypocrisy, Sam Avard, the apostate Mormon leader of the heinous diabolical Danites, was one of the chief witnesses for the prosecution, and he certainly showed no restraint in telling unbelievably vile and flagrant lies against the Church leaders. Even though the abominable and evil-minded Sam Avard had personally led a great many merciless and violent murderous raids on innocent Missourian citizens and had ruthlessly murdered a sizable number of them through the aid of his secret society, he was given complete immunity for his crimes in exchange for his testimony. In the most detestable an unbelievable breach of justice ever seen in a courtroom, he was set free and received total amnesty for his disgusting and egregiously false testimony against the Mormon leaders.

There were other traitorous apostates who also lied on the witness stand to save their own unworthy hides, with some reports saying that they had received bribe money for their perjury. Among these unworthy souls, was the Mormon Colonel, George M. Hinkle, along with his co-conspirators, Reed Peck and John Corrill. Brother Corrill had formerly been a counselor in the Presiding Bishopric. All of these backstabbing turncoats testified that Joseph Smith and his conspirators were planning to take over the world, either by conversion or by force and bloodshed. – 15

While summarizing the downfall of Far West and its sorrowful and disgraceful defeat, Brigham Young wrote in his discourses the following: "In the year 1838, in the month of March, in company with a number of brethren, myself included, Joseph arrived at Far West, Caldwell County, Missouri. We had not the privilege of staying there more than for a few months before the cry was raised against Joseph Smith, that he was guilty of high treason. This aroused the people and the government of the state;

and in October thirty-five hundred of the militia of the state of Missouri were marched against a few of us in Far West. They succeeded in taking Joseph and Hyrum and sixty-five others and putting them in prison. When Joseph had his trial, the great accusation against him was that he believed in the fulfillment of prophecy -- the prophecies that had been made by Prophets of old and contained in Holy Writ. When Judge King asked Joseph if he believed the predictions of Daniel the Prophet, that in the latter-days the God of heaven would set up a kingdom which should succeed and finally rule and hold dominion over all other kingdoms, Joseph replied that he did believe this scripture as well as the rest. This was considered treason! Joseph's lawyer turned to Judge King and said, 'Judge, I think you had better write it down that the Bible is treason,' and this was all they found against him. But the mob continued until they drove the Latter-day Saints out of the state of Missouri." - 16

*   *   *

1a. See History of the Church, Vol.3, Ch.13, p.178.

1b. See as above p. 191-196 Also BYU Studies 28(Winter 1988) p.5-41

2. See Life of Heber C. Kimball pp. 213-214

3a. See History of the Church 3:183

3b. History of the Church, Vol.3, Ch.15, p.220

4. See History of the Church 3:183-187

5. See History of the Church, Vol.3, Ch.13, p. 197

6. Samuel D. Lucas See History of the Church, Vol.3, Ch.13, p.198

7. See History of the Church, Vol.3, Ch.14, p. 202

8. See History of the Church, Vol.3, Ch.14, p.203

9. See "Life of Heber C. Kimball" p. 219

10. See History of the Church, Vol.3, p. 190, Footnotes

11. See "Autobiography of Parley P. Pratt" p. 192.

12. See Lucy Mack Smith, "History of Joseph Smith by His Mother" pp. 290-291

13. See "Life of Heber C. Kimball" pp.222-223

14. See Autobiography of Parley P. Pratt, pp. 228-230

15. See History of the Church 3:209-210

16. See FAR WEST Discourses of Brigham Young, p.472

*   *   *

Chapter Thirteen

CAPTIVITY & ESCAPE

*   *   *

On November 24th 1838, Judge King of Richmond Missouri released 23 of the original 56 Mormon prisoners after about three weeks of incarceration, stating that there was insufficient evidence to hold them. A few days later Judge King ruled that five of the remaining Mormon prisoners, which included Parley P. Pratt, would be held over for trial on the charge of murder. Although Parley had been taken prisoner with the original Joseph Smith group, the Judge now separated Parley into another group that was being indicted for murder at the Battle of Crooked River. This excerpt from an autobiography written by the daughter of Morris Phelps, one of the prisoners, reveals further explanation:

"My father was thrown into prison with Parley Pratt and four others at Richmond Jail, while Joseph and Hyrum Smith, with five others, were taken to Liberty Jail, Independence, the jail at Richmond not being large enough to hold them all. Father had his trial at the same time that Joseph

Smith had his mob trial at Richmond. He was told many times that if he would burn his Mormon Bible and quit the Mormon Church, he could go free; they said he had no business there, but he chose to be firm to his religion." – Taken from the Mary Rich, Autobiography, BYU Special Collections

And so it was that Parley P. Pratt was held over for trial in Richmond County jail with Morris Phelps, Luman Gibbs, Darwin Chase, and Norman Shearer, all of whom were being held over for trial for their involvement in a supposed murder of a Missourian. These Mormon prisoners had already been verbally harangued for more than twenty days with blatant in-your-face accusations and false testimony, and now they would continue to be held for further harassment in the Richmond Missouri jail for their supposed involvement in the alleged murder of a vigilante during the Reverend Bogart battle, also known as the Crooked River Battle. President David W. Patten was killed in that very same battle, but for some reason, no Missourian was even the least bit concerned over President Patten's death in that fray, nor were they troubled over the other two Mormons that were killed there. It was only the death of that one vigilante attacker that upset the Missourians. Supposedly the Mormons had murdered him unjustly, even though it was he that was shooting at the Mormons and trying to kill them at the time.

Meanwhile, after a few more days had passed, more than twenty additional Mormon prisoners were finally released to return to their homes, as there was no evidence against them either. This left less than a dozen of the top Mormon leaders still in jail out of the 56 Mormon captives taken, and so these dozen still remained in custody.

Unfortunately, and for what ever wholly arbitrary and illogical reasons, Parley P. Pratt and his four fellow prisoners remained incarcerated in the Richmond County Jail for nearly another five months without any actual evidence to hold them, and ultimately, on totally baseless charges. Some of Parley's compatriots were released in late April 1839, while Parley and Morris Phelps were kept until June of that year. – 1a

During the meantime, the most hated of all the Mormons, "Old Joe Smith," was being held in jail along with his first counselor, Sidney Rigdon, his brother, Hyrum, and three other church brethren, Brother Alexander McRae, Brother Caleb Baldwin, and the Mormon militia leader, Lyman

Wight. These last three brethren named were singled out especially because they were thought to have been the head leaders among the Mormon military Commanders; therefore they must be held culpable for their heinous crimes. Somehow, Joseph's secretary George W. Robinson was not held for trial at this time, possibly because he was not considered to be any more than just an ordinary clerk. Joseph and the others were now to be sent to Daviess County to be tried for the crime of treason. In the interim, all six of the now notorious Mormon leaders were to be held in the infamous Liberty Jail in Clay County just across the Missouri river from Independence. They were being held for an unspecified period of time before their trial, and they did not know for how many days or even months that would be. What they did know was that the authorities knew perfectly well, but ignored the fact, that the charges were based on little or no evidence. The injustice of being held in a barbaric dungeon under just plain miserable conditions and without their constitutional right to have "a speedy trial," and for something they didn't do, seemed overwhelmingly unfair and very disheartening to the Mormon prisoners. And to top it off there seemed to be little hope of being released any time soon.

And so as it was there in the infamous Liberty Jail that the Church leaders were being held in all reality in nothing more than a brutal cold dungeon. And the horrors suffered by the Prophet and his companions there were almost unfathomable. The jailers, who seemed less than human sometimes, showed no humanity or compassion whatsoever for the prisoners. The guards stayed on the top floor with the only access to the prisoners in the dungeon below being through a trap door in the floor. The dungeon walls were of very cold solid rock that were nearly four feet thick with a ceiling that was not even tall enough to allow the prisoners to stand up right. In addition, they found that the cold hard stone floor was barely covered with straw, no beds, an old wooden bucket had to do for a toilet, and to add to the misery, no heat was ever provided for the prisoners even through the long cold Missouri winter months.

It wasn't bad enough that the food itself was rancid and virtually inedible, but the guards would occasionally deliberately poison it. Hyrum Smith wrote; "Poison was administered to us three or four times. The effect it had upon our system was, that it vomited us almost to death; and then we would lie some two or three days in a torpid, stupid state, not even caring or wishing for life,--the poison being administered in too large doses, or it would inevitably have proved fatal." Fortunately for the Mormon prisoners, the poison was so overdosed that it caused immediate vomiting and thus it violently cleansed out their stomachs before the poison had a chance to be absorbed and seriously harm them.

At one point the guards had come across the body of a poor soul who had recently died. And so the ghoulish jailers decided as a sick joke to cut up a portion of this human body into a roast for the prisoners to eat. Being very hungry for some meat, Hyrum hurriedly and unknowingly tried to cut off a slice of the tainted roast. Oddly enough, the fork and knife awkwardly fell out of his hands twice before the Prophet loudly exclaimed, "Do not touch it, for it is human flesh!" Hyrum later testified; "We none of us partook of the flesh, except Lyman Wight. We also heard the guard, which was placed over us making sport of us, saying they had fed us on 'Mormon' beef." The depravity of the guards at Liberty jail was far beyond any human decency or any type of moral boundaries. – 1b

As the beleaguered first Presidency of the Mormon Church languished in Liberty jail, there were thousands of Saints starting their long wintery trek out of the State of Missouri as ordered by Governor Boggs and it was being brutally enforced by the Missouri State Militia who impressed no one with their compassion. The displaced and persecuted Saints scattered in several directions to get out of Western Missouri, but the vast majority of the Mormon refugees sought out the town of Quincy in west-central Illinois just across the Mississippi River on its east bank. The greater part of them had little or no money, carried with them very few earthly possessions, and most certainly exhibited the despairing and demoralized image of refugees in purse and spirit.

In January of 1839, Joseph sent a letter from Liberty jail to Brigham Young and Heber C. Kimball who were now the de facto leaders of the church. The letter stated that the responsibility for the Church was now in their hands, and thus they were mandated to see to the care of the overwhelming numbers of ten to twelve thousand Saints leaving the state and to oversee their safe and orderly exodus from Missouri using the assistance of the Twelve Apostles.

The few families that remained in Missouri were dirt poor and in many cases destitute. Some of the Saints had sold their property out of desperation with prime farmland having gone for as little as 50 cents an acre. Others had been forced to sign over their property at gunpoint without any compensation at all. The Missourians were completely merciless in their dealings with the Mormons and took full advantage of the Saints' desperate situation.

And so it came to pass, that Brigham Young, who had now become the most wanted man in all of Missouri, found himself forced to travel in disguise while he attempted to gather up the remaining leaders of the Church so that they could carry out the new responsibilities that the Prophet had placed upon them. When they were all gathered, Brigham presented them with a proposal stating: "I propose that we resolve this day to enter into a solemn covenant to assist each other to remove from this state, and that we resolve that we will never desert the poor who are worthy."

The body of men listening to Brigham's concerned words readily accepted the proposal. Seven of the brethren were chosen to be a special committee overseeing the aid to the poor and to see to their safe removal from the state. Thirty-three men signed the document that day and some reports say as many as 400 eventually signed it later. - 2

Emma Smith and her sister-in-law Mary Fielding Smith were both determined to not leave Missouri until they could make a trip to visit Joseph and Hyrum at Liberty Jail. It has been reported that Emma made at least two trips to the jail in December of 1838. In one of the trips she was reported to have brought along young Joseph the III to get a blessing from his father.

The journey to Liberty Jail was an exhausting 100 miles round trip, but Mary Fielding Smith was adamant that Hyrum should see his new baby son before they left the state. On January 29th 1839, Mary and her sister Mercy took baby Joseph F. Smith to his father at Liberty jail. Hyrum gave his new son a father's blessing, a blessing that would later be gloriously fulfilled when Joseph F. Smith became the sixth President of the Church. During the women's brief but welcomed visit, Joseph and Hyrum made it clear that their families must leave Missouri without delay for they would be prime targets for further harassment by the pitiless hard-hearted mobs. – 3a

On hearing of Joseph and Hyrum's serious concerns regarding their families, the Committee for Removal of the Saints decided that their first priority should be to get the families of the main church leaders out of the state of Missouri. Certainly, no one knew just when the vigilantes might single out these particular families for further persecution. Joseph's own parents had loaded up their belongings two different times in order to head east to Quincy Illinois, but both times their wagons were politely confiscated by the committee in order to accommodate Emma and her children, as well as to aid Sidney Rigdon's family in their move. Eventually Joseph's parents did make it out of Missouri with the help of their other grown children. – 3b

It was the Jonathan Holman family that escorted Emma and her own four children on their journey East to Illinois, along with the help of one of Joseph's trusted friends, Stephen Markham. After nine days of rough rutted roads and wet cold February weather, they finally spotted Quincy Illinois nestled on the other side of the Mississippi River just below the bluff. Since the wide and mighty river was frozen over, the ferry hadn't been able to operate for several days, which resulted in several wagonloads of families camped at the river's edge just waiting to cross the dangerously icy and very wide river. A few people had already dared to carry their belongings across the ice on foot, never the less, the thin ice cover simply wasn't thick enough that it could be completely trusted. This posed a very big question as to the wisdom of trying to cross over the thin ice on foot, for there was always the possibility of an unwary foot traveler breaking through the ice at any time and then having to struggle for their life in the freezing waters below.

However, Emma Smith was a determined woman and she stubbornly insisted on crossing the thin frozen ice of the mighty Mississippi River with her four young children. She also carried with her the translation of the Holy Bible manuscript tucked in a pocket under her skirts. She bravely held baby Alexander in one arm, two-year-old Frederick in the other, and then proceeded with great care and caution across the frozen river pulling along young Joseph III and her adopted daughter, Julia, while the two "youngins" tightly clung to her skirts. The river seemed to get wider and wider as she trudged along and Emma began to ache from the strain of carrying the two younger children in her weary arms. She grew more fatigued by the minute as the icy waters whirled visibly beneath the ice putting fear in her heart. After what seemed forever, Emma and the children eventually and gratefully reached the other side. When all of her little family miraculously made it across the river, Emma fell to her knees exhausted and thanked God for her ever so grateful deliverance and the safety of her young children. On arrival in Quincy, Emma and her children were able to temporarily move in with Judge John Cleveland and his wife Sarah who lived about 4 miles east of Quincy. – 4

As the months rolled by, Joseph and his fellow prisoners were kept in Liberty Jail from December 1, 1838 until April 6, 1839. It was more than four long months through the miserable cold Missouri winter. Sharing the depravity of this hellhole with the Prophet was his first counselor, Brother Rigdon, his second counselor, Hyrum, and three other ever so lucky fellow Church members who had the dubious but privileged honor of suffering there in Liberty Jail with the Prophet Joseph Smith. Lyman Wight, Alexander McRae, and Caleb Baldwin would never forget this very humbling and spiritual experience as they suffered along side of a Prophet of God.

Even though the conditions in the jail were nothing short of barbaric, some have called Liberty Jail "a Prison Temple" due to fact that Joseph as a Prophet had had so many important and divine communications within its crude walls. It was while the Prophet Joseph Smith languished in Liberty jail in March of 1839, that he prayed earnestly for deliverance and finally did obtain that most welcomed liberation from Hell's earthbound realm. His lyrical and sincere pleading words to the Lord are found in D&C 121, as well as the Lord's comforting and wise words of explanation of how He chooses whom He will, declaring that; "...many are called, but few are chosen; and why are they not chosen; because their hearts are set on the things of the world and the honors of men, that they do not learn this one lesson...the rights of the priesthood are inseparably connected with the powers of heaven, and...cannot be controlled nor handled only upon the principles of righteousness." These enlightening and powerful words from the Lord are found in Section 121:34-36.

After months of humble prayer, Joseph was told by the Lord that no matter how severe his tribulations were, even if he was cast into a pit, or the deep surrounded by billowing waves and fierce winds, "if the very jaws of hell shall gape open the mouth wide after thee, know thou, my son, that all these things shall give thee experience, and shall be for thy good. The Son of Man hath descended below them all. Art thou greater than he?" The Lord's full answer to Joseph's sincere prayer is given in a beautiful poetic form as found in Sec. 122. In Sec. 123, the Prophet gives his inspired instructions to the Saints and what their duty should be during their time of persecution. The poetic and inspiring words of the Prophet and the Lord in D&C sections 121, 122, and 123 are still available today for further perusing and pondering in the venerated Doctrine and Covenants.

Without question, the time spent in that filthy prison was cruel, harsh, and grossly inhumane, but it certainly was not wasted time for the Prophet by any measure. Some say Joseph came out of the crucible of Liberty Jail a more mature and seasoned prophet. He was now ready to be molded by the "Maker's Hand" into a more knowledgeable and better prepared servant of the Lord, and therefore more disposed to endure the many trials that were about to come upon him in the very near future.

Only a couple of weeks after Joseph's humble prayers, the Lord finally answered his pleas for deliverance from the grueling trials of liberty jail through a most unexpected and very unusual circumstance. At the Daviess County trial, the Mormon prisoners had been indicted on charges of murder, treason, arson, burglary, larceny, theft, and stealing. Joseph commented somewhat humorously that only a Missourian wouldn't know that larceny, theft, and stealing were all the same thing. None of the charges had any basis in reality and there was no evidence of any kind pointing to any actual crimes they had committed. In truth there was simply no hard facts to support the validity of holding them in jail any longer so that they could be legally convicted of anything.

The delicate matter of the Mormon prisoners having been held unconstitutionally in jail over an extended long period without a trial finally came to a head as the authorities ultimately realized that they themselves were breaking the law and trampling on the prisoner's constitutional rights; "the right to a speedy and public trial by an impartial jury." And so the Missourian law officials found themselves caught between a rock and a hard place, and it had the real potential of becoming a very sticky situation for the state, the local law officials, the local judges, and even for the Governor. There was no doubt about it, they were in violation of the prisoner's rights and just plain and simple had no solid evidence of any kind to convict the hated Mormon prisoners of anything and hence they simply could not hold them legally any longer.

However, if they just let them go free, the violent Mormon-hating mobs would have the heads of any body responsible for the release of the despised Mormon leaders. At the very least, any officials responsible would be politically crucified in the public arena resulting in an end to their careers. The political backlash and embarrassment alone would be considerable, not to mention the very real possibility of having lawless rioting and even mindless mob violence erupt and conceivably directed towards the officials themselves. And so they must now come up with a very clever plan to rid themselves of this extremely sticky situation of letting the Mormon prisoners go without "letting them go."

Thinking within the legal fringes, they came up with the notion that in order for their prisoners to have a "Fair and Honest" trial, then surely the prisoners must have a change of venue and be moved to another county, even at the risk of the prisoners possibly escaping somewhere along the way. It was Sheriff William Morgan that was put in charge of the escort and the logistics involved for the change of venue. He was told in a very confidential conversation with the Judge and in no uncertain terms that during this transfer of the prisoners for a change of venue, the prisoners WILL ESCAPE by whatever accidental means or if necessary, even contrived. The Sheriff was made to understand that it was an absolute priority to get rid of this very tricky circumstance of illegally keeping them in jail any longer, which was overriding the prisoner's legal rights. And so somehow, he must find a way to free them without turning them loose officially and he must avoid any appearance what so ever of having turned them loose by any official authorization as it might appear to the public. The Sheriff was to thoroughly understand that it was of a first rank priority to get rid of the tricky situation and do it permanently, because it had all just become an extremely "sticky-wicket" of a mess for all the officials concerned in the matter.

On their journey to Boone County, on April 15th and 16th of 1839, the Sheriff's escort group was executing the transfer for the change of venue for the Mormon prisoners. As a matter of course, they made camp by the roadside for the night. After supper, a jug of whiskey was passed around among the guards, which did a great job of thoroughly inebriating the lawmen. During the course of the evening, Sheriff Morgan made a point of loudly announcing that he was going to have a good healthy drink of grog and then go to bed to sleep it all off, and "the rest of you may do as you have a mind to."

And so it was that while their captor's were sleeping it off, the Mormon prisoners found themselves only loosely tied and blessed with horses that had already been saddled. It seems as though one of the guards had been very helpful in aiding their "accidental" escape. Joseph commented to his companions that it sure looked as though the Lord had provided them with a favorable opportunity to gain their freedom and they certainly shouldn't displease the Lord, so they very quietly took their leave of the premises. Later Hyrum Smith would write, "Two of us mounted the horses, and the other three started on foot, and we took our change of venue for the state of Illinois, and in the course of nine or ten days arrived safe at Quincy." – 5

Back in Daviess County, when Sheriff Morgan and his men returned to report the escape of the scoundrel Joseph Smith, the local citizens were so furious that they rode Sheriff Morgan out of town on a rail accusing him of taking a bribe to let the prisoners go. He couldn't tell them that he was only following unofficial secret orders. As matter of collateral retribution and in a case of dramatically misplaced anger, Sheriff William Bowman, who had nothing to do with the escape, was cruelly dragged by the hair of his head around the square of Gallatin in Daviess County. They accused Sheriff Morgan and ex-Sheriff Bowman of conspiracy in the escape of the Mormon leaders saying, "Bowman furnished the horses, and Morgan allowed them to escape." The pure unadulterated hatred for "Old Joe Smith" and the Mormons knew no boundaries or any semblance of rational thinking. – 6

Back in Far West, and before the news of "Old Joe Smith's" escape had got around, not every still standing healthy Mormon had yet completely abandoned the decimated city. Certain members of the Committee for Removal, and some of the Twelve hadn't been able to take their leave yet as they were still busy with cleaning up operations. Meanwhile, the most hateful of the Missourian ruffians were by no means finished harassing any unlucky Mormons they found still wandering about.

During this time period, Theodore Turley, a British convert who was on the Committee for Removal, was in his office when a group of eight

Missourian vigilantes burst in and demanded to know if it was true that Joe Smith was going to be brought back to Daviess county for trial. When Turley nodded yes, they exclaimed that was just great, because there were about fifty citizens of Daviess County who had vowed that if Joe Smith were ever brought back, they would not eat or drink until they had murdered him in cold blood. They also, had somehow, obtained a copy of "Old Joe Smith's" revelation, which declared that the Twelve Apostles would leave from the Temple lot in Far West on the 26th of April for their missions to England. See D&C Sec. 118.

One of the ruffians in a very loud and sinister voice referring to the revelation declared, "If they try to come here, they will be murdered." However, these Missourian ruffians simply had no idea of how persistent and dedicated Brigham Young would be in caring out and fulfilling that revelation. Even though the main body of the Quorum of Twelve Apostles of the Church had been decimated through a multiplicity of reasons such as apostasy, one jailed, at least one martyred, and a few still away on their missions, Brigham was insistent that the revelation would be carried out despite all the rational arguments against it being done. Brigham then determinedly saw to it that new apostles were called, plans were made, and all things were prepared and put in place to fulfill the decree of the revelation.

And so it was that on the 26th of April 1839, just as the revelation had declared, the Twelve led by Brigham Young met in the early morning hours before sunrise in Far West at the temple site. They held a hasty conference, and hurriedly laid down another cornerstone to the temple as they fulfilled the prophecy that said the Twelve would leave on their missions to the British Isles and, "depart to go over the great waters, and there promulgate my gospel." And so it was that they did leave from the temple site in Far West on the appointed day.

Some historians have thought that surely some of the Twelve on their way to Far West must have or should have passed by Joseph Smith and his escaping companions on their way out of the state while they were on the run as they left Missouri en route to Quincy. However, no such encounter ever occurred, but it stands to reason that Joseph and the other escapees would have stayed out of sight and off the main roads to avoid any unfriendly mobs or the law and therefore they probably would not have run into anybody or have ever been seen by anyone traveling on the normal roads. – 7

Meanwhile back in Quincy Illinois, the prophet's own mother saw her sons in a vision crossing the stark and cold prairie so weak that they could hardly stand up, sleeping for short periods of time, then struggling onward. Due to her prescient insight of her sons' plight, Mother Smith was unable to rest and she felt great uneasiness in not being able to help her sons in their hour of desperation and distress. When they finally arrived in Quincy on the 22nd of April 1839, it was in the afternoon just before the sunset, just as she had predicted, and it was on the same day that Mother Smith had said that they would come. Her two sons then verified to be true all that she had seen in her vision of their trials and suffering. – 8

And so they had finally arrived in Quincy, after enduring a very arduous journey of over 170 miles in ten days. It was a Church member by the name of Brother Dimick Huntington that was one of the first people to see the Prophet Joseph on his arrival in Quincy. He described Joseph's appearance as such: "He was drest in an old pair of boots full of holes, pants torn, tucked inside boots, blue cloak with collar turned up, wide brim hat, rim sloped down, not been shaved for some time, looked pale & haggard." Needless to say, none of the weary group of escaped prisoners was exactly looking their Sunday best when they arrived, never the less they had finally made it to Quincy to join the rest of the Saints in their new temporary home and a hoped for safe haven for the time being. – 9

Joseph and Hyrum briefly visited with their aging parents and then headed straight away to see their own families where they spent their first night. Emma was still at Judge Cleveland's home, and when she caught sight of Joseph coming down the road, she met him half way to the gate with wide-open welcoming arms. The next day, about thirty Smith family members gathered for a somewhat boisterous if not a very joyous reunion. It was only a short time before the word of Joseph and his companion's arrival in Quincy spread like wildfire inspiring hundreds of well wishers to flood Father and Mother Smith's family home, yard, and sidewalks. Joseph feeling the warm jovial mood of the occasion and in keeping with his warm and loving personality, attempted to greet and thank every last one of them.

*　　*　　*

1a. See History Of The Church Vol. 3 Chapter 14.

1b. See History of the Church 3:226-233 & History of the Church, Vol.3, Appendix, p.420-421

2. See History of the Church 3:249-254 - "Life of Heber C. Kimball" p237-239

3a. See "Life of Joseph F. Smith. Sixth President of The Church of Jesus Christ of Latter Day Saints" Desert News Press 1938 60

3b. See "History of Joseph Smith by His Mother" pp. 294-297

4. See "Church History, the Fulness of Times" p. 213. & "Joseph Smith III" p. 11

5. See History of the Church, Vol.3, Appendix, p. 423

6. See History of the Church 3:320-322

7. See History of the Church 3:335-340

8. See Lucy Mack Smith "History of Joseph Smith by his Mother" pp. 300-302

9. See Dimick Baker Huntington "Autobiography"

*   *   *

Chapter Fourteen

NEW BEGINNINGS IN ILLINOIS

*　　*　　*

After the Saints had been relentlessly harassed and persecuted for at least seven years in Missouri by way of the extreme violence of the unremitting "mobacrats," they were finally forced completely out of the state in the spring of 1839 by the well armed Missourian Militias as had been mandated by Governor Boggs. They had been willfully ignored by the federal and the state's unsympathetic political powers and thus they received absolutely no compensation for their valuable property or loss of life. The Saints then began their pressing and crucial quest to seek out a sanctuary, any sort of a safe haven where they could find some kind of peace and safety. As they desperately sought for a place of refuge where they might be accepted for who they were without any condemnation of their religion or culture, a few of them headed east to the bigger city of St. Louis. Some made their way into the Iowa territory, and others to the different parts of Illinois, but most of the Saints found their safe haven in the furthermost part of western Illinois along the east banks of the mighty Mississippi 140 miles north of St. Louis. Here they were able to finally find a place of refuge and a bit of peace on the serene banks of the Mississippi River in the quaint settlement of Quincy, Illinois.

That's where about 1500 altruistic locals took in 5,000 destitute Saints and showed them extraordinary compassion and great generosity as they gave them shelter, food, and clothing, and exhibited a true Christ-like kindness towards them. At the time, this was somewhat of a surprise to the Saints being that it was coming from complete strangers and it certainly was not familiar treatment as an unknown citizenry not of their religion was bestowing it upon them. It felt very curious, especially after the extreme ruthlessness and brutality they had previously been subjected to in Western Missouri.

The compassionate city officials in Quincy Illinois had officially encouraged its citizens to help the destitute refugees in any way they could. So the citizens of Quincy responded unselfishly with many individual instances of extreme kindnesses that included food, clothing, blankets, free rent, and there were even some job offers so the refugees could pay their bills and buy their necessities. Brigham Young acknowledged and commended this unusually kind treatment by the citizens of Quincy, as he contrasted it with the callous inhumane treatment the Saints had received at the hands of the Missourians, and he expressed his true feelings about both groups of citizens in the following comment:

"They (Missourians) succeeded, after killing many of the Latter-day Saints, men, women, and children, cruelly massacring them, in driving us out of the state to the State of Illinois, where the people received us with open arms, especially the inhabitants of the city of Quincy; for which kindness the hearts of our people who passed through these scenes have ever been lifted to God, petitioning for blessings upon them. And they have been blessed." – 1

So it came to pass that the Saints having a good deal of gratitude took great pleasure in the warm acceptance they received from the altruistic and compassionate citizens of Quincy. They were even further encouraged with much hope and optimistic expectations when the Prophet Joseph unexpectedly arrived in Quincy having recently escaped from Missouri. And so after having endured one ordeal after another in Missouri, now there came upon the Saints what felt metaphorically like a warm gentle rain after an extreme drought, falling gently and soothingly upon their souls bringing them tranquility in this welcoming place of refuge. This was a very welcomed feeling, which they hadn't felt in such a long time. And so it came to pass that the Saints then settled in to enjoy a beautiful spring of hope and relative tranquility in Quincy Illinois during the warming days of 1839.

Just a month later after Joseph's arrival in Quincy, following his rigged escape from the law officials in Missouri, the Prophet called for a May outdoors Church `Conference to be held in a large field known there about as the Presbyterian Campground. During the conference, Joseph profusely praised their neighbors in Quincy for their much-appreciated Christian generosity. However, at the same meeting, he declared to the Saints, "This cannot be our home, we cannot stay in Quincy. The Saints must have a place of their own so that this people can receive the full blessings of the Lord and build a house to His name." - 2

Even though the locals had truly gone out of their way to show their Christian charity in helping their neighbors, and they certainly had been more than generous in aiding the Saints in their time of need, unfortunately the situation would eventually become somewhat burdensome to the citizens of Quincy and just a bit more than they could manage. In a relatively short time, the circumstances in the small town had become more demanding and exhausting than the Quincy citizens could be expected to bear. There were just too many Saints trying to find too many places of shelter in too small of a community. And it was simply impossible to accommodate all of them. Many of the Saints were still living in tents even as more refugees still poured into the community looking for some type of shelter. The new comers were going to need a lot of help here in this small community that was now overwhelmed by the dozens upon dozens of new Mormon refuge families.

It was then that the Prophet Joseph made a surprise conference announcement. He declared that he and Hyrum had already located and purchased a piece of property forty or fifty miles north of Quincy on a beautiful bend of the Mississippi river called Commerce. During this May conference held in Quincy, it was also announced that the next Church conference was already being scheduled ahead of time and it was to be conducted in Commerce area 47 miles to the north of Quincy on the banks of the Mississippi River.

And so by the time the warm days of summer rolled around, most of the Saints had already left Quincy and were up the river busy building up the Commerce site or as it was soon to become known, "Nauvoo." It is not known exactly when Joseph Smith first used the particular name of "Nauvoo" for the site in Commerce, but the first time that it was seen in print was in August of 1839. The name was said to have meant "beautiful" in Hebrew and later on as Nauvoo grew into its prime, its name would soon become widely known as "Nauvoo the Beautiful." – 3

Although the location at Commerce was actually quite scenic being situated on a big bend of the Mississippi River, it did have a few serious drawbacks, which was why the property was so readily acquired from a local land man. Most of the purchased acreage was swampland that nobody in his or her right mind would want. However, this drawback was actually a point in its favor where the Saints were concerned. In spite of the negative connotation of swampland real estate being almost worthless, for their own purposes and for their peace of mind, the Saints actually didn't want this piece of real estate to seem desirable to anybody else, and they actually wanted it to seem worthless to any outsiders.

In light of his own extraordinary visionary ideas for the future, Joseph Smith had purchased land on both sides of the Mississippi river, which included Montrose Iowa. Some of the Saints were finding temporary shelter in the old barracks of Fort Des Moines, and that included Brigham Young, as well as Wilford Woodruff who had also moved to Montrose on the other side of the river from Commerce. Joseph's vision of the future of Nauvoo would include a long list of Mormon settlements spreading out like spokes around the hub city of Nauvoo on both sides of the river. Besides Montrose, Fort Des Moines, Zarahemla, Ambrosia, Nashville, Keokuk, and Potters Slough on the Iowa side of the river, there was on the other side in Illinois the settlements of String Town, Davis Mound, Pontoosuc, La Harpe, Fountain Green, Ramus, Plymouth, Bear Creek, Yelrome, Lima, Green Plains, Warren, Carthage, and Warsaw, all of which were within a 50 mile range of the Nauvoo hub. Unfortunately, some of these settlements would later become hotbeds of hard-core Mormon haters, most particularly found in the non-Mormon gentile settlements of Carthage, Green Plains, and Warsaw.

And so it was that very soon after the May conference, the Saints began the monumental task of digging long ditches and trenches that would empty into the river in order to drain the 800 acres of swampland at the Commerce site. There was one colossal drainage channel that they excavated that was some three quarters of mile long, which was virtually a huge canal 8 feet deep and 11 feet wide. It was located in the middle of the newly purchased real estate where there were plentiful swampy bogs of deep oozy black mud girded by a few scattered higher elevations of dry matted grass, and then accented by small ponds of open water.

Unfortunately, these particular natural features were very conducive to the hatching of hordes of blood sucking mosquitoes. This unanticipated fact would later prove to be a problem of disastrous consequences for the Saints. Many of them would become seriously ill and some would even die from the "Ague," which would soon bring all their hard working construction work at Commerce to a dead halt.

The Saints were unaware that the dreaded disease they called "Ague" or the "Shakes" was actually Malaria and was carried by the mosquitoes in the swamp. Malaria is not native to the United States, but many historians believe that it came to America with the captured slaves from Africa and then spread. The hazardous situation finally developed into a devastating epidemic effecting thousands of Saints, which impaired their overall health and well-being. And so as it came to pass, the building up of the city of Nauvoo was brought to its knees for many weeks by no less than the lowly mosquito.

Meanwhile, the grave health situation brought on by the mosquitoes certainly caused a great many serious illnesses among many of the Saints, as well as an unforeseen long travel delay for the departure of the Church's missionaries to the British Isles. During the first part of July, Joseph had given the Twelve Apostles missionary instructions and then blessed them so that they could soon depart for their anticipated proselytizing missions to England. Unfortunately, their travel plans were seriously delayed due to the many wide spread unexpected illnesses caused by the blood-sucking mosquitoes of the swamps.

By mid July of 1839, there was a full-scale epidemic of Malaria rampaging through Commerce and the surrounding communities. Every one of the Twelve apostles was either sick or had family members who were so seriously ill that they needed dedicated care. Joseph and Emma had moved into a tent in the yard so that their two-story log house could be used as a temporary hospital for the sick. Even though Joseph himself was very ill, he forced himself off of his bed, got up on his feet and went out among the Saints, and began straightaway to perform literally many dozens of blessings for the healing of the sick and the afflicted among his beloved Saints.

When Joseph heard that Brigham Young and many others were also down with the sickness on the other side of the river in Montrose, he and his companions went across the Mississippi to heal Brother Brigham and the others. There he commanded Brother Young saying; "Brigham Young, in the name of the Lord, I command you to leave that bed and to be healed of your illness. Come with us." Miraculously, Brigham instantly felt his energy come back, and so he joined with a few of the other Apostles and dutifully followed Joseph and went from house to house blessing and healing the sick.

One of the members who was extremely ill, was so close to death that his wife had already given up on him by the time that the Prophet arrived. Joseph took the man by his hand and asked him if he had the faith to be healed? The man weakly replied that he might have had if Joseph had arrived a little sooner, but it was too late now. Joseph then asked; "Do you believe in Jesus Christ?" Replying somewhat meekly, Elijah said; "Yes." In a voice so powerful, that it seemed to shake the very foundations of the house, Joseph loudly called out; "Brother Fordham, I command you, in the name of Jesus Christ, to arise from this bed and be made whole." Elijah Fordham then sat up from a point of very near death, swung his legs over the bed to the floor and not only began to walk, but asked his wife for some bread and milk, which he hungrily ate. Similar miracles of healing were repeated more than once among the Saints on that particular day. – 4

Joseph became so exhausted from going house-to-house healing the sick that he finally decided to place the responsibility for giving further blessings upon the shoulders of the Twelve. He told the brethren that were with him that they themselves held the same power of healing as Christ's Apostles had held anciently, and so they must therefore continue to go forth and bless the people, while he himself returned home to get some badly needed rest.

However, before he could even board the ferry, and while he and Wilford Woodruff were waiting to cross the river to Nauvoo, there soon came to his attention a particularly concerning and desperate request from a non-member. It was a ferry operator, who had two little twin girls that were seriously ill, who approached Joseph and begged for a blessing to heal his sweet little daughters. Since the ferryman lived some distance away and Joseph was dead tired, he handed Wilford Woodruff his red silk handkerchief and told Brother Woodruff to go and wipe the faces of the two little girls with the silk handkerchief. He then instructed Wilford to lay his hands up the girl's heads and bless them by the authority of the Priesthood. Even though the girls had been very seriously ill, Wilford's blessing worked wonders on them and the twins were healed almost immediately to the great joy of their father.

A little earlier at the time that Joseph had given Brother Wilford the handkerchief, he told Wilford to keep it as a bond between the two of them, which Wilford happily did, and he thus treasured that silk handkerchief for the rest of his life. Along with this miracle of the healing of the two little girls, many different people witnessed an untold number of other miraculous healings that day, and this led to the Saints calling July 22 1839 "a day of God's power." The numerous miracles of that day were all testified to by hundreds of seriously ill Saints who then were healed by faith and the power of the holy priesthood all overseen by a Prophet of God. - 5

By August of 1839, the Prophet was beginning to have strong impressions to get the Twelve on their way across the great waters to the British Isles to spread the Lord's word and take the gospel to the people in England.

On August 8th, John Taylor and Wilford Woodruff became the first of the apostles to leave Nauvoo even though their personal situations were not exactly favorable for leaving their families. Both men lived in Montrose on the other side of the Mississippi and both had family members who were very ill. Brother Woodruff himself was desperately ill and weak with the chills and was leaving behind a pregnant wife who was so sick that she had to have another family take in their little daughter. Brother John Taylor was also leaving behind his sick family who was living at that time in a single room in Montrose under very humble conditions. Despite the two apostles' great personal sacrifices and their worries over the truly distressing circumstances of their families, Brother Woodruff and Brother Taylor went ahead and left their families behind. They were only able to do this through their great faith that the Lord would take care of things as they left their beloved families in His hands, while they carried on to do the Lord's work and proceeded to carry out their missions to England. – 6

A little over a month later, Brigham Young and Heber C. Kimball, the two senior apostles of the church, prepared to leave on their own missions to England. Though Brigham was not fully recovered from the "ague," he asked someone to row him across the Mississippi in a small rowboat so he could meet with brother Kimball at his home. There he collapsed from the weakness caused by the "Shakes." He had reluctantly left behind his wife Mary Ann and their children who were so ill that none of them were even able to fetch a pail of water for the house.

Brother Heber Kimball was in no better shape and also violently ill, and his wife Vilate had just given birth to a son and was still in a very weakened condition. Their little four-year-old boy had it placed upon his small shoulders the burden of fetching food and water for the rest of the family. Meanwhile, the determined Mary Ann Young in desperation, despite her own ill health, persuaded a young man to row her across the river to the Kimball's home with the idea that she was going to nurse Brigham back to some kind of strength before he left. She was disappointed in attempting to carry out that intent as she had very little chance to take care of Brigham due to his own stubborn determination to get going and to proceed on his mission.

Even though neither Brigham nor Heber actually felt well enough to travel, Brigham insisted that they must be on their way, and so the two were helped into the back of a wagon to lie on quilts lining the wagon bed. As they reached the bottom of the hill below Heber's house, Heber yelled for the driver to stop. He proclaimed that this was no way to leave their families. The two apostles then struggled to their feet grasping on to each other for support, took off their hats as they waved them around in big circles, and yelled as loud as they could; "Hurrah! Hurrah for Israel! Hurrah! Hurrah for Israel!" The cabin door opened and Vilate and Mary

Ann appeared and bid their husbands good-bye as they tried to smile through their tears. – 7a

If the Twelve found that just getting started on their missions to England seemed like an exercise in futility, then making their way east to New York was of no less a challenge. There were transportation delays, the hassle of finding a place to sleep each night, the hardships in acquiring sufficient funds for their travel and the added chore and expense of procuring their daily meals. But even though the challenges were many, sometimes it became obvious the Lord had a hand in there and was helping them out.

At one point in their travels East, Heber and Brigham were doing some calculations regarding their meager budget. Something very odd was happening; there was a mystery concerning their budget; it just simply wasn't adding up correctly. Brigham thought Heber must have been adding to the budget out of a secret stash. Heber wasn't responsible and so denied that he had added any money. They had started out with $13.50, and now with one York Shilling left, they calculated they had already spent eighty-seven dollars in total with only 13.50 to start. How could that possibly be? They concluded it could only be explained by some type of a miracle like in the story of Elijah and the widow. Even though the needy widow had only enough oil and flour to share with Elijah for one meal, they somehow ate out of it for several days. - 7b

Added to the hassle of the traveling logistics, there were even some uncomfortable encounters dealing with unfriendly strangers and coping with the harassment coming from the locals they met concerning their unwelcome Mormon beliefs. Some of the anti-Mormons they ran across were accusing Joseph Smith of plagiarizing a previous work known as the "Spalding Manuscript." Never the less, when two professors at Oberlin College of Ohio compared the Spalding script with the Book of Mormon, they found that there was no resemblance what so ever in the material between the two books.

Other critics were insisting that Sidney Rigdon must have wrote the Book of Mormon because there's no way that an uneducated farm boy like Joseph Smith could possibly have done it. They were right about that; Joseph Smith did not write the Book of Mormon and couldn't have given his meager education. It was ancient authors of an antiquated civilization that wrote it, while the Prophet Joseph only translated the inspired writings he was given.

If these criticizing detractors had bothered to fully investigate the circumstances surrounding the coming forth of the Book of Mormon, they would have known that Sidney Rigdon was not even aware that there was any such book as the Book of Mormon at that time it was published. And it would be nearly ten months after the Book of Mormon was already published before he would even meet Joseph Smith. However, the Mormon haters were desperate to discredit Joseph Smith anyway they could, even if they had to make up their own facts to challenge the missionaries with their criticisms.

The different members of the Twelve arrived in New York in a wide spread array of varying dates that began with Wilford Woodruff on the 8th of October. Other arrivals, including John Taylor's, were delayed until December of that year. Parley P. Pratt and his newly reinstated apostle brother Orson, arrived separately in New York nearly three weeks apart.

Not wanting to wait any longer for the other missionaries, Wilford Woodruff, John Taylor, and Theodore Turley finally sailed from New York five days before Christmas. Elder Woodruff had already waited three months and decided he could not wait any longer for the other Nauvoo apostle missionaries to finally show up at the harbor in New York. So Wilford and his companion apostles became the first of the American missionaries to finally arrive in Liverpool England on the 11th of January 1840.

It turned out to be a wise decision to not wait for the other missionaries to arrive in New York, as the rest of the missionaries were delayed for some time. Those that were left behind to still come when ever they could get it all together, were Brigham Young, Heber C. Kimball, George A. Smith, and the two brothers, Orson and the Parley P. Pratt. This group was delayed in their departure for another six weeks, and then they ended up not arriving in Liverpool until the 6th of April 1840.

The voyage across the Atlantic Ocean for those early missionaries back in those days was no picnic. There were many inconveniences, dangerous encounters with immense storms, crowded overbooked ships, poor accommodations and bad food, and gut wrenching seasickness. Trans-Atlantic travel in the nineteenth century was still far from being comfortable yet, and felt more like a long, slow, crowded, stomach-churning, dangerous drudgery, rather than any kind of a vacation cruise. – 8a

Looking back on it all, the missionary experiences of the Twelve Apostles hadn't gone very smoothly at any time since their clandestine beginning in Far West, and so it was to be more or less expected that things just might not possibly go so perfectly well in England, either. An English paper accused the "Mormonites" of coming to Gloucestershire "for the express purpose of plundering the ignorant people in the neighborhood." Many of the criticizing and unduly concerned Ministers in Herefordshire petitioned the Archbishop of Canterbury to try to persuade Parliament to pass a law prohibiting the Mormons from even proselyting at all in England. The Archbishop not only declined their request, but insinuated that the haughty ministers might not lose so many of their own flocks if they themselves had done a better job of actually serving the people.

Often there would appear gangs of anti-Mormon hecklers at the baptisms who occasionally threw stones at the Mormons. In one case, during a shower of rock throwing, Wilford Woodruff was hit in the back of the head with a large rock and seriously hurt, as he was attempting to baptize his converts. His comment was; "But the Lord saved me from falling & I continued until I had closed my Baptizing & my mind was stayed on God." – 8b

However, if the Mormon missionaries were feeling beaten down, discouraged, and ready to give it all up, they didn't show it as they continued to carry on with their missions with stubborn persistence and a great resolve to carry on despite all their trials. Their faithfulness was beyond praiseworthy and commendable; it was meritorious. – 9

All in all, the enormous difficulties and the tremendous sacrifices that the Twelve made during those early days of the Church to fulfill their missions for the Lord seems almost beyond a modern day mind-set to even comprehend why they would continue to be so faithful, persistent, and dedicated in following through with their missions in the face of such severe trials. In fact, it is quite difficult for one to even imagine having to leave a poor sick family behind in America, and then having to endure many hardships to even get to their destination, and after all that, arrive in England only to undergo harassment and rejection. So why would one go through all these trails and difficulty just to bring the gospel to a resistant hostile audience, most of whom didn't want to hear any kind of preaching from any Mormon missionaries anyway? In the final analysis, one is tempted to ask the very poignant question; were all those hardships and sacrifices worth the trouble; was it all really worth all the battering of body and soul and the many severe trials that those early Church missionaries had to endure?

When all things are considered, and if it is indeed possible to measure the worth of their missionary efforts in the number of people they brought to the light of the Gospel of Jesus Christ, the final worth of their efforts is incalculable. In Wilford Woodruff's mission area alone, which was quite amazing in its own right, there were fifteen successful preachers who were respected church leaders of United Brethren Congregations that were miraculously converted and thus joined up and came into the gospel of Jesus Christ. And then to top it off, these same fifteen preachers proceeded to bring in approximately another 600 members of their own congregations into the Church. As amazing as these numbers are, that doesn't include the many other converts in those same areas, which came from a great many different denominations and were also baptized at that time.

The Twelve's success in England has been calculated to be somewhere in the substantial numbers of approximately six thousand converts, all brought into the Church as a direct result of the early apostles' efforts in the English mission. Thus it turned out to be not only a stunning success of missionary work, but also a significant boost to Church membership, and a very successful overall endeavor to build up the Kingdom of God and aid His important work to bring the gospel to the world. - 10

Meanwhile, it was in October of 1839, that Joseph Smith and his companions went to Washington D.C. to seek redress for the many crimes and wrongs committed against the Mormon people when they were cruelly forced out of Missouri. The small group got as far as Columbus Ohio when Sidney Rigdon became quite ill, enough so that the consensus was that he should stay in Columbus under the care of Doctor Foster while accompanied by Joseph's bodyguard, Porter Rockwell. The Prophet Joseph Smith and Judge Elias Higbee continued on to Washington D.C. on their own.

Just before they entered the city, the stage driver "got thirsty" and stopped into a "public house" for a drink of grog. Apparently, he had left the horses loosely tied, and when they became frightened for whatever reason, they "ran down the hill at full speed" as they dragged the stage behind them, jarring, tossing about, and putting a terrible scare into the passengers who were at the mercy of the run-away horses. Joseph not being a person to just do nothing in a desperate situation, climbed out the door and up and over the side to the driver's seat, where he grabbed the reins and after a considerable effort was able to pull the horses to a halt. No one was injured and the very grateful passengers proceeded to call Joseph a hero, including some congressmen who were also riding in the coach. They even proposed mentioning the heroic act in a session of congress, until they found out that their hero was the infamous Mormon Prophet, which immediately cooled their gratefulness. Joseph later wrote, "I heard no more of their praise, gratitude, or reward." - 11

Finally after arriving at the White House the next day, the "Mormon Caucus" requested an audience with the President. President Martin Van Buren was ostensibly sympathetic, but his final words were; "Your cause is just, but I can do nothing for you." Unfortunately, President Van Buren felt that the political expediency of courting the Southern voters in Missouri was of a much greater priority to him than the civil rights of any Mormons.

As it all turned out, the Saints neither received at any time, nor were they in any way rewarded with any type of compensation for their personal losses of their homes and private property, which was valued in the many hundreds of thousands of dollars. Despite the numerous violent and heinous crimes committed against the Saints and the very blatant violation of their constitutional rights, which were unmercifully trampled upon at the hands of their abusers, they never received any kind of justice, even though they were legal U.S. citizens and fully entitled to protection from discrimination and abuse. In summary, there was simply never any type of reparations, redress, or justice that ever came from any local, state, or federal government entity on behalf of the members of the Church of Jesus Christ of Latter Day Saints for their very abusive treatment. Being that the Saints were a non-violent, innocent, law abiding, and peaceful people, the discrimination and tyranny that was perpetrated upon them can be seen as nothing less than an abominable breech of justice. - 12

*   *   *

1. See Discourses of Brigham Young, p.473

2. See History of the Church 3:227-232, 345

3. See History of the Church 3:327-332 and 4:268 Also www. beautifulnauvoo.com

4. See Wilford Woodruff, "Leaves from My Journal" pp. 76-77.

5. See Wilford Woodruff, "Leaves from My Journal" pp. 78-79, also History of the Church, Vol.4, p.3, Footnotes

6. See Wilford Woodruff "Leaves From My Journal" pp. 83-84

7a. See Orson F. Whitney, "Life of Heber C. Kimball" pp. 265-266

7b. See LHCK see 7a. above, p.273 also See Elijah's miracle in 1 Kings 17:9-16

8a. See "Men with a Mission: The Quorum of the Twelve Apostles in the British Isles" pp. 78-80.

8b. See CHFT p. 230 and MWM pp 128-129

9. See "Men with a Mission: The Quorum of the Twelve Apostles in the British Isles" pp. 128-129.

10. See "Men with a Mission: The Quorum of the Twelve Apostles in the British Isles" pp. 301-302

11. See History of the Church 4:23-24

12. See History of the Church 4:141-142, 162-164

*   *   *

Chapter Fifteen

NAUVOO BECOMES A CITY

*   *   *

If the Saints and Church leaders thought they were completely through with the trials and worries of Missouri, they were wrong. Even in Nauvoo, rumors were flying about spreading the well-founded speculation that there was going to be further harassment by officials in the State of Missouri who were about to target the Mormon Church leaders for extradition. In fact, it was widely known that Governor Boggs under the relentless pressure from his constituents was determined to recapture the Mormon escapees. And as such, he had issued a warrant for Joseph and Hyrum Smith's arrest and was asking for their extradition back to Missouri. All these very troublesome rumors and the extreme likelihood of further harassment of Father Smith's two boys and the very real possibility of their extradition back to Missouri, had its accumulative and very detrimental effect on the mental and physical health of Joseph Smith Senior. He had seemingly worried endlessly about his sons and so his health continued to decline.

And so it was, by mid September of 1840, his physical and mental health was spent and he finally submitted to his deathbed at age sixty-nine.

Just before his passing, he had been attended to and comforted by all of his children and their families at which time he had called in each of his beloved children to give them a father's blessing. As he put his hands on the heads of Hyrum and Joseph, he prophesied that they would finish the holy work that they had been called to do. Father Smith died on September 14th of 1840, and Joseph and Hyrum fled the city almost immediately to avoid the presumed likelihood of being arrested and hauled away by the law officers sent by the unrelenting Missourian officials. – 1

However, the business of the Church was of a pressing concern and so it must be taken care of and soon. When Joseph returned to Nauvoo to preside over the October 3rd 1840 Conference, he proposed to the Saints a most surprising and a marvelous project for the members of the Church to think about, not only to think about, but to participate in, and to give of their service to a holy cause. It was at that time that he announced the beginning of the construction of a temple in the city of Nauvoo, a temple that would be dedicated to God and as the Lord had put it, "build a house to my name, for the Most High to dwell therein." And so it was that the Saints happily approved the proposal to begin the work on the Nauvoo Temple, a "House to the Lord." Soon thereafter, a stone quarry was opened up in the limestone cliffs on a bluff overlooking the Mississippi river, which was located just on the outskirts of Nauvoo, and in addition, the temple's basement excavation was also begun.

Meanwhile a new member of the Church and a very interesting character by the name of Doctor John C. Bennett came to Nauvoo in the late summer of 1840. Doctor Bennett's personal interests seemed to have focused outside of medicine and he had become something of a promoter having considerable interests in establishing public entities such as schools, universities, and other civic establishments. He was most particularly interested in the promoting of legislation to establish state militias in Pennsylvania, New York, and Illinois, all of which conveniently promoted his public image, his own pocket book, and his own self-esteem.

The Prophet Joseph Smith seeing possible usefulness in Mr. Bennett's many civic activities and interests, decided to give him the benefit of the doubt and thereby solicited his expertise in helping to establish the city of

Nauvoo as a legal entity. By December 1840, Bennett had drafted a charter for the city, and soon after, he became the primary impetus for getting the Nauvoo Charter through the Illinois legislature.

Under the rules of the Nauvoo Charter, the city was allowed to establish a militia overseen by a commanding general. For his role in getting the charter passed, Doctor Bennett was made Major General of the Militia and Joseph Smith became a Lieutenant General. Joseph's brother, Don Carlos, was given a commission as a Brigadier General, along with Wilson Law, who was a close friend of the Smith Brothers. Eventually the Nauvoo Legion would grow into a full military Brigade boasting as many as 5,000 militiamen backed up by some light artillery, which made them a formidable military presence throughout the entire area of Western Illinois. In April of 1841, the Nauvoo Legion proudly paraded through the streets of Nauvoo demonstrating their military form and polish as a apart of the ceremony for the laying of the cornerstones for the new temple. Around that same time, the Saints were also meeting together in their April General Conference. – 2

The thriving building activity in Nauvoo created considerable demand for bricks, stone, and lumber. Besides the vigorous activities in the local stone quarries and the extremely busy operations at the brick kilns in Nauvoo, the Church was also sponsoring and operating a large and ambitious lumber business by the fall of 1841. It was all sourced by the "Wisconsin Pineries" consisting of a lumberjack colony established on the Black River and the Roaring Creek tributary in Wisconsin. After the logs were cut down and dragged to the river, they were tied together to make gargantuan log rafts that were floated down the Mississippi River for a distance of over 400 miles to Nauvoo. Over a four year period in the 1840's, the church milled some one and a half million board feet of lumber, two hundred thousand shingles, and a considerable amount of logs, slabs, and other wood products, not to mention furnishing welcomed employment for many of the Saints. – 3

Meanwhile, the first apostles were beginning to return from their missions to England. Brigham Young, Heber C. Kimball, and John Taylor arrived on July 1st 1841. However, some apostles, for various personal reasons such as visiting their relatives on their way home, didn't make it back to Nauvoo until October. On July 9th of that year, Joseph received a revelation on the behalf of Brigham Young saying that Brigham's dedication, sacrifice, and labor were all very pleasing and most acceptable to the Lord and so it would not be necessary for Brigham to serve any further foreign missions that took him so far from his family and home. – 4

The returning missionaries took many different routes and some even made wide detours on their way home. The Apostle Orson Hyde didn't return to Nauvoo until December of 1842 due to his having made a year and a half long side trip to several different countries including Palestine. On the auspicious occasion of the 24th of October 1841, having been directed to do so a year earlier by the Prophet Joseph Smith, Orson went to the top of the Mt. of Olives and dedicated the Holy Land for the return of the Jews. Orson had a personal interest in doing so as he was of Jewish descent. Ten years before this, the Prophet Joseph had prophesized in a blessing on the head of Orson Hyde that the time would come when he would go to Jerusalem, "the land of his fathers, and be a watchman to that people…and greatly facilitate the gathering together of that people." After fulfilling that prophecy with his notable visit to Palestine, Orson continued his travels for more than a year, finally returning home by way of Egypt and Europe and eventually making his way back to Nauvoo after completing a legendary odyssey of over 20,000 miles across the wide expanses of three different continents.

President Ezra Taft Benson said that; "In Elder Hyde's prayer of dedication on the Mount of Olives, he prayed that the bareness and sterility of the land would be removed, that springs of water would burst forth, that the land would become fruitful again, that the Lord would subdue their unbelief and 'incline them to gather in upon this land.' He also prayed that God would inspire the kings of the earth to help bring about the promises made to Judah."

It was also mentioned specifically in this same prayer that Great Britain would play a significant part in the return of the Jews, and so it came to pass that that particular part of the prophecy was fulfilled. The British government had ruled over Palestine from World War I until 1948 at which time they voluntarily turned over sovereignty to Israel to become its own state and a homeland for the return of the Jews. Elder Orson Hyde's blessing on Palestine has since been largely fulfilled on behalf of the Jews despite the great strife and the extremist Muslim resistance coming from the opposition.

Parley Pratt's own brother, Orson Pratt, returned to Nauvoo a couple of weeks after Brigham Young had arrived, but Parley himself remained in England until October of 1842 and then finally arrived back in Nauvoo bringing with him a group of enthusiastic converts in February of 1843. Parley was the last of the twelve to return from the English mission. – 5

Meanwhile in Nauvoo, the Prophet Joseph received a rather lengthy revelation on the 19th of January 1841, which is now found in D&C Sec. 124. The Prophet Joseph Smith was commanded to "make a solemn proclamation" and testimony to kings, presidents, and "the high-minded governors of the nation in which you live," and to all nations of the earth, "For behold, I am about to call upon them to give heed to the light and glory of Zion, for the set time has come to favor her." and "If they reject my servants and my testimony which I have revealed..,. the day of my visitation cometh speedily in an hour when ye think not...."

In addition to the profound admonitions made in this solemn proclamation, there were also given some important commandments to be carried out by the Saints regarding the building up of the city of Nauvoo itself. In this revelation was a mandate from the Lord to build a boarding house for strangers and for visitors to the city of Nauvoo that would be called the "Nauvoo House." Additionally, there was the commandment to construct a beautiful temple to the Lord where the performances of certain sacred temple ordinances could be conducted, such as the ordinances of washing and anointing, the ordinances of the endowments, a directive for solemn assemblies, vicarious baptisms for the dead, and other "things which have been kept hid from before the foundation of the world..." – 6

In regards to the vicarious baptisms for the dead, which outsiders have mocked, the Apostle Paul spoke of baptism for the dead in the New Testament indicating that the ordinance was an original part of Christ's Primitive Church. "Else what shall they do which are baptized for the dead, if the dead rise not at all? Why are they then baptized for the dead?" - 1 Corinthians 15:29 And so the Saints did do baptisms for the dead.

It was at a young boy's funeral that the Prophet Joseph first taught about baptism for the dead in August of 1840 in order to comfort a widow whose son had died without being baptized. After the importance of this revelation on baptism for the dead was stressed by Joseph and later published in the "Times and Seasons" in 1841, there were many of the Saints who felt a compelling obligation to do baptisms for the dead, even if the baptisms had to be conducted in the muddy Mississippi River being that the temple baptismal font was still not completed. However, the Lord then specified later that this ordinance "belongeth to my house," and so "baptisms for the dead" in the river, as it turned out, were only done for a very short time and then forbidden thereafter on the completion of the baptismal font at the Nauvoo temple. By the time of the Prophet's martyrdom in 1844, there had been an amazing 15,722 vicarious baptisms for the dead performed in the temple located there in the city of Nauvoo. – 7

Meanwhile, very few people would argue against the fact that life can be somewhat challenging at times and often full of disappointment, and sometimes can even bring overwhelming tragedy and deep sorrow to a family. Rarely is there any family completely immune to grief and unexpected tragedy, but once in awhile, certain families seem to experience more than their fair share of trials in a short period of time. From September of 1840 to September of 1841, in just one year's time, the Smith family suffered six different deaths among its own family members. It started with the Prophet's own father, Joseph Smith Senior, then Joseph's brother Samuel's wife, next was the death of Joseph's brother Don Carlos, and only a few days later, the Prophet's own little Don Carlos, followed up by Hyrum's brother-in-law, and then in a final blow to the family, the rash of deaths ended tragically with Hyrum's own seven year old son.

Perhaps most devastating of all to the Prophet were the deaths of his brother Don Carlos and his own son, little Don Carlos. Those two deaths were particularly difficult for Joseph to accept. As devastating as his son's death was, the death of his brother Don Carlos struck Joseph particularly hard because Don Carlos had been an exceptionally close and supportive brother, and Joseph was very proud of his accomplishments. Don Carlos had been the president of the High Priest in Kirtland and in Nauvoo, a member of the Nauvoo City Council, a Brigadier General in the Nauvoo Legion, and the first editor of the "Times and Seasons." After his very untimely death from symptoms of pneumonia, the Prophet often times reflected upon the life of his beloved brother and he frequently mentioned how much he missed Don Carlos. Unfortunately for the Prophet, the losses of his beloved brother and his own little son would not be the end of tribulation in his all too short life.

Never the less, there were a few encouraging things going on in the Prophet's life such as the work on the temple, which was progressing briskly and for the most part, quite smoothly. Joseph was promised in a revelation that is found in D&C Sec. 124, "And I will show unto my servant Joseph all things pertaining to this house, and the priesthood thereof, and the place whereon it shall be built," and by inspiration, the architectural design would be given him, even such details as those impractical round windows on the broad sides of the building that were opposed to by the temple architect, William Weeks. To aid the Prophet in the construction of the holy edifice, a building committee composed of Reynolds Cahoon, Elias Higbee, and Alpheus Cutler was appointed. The three proved to not only be quite competent, but very supportive to the Prophet, and overall, very helpful during the construction of the new temple. At this time the Lord did pardon the Saints from having to build the temple in Jackson County, Missouri, excusing them due to the severe opposition and oppressive interference coming from their enemies.

The Nauvoo temple was larger and a bit more ornate than the one built in Kirtland. Its tower and spire were visible from a distance of over twenty miles, and the building stood out as the principal structure of the city of Nauvoo as it faced west standing on highest part of a gently sloping bluff overlooking the entire city and the mighty Mississippi River. The temple was built from a high-quality grayish-white to tan limestone with walls three feet thick at ground level. Some of the monstrous stone blocks weighed as much as 4,000 pounds each. The building was 128 feet long and 88 feet wide and graced by a frieze consisting of sunstones, moonstones, and stones of the stars that symbolized the three degrees of glory. It's tower stood 158 feet above the ground and was topped off by a golden figure of an angel flying in a horizontal position giving the entire view of the magnificent edifice a most outstanding architectural look and a very striking sight to behold. – 8

Somewhat surprisingly, a few endowment ordinances were performed before the temple was even completed. The Prophet had a real fear that he might not live to see the temple finished, so in case that should happen, which it sadly did, he proposed and prepared for an auxiliary location for the endowment ordinances to be performed. As somewhat of a surprise to some members, the alternate location turned out to be situated on the upper floor of what was then known as the Red Brick Store. The store had a large open top floor that was set up to resemble what Joseph had envisioned to be what the interior of a temple should be like. Canvas partitions separated it into several sections each representing a different stage of man's progression from his creation to his potential place in the Celestial Kingdom. It was here in the Red Brick Store that the Prophet administered to a few especially chosen worthy members, the ordinances that today are associated with the endowment ordinance. – 9

The Red Brick-store was the very first place where the full endowment was performed, but later three other locations were also used before the temple was finally completed. Even though these other places had a limited amount of usable space, they were still considered as holy places of the Lord. The three other special localities chosen for those early endowments were in Joseph Smith's first home in Nauvoo known as the "Old Homestead," a second location was in Joseph' and Emma's Mansion House, and finally a few endowments were conducted in Brigham Young's own personal residence. When the Nauvoo Temple itself was finally ready for use, it provided considerably more space and a much more enhanced experience for the patrons who were participating in the sacred rites involved in the temple's ordinances. – 10

In addition to the beautiful Nauvoo Temple, there were other buildings in Nauvoo that were of significance to the members of the Church, and which would also become of some notoriety in Church history. Joseph Smith's Red Brick Store mentioned earlier, was built in 1842 and was definitely one of the most famous structures in Nauvoo. The store provided a place for many social activities and other services for the entire city and even the entire region round about, as it became a major and well-used center of social, economic, political, and religious activity for the Nauvoo community. An office and meeting room on the second floor was set aside for the Prophet, and served for all intents and purposes as the official headquarters of the Church.

Among the other significant activities that were conducted at the Red Brick Store; the second floor was the first site of the very first full endowments performed outside the temple, as previously mentioned. And adding to its special significance, the Red Brick Store was also the site of the very first Relief Society meeting of the Church. The Relief Society's initial organization was carried out there in 1842. Joseph himself presided over the first meeting there in the Red Brick Store and at that time Emma Smith was voted in as the first Relief Society President. – 11

Another very prominent and significantly famous structure in the city was the city's main hotel, the "Nauvoo House." The same architect that supervised the construction of the Nauvoo temple, William Weeks, also helped design the Nauvoo House at the end of Main Street very near the river in Nauvoo. Many Latter-day Saints had purchased stock of $50 per share in this first-rate hotel. The Lord was the one who set the share price and He even specified the identity of some of the Saints who should invest in it, including Hyrum and Joseph. The money was used to pay for labor and building materials. As has been stated in D&C 124:60, this grand hotel was designed to be "a delightful habitation for man, and a resting place for the weary traveler." The Lord desired that the Saints should not isolate themselves from the world, but that they should build attractive accommodations for strangers and tourists where they could "contemplate the word of the Lord; and the corner-stone I have appointed for Zion." - See D&C 124:23.

The design for the Nauvoo House called for an L-shaped brick building forty feet long and three stories high and was begun in the spring of 1841. The construction continued into 1845, at which time the work was halted in an effort to more closely focus on the bigger priority of the completion of the Nauvoo Temple. When the Saints were hurriedly forced to leave Nauvoo in 1846, the walls of the Nauvoo House were still only up as high as the second story windows. This unfinished building on south Main Street, facing the Mississippi River, then became the property of Emma Smith who stayed in Nauvoo after the rest of the Saints had left for the Rocky Mountains. In December of 1847, she remarried. The man who became Emma's second husband, Lewis C. Bidamon, remodeled the structure and used the bricks to construct a smaller hotel that became known as the Bidamon House, or called by some, the Riverside Mansion. After Mr. Bidamon passed away, the Reorganized Church of Jesus Christ of Latter day Saints purchased the Nauvoo House and still own it today.

The RLDS Church would become the "Community of Christ" Church in April of 2001. – 12

Back in those early days of settling Nauvoo in 1839, Emma and Joseph had originally moved into a small log house near the river, which would later become famously known as the "Old Homestead." It was near the southern edge of the city and became the sentimental favorite home where they first began their life in Nauvoo. That first cabin would eventually be replaced as their personal living quarters when they built the considerably larger home they called the "Mansion House." In Joseph's own words, he commented somewhat on the problems that came with the Mansion House, and why he had to eventually convert it into a hotel:

"In consequence of my house being constantly crowded with strangers and other persons wishing to see me, of who had business in the city, I found myself unable to support as much company free of charge, which I have done from the foundation of the Church. My house has been a home and resting-place for thousands, and my family many times obliged to do without food, after having fed all they had to visitors; and I could have continued the same liberal course, had it not been for the cruel and untiring persecution of my relentless enemies. I have been reduced to the necessity of opening 'The Mansion' as a hotel. I have provided the best table accommodations in the city; and the Mansion, being large and convenient, renders travelers more comfortable than any other place on the Upper Mississippi." - 13a

Joseph and Emma moved into the Mansion House in August 1843. Later they would add a wing to the east side of the main structure bringing it to a total of twenty-two rooms. Like the Nauvoo House, it would eventually serve as an inn or hotel for weary travelers. Beginning in January 1844, Joseph recorded: "Monday, 22.--Rainy; wind easterly; mud very deep. Rented the Nauvoo Mansion and stables to Ebenezer Robinson for one thousand dollars per annum and board for myself and family and horses, reserving to myself three rooms in the house."- 13b

After Joseph's death in June of 1844, Emma Smith married a non-Mormon, Lewis C. Bidamon in 1847, just three years after the Prophet was gone. The two lived in the Mansion House until 1869, at which time she and Mr. Bidamon moved into the Nauvoo House and remained in the Nauvoo House until she died in 1879. Lewis Bidamon continued to reside at the Nauvoo House until he died in 1891; that's when the property was deeded to the RLDS Church by Joseph Smith's grandson. – 14

By the mid 1840's, Nauvoo had become a city of thriving activity with three brickyards, a half dozen or more stores, two blacksmith shops, a gunsmith shop, and several woodworking shops, not to mention some schools and even a few two story red brick houses. The Mansion House, the Nauvoo House, the Red Brick Store, and the Old Homestead were all located in the south part of town on the south bend of the river and within couple of blocks of each other. The Nauvoo House was the farthest south located on the north-south running Main Street closest to the river and near the steamboat dock so that visitors could have easy access to the arrangements at the hotel. It was especially suitable for those who were seeking the nicer accommodations of a grand hotel near the docks as they visited the beautiful city. Also on Main Street, and one block north of the Nauvoo House was the Smith's Mansion House. Just west of the Nauvoo House, also near the river, was located the Old Homestead. Northwest of the Old Homestead at the corner Water Street and Granger was the Red Brick Store located on the east-west running Water Street. Just a couple of blocks to the north was Brigham Young's home. All five of these soon to be historic buildings were within walking distance of each other and the river. The Temple itself was about ten blocks to the north on a bluff overlooking the city.

Nauvoo was widely acclaimed as one of the most beautiful cities west of the Eastern seaboard and by 1846 it had built up a population of 12,000 citizens, which at the time rivaled Chicago for being the largest city in Illinois. There was one very impressed visitor to Nauvoo who gave a delightful description of the famed Mormon City. The following is what a Methodist minister, a Mr. Briar, wrote about Nauvoo before the Saints were forced to leave it:

"Here is the proud and gallant Mississippi, with her rapid current, tumbling to the broad Atlantic, seeming to say las she quickens her pace over the rugged rocks of the lower rapids just opposite to our beautiful Nauvoo. Instead of seeing a few miserable log cabins and mud hovels, which I expected to find, I was surprised to find one of the most romantic places I had visited in the West. The buildings, though many of them were small and of wood, bore the marks of neatness which I had not seen equaled in this country. The far spread plain at the bottom of the hill was dotted over with habitations of men with such majestic profusion that I was almost willing to believe myself mistaken; and instead of being in Nauvoo, Ill., among Mormons, that I was in Italy at the City of Leghorn.... I gazed for some time with fond admiration upon the plain below. Here and there arose a tall, majestic brick house, speaking loudly of the untiring labor of the inhabitants, who have snatched the place from the clutches of obscurity, and wrested it from the bonds of disease; and in two or three short years rescued it from a dreary waste to transform it into one of the first cities of the West."

And so it would seem that the name, "Nauvoo, the Beautiful," was a fitting and an appropriate title for the great Mormon city located directly across the river from the eastern boundary of the wide-open expanses of the Wild West. Sitting there on the east banks of the mighty Mississippi, Nauvoo as a fledgling city had grown rather quickly compared to most, yet it soon rivaled even the larger cities in the "East" in size and beauty, even challenging Chicago as Illinois' second city. Unfortunately, its glory days like the Prophet Joseph Smith's own days were numbered, and so it was to be that Nauvoo's days too would be cut short all too soon. - 15

* * *

1. See Lucky Mack Smith "History of Joseph Smith by His Mother" pp. 307-314

2. See History of the Church 4:326-331

3. See Dennis Rowley, "The Mormon Experience in the Wisconsin Pineries" 1841-1848 pp. 119-148

4. See D&C Sec. 126.

5. See "Men with a Mission: The Quorum of the Twelve Apostles in the British Isles" pp. 304-308.

6. See D&C 124:22-41.

7. See "A Most Glorious Principle": "Children of the Covenant" pp.129-130.

8. See Encyclopedia of Mormonism, Vol.3, NAUVOO TEMPLE.

9. See History of the Church 5:1-2. & John Taylor, "The Gospel Kingdom" pp. 286-287

10. See Joseph Fielding Diary, "Nauvoo Journal," BYU Studies 19 (1979), p.159 Footnote 77.

11. See Encyclopedia of Mormonism, Red Brick Store B. H. Roberts collection.

12. See Encyclopedia of Mormonism, Vol.3, NAUVOO HOUSE

13a. See History of the Church, Vol.6, Ch.2, p.33.

13b. See History of the Church, Vol.6, Ch.8, p.185

14. See Encyclopedia of Mormonism, Vol.3 NAUVOO HOUSE, and SMITH, EMMA HALE

15. See Levi Edgar Young, Conference Report, October 1950, p.117

*   *   *

Chapter Sixteen

———∽∾⌒◦⌒◦⌒◦∾∽———

PERSECUTION
SUBVERSION
AND BETRAYAL

*　　*　　*

Back in the early days of Church history during the early 1840's and in the beginning days of Nauvoo, things weren't quite as turbulent and violent as they had been in the Missourian period of the late 1830's. So the Saints were able to settle in and build their homes with high hopes at the very edge of eastern civilization along the banks of the Mississippi River in expectations of a brighter more peaceful future. The west side banks of the Mississippi River marked the boundary of the sparsely populated countryside of what was then called the "Western Frontier." It was the boundary, which separated the lively civilized urban area on the east bank from the drastic contrast of the wide-open spaces. Nauvoo at that time was a unique settlement that was quickly growing into a major city of the West, and as far as the normal vitality and activities that sustains the courses of commerce goes; the new city was doing quite well.

Regrettably though, and in spite of the fact that the city was doing just fine in a secular businesslike way, not every thing was going as smoothly and as free from turmoil in Nauvoo as they had dreamed that it would be in their newest sanctuary home. Even though the Saints had high hopes that they had finally settled into a safe place with a presumed degree of security for their families, there would inevitably appear upon the scene those ubiquitous spoilers who simply could not let the Mormons alone to just practice their religion without interference and simply let them live in peace. No matter where they settled, there always seemed to be certain outsiders who just "could not leave them be." As usual, these outsiders were more than eager to show their disapproval of the Saint's religious practices, and it certainly seemed like these outside interest were also being unreasonably pigheaded in their opposition to any kind of secular or economic progress that would encourage the Mormons to settle permanently in the area right there among the local Illinois residents.

However all this did not dissuade Joseph Smith from his vision and resolve to establish many Mormon settlements radiating out from Nauvoo like the spokes of a wheel. Some say there were as many as seventeen of these settlements. And so it was that the Prophet followed up on his vision of the future by sending out a number of the Saints to settle these many different outlying communities. Many of these towns were Mormon friendly because they were predominately settled by the Saints, but unfortunately, there were a few of these towns that were teeming with the worldly culture of an intolerant gentile population and they soon grew into hotbeds of anti-Mormon sentiment.

In one of the neighboring gentile towns called Warsaw, located just sixteen miles south of Nauvoo, there was a young ambitious newspaperman who was the chief editor of the "Warsaw Signal" newspaper. Thomas C. Sharp's intense, ardent, and impassioned personal views created a newsman that was simply unreceptive to any ideology or any person who he found to be incompatible with his own strong opinions and beliefs.

However, being that he was a legitimate local news reporter in this area, it was only natural that Sharp should be amicably invited to Nauvoo to observe the laying of the cornerstones for the Nauvoo temple in 1841.

After he attended the special event and listened carefully to the ceremonial speeches concerning the predestined and inevitable domination of the Kingdom of God, he became unduly upset with what he had heard. He then put his own skewed interpretation upon this harmless religious rhetoric that was merely foretelling the future of the world through scriptural prognostication. As he let his imagination broaden into the many possibilities, he became unjustifiably and irrationally frightened by the potential of a great Mormon Empire becoming the dominating political power in Illinois, or maybe even the entire rest of America. Sharp saw Mormonism as much more than just a religion, and he was convinced that Joseph Smith intended to create a political and religious empire that had the alarming ambition of completely ruling over the United States and possibly even the world.

Consequently, while he was entertaining his own delusions, Thomas Sharp proceeded to publish his unfounded opinions and exaggerations in the "Warsaw Signal" paper warning the public of the dangers of their citizenry being ruled by the evil hand of a false and dangerously deranged man, the Mormon Prophet, Joseph Smith. Attempting to convince others of the peril at hand, he backed up his manufactured case by publishing what he considered as the all too loose and dangerously liberal regulations of the Nauvoo Charter. And he most certainly didn't leave out the great potential dangers that might come from everybody being under the heavy-handed jurisdiction of the formidable 5,000 men of the Nauvoo Legion militia. He exaggerated the very frightening prospect of the Nauvoo Legion enforcing Mormon law on everybody in the area and subjugating them to Joseph Smith's rule, or so it would seem in his over-dramatized and unfounded fearful thinking.

In an attempt to show proof that the Prophet was a fraud with nothing less than evil ambitions, he tried to pressure "Old Joe Smith" into admitting he was not really a prophet and so challenged Joseph to bring the Gold Plates forth and put them on display before the public. That way all could see them, and then if they were actually real, legitimate experts could retranslate them correctly. Of course when Sharp realized that "Old Joe Smith" wasn't even going to consider such an absurd challenge and condescending scenario, he declared Smith to be nothing more than a coward and a shameless fraud.

And so it seemed inevitable that the "Warsaw Signal" would soon become a prime source for creating a great deal of hatred towards the Mormon Prophet and his followers in Illinois, most particularly in the neighboring non-Mormon communities surrounding Nauvoo. Thomas Sharp went even further with his hostile ambitions and proceeded to establish an Anti-Mormon political party in Hancock County, Illinois. And thus he became a very avid anti-Mormon political activist. This obsessed Mormon hater and rancorous newspaperman soon became a tireless source of slander and verbal harassment as he spewed out a litany of lies attempting to defame Joseph Smith and his church. His obsession went way beyond normal thinking and reasoning and so he most definitely became the major source of the hatred that was misrepresenting the Latter-day Saints in Illinois. And thus he contributed greatly to their unpopular image and he purposely stirred up as much of the local hostility towards the Mormon people as he could stir up.

Later on, it was Sharp that would be given credit for leading one of Warsaw's murderous vigilante groups to Carthage to participate in the murder of Joseph Smith. Sometime after that, he was indicted by a grand jury for murder and his own active participation in the killing of the Smith brothers. However, as with all the other participants in that heinous crime, he was never found guilty or punished in any way for his part in the assassination of Joseph Smith. – 1

If the Saints didn't have enough problems dealing with the opposition from outsider antagonists like Sharp, there were plenty of problems to deal with right within the Church itself. There were several ill intentioned wayward members who seemed to ostensibly support the Prophet and the Church, but instead they pursued their own shady, devious, hateful, and selfish interests as they worked behind the scenes. And so it was that among their plans and their fiendish aspirations was the dedicated ruin of Joseph Smith and his Church.

Joseph Smith was a true prophet, a seer, and a revelator who had proven himself as such by the actual fulfillment of many of his prophecies and by his far-reaching visions concerning the unpredictable future. One such example of his ability as a prophet and Seer was the foretelling of the details of "the who, the where, and the when" of the Civil War some 30 years before it even happened. He not only specifically named South

Carolina correctly as the place where the war would begin its hostilities, he also named the combatants in the conflict as being the southern states divided against the northern states over the question of slavery. He also prophesized correctly that it would eventually result in an extraordinary loss of life on both sides. He even added the detail of the South calling upon Great Britain to help them in the war against the North, which they did. This amazingly precise revelation was given as a prophesy by Joseph Smith in December 1832 at Kirtland nearly thirty years before that devastating war ever began. – See D&C 87:1-4

Just two months after he had given the Civil War revelation, he delivered another far-reaching revelation concerning the health of the Saints. This "Word of Wisdom" health code would benefit the Saints then and into the future and beyond. This inspired health advice more than hundred years later, would eventually be found by health researchers to not only be a valid health guide for the Church's membership, but also in truth, to be wise and sound health counseling for the general population. So in light of these two amazing revelations, it would seem reasonable that the Civil War prophecy and the "Word of Wisdom'" revelation alone would confirm that he was a true "Seer." - See D&C Sec. 89

Adding to this body of solid prophetic evidence are the great many testimonies of the many eyewitnesses who had observed him miraculously healing the sick and the afflicted. One good example was the incredible and miraculous healing of Elsa Johnson's long time lame arm at the Whitney home in Kirtland. And then there was the most astonishing and remarkable healing of Elijah Fordham who after being blessed by the Prophet got up off his own deathbed and began to walk and talk, and then proceeded to eat some bread and milk during the malaria epidemic at Commerce. These many and various miracles a long with an abundance of other incidents of healing truly showed that the Lord's power and strength were in fact with Joseph Smith the Prophet.

Yet, for some unexplainable reason and for all his apparent prophetic foresight, he seemed sometimes to have been completely blinded to the flaws of certain men that were closely associated with him. Even his own counselors that had bonded with him by sharing many spiritual experiences, eventually lost faith and turned their back on him. And so it was that he seemed blinded when it came to perceiving the "true heart" of

John C. Bennett, the Church's most infamous scoundrel. Joseph's prescient sight seemed to be dulled and ineffectual in judging John Bennett, at least in their beginning relationship. Elder J. Golden Kimball humorously once said; "Most of our leaders are sent here by God to lead us. Others are sent here to try us." In the case of John C. Bennett, that observation may have been more profound than humorous.

In truth John C. Bennett had actually served the Church and his fellow citizens very well at one time, especially in his invaluable help in the drafting the Nauvoo City Charter. With admirable determination he single handily pushed it all the way through the Illinois legislature. He later became one of Nauvoo's most prominent and respected citizens as he served as the first Mayor of Nauvoo and the first Major General of the Nauvoo Legion as well as having served the citizenry as a highly respected practicing and prominent doctor in the community. And at one period of time, he had even served as a counselor to Joseph Smith in the First Presidency when Sidney Rigdon became ill. So just how is it possible that a man so very accomplished, so very talented, and so widely respected by the citizens of Nauvoo, and who had served the Church so well in so many capacities; how was it possible that he could fool so many people and sink so far into the depths of Hell to become such an unmitigated scoundrel? And why wasn't Joseph able to perceive his vital flaws beforehand?

In addition to his other very long list of scandalous crimes, John Bennett turned on the Prophet and publicly lied and charged Joseph Smith as being "one of the grossest and most infamous impostors that ever appeared upon the face of the earth." It all turned out that his unbelievably vile accusations against the Prophet Joseph Smith and the other Church leaders were all perpetrated by him to merely cover up and distract the public's attention away from his own repulsive and absolutely despicable sins. – 2

At one point, the Prophet Joseph received an anonymous letter stating that John C. Bennett had left behind and abandoned a wife and three children back in Ohio. Further investigations by Brother George Miller and Hyrum Smith corroborated those accusations made in the letter. However damning this particular letter may have been, it only scratched the surface of all the misdeeds and transgressions of John Bennett, and further investigations would reveal a man plagued with unbelievable sins and blatant dishonesty. – 3a

When the Prophet confronted Bennett point blank concerning his profuse lying, his many fraudulent activities, and the prolific accusations by many witnesses concerning his highly immoral behavior, he at first denied everything. Joseph then chastised him very severely for using the Church leaders for his excuse to justify his own sins. He had actually been claiming that he had received confidential sanctions for his illicit activities directly from the Church leaders themselves to commit these unconscionable sins. At this point, as he came face to face with the Prophet's censure, Bennett broke down and begged for forgiveness and mercy from the Prophet. He pretended to be ever so humble and asked most submissively to be pardoned for all his sins and then promised that he was done with all that and that he was most assuredly a completely changed man now.

However, as the Prophet pointed out, the seriousness of his sins was beyond any "behind closed doors" forgiveness at this stage of the game, and so his actions must be made public so that he could rectify his many lies and the detestable transgressions made against his victims and against the Church leaders. Joseph asked; "Doctor! Why are you using my name to carry on your hellish wickedness? Have I ever taught you that fornication and adultery were right, or polygamy or any such practice?" And Bennett replied, "You never did." -3b

It is not known whether Bennett's self-abasement, which took place soon after that chastising conversation with the Prophet, was merely a contrived attempt to gain sympathy or was an actual act of sincere regret. However it was, Bennett did attempt suicide at about the time that Joseph was preoccupied with the critical illness of his brother Don Carlos. Due to his supposed great remorse over his shameful deeds, Bennett ostensibly tried to take his own life, but he somehow survived the self-administered poison of his suicide attempt. Whether it was all just a sham or not, is not known, but there were many who suspected that as a doctor, he would have had the medical knowledge to know how to survive any poisonous ingestions. Yet, if there was ever any true humbleness and repentance on his part, they were short lived, and so he went on from there to extend his sins to an even greater magnitude and to further escalate his vile vindictive accusations against the Prophet.

During those early days of the Church when the principle of plural marriage was being selectively introduced to the Saints, the very controversial and delicate subject was confined to a few trusted members of the Church leadership only. John C. Bennett took advantage of the strict confidentiality of the situation and proceeded to institute his own personal version of the plural marriage principle. He twisted it into something so vile that even today its discussion is very uncomfortable and nothing short of shocking as it reveals the unmitigated and depraved lechery of this man. In his own warped and distorted version of the plural marriage principle, Bennett taught the doctrine of "spiritual wifery" where he would persuade trusting "church-going" women into having illicit sexual relationships with him as he convinced them that they were spiritually married to him and therefore effectively his wives. He would tell them that they had been especially chosen for this very special privilege to be sacredly and "spiritually married" to him and it was a great honor to be chosen. He convinced those women that it was all in a very hallowed and sacred trust, but never the less, it must be kept very confidential. Therefore, even if it wasn't quite an official ordinance according to the Church or any law of the land, it was very sacred, and for sacred reasons it was to never be known publicly among the Saints.

In truth, it was nothing short of absolutely amazing as to how this deceiving charlatan could dupe and so skillfully charm so many supposedly good churchwomen into believing that it was all on the up and up and approved by the Prophet. He convinced them that even Joseph was supposedly engaging in this same ordinance of "spiritual wifery." He asserted that the Prophet Joseph Smith had selectively introduced these very special "spiritual-wife" arrangements to an especially chosen few leaders in the Church, and most specifically to Bennett himself because of his extremely close relationship to the Prophet. Bennett went on to brag about the honor of having been so very fortunate to have been selected as one of the very special chosen few to have the distinct privilege to practice "spiritual wifery."

Bennett not only perpetrated a great many blatant unmitigated lies and heinous acts of deceit, but he also committed a surprising number of undeniable acts of adultery as he duped several women into sinning with him. To add to his other scandalous crimes, as a doctor it was also reported that he had performed abortions for some of his victims to cover up his and their misdeeds. If all these deplorable and very shameful acts weren't bad enough, there were also rampant rumors going around town that he had been running a secluded secret brothel down by the river, which was supposedly frequented by other rather prominent men in the community. As egregious as all this was, right at the top of his most unconscionable sins list, were the false accusations and outrageous lies that he made against the Prophet Joseph Smith and the Twelve Apostles. – 3c

Regrettably, John Bennett was also very persuasive in convincing other sinners that the Prophet had no right to judge them in their misdeeds and thus he became not the only apostate who had grievances against Joseph Smith. They in turn tried to justify their own guilt by accusing the Prophet of being a charlatan, a fake, and a despot. These other perverse transgressors who hated the Prophet, expressed their petty grumbling against him almost daily and claimed they were only doing what the Prophet was doing, or so said Bennett. They were saying he was being much too strict about their misdeeds and most certainly way too harsh in his judgments, and he really had no right to judge their private activities. Consequently, and in collusion with John Bennett, these shadowy enemies of Joseph Smith Jr. contrived an evil plot to actually assassinate a Prophet of the Lord.

On the 7th of May 1842, several hundred men of the Nauvoo Legion participated in a grand parade and performed an exciting sham battle for the entertainment of the local citizens. General John C. Bennett, while trying hard to cover up his own arrogant hatred, approached the Prophet and suggested that he should take leave of his wife, his guests, and his guards, and leave them behind just where they were seated, so that the Prophet himself could take up his official position as a commander mounted among the troops in the Nauvoo Legion. Thereby the Prophet would be mounted right in the midst of the cavalry and would be able to more closely observe how the men would perform.

In all reality, this all was a well-conceived plot by Bennett and his co-conspirators, the Higbee brothers and Dr. Foster, to put a quick and bloody end to the Prophet's very life during the activities of the sham battle. They had been colluding and carefully scheming to manipulate the Prophet into a position where he would be accidentally shot by an unknown shooter or unintentionally ran through by a sharp saber during the confusion of the mock battle.

When Joseph declined the suggestion of directly participating in the battle, Bennett was undeterred and resorted to plan B. He then urged the Prophet to instead take up a position where he would be mounted prominently at the far end of the battlefield by himself where he would have an even better view of all the action. Once again Joseph declined the suggestion saying that he really thought his proper place should be with his wife and his other VIP guests. – 4a

After having plan B thwarted so easily, Bennett jerked his horse around and left in disgusted disappointment, and then with profound dissatisfaction he shouted the word to his men to proceed with the entertainment of the sham battle. The evil plot had been foiled. It was then that the Prophet slowly leaned over towards his two brothers and quietly said to Hyrum and William; "The gentile breathings of the Spirit whisper that there is mischief in this sham battle and I think John C. Bennett is behind it. And if I am not wrong, time shall prove me right about his character." - 4b

Sometime later, John C. Bennett wrote a treacherous letter to Sidney Rigdon, a letter that conveyed his true and hateful feelings towards Joseph Smith, and thus he openly revealed his completely loathsome and traitorous attitude towards the Prophet. Having obviously now exposed his lack of fidelity to the Prophet, Bennett himself was just a little surprised when he found Sydney to actually be somewhat sympathetic towards those antagonistic feelings. Not only didn't Sydney find Bennett's disloyalty inappropriate, but in addition, he most surprisingly proceeded to express his own personal disloyal thoughts and doubts about Joseph.

At this time Sydney Rigdon was still Joseph's counselor in the First Presidency and thus certainly thought to have been loyal and supportive to the Prophet, certainly not antagonistic. However, due to the influence of his own self-absorbed personal interest and his infidelity, it came to pass that Sydney negligently refrained from passing this conspiratorial and potentially dangerous information in the letter on to the Prophet. It seems as though for some time, Sidney had actually been wrestling in his own mind with mixed personal feelings towards the Prophet and he couldn't quite decide to whom he should side in with, Joseph or Joseph's evil distracters.

It all finally came to a head in 1843 when the discovery of Sidney Rigdon and John C. Bennett's subversive activities and closet collusion caused the Prophet to formally ask for the removal of Sidney from the First Presidency. However Sidney's supporters somehow surprisingly persuaded the Prophet to not drop him from the presidency position at that particular time. Shortly thereafter, Sidney ended up traveling to Pittsburg to establish his own campaign to be the Vice President of the United States under the presumed Presidential candidacy of Joseph Smith.

Just before his trip to Pittsburg, Sidney Rigdon had discreetly handed the subversive letter to Orson Pratt who had previously been disfellowshipped and was thought by Sidney to have been somewhat sympathetic in the criticism of Joseph Smith. Orson, however, surprised him and unexpectedly took the letter directly to the Prophet. Ironically in an upside down twist of fidelity, Sidney Rigdon, which should have been one of Joseph's most loyal and trusted friends, had deliberately withheld this potentially dangerous and vital information from the Prophet. On the other hand, Orson Pratt, who was at the time a fallen Saint, immediately and in an act of laudable loyalty made Joseph aware of the conspiracy that was being plotted against him. This critical act of trustworthiness showed the Prophet that Orson Pratt had become not only humble, but a loyal supporter and ready to come back into the Church, and so Joseph with welcoming arms of joy and a great deal of satisfaction accepted him and his wife back into the fold.

Meanwhile, Mr. John C. Bennett was certainly nowhere near in his own thinking, to be doing the right thing, and he was definitely not in any frame of mind to apologize to Joseph or make his way back into the fold, nor did he do any manner of repenting; instead he only escalated his vendetta against the Prophet. A short time later, the immoral and sin plagued John C. Bennett was forced to leave the Church and in a further humiliation, he was compelled to turn in his resignation as the Mayor of Nauvoo. In addition to these humiliating and disgraceful consequences, it was also rumored that the Masonic Lodge had also repudiated him as well. Due to his many abominable indiscretions, he was finally and officially excommunicated from the Church on May 11, 1842.

However, given the well-deserved consequences of his actions and the many lessons that should have been learned from his scores of bad choices, it all just never seemed to quite sink into his numb ethics or his desensitized conscience. He had become literally his own worst adversary. Therefore these fitting and deserved consequences never brought about any sort of repentance to Bennett's darkened soul. Years later, while he was a member of the James Strang religious group, he once again had further embarrassing indiscretions exposed and thus was excommunicated from the "Strangites" for very similar transgressions that he had committed while he was with the Saints. The "Strangites" group that he had joined was a Mormon off shoot group that was led by James Strang, a delusional pseudo prophet, who had relocated from Illinois to Beaver Island in Michigan. However, the movement didn't last long. The Strangite group uneventfully faded into the forgotten annals of history after James Strang was assassinated by one of his own followers.

If John Bennett ever did repent, it certainly was not obvious from his subsequent actions. John Taylor commented that John C. Bennett continued to slander Joseph Smith and "went lecturing through the country, and commenced writing pamphlets for the sake of making money. He was charging so much for admittance to his lectures, and selling his slanderous accusations in a series of letters in a Springfield, Missouri newspaper. His remarks, however, were so bad, and his statements so obscene and disgraceful, that respectable people were disgusted." – 5

Then out of pure vindictiveness, Bennett put considerable efforts into attempting to have Joseph Smith extradited to Missouri for trying to assassinate Governor Boggs. He was also given credit for negatively influencing another prominent member in the Church, William Law. Elder Law, who had been a counselor to Joseph Smith in the First Presidency, sadly fell under the spell of Bennett's mastery of words and charm, and as a result became another one of Bennett victims and another lost soul becoming a devious traitor to the Prophet. The majority of Joseph's traitors had all been highly influenced by Bennett's persuasive words of sedition and personal malice.

Regrettably, there were others who became seditionist. There was William Law's brother, Wilson, who had been a general in the Nauvoo Legion, and who also surrendered to going along with the accusations and treachery against the Prophet. Another one of traitors that belonged to the Judas gang was Dr. R. D. Foster, a man of some wealth but of highly questionable character. He too became an unscrupulous conspirator along with the Higbee brothers, the very devious Francis and Chauncey Higbee. These two brothers were the wayward sons of the respectable and very honorable Judge Elias Higbee who had previously passed on. In the Judge's death, he was mercifully saved from the shame that his two sons had brought upon themselves and their family. All of these dishonorable and roguish enemies of the Prophet in Nauvoo were now colluding among themselves and were very determined to completely destroy Joseph Smith and the Church.

For whatever crazy reason that no one has ever quite explained, John C. Bennett unexpectedly did do one honorable thing in his life to partially redeem himself; perhaps he had found it impossible to sleep under his guilty conscience. Thus he surprisingly and officially exonerated the Prophet Joseph Smith by saying that the Prophet had never sanctioned his licentious deeds. The following is an actual deposition made by Bennett in front of a Nauvoo City Alderman:

"State of Illinois, city of Nauvoo, personally appeared before me, Daniel H. Wells, an Alderman of the said city of Nauvoo, John C. Bennett, who being duly sworn, according to law, desposeth and sayeth, that he was never taught anything in the least contrary to the strictest principles of the Gospel, or of virtue or of the laws of God or man, under any circumstances, or upon any occasion, either directly or indirectly, in word or deed, by Joseph Smith, and that he never knew the said Smith to countenance any improper conduct whatever either in public or private; and that he never did teach to me in private that an illegal, illicit intercourse with females, was under any circumstance justifiable, and that I never knew him to so teach others." Signed - JOHN C. BENNETT. – 6

John C. Bennett charmed and fooled even the most elect among the Saints, and presumably, he very much disappointed the Lord. The Lord had spoken to the Prophet Joseph on behalf of Bennett in D&C 124:16-17. Here the Lord made a promise to Bennett; "Again let my servant John C. Bennett help you in your labor in sending my word to the kings and people of the earth...and his reward shall not fail if he receive counsel.

And for his love he shall be great for he shall be mine if he do this…and will crown him with blessings and great glory."

Obviously Bennett didn't follow through with his part of this promise regarding the Lord's expectations. He certainly did not commit to labor with the Prophet nor did he accept any counsel from the Prophet or from the Lord, for that matter. However, as one reads this promise from the Lord in the Doctrine and Covenants, which was given especially to Bennett, one has to wonder why would the Lord give such a promise to Bennett if he truly was such a corrupt human being from the very beginning. Is it possible that for a short time in his life, John C. Bennett was not a complete hypocrite? Is it possible that he may have even been sincere in the very beginning of his Church service and activity, all before his own unfettered appetites and lust corrupted him and took over his soul?

If this is actually true, then there is a great lesson to be learned in all of this; which is that even the most elect can fall in front of worldly temptations unless they are constantly vigilant in avoiding immoral enticement and their succumbing to baser instincts and worldly appetites. The truth of this statement is powerfully illustrated in the unfortunate and very disappointing downfall of the great King David. He was a "righteous man after the Lord's own heart," yet he yielded to his lustful desires for Bath-Sheba and consequently committed adultery, and then to cover it up, he had her husband deliberately placed in such a dangerous situation, that he was killed. It was all done because he let his baser appetites overpower his higher morals. These two examples about King David and John C. Bennett illustrate that it can happen to anyone who is not on their guard against the insidious worldly appetites that relentlessly tempt the natural man.

As an interesting post note, John C. Bennett did not just dry up and blow away in the wind after he left Nauvoo. The talented, accomplished, and intelligent Doctor, though of weak moral character, went on to advocate health issues such as the benefits of tomatoes, the advantages of chloroform as an anesthetic, and to establish medical colleges, even though only one of them survived his questionable reputation. He also branched out into experimenting with the breeding of a new type of chicken, one of which was a new breed called the "Plymouth Rock Foul," which was exhibited in Boston in 1849. Later he served as a Union Army commander while fighting in the Civil War, and then quietly passed away in August of 1867. – 7

John C. Bennett was only one of a dozen men who had colluded with the authorities in Missouri to extradite Joseph Smith back to Missouri. This dishonorable persistent faction of the Prophet's enemies would continue to be an unrelenting thorn in Joseph's side until he was finally martyred. It was only a short time after the infamous attempt to assassinate Lilburn Boggs that the calculating ex-Governor of Missouri, a sworn enemy to Joseph Smith, tried to get the Prophet indicted. This unscrupulous politician immediately placed suspicion upon the Mormons, and most particularly and directly upon the head of Joseph Smith, and then he actually swore to the fact that Joseph Smith was the man responsible for the assassination attempt made upon his person even though Joseph Smith wasn't even in Missouri at the time. Mr. Boggs proceeded without conscience with his false testimony and made the accusation quite clear in this deposition:

"Lilburn W. Boggs, who being duly sworn, doth depose and say that on the night of the 6th day of May, 1842, while sitting in his dwelling, in the town of Independence, in the county of Jackson, he was shot with intent to kill; and that his life was despaired of for several days; and that he believes, and has good reason to believe from evidence and information now in his possession, that Joseph Smith, commonly called the 'Mormon Prophet,' was accessory before the fact of the intended murder, and that the said Joseph Smith is a citizen or resident of the state of Illinois." – 8

Soon after this, a Deputy Sheriff of Adams County arrested the Prophet and Orrin Porter Rockwell in Nauvoo on the 8th of August 1842 on charges that they attempted to assassinate the Governor. The falsely accused Mormon prisoners made no attempt to resist arrest, but immediately applied to the municipal court in Nauvoo for writ of habeas corpus. The Deputy Sheriff refused to recognize the authority of the municipal court but left his prisoners in the hands of the City Marshal anyway, and then left Nauvoo. Two days later he returned and was very determined to take the Prophet from Nauvoo under the guise of a very questionable legal document to deliver Joseph to the authorities in the state of Missouri. However, the Prophet was somehow able to avoid the physical arrest, and in as much as discretion is the better part of valor, Joseph went into seclusion until the legal red tape was taken care of, which was then brought to a conclusion with the witnesses for the defense testifying to the truth of his alibi and proved his innocence and thus the whole matter was finally straightened out.

Despite what the Missourian extradition papers stated, it was common knowledge both in Missouri and in Illinois that Joseph Smith had not been in Missouri for at least three years at the time of the assassination attempt upon Governor Boggs. It was also confirmed that on the day of the assassination attempt, when Boggs was hit by the buckshot, that Joseph Smith was elsewhere and was witnessed to be present at an officer's drill in Illinois, and therefore not anywhere near Missouri. Accordingly so, Joseph Smith was not legally extraditable under the law on those charges, and therefore he was not legally bound to present himself in Missouri.

Of course, the Missourian authorities were nowhere near satisfied with this development and they proceeded instead to go after Joseph's good friend, Porter Rockwell. Porter was charged as a paid accomplice in the conspiracy that was supposedly arranged by his boss, Joseph Smith. Porter was well known to be a close friend, bodyguard, and protector of Joseph and so it was no surprise that he was accused of perpetrating such a dirty deed as the scandalous assassination attempt on the Governor at the bidding and bribery of his Mormon prophet boss. Rockwell wrote in his own words: "I, Orrin Porter Rockwell, was on my way from New Jersey to Nauvoo; and while at St. Louis, on the 4th March, 1843, was arrested by a Mr. Fox, on oath of Elias Parker, who swore I was the O. P. Rockwell advertised in the papers as having attempted to assassinate Lilburn W. Boggs, and was taken before a magistrate in St. Louis." - 9

Even though Porter was arrested and was eventually taken to Jackson County Missouri for trial, the authorities had to acknowledge "there was not sufficient proof adduced against him to justify an indictment for shooting at the ex-Governor, Lilburn Boggs, and the grand jury therefore did not indict him for that offense."

Speaking in his own defense, it was reported that Porter Rockwell said somewhat humorously that if he had been the one who had tried to shoot Boggs, Boggs would now be very dead. This was not just bragging; everybody knew it to be true that Rockwell was widely known as a dead shot and rarely missed anything he shot at. When Joseph was questioned about Porter's guilt, he stated that Rockwell did not have any thing to do with it, and was completely innocent of all charges. They asked; "How can you be so confident?" In light of the governor's survival, Joseph answered, "He's still alive, aint he?" His meaning was clear, that the accusation of guilt against Porter for trying to assassinate the Governor was just not plausible. The simple fact was; if Porter had been the one who had shot at the governor, the governor would now be six feet under pushing up daisies.

The Missourians deliberately kept Porter in jail on trumped up charges and put into play any further delays they could think of to keep Rockwell unjustly in jail for more than nine months, all under the extreme duress and cruelty of continuous harassment from his jailers. In addition there were constant threats from vigilantes expressing a strong determination to hang him without a trial. He was stuck in jail "without even the form of an inquiry, chained double in a filthy, damp, unventilated dungeon, chained hand and foot, so that he could not straighten for months, till his body was reduced to a mere skeleton, and he unable to walk when the irons were taken off, and he had to be led, half fed on the refuse of what dogs would not eat: his case presented to a Jackson county grand jury, and not evidence enough to warrant them in even finding an indictment." – 10

The Prophet became quite concerned about his friend Porter and thus sent $200 to Porter's mother for legal fees. The Judge appointed General Doniphan, the same attorney who had defended Joseph Smith in the past, to be Rockwell's counsel. The lawyer Doniphan was able to get a legal change of venue from Independence Jackson County to Liberty in Clay County. However, it was very plain to see, especially to Rockwell's Attorney, that although the Missourian authorities had no case whatsoever against Rockwell, they were very determined to keep him in jail indefinitely, even if it was quite obvious that it was illegal and without cause.

The Attorney Doniphan then gave Rockwell some very good practical advice, even if it was somewhat questionable as far as any kind of sanctioned legal advice. Mr. Doniphan knew the Missourian authorities were determined to hold on to Porter whether they legally could or not, so he then advised Rockwell to do what ever he had to do to escape. Rockwell wrote about it saying, "About 8 p.m. on December 13th, General Doniphan took me out and told me I must take across the country on foot, and not walk on any traveled road, unless it was during the night, as they would be apt to follow and again take me, as they did not care on what grounds, so they could make me trouble." – 11

And so with the help of his Attorney, Porter Rockwell did somehow escape the unrelenting clutches of the Missourian authorities and drudgingly walked most of the way from Liberty Missouri to Nauvoo Illinois, traveling night and day as he hid behind trees and "traveled in the fields by the side of the road." On occasion, he was able to receive kindness and food from strangers living along the way. Though he was very weakened from his ordeal in jail, he was unremitting in his determination to make it to Nauvoo.

Joseph and Emma had moved into the Mansion house just four months earlier and were now celebrating the holidays with their guests when Porter finally trudged into Nauvoo. His unexpected arrival at the Smith's Mansion House on Christmas day during their Christmas celebration makes for an interesting story.

"During the Festivities, there came sounds from the hallway of loud voices and scuffling. A voice said; 'Sir you can't go in there. This is a private party.' Joseph and the City Marshall went to investigate. A stranger in dirty buckskins, tattered hat, matted hair and a scruffy beard came down the hall towards Joseph. Someone yelled; 'Look out; it's a Missourian.' The Marshall tried to stop him but the stranger pushed the Marshall aside, and grabbed Joseph by the lapels."

In his own defense, Joseph grabbed on solidly to the coat of his offender to prepare for a wild tussle. However, he was quite surprised to hear the response; it was the hardy laughter of the shabby stranger and a laugh that Joseph would have recognized anywhere. Sure enough, it was his longtime and beloved friend and bodyguard who had been in a cold dirty Missouri jail for nearly a year, and now had traveled night and day on foot over two hundred miles to see Joseph. "It was Porter Rockwell, one of the best Christmas presents Joseph could have asked for." - 12

Most historians believe that this was the very same occasion on which Joseph foretold Porter that his life would never be taken as long as he would never cut his long hair. Joseph promised; "…so long as ye shall remain loyal and true to thy faith, need fear no enemy. Cut not thy hair, and no bullet or blade can harm thee." - 13

This was another one of Joseph's prophecies that came true and was fulfilled even though Porter engaged in a lifetime of risk taking and wild adventure. Though having some very dangerous confrontations with several vicious men who desperately wanted to do him serious harm, Rockwell was able to survive several gun battles and other perilous skirmishes in which he never received a scratch. Porter Rockwell became famous as a gunfighter, a religious enforcer, Joseph's personal bodyguard, and a loyal defender of the Church and thus was aptly dubbed by some as the "Mormon Destroying Angel." Without really intending to do so, he had accrued a number of enemies who would have been delighted to nail his tough old hide to the side of a barn and just shoot it "plum" full of holes. However, as he spoke in his own defense, he famously said, "I never killed anyone who didn't need killing."

Though he had a great many adversaries who in point of fact wanted to shoot him dead, he went on to live a very full life. While living in Utah, he ran the Hot Springs Hotel and Brewery business at "the point of the mountain" at the southern end of the Salt Lake Valley. He later became a deputy marshal, fathered seven children, and died at the ripe old age of 64 of natural causes. Porter Rockwell is widely recognized as a legendary character of the Old West in modern movies, books, and western lore. He was well known in the Church for being a heroic, faithful, and a loyal bodyguard to the Prophet Joseph Smith and also to Brigham Young. Rockwell was most definitely one of the most fascinating and interesting characters in the history of the Church. – 14

*   *   *

1. See History of the Church, Vol.4, Ch.28, p.489 & H of the C, Vol.7, Ch.6, p.60

2. See Encyclopedia of Mormonism, Vol.1, ANTI-MORMON PUBLICATIONS

3a. See History of the Church 5:36-37, 42-43.

3b Joseph Smith Papers 1 Aug, 1842 p.871

3c See "The Saintly Scoundrel: The Life and Times of John Cook Bennett" by Andrew F. Smith pp 118-124

4a. See Joseph Smith Papers Saturday 7 May 1842

4b See History of the Church 5:4-5

5. See History of the Church, Vol.5, p.79, Footnotes.

6. See History of the Church, Vol.5, Ch.1, p.11 also History of the Church, Vol.5, Ch.4, p.71, also see Daniel Bachman "A Study of the Mormon Practice of Plural Marriage Before the death of Joseph Smith" (Master's thesis, Purdue University 1975)

7. See Wikipedia – JOHN C. BENNETT

8. See History of the Church, Vol.5, Ch.12, p.226

9. See History of the Church, Vol.6, Ch.6, p.135.

10. See History of the Church, Vol.6, Ch.6, p.151

11. See History of the Church, Vol.6, Ch.6, p.141

12. See History of the Church, Vol.6, Ch.6, and p.134-135.

13. See Richard Lloyd Dewey, "Porter Rockwell: A Biography" pp. 73-77

14. See-www.wikipedia/-Porter-Rockwell

*   *   *

Chapter Seventeen

———~~∙᠀᠀᠀᠀᠀~~———

MUMMIES AND
PLURAL WIVES

*   *   *

During the General Conference of April of 1842, the Prophet Joseph gave a scathing sermon to certain unspecified attendees seated among the rest of the Saints in the grove near the Nauvoo temple. Among other things, he declared that the Church must be cleansed and that hearts filled with evil have no room for good, or even for studying good. Joseph summarized this sermon in his history by commenting; "I preached in the grove, and pronounced a curse upon all adulterers, fornicators, and unvirtuous persons, and those who have made use of my name to carry on their iniquitous designs." - 1

Without having named anyone specifically, Joseph's words clearly stung certain individuals hard with words that were meant to prick their guilty consciences. And so they found themselves feeling humiliated, guilty, and sheepish, and their hostility increased to new levels of bitterness before his scathing reprimand, and thus their hatred grew even greater than before towards the Prophet. Shortly thereafter, the dissidents became resolute in convincing themselves that he was truly a fallen prophet and needed to be disposed of in accordance with their personal perception of justice, their religious duty, and their obligation to execute his overthrow by the righteous indignation of their own hand. And so it was that Joseph's dedicated enemies rationalized their hatred and became dangerously conspiratorial and plotted against him with an increasing spirit of venomous rancor, and in the end, they would come to a final and absolute determination to assassinate him.

Fortunately, there were other Saints that felt quite differently about the Prophet and they knew in their heart and with out any doubt that Brother Joseph was a rare leader and true prophet. One such Nauvoo Saint had a personal experience that dramatically revealed to him that Joseph Smith genuinely had the abilities of a seer and a prophet. His personal story is truly inspiring and is a strong faith builder for those who are in tune with this special testimony of the Prophet's prophetic powers.

Israel Barlow was a faithful member of the Church and at this time was serving in the Church as one of the teamsters hauling the huge limestone blocks from the bluff quarry on the Mississippi river to the Nauvoo temple site. The temple sat upon the hill overlooking the city and required many huge stones to be hauled by horse and wagon to the work site during its highly laborious construction period.

Israel was the proud owner of a team of two matching black mares, which he doted on. The other teamsters often teased him about getting a buggy whip to whip his spoiled and spirited horses into a more disciplined and yielding behavior. All of this teasing only caused him to become more resolved in ignoring their advice and in the meantime he became very defensive and quite touchy in regards to the whole idea of ever whipping or punishing his precious horses.

One day when the Prophet was doing a routine inspection of the work in the quarry and observing how the temple's construction was progressing, he greeted Israel with a casual hello as he passed by his wagon. Then suddenly, Joseph stopped in his tracks, turned around and walked back to Brother Barlow's wagon and spoke in a very serious manner, saying; "Israel, after you drop that block off at the temple, go by the store and purchase a buggy whip."

Israel thought at first that Joseph was just teasing him and replied that the Prophet should know that he never ever whipped his horses. The Prophet then looked Israel square in the eye and very sternly repeated the abrupt request. It was such a powerful directive from the Prophet that Israel yielded and submissively said that he would do it. Later that day when Israel showed up at the quarry with a new buggy whip stuck in his whip holder, the other teamsters once again began their teasing. Israel shot back that the Prophet had said only that he should buy the whip, but not necessarily that he had to use it.

That very afternoon, Israel was backing his team up to the edge of the steep drop off at the quarry rim in order to load up the next huge temple stone for delivery, when suddenly a couple riding in a buckboard came trotting into the quarry yard and inadvertently came too close to Israel's horses and spooked his already skittish team. The two spirited mares began rearing up in a snorting panic, pawing in the air, their nostrils flaring, and no amount of coaxing from Israel was calming them down. Each time they reared up, they dangerously inched the back of the wagon closer in the direction of the steep rim of the quarry cliff. Israel yelled until he was nearly blue in the face, and then just before the rear wagon wheels reached the very edge of the dangerous precipice, he grabbed for and yanked the buggy whip out of its holder and smacked it across the rump of one of the mares. These horses had never felt the sting of the whip before, and this new experience in pain along with another snap of his whip brought about a quick reaction, which spurred the mares to suddenly jump forward hard, each one pulling her companion with her. They then began to run away in a frenzied panic. Only after a long hard run, was Israel able to finally calm them down and bring them to a slow stop. He then pensively put the buggy whip back in its holder and then just sat there for a few moments reflecting on all the possibilities of what could have happened if he hadn't obeyed a Prophet of God. How was it possible that Joseph knew Israel was going to need that whip to save his very life that very afternoon? – 2

This was only one of many proofs that Joseph Smith was a Prophet. Another corroboration of the evidence came in the form of his extraordinary translating abilities and how he was able to transliterate the inspired Pearl of Great Price into English from the mysterious markings found on the ancient and virtually unintelligible papyrus rolls. The curious, mystic, and archaic text rolls had been found stowed away with some long ago buried Egyptian mummies.

In the year 1828, a French explorer called Antonio Sebolo received permission from the Viceroy of Egypt to explore for antiquities in that country. Three years later he discovered some catacombs in Egypt near where the ancient city of Thebes once stood. Eleven of the mummies that he uncovered were in a perfect state of preservation and were taken to Paris. After Sebolo died, the mummies finally made their way to New York and ended up in the hands of a nephew named Michael H. Chandler where the caskets were first opened.

An observer standing near by at the time of the public display of the papyrus rolls, recommended to Mr. Chandler that he should take them to the Mormon Prophet, Joseph Smith, as he might be the only man who could actually translate them correctly. However, Mr. Chandler had other ideas about how he could best use them, and so instead began to exhibit the mummies around the United States. In the process of his travels, several experts assured him that both the mummies and the papyrus rolls were truly genuine, and subsequently he did receive certificates testifying to their authenticity. Before finally selling his archaeological treasures, he exhibited them throughout the Northeastern United States where many hundreds of curious onlookers viewed them with great interest. – 3

It was not until July 3, 1835, that Mr. Chandler finally arrived in Kirtland, Ohio, and met with Joseph Smith personally and asked him; "If he had a power by which he could translate the ancient Egyptian? Mr. Smith replied that he had."

Shortly thereafter, Chandler turned over the Egyptian mummies and the papyrus rolls to some associates of the Prophet Joseph Smith for the sum of $2,400. The Prophet subsequently translated the Egyptian characters on one of the scrolls and found it to be a first person account of Father Abraham's experiences in the course of his sojourn to Egypt during ancient biblical times.

The Prophet in his own words wrote the following: "Soon after this, some of the Saints at Kirtland purchased the mummies and papyrus, a description of which will appear hereafter, and with W. W. Phelps and Oliver Cowdery as scribes, I commenced the translation of some of the characters or hieroglyphics, and much to our joy found that one of the rolls contained the writings of Abraham, another the writings of Joseph of Egypt, etc., a more full account of which will appear in its place, as I proceed to examine or unfold them. Truly we can say the Lord is beginning to reveal the abundance of peace and truth." – 4

The Prophet went on to tell us, "he (Mr. Chandler) discovered that in connection with two of the bodies, was something rolled up with the same kind of linen, saturated with the same bitumen, which when examined, proved to be two rolls of papyrus." These rolls of papyrus were beautifully written, "With black, and a small part red, ink or paint, in perfect preservation." Shortly thereafter, the Prophet translated the mysterious text. And thus were the writings of Father Abraham soon brought to the members of the Church in the form of an officially canonized scriptural book called the Pearl of Great Price. – 5 & 6

At one point during the translating process, the Prophet presented his own version of the translations of the Egyptian characters to Mr. Chandler so that a comparison could be made with the expert versions. And thus the Prophet's translations were discovered to be surprisingly accurate in their agreement with the interpretations given by the expert archeologists in other cities where the mummies and papyrus rolls had been exhibited. Mr. Chandler then turned over to the Prophet Joseph Smith a certificate stating the facts of the comparison, which verified the agreement between Joseph's translations and those of the expert archeologists.

Years later uninspired and very skeptical critics would claim Joseph Smith had really done nothing more than just simply translated Egyptian funerary texts. These uninformed critics seemed to have completely ignored the fact that genuine archeological experts, who had actually seen the Egyptian characters with their own eyes and had compared their interpretation to Joseph's translation, had then judged Joseph Smith's interpretation to be an accurate translation. If Joseph had merely dreamed up the Abraham story out of his own imagination, wouldn't the experts have felt obliged to expose him as a fraud rather than proceed to actually verify his work?

In March of 1842, the Church's Nauvoo news paper, the "Times and Seasons," published a very significant issue, which contained parts of what would later be canonized as the Pearl of Great Price scriptures. Included in these articles were not only the fascinating writings of Father Abraham, but they also contained a very significant section in regards to the Church of Jesus Christ's actual beliefs that were presented to the public for the very first time. They were called the Articles of Faith of the Church of Jesus Christ of Latter Day Saints and they clearly stated the fundamental beliefs of the so-called "Mormons" as the members of the Church of Jesus Christ of Latter Day Saints believe them to be.

The Articles of Faith had originally come through Joseph Smith by way of a seemingly inconsequential personal letter, which had been cordially written as a reply to a request from John Wentworth, the editor of the "Chicago Democrat" newspaper. Wentworth had sincerely wanted to know more about the true facts concerning what the "Mormons" actually did believe. Therefore Joseph gave him honest answers in what would become known as the famous Wentworth letter, which clearly stated in a summarized list the basic beliefs of the Church. Those beliefs as given by Joseph the Prophet in the "Thirteen Articles of Faith" are presented here in a paraphrased summarized short version:

1. We believe in the father, the Son, and the Holy Ghost.
2. We believe men will be punished for their own sins, not Adam's.
3. We believe in the Atonement of Christ and that all men will be saved.
4. We believe in the principles of faith, repentance, baptism, and the laying on of hands.
5. We believe a man must have authority to preach and administer ordinances.
6. We believe in same organization as Christ's primitive Church.
7. We believe in gift of tongues, prophecy, revelation, visions, healing, and interpretation.
8. We believe the Book of Mormon & Bible as the word of God as translated correctly.
9. We believe God does now reveal and will reveal many important things.
10. We believe in a literal gathering of Israel, the ten tribes, & Christ will reign upon the earth.
11. We claim privilege of worshiping freely by dictates of our conscience & allow all men the same privilege.

12. We believe in being subject to kings & governments and obeying the law of the land.

13. We believe in being honest, chaste, benevolent, virtuous, and in doing good while seeking things lovely, praiseworthy, and of good report.

*   *   *

In addition to these "Thirteen Articles of Faith" presented in his letter to Mr. John Wentworth in March of 1842, Joseph Smith also made a somewhat controversial prophecy aimed at the non-Mormon population: "No unhallowed hand can stop the work from progressing; . . . the truth of God will go forth boldly, nobly, and independent, till it has penetrated every continent, visited every clime, swept every country, and sounded in every ear, till the purposes of God shall be accomplished, and the Great Jehovah shall say the work is done." – 7

In addition to his prophetic blessings, his prophecies, his visions, and other divine manifestations, the Prophet Joseph Smith also was able to see with his prophetic foresight that the Church would never be fully organized until the women of the Church were also fully organized. Joseph's first appreciation for the amazing abilities of the women of the Church to self organize came as far back as at the time of the building of the Kirtland Temple in Ohio. The ladies of the Church had loosely organized themselves during that time into a group that generously donated money and materials for the temple construction. Meanwhile as they sewed clothing for the men working on the temple, they also happily stitched the sacred veils for the interior of Kirtland temple. This early and loosely put together organization of women would become the rudimentary beginnings of the Church's Relief Society.

A few years later during the construction of the new Nauvoo temple, the ladies once again would show their organizational abilities as they gave of their time and self-sacrificing contributions towards the building of the Church's newest temple. And so once more they were happily doing their Church service as they proceeded with similar types of projects as they had previously carried out in Kirtland. Sarah Kimball, the wife of Hiram Kimball organized a neighborhood group to sew shirts for the hardworking men constructing the temple in Nauvoo. It was just one of the many different service projects that had been put together by these dedicated women of the Church at that time.

During this happy, satisfying, and contented time of Church service, the women worked as diligently as the men to do volunteer work on the new temple. It was sister Eliza R. Snow that was asked to write up a constitution and a few bylaws for the ladies' service group. After her draft was shown to the Prophet, he not only wholeheartedly approved of it, but also then proceeded to invite a select group of women to come up to the upper room of the Red Brick store for a special meeting. It was at this very meeting that they would organize "the women under the priesthood after the pattern of the priesthood." This was on March 17ᵗʰ 1842, at which time about twenty women met with the Prophet Joseph Smith, along with John Taylor and Willard Richards in the "assembly room" of the Red Brick store to organize the women's Relief Society of the Church of Jesus Christ of Latter Day Saints.

Joseph presided at the meeting as he stood up and gave the sisters a short tutorial on parliamentary procedure and then suggested that they elect a president and two counselors. In the first order of business, it was motioned that Emma Smith should be elected as the first president of the organization at which time the motion was seconded, and then unanimously approved. Emma chose Sarah Cleveland and Elizabeth Ann Whitney as her counselors as they patterned their presidency after the Church's priesthood quorum presidencies. The Prophet then called for Elder John Taylor to come forth so that he could have the honor of giving "Emma a blessing, and then he was asked to ordain and bless Sisters Whitney and Cleveland to their callings" in this new presidency. Emma had previously been "ordained" at the hands of her own husband as mentioned in D&C 25:7. And it should be noted that this revelation to Emma through the Prophet does use the term "ordained," however, there is a footnote of clarification referring to the term as being "set apart." This same revelation in addition, also gave two very important assignments to Sister Emma Smith, "to be a scribe for him," and "to make a selection of sacred hymns, as it shall be given thee,...." Emma followed through with these two assignments as she had already been Joseph's first scribe, and in addition, she then put together an historic selection of sacred hymns for the Church. See D&C 25:6 & 11

After the setting apart of the two sister counselors, John Taylor explained that even though the activities just conducted were called ordinations, they should not be confused with priesthood ordinations, but were more like a setting apart to an office and calling by the hands of the priesthood. Some historians say that John Taylor's explanation about the setting apart versus priesthood ordinations was given at a later date. – 8

Joseph then commented to those present at that particular meeting, that the Lord had called Emma "an elect lady" and this calling was now the fulfillment of that 1830 revelation found in D&C 25:3,7-8. As an Elect Lady, Emma was counseled to preside over the Relief Society "during good behavior" and "as long as [she] shall continue to fill the office with dignity." Some would later criticize Emma as they thought she seemed to have forgotten those particular words, "during good behavior," and a few others apparently thought she did not fulfill the admonition to "fill the office with dignity." - 9

Although a number of different names were proposed at the meeting for the new women's organization, Emma's own suggestion prevailed, and the name "The Female Relief Society of Nauvoo" was unanimously accepted. From March of 1842 through the next couple of years, Emma became the most revered woman leader in the Church. The Prophet frequently attended their meetings and counseled the women on the important charitable mission of their society and how they would "come in possession of the privileges, blessings, and gifts" associated with the priesthood. – 10a

Despite the auspicious beginning of the Relief Society, there were signs that there just might possibly be some controversy coming in the future to this women's organization. It seemed like there was something just peeking over the horizon at this point. Shortly after being organized, on one particular occasion and at the conclusion of a very much-criticized Relief Society meeting, some of the sisters present approached Emma Smith and requested a blessing of comfort and health, and they specifically asked that Emma and her counselors should administer the blessings. It was reported that Emma and her counselors then proceeded to anoint the women with oil and laid their hands upon the ladies' heads and gave the women each a blessing, a blessing which appeared to be very much like a priesthood blessing. Needless to say, this particular incident brought about a great debate in the community as to whether Emma had greatly exceeded her authority.

In response to the troublesome controversy, Joseph would himself later speak to the sisters of the Relief Society in an attempt to relieve their consternation and to more or less defend the actions of Emma and her counselors. In his explanation, the Prophet quoted some scripture saying; "And these signs shall follow them that believe: In my name shall they cast out devils; they shall speak with new tongues; they shall take up serpents; and if they drink any deadly thing, it shall not hurt them; they shall lay hands on the sick, and they shall recover." – Mark 16:17 & 18

He then added; "No matter who believeth, these signs, such as healing the sick, casting out devils, etc.," the signs would follow all that believe, whether male or female. "He asked the women if they could not see by this sweeping promise, that wherein they are ordained, if it is the privilege of those set apart to administer in that authority, which is conferred on them; and if the sisters should have faith to heal the sick, let all hold their tongues, and let everything roll on." He then told the women, that if these blessing came to a realization by way of the great faith of Emma, her counselors, and the faith of the sisters receiving the blessings, then "who are we to condemn any such activity." - 10b

He added for further clarification; "I will say, it is not the calling of these sisters to hold the priesthood, only in connection with their husbands, they being one with their husbands." The Apostle George A. Smith later further clarified to the Church members that in defending the women that gave these blessings of healing, the Prophet was speaking about the healing of the faithful by the laying on of hands and through the strong faith of the sisters present, and not by any assumed priesthood power of the ladies that appeared to be conducting a women's priesthood ordinance. – 11

Unfortunately, this particular incident would not be the end of the controversies that would come about in the early days of the Relief Society. To the surprise and shock of many, just two years after the "The Female Relief Society of Nauvoo" was organized, its meetings were suspended without further notice and there were no more Relief Society meetings held for more than two decades after 16th of March of 1844.

Interestingly enough, there has been more than one narrative used to explain "the who and why" of this suspension of Relief Society meetings in the Church. Although it is not fully known for certain what direct involvement Joseph had in the termination of the Relief Society meetings, there is at least one account that says it was Joseph himself that actually called for the stoppage of the meetings of the Relief Society.

Another version of the story, which some have called suspect, claims it was actually Emma who stopped the meetings in order to spite the very critical Church leaders. She was definitely upset with all of them for all the criticism that had been coming from the apostles over her using the Relief Society meetings as a platform to speak against plural wives.

A third and more widely publicized version of the story surrounding the suspension of Relief society meetings, explains that it was in all reality just out of concern for the safety of the sisters and the fear of antagonistic outsiders carrying out some type of harassment during the meetings. Persecution coming from the anti-Mormons faction in the area had been somewhat of a concern, however, one might think that the priesthood brethren would have been more than willing to escort the sisters to and from their meetings and stand guard over them while they were meeting, just as the priesthood brethren sometimes do today when asked to chaperone some relief Society meetings.

After all speculation is considered and when all is said and done, John Taylor's explanation seems to be the most likely explanation. He later attributed the suspension of the Relief Society to Emma's public opposition to plural marriage, or as it was to become more commonly known, polygamy. Brother Taylor put it this way, "Sister Emma got severely tried in her mind about the doctrine of plural marriage and she made use of the position she held to try to pervert the minds of the sisters in relation to the doctrine." - 12

At that time, there were actual real concerns coming from certain Church leaders regarding Emma using the Relief Society as a platform to aggressively preach against plural marriage. Although the Relief Society meetings were for all intents and purposes suspended a few months before Joseph was martyred in June of 1844, it did not actually become official until 8 months after the Prophet's death at which time Brigham Young formally suspended the meetings as of March 9th, 1845. – 13

As it all turned out, there was no actual formal organization of the

Relief Society in the Church after mid 1844 for a span of some twenty-three years. Then following that significant hiatus it was once again reestablished in the year 1867. During the suspension time there were a couple of unofficial Relief Society meetings, such as the ones at Winter Quarters during the exodus, and again in Utah during the 1850's. While in Salt Lake Brigham Young requested that the sisters should loosely organize themselves in order to provide clothing and food for the Native American children. However, these particular women's meetings were only temporary and unofficial.

Finally after a long hiatus, on December 8th 1867 in Salt Lake City, Brigham Young was inspired to institute the Relief Society organization once again into the Church along with the aid and strong support of sister Eliza R. Snow. He then officially asked the Bishops of the Church to each one organize a Relief Society organization in their individual wards. The importance of Eliza R. Snow's personal involvement in restoring the Church's Relief Society can't be over stated. Having been married to Joseph Smith at one time and then later as a widow, married Brigham Young, she played a major role in helping President Young reinstate the Relief Society into the Church of Jesus Christ of Latter Day Saints. In addition to her vital part in reestablishing the Relief Society, Eliza R. Snow and her counselors would later be instrumental in establishing the Young Women's organization and the Children's Primary. The Relief Society of the Church of Jesus Christ of Latter Day Saints has since those times become the largest women's organizations in the world and one of the most highly respected women's groups around the entire globe with over seven million female members. - 14

Emma Smith's personal culpability and the strong suggestion that she was totally responsible for the suspension of the Relief Society after having been its premier leader is a very controversial issue and maybe just a little vague in all the facts. The full story of Emma and the suspension of the Relief society is somewhat complicated and certainly not clearly laid out even today with its many explanations.

Any one who knew Emma Smith would not contradict the fact that Emma had been a loyal and faithful wife, a good mother, and a true believer in her husband's divine calling, but never the less, she certainly did most strenuously oppose polygamy. Emma was a strong willed woman and an individual with great inner strength as she had proven so many times during her many trials, having lost several homes, six out of her eleven babies, her beloved husband, and in the end, even her church. Although she was consistently a very great support to her husband during the Prophet's many trials, she just simply could not accept the principle of plural marriage even though Joseph strenuously maintained that God had commanded the principle to be instituted in the Church at that time.

In the very beginning, Emma was somewhat ambivalent in her opinion towards the principle of plural marriage, which enabled Joseph during a very brief period of her passive acceptance to initiate the doctrine and to take additional wives to himself. Never the less, she came to abhor the idea of plural wives even though she was well aware that Father Abraham had two wives, that Jacob the patriarch of Israel had four wives, and King David had at least two wives, all under the auspices of the Lord. She just could not bring herself to accept the doctrine of plural marriage, except for that short period in the beginning when she seemed to tolerate it, but then subsequently rejected it wholly. Whether Emma's opposition to polygamy is totally responsible for the suspension of the Relief Society in the early days of the Church or not, has never been fully established.

It is thought that plural wives principle may have first been introduced to the Twelve privately after their return from their English missions. And there is some evidence that suggests that the idea of plural marriage was first revealed to the Prophet in connection with his study of the Bible as early as 1831.

On July 12, 1843, the Prophet Joseph Smith dictated a lengthy revelation on the doctrine of marriage for eternity and the law of plural marriage in D&C 132:61-66. This revelation taught that under specified conditions through the auspices of the Lord, a chosen man might be authorized to have more than one wife without committing adultery, as has been evidenced through the example of God's prophets in the Bible such as Abraham, Jacob, King David, and Solomon. The following scriptures found in the Doctrine and Covenants were the Lord's answer to Joseph's questions concerning ancient prophets having multiple wives. – 15a

D&C 132: 1 "Verily, thus saith the Lord unto you my servant Joseph, that inasmuch as you have inquired of my hand to know and understand wherein I, the Lord, justified my servants Abraham, Isaac, and Jacob, as also Moses, David and Solomon, my servants, as touching the principle and doctrine of their having many wives and concubines."

132:2 "Behold, and lo, I am the Lord thy God, and will answer thee as touching this matter."

132:3 "Therefore, prepare thy heart to receive and obey the instructions which I am about to give unto you; for all those who have this law revealed unto them must obey the same."

132:4 "For behold, I reveal unto you a new and an everlasting covenant; and if ye abide not that covenant, then are ye damned; for no one can reject this covenant and be permitted to enter into my glory."

132:61 "And again, as pertaining to the law of the priesthood--if any man espouse a virgin, and desire to espouse another, and the first give her consent, and if he espouse the second, and they are virgins, and have vowed to no other man, then is he justified; he cannot commit adultery for they are given unto him; for he cannot commit adultery with that that belongeth unto him and to no one else."

132:62 "And if he have ten virgins given unto him by this law, he cannot commit adultery, for they belong to him, and they are given unto him; therefore is he justified."

*   *   *

As a result of Emma's abhorrence towards polygamy and her strong feelings of jealousy, she was not so very friendly to some of Joseph's other wives. There are several accounts from early Church history and a few other non-LDS historical sources that claim that Emma Smith in a fit of jealousy attacked a pregnant Eliza R. Snow and pushed her down the stairs in their shared home in Nauvoo.

Eliza R. Snow was not the only one to experience the wrath of Emma Smith's animus regarding polygamy. During the summer of 1843, Hyrum suggested to the Prophet, that if Joseph would write down the revelation concerning "plural wives" on a piece of paper, Hyrum himself would present it to Emma and he assured Joseph that with the revelation in hand, he could convince Emma of the authenticity of its divine nature. Joseph replied; "Hyrum, you don't know Emma like I do."

Hyrum returned from his short and very volatile meeting with Emma in somewhat of a humbler mood, saying that he had never had such a "Tongue Lashing" in his entire life. Joseph didn't say much, but it was obvious that Hyrum's skilful salesmanship and Emma's supposedly open mindedness and demure nature were not exactly compatible on that particular day. Hyrum never brought up the subject to Emma ever again.

It is now agreed, by most historians, that the reason the Relief Society was suspended for some twenty-three years was due to Emma using her position as president of the Relief Society to preach against plural marriage. Never the less, Emma Smith did have her supporters in Nauvoo. This made the whole issue even more contentious and divisive during that time in the Church, just exactly as Joseph had feared it would be before the practice was initiated.

Just as there are in any number of controversial issues, there is more than one point of view to be considered by any open-minded person in judging any particular issue, and this includes the principle of plural marriage. Naturally there were then and still are today those who would accuse Joseph Smith of simply being a lecherous man with an uninhibited lust for women, and if the truth were told they say, the only reason he came up with the plural wives revelation was to facilitate his own true lascivious nature.

However, in stark contradiction to that particular view, when Joseph honestly shared his true inner feelings in private with his most trusted friends, he expressed extreme repugnance in the beginning for the whole idea of plural marriage. He at one time stated that he had even pleaded with the Lord to not make him go through with it as he could perceive that the future controversy surrounding it would be clouded with much division and anguish among the members of the Church, and that it would bring even more hatred from the outside world to the Saints.

Joseph then solemnly declared before witnesses that an angel of the Lord had come to him on three different occasions demanding that he either carry out this specific command to initiate plural marriage, or his office would be taken from him and given to another. "During the third and final appearance, the angel came with a drawn sword, threatening Joseph with destruction unless he went forward and obeyed the commandment fully." - 15b

He ultimately came to terms with it and accepted it as being as one of those unconditional non-debatable commandments from the Lord and he realized the Lord was not going to accept "No" as an answer nor was He going to change His mind. Even as Joseph could see the negative consequences, he finally came to the realization that God did have His purposes for plural marriage. – 15c

The Prophet Lorenzo Snow recalled vividly a conversation with the Prophet Joseph describing the battle Joseph waged "in overcoming the repugnance of his feelings" regarding plural marriage. "He knew the voice of God—he knew the commandment of the Almighty to him was to go forward—to set the example, and establish Celestial plural marriage. He knew that he had not only his own prejudices and pre-possessions to combat and to overcome, but those of the whole Christian world...; but God...had given the commandment." – 16

The Prophet Joseph certainly was not the only Church leader who had some serious reservations concerning plural marriage, and who even felt a repulsion and abhorrence for the very concept in the beginning. When Brigham Young was taught plural marriage, he said it was the first time in his life that he had "desired the grave." For days he longed for death rather than face the prospect of breaking the heart of his beloved Mary Ann. However, to his great relief and somewhat of a surprise, Mary Ann eventually gave her full consent to share her husband with other sister wives, and she remained faithful thereafter in her loving understanding for her beloved Brigham. He eventually married 55 women and had 59 children by 17 of his wives. It should be noted that these particular numbers might vary slightly as they come from various reference sources.

Then there was the case of Heber C. Kimbal, Brigham's former missionary companion and good friend, who also experienced a great deal of anguish in accepting the idea of polygamy. Joseph Smith taught Elder Heber the principle of plural marriage privately, and pointed out that it was the Lord Himself that was asking Heber to marry a woman who had previously been abandoned by a drunkard husband and left with a number of children to take care of and now she desperately needed Heber's care. After his initial resistance to the idea, Elder Kimball finally married his second wife, Sarah Noon. His agony over keeping the second marriage a secret from his wife Vilate was brought to a happy conclusion by a surprising event. Vilate revealed to Heber that she had actually received a vision from the Lord concerning eternal marriage and thus had it revealed to her how the Lord sanctioned plural marriage, and it was through that understanding that Vilate was able to accept Heber's second wife as a sister.

Heber eventually came around to seeing plural marriages as a religious obligation, a true act of charity, and as an unconditional commandment from God, and at some point, he certainly must have accepted the principle with some enthusiasm as he married forty-three wives. Although he was not entirely intimate with each one of them in the full marriage sense of the word, he did follow through with his obligation to all of them, seeing to their care, their health, and their welfare and he was truly committed to accepting the fact that they were each one his responsibility to take care of, being that they were his wives. Never the less, he did somehow find the time to live the principle of plural marriage more fully with seventeen of his wives by fathering sixty-five children. Again the actual numbers may vary according to the source. – 17

Joseph Smith felt a need to set the example for plural marriage as God had specifically commanded him to do so. There is an affidavit from his own private secretary, William Clayton, which testifies that Clayton personally was the one who wrote the revelation down just as it was given through the lips of the Prophet. Brother Clayton also verified Joseph's marriages to Eliza R. Snow, Sarah Ann Whitney, Helen Mary Kimball, Fanny Young, Lucy Walker, and Rhoda Richards. These faithful sisters were sealed to the Prophet Joseph Smith in Nauvoo, and they testified to it by their own lips during the lifetime of the Prophet, giving names and dates, and swearing under oath, that they were truly sealed to the Prophet Joseph Smith. The Prophet was reported to have had 33 wives ranging in age from a 20 year old to the 56-year-old Fanny Young, but again these numbers concerning the total number of wives can vary according to different reference sources. In many of the cases, the Prophet was only married symbolically to some of the women for their own personal need of fulfillment and comfort, and thus he was only sealed ceremoniously to these women for "Time and Eternity," without ever having actually lived with them in what would have been considered a normal marriage relationship. – 18

Some people are able to accept the idea of plural marriage by simply saying; "It doesn't need to be justified any more than any other commandment from the Lord does," and in the end, it is all simply a matter of being obedient to the Lord regardless of any personal feelings, judgments, or opinions. And they say if Joseph the Prophet said it came from God, then it came from God and it shouldn't be questioned.

Others just simply cannot accept the idea of a man having more than one wife at a time for any reason. They may even think it is immoral and they just can't justify it in their mind in any way, shape, or form, and just can't believe God would demand such a thing.

Another more practical thinking group can justify the plural wives principle as simply being a case of a practical and logical necessity at the time and view it as a matter of being a realistic and sensible solution to a pressing crucial problem in the Church. It seemed during that period of time, it was badly needed to take care of abandoned widowed women and their children. In making any fair judgment, one should keep in mind that during the early days of the Church there was no such thing as any kind of government welfare available, nor any kind of social security benefits for anybody anywhere in the United States, no unemployment benefits, and there wasn't even an official welfare program in the Church as of yet. Sadly there simply was no public, state, church, or government established financial subsistence aid for widowed women and their children to fall back on for their survival. In actuality, there was very little or nothing for them to survive on in a day-to-day existence after loosing their husband and the father of their children. And it became an especially grievous situation after those murderous days in Missouri when many of the Mormon men were killed. As it turned out, taking care of these women and their children by a polygamist husband became a great blessing to these particular needy sisters and their kids.

Even as controversial as it was, polygamy was certainly a godsend for these desperate women and their little ones. On another practical point, the charity and sympathy coming from their neighbors, the emergency help from the Church leaders, and the handouts from the local members could sustain them only for so long before all the good intentions, the temporary charity, and the generous donated goods would eventually run out and the sustaining succor from their benefactors would finally just phase out.

And then there were those few women among the Saints who seemed like they were to be destined to live life without a husband and family. Even though they sought after a better life style to sustain their very survival, as they looked around at the very limited and disappointing options, the future sometimes looked awfully bleak. When they looked at the unlikely possibility of finding a non-Mormon husband who wouldn't be biased against a Mormon woman, it soon became quite clear that polygamy was one of the few viable options available for them. It then became quite apparent that in all reality that it was probably only a polygamist husband that could fill the void in their quest to find a more dependable means of existence. A committed polygamist husband would provide permanent financial support and could become a real blessing to a single woman in order for her to have a dependable marriage commitment that would sustain her in her need for companionship and having a family.

Even though a great many people will always be skeptical of the true reasons that Plural Marriage came into practice, it was most definitely a blessing to a great many women in need of food, shelter, clothing, and a dependable means of acquiring their daily needs for them and their children. This was the reality of the uncertainty and crucial needs for single women and widows at this time in Church history.

Now as one takes a little closer look at the men's side of the polygamy issue; in actual fact, for these men who were practicing polygamy, it was a substantial financial burden not to mention having the added worry of providing for the housing, the health, and the safety of these large families all placed upon their minds. It required a strong faith, a charitable soul, and a religious dedication that not every man had it in him to do, and certainly not every man was simply willing to bare the burden of the responsibilities associated with polygamy. Although for the most part, these needy abandoned women were hard workers and they did try earnestly to do their share to support their polygamist families, the ultimate responsibility was still on the backs of these polygamist men. The brethren who took on these huge obligations and who accepted the additional load placed upon their shoulders, found that the extra burden placed upon their backs went far beyond any gratuitous superficial marital privileges received in compensation for their hard work, especially if the only reason for taking on the burden was to appease their baser masculine appetites.

The preponderance of people outside the Church and even most

Church members today are not completely aware of the fact that the biggest share by far of the early Saints never actually practiced polygamy and the great majority were never really involved in the implementation of the doctrine of plural marriage. In all truth, there was never more than a small percentage of the Church members at any one time that ever engaged in the practice of polygamy, and by some estimates, never more than 25% of the Mormon men ever had more than one wife. N. Eldon Tanner claimed that even less than that were involved saying; "Polygamy was officially outlawed more than seventy years ago and less than 3% of the Mormon community ever indulged in it." - 19

Even though the principal of plural wives was only practiced for a limited time and only practiced by a relatively small percentage of the Saints as they were commanded to do so by the Lord, and for only a period of about fifty years, the overall public perception of polygamy became quite vexing to the Saints and created bad publicity for the whole Church. The practice of plural marriage brought upon the general body of the Church an inordinate amount of strife and a significant amount of persecution from the outside world. The Saints were entirely run out of the state of Illinois, at least in part because of polygamy. Even after they settled in the peaceful mountains of Utah, the Saints were still not left alone to live in peace, and it was mostly due to the plural wives principle that they were practicing up until 1890.

It was polygamy that became the main impetus for the so-called Utah War, which brought Johnston's Army to the territory to put the Mormons under strict law and order, and caused President Buchanan to depose Brigham Young as territorial governor. The practice of Polygamy also brought about criminal charges and the actual imprisonment of many Church Leaders, as well as an on going threat of Church property being confiscated by the government. Lastly, it caused a long delay in Utah becoming a bona fide state of the Union.

Finally, on October 6th, 1890, President Wilford Woodruff of the Church of Jesus Christ of Latter Day Saints issued an official declaration, commonly called the "Manifesto," that the Church forbade any marriage forbidden by the law of the land. And thus it became official; the practice of polygamy was ended throughout the Church and finished as an accepted or sanctioned practice.

Naturally many of the Saints practicing polygamy in the Church at that time could not accept the idea of just up and abandoning their large families. So they hid out or headed for the Arizona border to hide from the law. Even though it might have been against the law, the evasive actions by polygamist husbands to preserve their families can certainly be sympathized with as these polygamist fathers just couldn't ignore the reality of having a responsibility for their wives and children. After all they were thoroughly committed to their plural marriage families and actually loved their wives and children; how could they just forsake them now. How could the U.S. government possibly expect them to virtually overnight, desert and disown their loved ones?

Six years later in 1896 after the Church abandoned polygamy, Utah finally and officially became a fully accepted and legitimate State of the United States of America bringing to the citizens of Utah a great sense of pride and considerable jubilation. Meanwhile, even though it has been abandoned for over one hundred and thirty years, the very touchy issue of Polygamy continues to be a most fascinating slice of Church history. And even today it continues for the most part, to remain a controversial and a hotly debatable issue among a great many Latter Day Saints and also amongst many outsiders even though it has been well over a century since it was ended.

Somewhere along the line in the early church, some members of the church erroneously got the idea that Celestial marriage and plural marriage were the same thing, even thinking incorrectly that a man had to have many wives to enter into the Celestial Kingdom. In 1933, the First Presidency of the Church of Jesus Christ of latter Day Saints corrected this thinking and declared officially that Celestial marriage and plural marriage were not synonymous, and it was not required for any man to have more than one wife for his exaltation.

The justification of polygamy as having been a practical and necessary need during those hard times in the early Church, as well as the criticism of its moral standards and its societal ethics is still a very much-debated subject even today. The final judgment of whether it truly was commanded by God for His divine purposes, should possibly be left to one better suited to judge its overall merit, its social ethics, and its value as a practical and sincere need in the Church at that time. Some good advice for judging the implementation of the "Plural Wives" principle, maybe that the judgment should be based on a much bigger picture than the rest of us can actually see or comprehend; and that would seem to leave the final judgment to the Lord Himself.

*   *   *

1. See History of the Church 4:587-588.

2. See Ora Haven Barlow, "The Israel Barlow Story and Mormon Mores" pp. 195-196

3. See William J. Critchlow, Jr., Conference Report, October 1966, p.30

4. See History of the Church, Vol.2, Ch.16, p.236.

5. See LeGrand Richards, A Marvelous Work and a Wonder, Ch.29, Footnotes, p.404. See also HC 2:235 & P. Pratt, Millennial Star, July 1842

6. See William J. Critchlow, Jr., Conference Report, October 1966, p.30

7. See History of the Church, 4:540 and Harold B. Lee, Conference Report, October 1955, p.55.

8. See "Women's Exponent 9" 1 September 1880 pp. 53-54

9. See Minute Book & Record of the Female Relief Society of Nauvoo, p.8

10a. See Kimball "Auto Biography", p.51. Also see (HC 4:602).

10b. See LDS Library- "Gifts of the Gospel"

11. See History of the Church 4:607 and "The Words of Joseph Smith" pp 119, 1 42. Also Teachings of the Prophet Joseph Smith, Section Four 1839-42 p.224

12. See Relief society Record 1880-1892, Eliza R. Snow.

13. See Association], July 17, 1880, reported in the Woman's Exponent 9 [Sept. 1, 1880]: See also Encyclopedia of Mormonism, Vol.3, SMITH, EMMA HALE

14. See Brigham Young Discourse March 9, 1845 & December 8, 1867. Also see Deseret Evening News April 18, 1868, See also "The First fifty Years of Relief Society" Church History Department

15a. See Encyclopedia of Mormonism, Vol.3, PLURAL MARRIAGE

15b. Daniel W. Bachman, See "A Study of the Mormon Practice of Plural Marriage Before the Death of Joseph Smith" pp. 74-75

15c. See Encyclopedia of Mormonism, Vol.3, PLURAL MARRIAGE,

16. See Encyclopedia of Mormonism, Vol.3, PLURAL MARRIAGE: Daniel W. Bachman, See also "A Study of the Mormon Practice of Plural Marriage Before the Death of Joseph Smith" pp. 74-75, Also The Biography and Family Record of Lorenzo Snow, pp. 69-70 (Salt Lake City, 1884), and Brigham Young Discourse,   Oct. 8, 1866

17. See Encyclopedia of Mormonism, Vol.2, KIMBALL, HEBER C.

18 See Joseph Fielding Smith, Gospel Doctrine, p.489 - p.490

19. See N. Eldon Tanner, Conference Report, April 1962, p.52

*   *   *

Chapter Eighteen

NO REDRESS, EVIL PLOTS, NEW DOCTRINE

*   *   *

Sometime in December of 1843, Joseph and the Twelve became absorbed in the possibility of obtaining legal reparations for the Saint's extensive losses after they were literally and violently ran out of the state of Missouri. So the Brethren made the decision to personally contact all five of the leading candidates running for President of the United States to see what each of them might be able do for the Saints. The nagging question that came to their minds was, "Would there be any of these politicians who would even attempt to help the Saints?"

Would the government in anyway help them get some kind of redress for the loss of their property, their lost homes, the many lost lives, or even the recognition from government officials that their Constitutional rights as U.S. citizens had been seriously trampled and infringed upon in Missouri? Most sadly, the answer to all these questions would be an emphatic no.

Senator John C. Calhoun was one of the very few candidates who even bothered to respond to their request, and even his response was very disappointing. The Senator declared that the Mormon's grievances did not fall under the jurisdiction of the Federal Government; the local law enforcement was over these things, and so there was just nothing that could be done for the Mormons by any Federal elected officials at this time. Unfortunately, they were to find out that this view was representative of the political and personal attitude of the great majority of the federal government officials and of the state authorities also, at least as far as any type of actual compensation for the Mormons went. The Prophet was so incensed by the dismissive reply that he wrote a scathing letter to Senator Calhoun regarding the Senator's responsibility and his sacred oath to protect the rights of the citizens, all the citizens of the United States under the Constitution. – 1

Soon after weighing the implications of these very discouraging responses coming from the unsympathetic politicians and presidential candidates, Joseph realized they would have to rethink their strategy and go another route. Realizing this kind of apathy would more than likely be the typical dismissive attitude across the board of government officials, as well as that of all the other unconcerned political candidates, Joseph Smith decided that he himself would have to run for President of the United States if the Saints were ever going to get any kind of satisfaction. With the help of W.W. Phelps and John M. Bernhisel, the Prophet Joseph Smith put together a viable political platform. The platform included the salient points of the basic purposes of the government, a reduction in the size of congress, prison reform, the abolishment of slavery, reform of military justice, fiscal responsibility with lower taxes, and a national bank with a standard medium of exchange. – 2a

Even though Joseph's well thought out and practical platform was accepted and endorsed by the Twelve Apostles, and then enthusiastically applauded when it was read aloud in public by W.W. Phelps in the assembly room of the Red Brick Store, very few voters would ever even know about Joseph Smith's very feasible and exceptionally well put together platform.

"On Friday, May 17, 1844, the State Convention met in the assembly room. It was moved, seconded, and carried by acclamation, that General Joseph Smith, of Illinois, be the choice of this convention for President of the United States. It was moved, seconded, and carried by acclamation, that Sidney Rigdon, Esq., of Pennsylvania, be the choice of the Convention for Vice-President of the United States." And so that was the way it was recorded in Church History. - 2b

Yet as good as Joseph's ideas were, as it all turned out, the greatest majority of American's citizens would never even hear about Joseph's candidacy for the President of the United States. As one Nauvoo citizen put it; "Of course there could be no hope seriously entertained that he would be elected; but, as explained by an editorial in the Times and Seasons, if the Saints could not succeed in electing their candidate, they would have the satisfaction of knowing that they had acted conscientiously; they had used their best judgment, under the circumstances, and if they had to throw (away) their votes, it was better to do so upon a worthy than upon an unworthy individual...," and as disappointing as it was, that was the feeling. This came from an Editorial Comment in the Times and Seasons.

It wasn't until 160 years later that a Mormon Church President would actually be in the White House, and it would be as he stood in recognition in front of the entire nation. At that time, Church's President Gordon B. Hinckley stood before U.S. President George W. Bush to be honored, recognized, and awarded the "Medal of Freedom" on June 23rd, 2004. It was the Nation's most prestigious civil award being presented by the President of the United States to the President of the "Mormon Church." It was President Bush that then praised President Hinckley with these words: President Gordon B. Hinckley is one who through "his tireless efforts has inspired millions" and has "spread the word of God" to "promote good will having strengthened his faith, community and our nation."

As a result of this national spotlight, President Hinckley received very positive and surprisingly upbeat publicity from all of the national news services and he was even shown on network television receiving this prestigious award. It resulted in a rare and unusually favorable image for the "Mormons" and most particularly for the President of the Church of Jesus Christ of Latter Day Saints. – 3

Meanwhile, back in Nauvoo at about the same time that Joseph Smith was thinking about presidential politics, there was a deep dark conspiracy a foot in a most sinister and menacing way taking its form in the shady back rooms of Nauvoo. Suspecting that there really was some subversive plotting against him and then having that information verified by others, Joseph informed the Nauvoo Police Force that there was a Judas dwelling among the Saints who had ominous intentions. This sent the dissidents, who thought they were operating in complete secrecy, into a near panic as they realized that their nefarious activities had been exposed. Consequently in their paranoid hateful state, they went on the offensive and tried to turn the tables on the Prophet with their own accusations by bringing the matter before the city council and blatantly accusing Joseph Smith of ordering the police to kill William Law and William Marks. They made it all sound quite heinous, dark, and downright loathsome even though Joseph had most certainly not done any such thing nor had he ever mentioned the killing of those men or any one else for that matter.

Seeing it all as nothing more than merely inflammatory gossip, the council subsequently dropped the whole matter. One month later due to that particular incident along with William Law's other dissident transgressions, President Law was dismissed as the second counselor in the First Presidency of the Church for his blatant disloyalty and his suspected association with other subversive groups plotting against the Prophet. It is believed that it was John C. Bennett, himself, that had had such a significant influence on William Law's sedition and his disloyalty to the Prophet.

Soon after that, William Law being well steeped in his vindictiveness and his own wrath, became a bitter enemy of the Prophet and he proceeded to draw other previously good men into his dark evil web with his devious conspiratorial scheming against Joseph. One of these other deluded and bamboozled souls included William's own brother, Wilson Law, as well as the devious Doctor Robert Foster and his brother, and in addition Charles Foster, and the Higbee brothers, Francis and Chauncey.

Looking beyond the darkness of these particularly hateful and better-known apostates, there were a few other misled brethren who had also been brainwashed, and they were now willing to participate in mischief, slander, and even doing serious harm to the Prophet. Found buried in annals of Church history are the names of these other dissidents who were not so well known, but just as underhanded and every bit as much of a turncoat. The names that would carry the disgrace and shame of turning on the Prophet Joseph Smith as apostate members of the Church and traitors are Leonard Soby of the high council, Austin Cowles, Joseph Jackson, Charles Ivin, and most surprisingly, even the Nauvoo Stake President, William Marks.

Joseph H. Jackson stood out among the others as one particular apostate that was constantly threatening to do harm to the Prophet Joseph Smith. This very menacing and hostile apostate said that "Joseph Smith was the damnedest rascal in the world, and he would be damned if he did not take vengeance on him, if he had to follow him to the Rocky Mountains."

Subsequently this vile apostate made many more such loathsome threats against the Prophet. A respected and reliable witness, a Mr. Heaton, told Joseph Smith that he had heard Jackson declare "that there should not be one of the Smith family alive in a few weeks." That ominous threat by Jackson never materialized under his own hand, even though it was only a few weeks later that Joseph and Hyrum Smith were martyred by the mob at Carthage.

It seems so ironic that nearly all of these apostates involved in this underhanded treachery against the Prophet were at one time considered to be upstanding members of the Church; one had even been a counselor to the Prophet, and another had been a Stake President. So it would seem that even people who might think of themselves as being good upstanding members of the Church are not necessarily immune to Satan's cunning influence. Having disloyal thoughts and being critical of Church leaders can be subtly insidious so that even today any Saints who discover themselves to be overly critical of their leaders can easily find themselves being swayed by the dark forces. And if they are not constantly vigilant and conscious of this negative attitude coming into their thinking, and if they do not turn to the greater spirit of a strong testimony that must be nourished regularly, they soon may find themselves treading upon the extremely destructive and dangerously thin ice of the seductive and sinister thoughts of apostasy.

As a side note, it should be noted that President Marks was actually reluctant to join with the dissidents in the evil conspiracy against the Prophet, and he did not feel quite right about the disloyalty and the whole situation. Never the less, he was eventually excommunicated after the Prophet's death for sympathizing with and for joining up with the James Strang cult that turned out to be a very bad idea for him and every one else who was ever involved in it.

The rest of that subversive pack of deceitful wolves dressed in sheep's clothing conspired with each other and covertly planned a malicious plot having the ultimate goal, "to bring down the Prophet and his church with him." Spurred on by their depraved thinking, they swore an oath to carry out and do serious bodily harm to the Prophet Joseph Smith and get rid of him once and for all.

In the spring of 1844, several of these dissidents in their diabolical scheming made hateful oaths and they proceeded to combine their forces to join with an anti-Mormon group in Warsaw to bring together an evil campaign and a malicious offensive against Joseph Smith. It was the nefarious Doctor Robert Foster of Nauvoo that initiated a most sinister dialogue with Thomas Sharp of the "Warsaw Signal" newspaper to carry out an evil plot against Joseph Smith. This newspaper was located in the nearby growing hotbed of anti-Mormonism in Warsaw just south of Nauvoo.

On the ninth of March 1844, the good Christian citizens of Warsaw, egged on by Thomas Sharp and Doctor Foster's false reports and unfounded accusations, held a religious fast to ask God Himself to completely destroy the Mormon Prophet and his church. After this unholy religious fast, they held a very rowdy and out of control rally that bordered on nothing less than a wild gathering of ranting extremists manifesting an intense hatred towards Joseph Smith and the Mormons.

In the early spring of that fateful year of 1844, the Prophet was having some premonitions regarding his own imminent death. In preparation for such a course of events and any future persecution upon the Church, he felt compelled to instruct the Twelve to organize an exploratory expedition to search out a new home for the Saints in the far away Rocky Mountains. Although there were some preliminary plans made to do this, the expedition was never undertaken due to the unusual and preoccupying circumstances that were about to take place.

At this time the Prophet's mind was very much pressed upon to make sure that the Twelve Apostles would be able to fully function without him being at the head of the Church. In March of 1844, he finally alleviated his uneasiness by putting the responsibility for the Church upon the shoulders of the Twelve as he solemnly and officially conferred upon the Quorum of the Twelve Apostles all of the ordinances, keys, and power of authority that he personally possessed.

Wilford Woodruff said it best when he reported that Joseph Smith "lived until every key, power and principle of the holy Priesthood was sealed on the Twelve and on President Young, as their President." Wilford then quoted the Prophet's saying; "I have lived until I have seen this burden, which has rested on my shoulders, rolled on to the shoulders of other men; …the keys of the kingdom are planted on the earth to be taken away no more for ever…. You have to round up your shoulders to bear up the kingdom. No matter what becomes of me." – 4

Meanwhile the nefarious and scheming conspirators were holding secret meetings and proceeded to eagerly plan just how they were best going to permanently dispose of Joseph Smith. Catching them all off guard one day, the Prophet publicly stunned the unsuspecting conspirators by announcing to a small group of the more faithful Saints that there was a conspiracy being planned against his very life. This ominous announcement obviously upset a great many of the faithful Saints, but most particularly his own brother, Hyrum, who became extremely concerned about his beloved little brother. As Joseph tried to quietly reassure Hyrum, he said somewhat humorously, "That bunch couldn't scare off an old setting hen."

Some historians think that it is possible that Joseph's chief source of information regarding the conspiracy plot may have come mainly from two young men known as Dennison Harris and Robert Scott. These two lads by happenstance had actually been invited by the apostates to join them in the conspiracy, and when the two boys later went to the Prophet and asked what they should do about it, he advised them to go ahead and attend the meeting, but told them that under no circumstances should they ever agree to any oaths or covenants.

At the secret meeting, all those present were required to swear an oath on the Bible and swear before holy angels that they would not rest until Joseph Smith was dead. The boys were shocked at this, felt on edge, and even in danger. This shocking fiendish oath went far beyond most people's comprehension to even conceive of such a satanic goal and purpose.

However, these apostates, formerly good members of the Church, had now turned traitorous, and were so hateful, so evil, so brainwashed, and so bloodthirsty, that they did actually plot to murder a Prophet of God. The two boys refused to make the oath and thus had their very own safety placed in jeopardy as they barely escaped with their lives. When they reported to Joseph what had happened, he made them swear to keep this information a secret for at least twenty years until all the conspirators were gone and the boys were safe from retaliation. – 5

When the conspirators finally came to the full realization that the Prophet was very well aware of their subversion and was wise to their evil plotting, they then became quite brazen and began to openly show publicly their own hateful opposition to the Prophet. They now were aware that he had solid evidence regarding their seditious agenda, and so they began to publicly slander him and they proceeded to openly recruit other members of the Church to join with them in their unholy alliances. They actually formed a committee to go door to door to different homes in Nauvoo in a campaign to try to persuade other Church members to join them. In their attempt to make mischief for the Prophet, they went about spreading vicious rumors about him, including a rumor that Emma was going to leave Joseph because of his stubborn pursuit of those other so-called spiritual wives. Their contemptible lies had no boundaries.

Finally things came to a head after the April conference of 1844. About a week later, there was enough evidence gathered against three of the conspirators to have them unanimously and officially excommunicated from the Church. The three fallen and dishonored brethren were the two Law brothers, Wilson Law and William Law, along with William's wife Jane Law, and the third was the notorious Doctor Robert D. Foster. About a week later, there were three more of the dissidents who also met with a measure of justice. Robert and Charles Foster, and Chauncey Higbee had to be forcefully disarmed by the police and then arrested after they had the audacity to violently threaten to kill the Prophet with a loaded gun right inside the Mayor's office.

All of these unsettling events started to create an undue anxiety in the city and the tension level in Nauvoo rose to an almost a palpable intensity creating a great uneasiness among the citizens of Nauvoo. The apostates continued with their subversive activities and carried it just one step farther when they met at Wilson Law's home one Sunday evening in an attempt to form their own church. As it turned out, William Law, who had been the former second counselor to the Prophet Joseph Smith, and now a known adulterer, was chosen as the new president of this unholy apostate church. It almost seemed as though there was some kind of an unwritten rule to be a leader in this ill-conceived church; that you must be a hypocritical egregious sinner to qualify for a position. It was like some kind of a badge of honor. Wilson Law, William's brother, and his friend Austin Cowles became counselors in this dubious and ill-fated organization. Ironically, and almost humorously considering their very shady credentials, the nefarious Doctor Foster and the roguish Francis Higbee, both very well known for their many questionable deeds, were then nominated to be apostles in the new church of the apostates. With these types of odious men leading the ill-fated church, how could they ever possibly accomplish anything of "Good Report," beyond just for show or just pretending to worship God in their shallow sanctimonious way? They certainly could not have been engaging themselves in any kind of a genuine religious worship nor could they have possibly had any serious devoutness to any real theological doctrine given their focus on revenge and murder.

This newly established church of the dissidents eventually became like a noxious pervasive weed in the community and they vigorously tried to draw off and subvert the thinking of many of the Saints in Nauvoo. And they proceeded in earnest to persuade the citizens of Nauvoo to join in their apostasy against the Church. This church of the apostates was most certainly a tainted influence on the community and thus became a serious nuisance in Nauvoo. However, as it all turned out, it in of itself was not the most threatening development to the overall peace in the city. That honor would go to the establishment of the apostate's opposition newspaper, which would soon come to Nauvoo and create nothing less than civil chaos in the city. – 6

Even though these misguided and evil-intentioned apostates were absolutely insisting that Joseph Smith was a fallen prophet, the main body of the Saints was experiencing a reaffirmation of their faith in the Prophet Joseph Smith as they sat and listened to him in the 1844 April Conference. During the second day of the conference, Joseph gave a sermon on God and mankind's destiny that would not only become one of the more controversial teachings of the Prophet, but would also establish a whole new precept in the Church. It became known as the famously profound "King Follett Discourse."

King Follett was not really a king or any kind of royalty, but just an ordinary Elder of the Church and also a Nauvoo Constable whose first name happened to be King. He had recently been accidentally killed in his own water well by some falling rock. Joseph had missed the funeral due to an illness, but later decided to pay a tribute to Brother Follett as he spoke in this conference.

On that day he started out on the subject of death and man's pattern of parentage, but soon transcended into the subject of the character of God and man's destiny to follow in God's footsteps being His literal spirit children. The most poignant and controversial point of the long discourse was the doctrine that God is an exalted man and as His children; man himself may someday become a God also.

Joseph declared; "We may now be young in our progression, juvenile, even infantile, compared with Him. Nevertheless, in the eternities to come, if we are worthy, we may be like unto Him, enter His presence…. and receive a fullness." The Prophet further elaborated by saying; "God himself was once as we are now, and is an exalted man, and sits enthroned in yonder heavens!"

Not only was the King Follett Discourse somewhat astonishing to the majority of the Saints in the Church who heard it for the first time, but it also would become an extremely controversial teaching after it was heard among the gentiles in the Christian world. However, the Prophet backed his theology with some references found in Matthew, Romans, Revelation, John, and D&C 132. The bottom line from the Prophet was that he was saying that just as the son of a King can someday follow in his father's footsteps and become a King also, so it is that man himself can become an heir to the King of Heaven, and thus follow in the steps of his Father in Heaven and become a God also. Joseph used the following scriptural references to support his position that men are the heirs of God.

Romans 8:16 "The Spirit itself beareth witness with our spirit, that we are the children of God:"

8:17 "And if children, then heirs; heirs of God, and joint-heirs with

Christ; if so be that we suffer with [him], that we may be also glorified together."

D&C 132:20 says: "Then shall they be gods, because they have no end; therefore shall they be from everlasting to everlasting, because they continue; then shall they be above all, because all things are subject unto them. Then shall they be gods, because they have all power, and the angels are subject unto them."

*   *   *

There were back then in the 1800's and still are today some very strong critics of this doctrine of man being able to become a God. Throughout the Christian world they simply find Joseph Smith's so-called "God Maker" belief to be nothing short of pure heresy. Never the less, this doctrine that states that God is an Exalted Man and that man himself can follow in His footsteps and become a God also, has become accepted doctrine in the Church of Jesus Christ of Latter Day Saints. It was President Lorenzo Snow that made the "man's succession to God" quote a renowned saying in the Church; "As man now is, God once was; as God now is, man may be."

Later, the Prophet Spencer W. Kimball would also attest to the same principle by saying, "Man can become like God. In each of us is the potentiality to become a god -- pure, holy, influential, true and independent of all these earth forces." – 7

This particular doctrine of man having the potential of becoming a god was certainly not the only teaching of the Prophet Joseph Smith that set the Christian world on its ear and raised their unyielding difference of opinion. Another of his teachings, which also upset many Christians, was his teaching concerning a "plurality of Gods." Even though there is actually good solid evidence in their own Bibles to support this reasoning and conclusion, they refused to accept it. Yet, as it is found in the understanding of Genesis in the Holy Bible, a plurality of gods is clearly implied in Genesis chapter 1, verse 26, where it says, "And God said, let us make man in our image, after our likeness,…" And then again it seems very clear in Genesis 3:22, where it says; "And the Lord God said, Behold, the man is become as one of us, to know good and evil." So just whom are those pronouns "Us" and "Our" in those particular verses actually referring to, if not the other Gods in the Godhead?

Joseph Smith continued to upset much of the traditional Christian world even further when he declared that in all reality the Father and the Son both have separate bodies, and each has His own body of "flesh and bones as tangible as man's." This controversial idea of both the Father and the Son having bodies of flesh and bones seems to have been every bit as theologically upsetting to the rank and file traditional Christians as Joseph's other two very controversial ideas, that is his "God Maker" theology and "the plurality of Gods." Most certainly, none of these disputed theological ideas endeared the Prophet Joseph Smith to the established Christian world and thus there would soon come to be an even a greater gulf between the "Mormons" and the rest of the traditional Christian world. – 8

This disagreement in theology with the rest of the traditional Christian world is not necessarily a circumstance that must be remedied right away. It is not an unexpected state of affairs in the world. Its resolution will come in the Lord's own good time. "For thou art an holy people unto the lord thy God, and the Lord hath chosen thee to be a peculiar people unto himself, above all the nations that are upon the earth." - Deut. 14:2

$$* \quad * \quad *$$

1. See History of the Church 6:155-60.

2a. See "Restoration" pp. 269-270.

2b. See HC Vol 6, Ch. 18 p 390.

3. See "LDS Church News", Lee Davidson "Medal of Freedom" June 26, 2004

4. See Journal of Discourses 13:164, and Encyclopedia of Mormonism, Vol.3, QUORUM OF THE TWELVE APOSTLES.

5. See Restoration" pp. 590-591.

6. See History of the Church, Vol.6, Ch.16, p.348-349, and p.152. Also Joseph Fielding Smith Jr., Doctrines of Salvation, Vol.1, p.256

7. See Conference Report 1984, p 83. Also the History of the Church 6:302-17. See also "Teachings of the Prophet Joseph Smith" - section 6, and The Teachings of Spencer W. Kimball - Chapter 2 - "The Plan of Salvation"

8. See D&C 132:20 and D&C 130:22 and also Encyclopedia of Mormonism, Vol.1, DOCTRINE

*   *   *

Chapter Nineteen

A CITY ON THE EDGE

*　　*　　*

The full extent of the extremely tense atmosphere that existed in Nauvoo of 1844 cannot be overstated. Eventually as the knowledge of the private teachings concerning plural marriage leaked out publicly into the community of Nauvoo, it was inevitable that it would also leak outside the city into the non-Mormon Gentile communities. It was then only a matter of time before there arose a profusion of extreme criticisms, distorted interpretations, unfounded conjecture, and the spreading of vile rumors concerning the shameless immoral behavior of the Mormons. The malicious gossip found in this tense atmosphere of derogatory reports and distorted opinions proliferated throughout the state of Illinois stirring up a considerable amount of hostility, disgust, and even hatred towards Joseph Smith and the "Mormons."

Sadly, it wasn't all just outsiders that this very harsh condemnation was coming from; many of the Saints themselves were also very troubled and unduly disturbed by the gossip surrounding the plural wives rumors. Even as the Prophet tried to faithfully pursue his duties as the head of the Church, there regrettably arose a series of unwarranted condemnations and words of extreme criticism against him coming from many of the Saints right within the Church. The continuing negative rhetoric spewed out by William Law and the other subversive apostates was very persuasive and was very effective in swaying additional malcontents whose faith was already in a state of wavering. These wrongly opinionated critics under their false and unjust perceptions brought about even more hatred and serious condemnation of the Prophet. Elder Law who had been rightfully kicked out of the Church now found himself severely dishonored and thus proceeded to look for revenge. Thus by way of his own embitterment, he put together a group of like-minded men who also wished to do harm to the Prophet. That action produced a faction of many dissidents who would now become bent upon the final undoing and the hoped for disgraced ruin of the Prophet Joseph Smith.

Meanwhile, outside the Nauvoo community and throughout most of the non-Mormon settlements, there was a growing outrage over what they considered as the unacceptable and immoral behavior found among the Mormons and their practice of polygamy. This gave birth to a great many denigrating rumors that only served to further intensify the adverse atmosphere of the threatening criticism that was being spewed out by a handful of hateful anti-Mormon mobs. All this very sinister and menacing talk along with the anti-Mormon newspaper's rhetoric only added to the local political group's becoming increasingly hostile. This moral outrage not only negatively influenced the opinions of the local authorities, but also grossly misinformed other government officials who were now becoming highly critical of the Mormons in general. These officials would become very antagonistic toward the Saints due to what they considered to be the very appalling and evil practice of plural wives. And so it all began to escalate to the point that the greatest part of these many different hostile groups were becoming absolutely determined to see Joseph Smith either in jail or see him dead.

In the meantime back in Missouri, the state authorities tried three different times to extradite Joseph from Illinois and bring him back to Missouri, which was causing him considerable worry as to the possibility of being hauled off to Missouri to be hung or stood in front of a firing squad. All this unnecessary harassment brought to the Prophet's very front door the nuisance of having to deal with sheriffs, lawyers, biased judges, and a continuing array of ongoing legal worries for the Prophet. And then due to his personal loss of property as a result of the on going persecution, he was frequently unable to pay his debts and consequently had many creditors harassing him in addition to his various other trials. All of these unabating distractions became more than just an annoyance and thus these diversions often kept him from carrying out his Church duties more fully as he would have liked to have done. It must have seemed like to Joseph the relentless arrows of Satan were all coming at him at once and from every conceivable direction.

As if there weren't already enough things for the Prophet to worry about, many of the political leaders in Illinois showed not only flagrant prejudice against the Prophet himself, but they frequently showed an undisguised adverse bias towards the entire Latter-day Saints religion as they dealt with the Saints in civil disputes and local political matters. The majority of these very negative stories about the Mormons had been over-dramatized and highly tainted by phony political reports as well as derogatory, exaggerated, newspaper articles, which were routinely blatantly false and always very disparaging. – 1

During the very fateful month of June of 1844, there came about a particular chain of events that would be the beginning of the end for the Prophet Joseph Smith. It all started with a group of the Church's apostates coming together to collude with Thomas C. Sharp, the editor of the "Warsaw Signal" paper, and they had just one thing in mind, the express purpose to shame and defame Joseph Smith. Their devious plan was to vilify the Prophet to the citizens of the city of Nauvoo itself through the use of an opposition newspaper printed right in the city of Nauvoo. Thus they spewed out many venomous lies in their anti-Mormon publication, and it seemed to be deliberately placed most impudently right under Joseph's own nose. These conspirators intentionally attempted to stir up as much unrest as they could possibly instigate throughout the community of the Nauvoo Saints. There was no question about it; the local publishing of the "Nauvoo Expositor" was specifically and chiefly designed to attack the Church and its leaders, to make ridiculous charges against the Prophet

Joseph Smith, and to stir up as much dissension as possible within the city and the Church itself. This was truly their dedicated and diabolical aim and purpose.

When the first and only edition of the "Nauvoo Expositor" was published on June 7th 1844, it was represented as being edited by Sylvester Emmons, a former Judge in Nauvoo. In reality, the paper was funded, sponsored, and legally owned as the property of William Law, Wilson Law, Charles Ivins, Francis M. Higbee, Chauncey L. Higbee, Robert D. Foster, and Charles A. Foster, all of whom were using Judge Emmons as a front for their devious printed lies. There was certainly no doubt that every last one of them was a sworn enemy of the Prophet Joseph Smith and they were determined to use their news paper as a public weapon against him.

The "Nauvoo Expositor" not only blatantly disparaged Joseph Smith in several questionable articles with its false accusations, but even more exasperating, they falsely advertised their notorious lies as being backed up by a variety of dubious and anonymous eyewitness testimonies. The derogatory news articles even sunk so low as to cite stories stating that Old Joe Smith was often engaged in unseemly activities with the female members of his church. Escalating their lies even further, they accused Joseph Smith of soliciting females from foreign countries with the lure of his religion and then enticing them to journey to America to the city of Nauvoo for his dubious purposes. There in Nauvoo, in a secret place down by the river, the paper insinuated that he supposedly met with the foreign women to ostensibly give them a blessing, and then proceeded to pursue them through his very persuasive talents to become his spiritual wives under threat of damnation if they didn't submit to him. Of course, all these lies were supposedly backed up with the testimonies of eyewitnesses, but in actuality it was with nothing more than unsubstantiated accusations by dubious and always anonymous witnesses. The false stories were only a small part of the very dishonest and deplorable apostate agenda to destroy the Prophet Joseph Smith.

The odious Francis Higbee, a close associate of the editor Judge Emmons, deemed himself as one of the proprietors of the Expositor newspaper and so as an owner, he attempted to sue Joseph Smith for $5,000 in his failed libel suit. As a matter of routine, Francis Higbee often made threats against the Prophet and at one point; he very offensively described Joseph Smith as being "the biggest villain that goes unhung." – 2

The apostates made no bones about what they wanted. The Expositor decreed the following intents and purpose: "THE UNCONDITIONAL REPEAL OF THE NAUVOO CITY CHARTER, to restrain and correct the abuses of the UNIT POWER, to ward off the iron rod which is held over the devoted heads of the citizens of Nauvoo and the surrounding country, to advocate unmitigated DISOBEDIENCE TO POLITICAL REVELATIONS, and to censure and decry gross moral imperfections wherever found, either in the plebeian, patrician or the SELF-CONSTITUTED MONARCH....." - 3

Their reference to the "SELF-CONSTITUTED MONARCH" was a direct accusation and indictment of the Prophet Joseph Smith accusing him of being a religious dictator. The meaning was clear; they considered Joseph Smith to be a lecherous tyrant despot who ruled with absolute control over his people and often mixed state and religion for his own diabolical purposes.

As a result of the Expositor's incendiary and very seditious publications, the mood of the entire city of Nauvoo was thrown into a frenzy of unsettling chaotic rumors, much apprehensiveness, and worst of all, the increasingly growing doubts concerning the Prophet's true character. Along with this elevated state of wide spread uneasiness, it was bringing upon the entire community an unwanted air of disunity and a great deal of discord. All this discord of course, was brought on by the "Nauvoo Expositor's" anti-Church articles and their vile accusations against the city council, not to mention their seditious and unrelenting vendetta against Joseph Smith.

Along with these inflammatory accusations against the Prophet himself, the Expositor's first issue also viciously attacked the Nauvoo city council. Consequently, the city council felt that they had a civic duty to address the very troubling situation. And so they met together over a two-day period to discuss the troublesome matter as they debated just what to do about the Expositor's inflammatory publication and the civil unrest it was causing in their city. At the conclusion of their lengthy discussions, they finally made their controversial decision and declared that their final judgment was and rightfully should be, to order the elimination of the

Expositor newspaper; and the order did clearly state that specific intention as recorded in the following statement:

"Resolved, by the City Council of the city of Nauvoo, that the printing-office from whence issues the Nauvoo Expositor is a public nuisance and also all of said Nauvoo Expositors printed material which may be or exist in said establishment; and the Mayor is instructed to cause said printing establishment and papers to be removed without delay, in such manner as he shall direct." - 4

Consequently, as the Mayor of Nauvoo, Joseph Smith was obligated to follow the directive of the city council and he dutifully followed their instructions and thus gave the following order to the city Marshal, John P. Greene: "You are here commanded to destroy the printing press from whence issues the Nauvoo Expositor, and pi or scatter the type of said printing establishment in the street, and burn all the Expositors and libelous handbills found in said establishment; and if resistance be offered to your execution of this order by the owners or others, demolish the house; and if anyone threatens you or the Mayor or the officers of the city, arrest those who threaten you, and fail not to execute this order without delay, and make due return hereon." - 5

It was just a few hours later when the city Marshal returned with his own message to Mayor Joseph Smith saying very succinctly that the Mayor's order had been fully carried out on the 10th day of June 1844 at about 8:00 p.m. It was signed John P. Greene, City Marshal. And so the Expositor office was completely destroyed, its letterpress type scattered, and its libelous handbills burned.

If Joseph Smith and the city council had known the extent of the clamor, the furor, and the outcry that would soon come from them ordering the destruction of the Expositor newspaper, they may have tried a little harder to come up with a different solution in order to shut down the yellow journalism of the outrageous paper. At the time they had no idea how loud the outcry would be, or how far it would go, or how wide it would spread.

One of the most irritating and hypocritical things about the "Nauvoo Expositor" was that underneath the title of the newspaper, and brazenly printed on the masthead, their motto was expressed as "The Truth, The Whole Truth, and Nothing but The Truth." However, nothing could have been more laughable or insulting to the intelligence of the exasperated Saints in Nauvoo!

As the news became widespread through out the state concerning the destruction of the "Nauvoo Expositor" newspaper, and the publicized fact that it was reported to have been destroyed through the cooperation of the Nauvoo city council, their complicit city mayor, and their dutiful city Marshal, there arose a great indignation throughout the state. Crazy rumors flew around everywhere spreading like wildfire, and the opposition wasted no time coming up with wildly speculated opinions on the different possible acts of retaliation that must surely be meted out to the city officials in Nauvoo.

There was even talk of a large mob coming out of Carthage that was preparing to attack and ravage the city of Nauvoo itself, and in addition, there was also a rumor that more than 1500 Missourians were coming across the river to join with the Warsaw anti-Mormon war party. As it turned out, it was all just inflated gossip and rumors, and there never was any menacing and destructive rabble from Missouri that ever showed up in Nauvoo. If the Missourian rabble really had shown up, the 5,000 men of the Nauvoo legion could have easily changed their vengeful minds and sent them all back to Missouri with their tails between their legs.

Meanwhile, the very sinister and disloyal Law brothers, the scheming Higbees, and that devious Foster brother duo were all determined to retaliate for their smashed up news paper office. In planning their revenge, they were determined to smash up one of the Nauvoo's most prominent printing presses, the "Times and Seasons," in order to exact justice for the destruction of their Expositor's press office. And they also fully intended to completely destroy the offices of the local paper called "The Nauvoo Neighbor." As a precaution, Joseph ordered the city police to post guards at these two printing offices as well as at most of the city's other businesses.

Just twenty miles away from the city of Nauvoo, Thomas Sharp of the "Warsaw Signal" was whipping everyone within earshot into a vengeful frenzy in order to "get old Joe Smith." In his bitter opinion "Old Joe" had supposedly perpetrated a complete obliteration of the Constitutional rights awarded to the "Freedom of the Press." Sharp was actually calling for in his very own newspaper some serious acts of violence aimed at the Prophet. He made a powerful summon for all the citizens of Western Illinois to rise up and exterminate Joseph Smith as well as all of his church leaders, and to drive the Mormon people completely out of the entire state of Illinois. This was far beyond the pale of just criticizing and having a civilized disagreement. Thomas Sharp had now just completely lost any kind of sensible reasoning or logical thinking that he may have ever had, and thus had let hate take over his very soul.

In this tense atmosphere of hysteria resulting in a completely ridiculous frenzy of craziness and demagoguery, Joseph put the Nauvoo Legion on alert to guard the roads into Nauvoo and deter any mischief-makers, and he also ordered the local police out to especially protect the city's property from any dissident vandalism. Ironically, this seemingly perfectly rational and reasonable action of calling out the Nauvoo Legion to bring order to the city and keep the peace in the community was actually used later as a legal indictment against Joseph Smith. In the State's criminal case against Joseph, they accused him of "Treason" against the State of Illinois and its troops by calling out his Nauvoo Legion to oppose the State Militia. Of course, he had had no intentions of the Legion's troops confronting the State Militia or any other such thing. In all reality, he had only deployed the Legion troops to merely keep the peace in the city of Nauvoo.

With the city on the edge of pandemonium, on June 18th 1844, Joseph wisely decided to put the city of Nauvoo under martial law. He then proceeded to address the 5,000 men of the Nauvoo Legion in hopes that peace and order in their city could somehow be maintained. In his address, he first outlined the threat to their city and the dangerous unrest that existed all about them. Then he made a personal statement saying; if the enemy would actually accept him personally as a sacrificial lamb and deem his own surrender to be some kind of justice and sufficient retribution for their grievances, and in return, they would promise to leave the city of Nauvoo alone and let the rest of the Church members live in peace, he would gladly submit to the authorities and sacrifice himself without hesitation.

However, as he frankly and honestly pointed out, any act of a submission and surrender by him in return for some kind of a reciprocal favor was not a plausible reality. They would most certainly never treat him with any kind of fairness or render to him any kind of a good faith act. He pointedly declared that the enemies of the Church are the "adversary of all righteousness" and they are moved upon by an evil spirit, and they will never rest until every man and woman of the Mormon Church is destroyed or removed from the state.

He also firmly stated and emphasized that in true fact the members of the Church have not violated any laws of the state or of their country in any way. They therefore should by all legal and moral standards be fully protected by their rightful and legally recognized civil rights as clearly stated under the Constitution of the United States, which the State of Illinois should be obligated to uphold. Upon hearing this penetrating and perceptive statement from the Prophet Joseph Smith, there was loud applause, lots of foot stomping, and even some noisy leg slapping by the legion troops. As the applause quieted down, Joseph asked if the Nauvoo Legion would stand by him to the death, and thousands of voices yelled the heartening reply, "Aye!" Sadly as things turned out, this was not only his last address to the Nauvoo Legion Troops, but it would also be the last and final public words of the Prophet Joseph Smith to any gathering of the Saints while he was still on this earth and in his mortal state. - 6

*   *   *

1. See Encyclopedia of Mormonism, Vol.3, SMITH, JOSEPH

2. See History of the Church, Vol.7, Ch.6, p. 67 – also Encyclopedia of Mormonism, Vol.3, NAUVOO EXPOSITOR

3. See History of the Church, Vol.6, Ch.21, p.443-4

4. See History of the Church, Vol.6, Ch.21, p. 448

5. See History of the Church, Vol.6, Ch.21, pp. 432-448.

6. See History of the Church 6:497-500.

*   *   *

Chapter Twenty

THE FINAL DAYS
OF A PROPHET

*　　*　　*

After hearing all about the news of the trouble and great civil unrest occurring in Hancock County in the Mormon city of Nauvoo, Governor Thomas Ford sitting quietly in his office in Springfield determined that this matter was going to require his personal attention. Selecting the community of Carthage for his base of operations, which was about twenty miles outside of Nauvoo, the Governor decided to use the small town as the site from which to monitor the situation. Meanwhile, when Joseph heard about the Governor's request to hear the Mormon's version of the conflict, the Prophet sent the apostle John Taylor and Dr. John Bernhisel with a letter and some documents to Carthage to plead their case before the Governor.

The pair left late at night for Carthage and after reaching their hotel that night, a couple of devious Church apostates tried to bamboozle them in order to keep them from talking to the Governor. Chauncey Higbee was accompanied by the vicious bully Joseph H. Jackson, and they attempted to separate the two Mormon emissaries with a ruse about bailing out a fellow Mormon from jail. The two brethren did not fall for it, but laid awake most of the night in the hotel with their pistols at the ready.

At the meeting with the Governor the next morning, the two brethren found to their dismay that there were already present in the room about twenty apostates and other Mormon haters in the company of his Honor. Frank Worrell, an officer of the very militant Carthage Greys made himself conspicuous and apparent, and so with his bellicose attitude and interruptive utterances, he attempted to thwart the Mormon presentation and sway the Governor.

There was no doubt that all the nonessential bit players in the room were bitter enemies of the Prophet. The belligerent rowdy crowd would not let John Taylor get two words in edge wise without interruption. Finally the frustrated Governor declared that the only way to satisfy all parties was to require Joseph Smith to come to Carthage to answer to the charges of rioting and destroying the free press of a public newspaper.

However, Brother John Taylor made it known to the Governor that he had some serious concerns regarding the Prophet Joseph's personal safety in coming to Carthage. Governor Ford's response seemed to be to Brother Taylor very unsatisfactory in addressing those concerns. Never the less, the Governor then made a pretentious pledge of what would soon prove to be no more than a lot of hot air, just so many empty words.

"Mr. Smith and those who come with him shall be protected. I guarantee your perfect safety," pontificated the Governor. After the unproductive and very disappointing meeting, the Governor, for whatever reason, deliberately delayed the brethren's departure to Nauvoo by several hours by keeping them waiting for the official letter to be delivered to the Prophet. – 1

When the Mormon emissaries returned to Nauvoo to report to Joseph the bad news, the other brethren were stunned by the lack of compassion coming from Governor Ford concerning Joseph's safety and their own. Hyrum commented, "Just as sure as we fall into their hands we are dead men." Joseph then asked his older brother the perplexing question, "Yes; what shall we do, brother Hyrum?" After some deep thought by both

Hyrum and Joseph, suddenly the Prophet brightened up and answered his own question. "We will cross the river tonight, and go away to the West."

At this time, he also requested that his friends should put his and Hyrum's families on the "Maid of Iowa" steamer and send them down the Mississippi to Cairo to the confluence with the Ohio River and then up the Ohio River to Cincinnati and to Portsmouth. There, their wives would be able to wait in safety for any word from their husbands. However, due to unfortunate and unforeseen circumstances, all these plans would soon go by the wayside. – 2

Joseph and Hyrum humbly and tearfully said their good-byes to their families at the Mansion house and at Hyrum's home. They reasonably assumed that it would be some time before they would ever see their families again. Late that night, and in the early morning of June 23rd 1844, the Prophet, his brother Hyrum, Brother Willard Richards, and Porter Rockwell all crossed the Mississippi River in a leaky rowboat, which required the unwanted water to be bailed out with their boots.

On the other side they were welcomed and provided board and room at a member's house in Montrose Iowa. Meanwhile, the ever-faithful Porter Rockwell went back across the river to get some horses and other supplies while the refugees awaited his return. While Porter was in Nauvoo getting the horses, he learned that the Governor had sent a posse of law enforcement officers to arrest Joseph Smith. When the posse found their intended captive had flown the coop, they were very angry and attempted to intimidate the local population into thinking government troops would now come and put the city of Nauvoo under siege.

When Porter Rockwell returned from across the river to Montrose to meet up with his waiting friends, he was accompanied by a delegation of Church brethren from Nauvoo who attempted to convince the Prophet to return to the city. They grumbled and whined that if he didn't, their property would be destroyed and they would be left without house or home. In their highly emotional state, Reynolds Cahoon, Lorenzo D. Wasson, and Hiram Kimball went on to actually accuse the Prophet Joseph of cowardice in leaving his people behind, unprotected, and at the mercy of the mobs and state militias.

It was at this point that they produced a note from Emma. It is not known exactly what the words of Emma's note said, but her presumed plea to come back was enough to finally convince the Prophet to return and face the almost certain possibility of long term incarceration or worse, conceivably even execution. Joseph was visibly shaken by the accusations of cowardice from the brethren and by Emma's plea, and he showed that he was somewhat emotionally unstrung when he replied: "If my life is of no value to my friends, it is of none to myself."

He then turned to Hyrum saying; "Brother Hyrum, you are the oldest, what shall we do?" Hyrum said, "Let us go back and give ourselves up, and see the thing out." At this point, Joseph turned to brother Cahoon and asked him to go ahead and request that Captain Daniel C. Davis should have a boat ready at half-past five to cross the river for their return to Nauvoo, and so it was that the fateful decision was made. - 3

Before crossing back across the river to give themselves up, Joseph and Hyrum wrote a letter to be delivered to the Governor saying that they were on their way and ready to come in peaceably. When they arrived in Nauvoo, Joseph sent Theodore Turley and Jedediah Grant to personally deliver it to the Governor waiting in Carthage. The Governor responded with a return message demanding that Joseph show himself in Carthage by ten a.m. the next day, and without any escort or there would be serious consequences.

As they came back across the river, there were more painful farewells to their families in Nauvoo as the two Smith brothers prepared to ride to Carthage for their official surrender. On their way out of the city as they rode past the Temple, Joseph paused, looked upon it with much admiration, and then looked upon the city itself, and remarked, "This is the loveliest place and the best people under the heavens; little do they know the trials that await them." – 4

"When Joseph went to Carthage to deliver himself up to the pretended requirements of the law, it was two or three days prior to his assassination," but he knowingly made a statement that proved to be very prophetic: "I am going like a lamb to the slaughter; but I am calm as a summer's morning; I have a conscience void of offense towards God, and towards all men. I SHALL DIE INNOCENT, AND IT SHALL YET BE SAID OF ME--HE WAS MURDERED IN COLD BLOOD." Once again the Prophet showed that he was truly a prophet and seer, and that he was fully aware of the fate that awaited him in Carthage. - See D&C 135:4

Even though he was a Prophet of God and fully believed God was in control of all things, he was still a mortal man who could feel the very human pangs of fear, disappointment, and genuine discouragement at times. His very human feelings are revealed in the following off hand remark: "Oh! I am so tired, so tired that I often feel to long for my day of rest. For what has there been in this life but tribulation for me? From a boy I have been persecuted by my enemies, and now even my friends are beginning to join with them, to hate and persecute me! Why should I not wish for my time of rest?" - 5

About four miles out of Carthage, a Captain Dunn of the Augusta Union Dragoons and his troops, having been sent by the Governor, met up with Joseph Smith's party on the road. Although Captain Dunn's troops were somewhat skittish knowing that Old Joe Smith had a full complement of 5,000 Legion troops at his beck and command, Joseph assured Captain Dunn and his men that they had nothing to fear. Joseph then reaffirmed that he and his friends were only on their way to submit themselves peacefully to the Captain's custody as ordered by the Governor. Captain Dunn, who was an honorable man and a gentleman, then declared somewhat reluctantly that he had an additional order from the Governor and he suggested that they retire to a nearby farmhouse to discuss it.

Although the Captain was polite, the new unconditional order was not well received by the Mormon prisoners. The new additional request from the Governor asked for the Nauvoo Legion to turn in all the weapons that they had in their possession that had previously been supplied by a grant from the state of Illinois, and do so immediately. Even as Joseph's companions audibly opposed the new directive, Joseph declared to Captain Dunn that he himself would return to Nauvoo with the Captain to see that the Nauvoo Legion did not oppose the troops and that the order would be carried out peaceably. – 6

Due to the additional time that it took to make the trip back to Nauvoo for the surrender of the Legion's weapons, Joseph's own surrender in Carthage was necessarily delayed. So the long column of troops escorting Joseph's party did not arrive in Carthage until late that night. Unexpectedly, being as late as it was, there was a raucous crowd of Mormon haters waiting for the despised Mormon leader. It consisted of a drunken rabble of clamorous yelling "vigilantes," some very noisy and vulgar talking Carthage militiamen, and even quite a few curious jeering onlookers. In addition to this unseemly crowd, there were a number of different companies of state militia troops posted around the town having been ordered to come to Carthage from various parts of the State. All of these noisy and different groups together generated a very loud and very boisterous commotion, which effectively created a circus like atmosphere in Carthage that night. Never the less, through all this profanity, angry threats, and name calling, Captain Dunn and his armed men kept his promise to protect and escort the prisoners safely even as they maintained their military composure and marched stone-faced right past the belligerent Militia of the Carthage Greys, who seemed to be even more boisterous and abusive than the rest of the disorderly crowd.

The next day, Governor Ford agreed to meet with and have an interview with Joseph Smith. The following account comes from John Taylor and shows how there was very little understanding or sympathy coming from Mr. Ford.

Governor Ford: – "General Smith, I believe you have given me a general outline of the difficulties that have existed in the country, in the documents forwarded to me by Dr. Bernhisel and Mr. Taylor; but, unfortunately, there seems to be a discrepancy between your statements and those of your enemies…The press in the United States is looked upon as the great bulwark of American freedom, and its destruction in Nauvoo was represented and looked upon as a high-handed measure, and manifests to the people a disposition on your part to suppress the liberty of speech and of the press. This, with your refusal to comply with the requisition of a writ, I conceive to be the principal cause of this difficulty; and you are moreover represented to me as turbulent, and defiant of the laws and institutions of your country." – 7

The governor had been obviously swayed by the many misleading rumors and he was just assuming that these many blatant lies were the truth, and now he himself was using unnecessary demagoguery of his own to unfairly characterize the Prophet. Thus Joseph being falsely judged by the Governor and receiving absolutely no quarter from him, was promptly incarcerated along with his three companions in the Carthage jail without bail. Although the unfairness was obvious, there was little they could do about it. Any perceived resistance from them could have resulted in the very real possibility of all four being summarily executed without a trial and being shot on the spot.

However, in the end, their full cooperation mattered little because it was only a few days later that the Smith Brothers were summarily and illegally executed by an enraged vicious bloodthirsty mob. Their fate had been set by providence.

During the meantime, while Joseph and his companions were languishing behind bars, they had several visitors, one of which turned out to be a nice surprise for them. Uncle John Smith came from Macedonia to see his two nephews, Joseph and Hyrum. On the way, the "mobbers" and others who recognized him as a Smith family relative, threatened him, and if that wasn't bad enough, the guard at the jail refused to admit him. Joseph happened to see him through the jail window, and said to the guard, "Let the old gentleman come in, he is my uncle." The guard replied that he "didn't care who the hell's uncle he was," he wasn't allowed to go in. Joseph then spoke to the guard with disarming firmness, "You will not hinder so old and infirm a man as he is from coming in," and then said, "Come in, uncle."

After searching the old man thoroughly, the guard reluctantly let him pass into the jail, where John stayed for nearly an hour. During their goodbyes, Joseph asked his uncle to pass on a message to Almon W. Babbitt; "I want him to come and assist me as an attorney at my expected trial tomorrow before Captain R. F. Smith." - June 26, 1844. – 8

Among the other visitors that came to the jail, were Colonel Markham and Brother Cyrus Wheelock who out of nothing but good intentions, brought Joseph a six-barreled pistol called a "pepperbox," which Brother Wheelock had hidden underneath his raincoat. Later on when the two visitors left the jail to take care of some errands, one of which was to fetch some medicine for brother Richard's stomach ache, neither one of them was allowed to return to the jail and they were promptly ran out of town at the end of a bayonet. - 9

In a letter Joseph sent to his dearest Emma, and without realizing it himself, he unknowingly revealed the Governor's underlying diabolical intentions and his deceitful agenda planned for the next day. The underhanded negligent action would in the end result in a disastrous and fatal circumstance for the Prophet at Carthage jail. Joseph wrote to Emma:

"P.S. -- 20 minutes to 10. -- I just learn that the Governor is about to disband his troops, all but a guard to protect the peace and us and come himself to Nauvoo and deliver a speech to the people. This is right as I suppose." - 10

The deadly circumstances, which would result in the martyrdom of Joseph Smith, were all set in motion by Governor Ford's betrayal of the Mormon prisoner's safety when he intentionally removed from the town of Carthage all and any legitimate and effective protection for the Mormon prisoners. This left behind as the only protection for the prisoners, the menacing and hateful Carthage Greys who were suppose to safeguard the Prophet and his companions from the pressing violent mobs. The Governor had to have known that this was akin to leaving behind a hungry chicken-eating badger to protect defenseless chickens, never the less, he seemingly deliberately sat up this perilous and unpredictable situation without any real regard for the prisoner's safety.

On Thursday, June 27th 1844, the day of the martyrdom, Governor Ford fully aware of the volatile situation and knowing the consequences of what he was doing, ordered Captain Dunn and his company to leave Carthage and escort his Honor to Nauvoo. He was deliberately leaving behind Joseph and his companions to be guarded only by the infamous Mormon hating Carthage Greys. To assume Governor Ford was just being naive and unaware of the reality of what he was actually doing, is contradicted by the following statement from a deposition by Brother Alfred Randall who overheard a conversation between a soldier and Governor Ford.

"In a few minutes Randall went to another crowd of soldiers, and heard one say, 'I guess this will be the last of old Joe.' From there Randall went to Hamilton's Hotel, where Governor Thomas Ford was standing by the fence side, and heard another soldier tell Governor Thomas Ford, 'The soldiers are determined to see Joe Smith dead before they leave here.' Ford replied, "If you know of any such thing keep it to yourself." - 11a

Governor Ford intentionally took any and all legitimate protection for the Mormon prisoners with him to accompany his entourage to the city of Nauvoo. While the prisoners were left in the hands of a dangerous and hostile crowd protected only by a handful of guards, his Honor was some distance away speaking at the Mansion House in front of a large crowd of the Saints. That's where he made one of the most insulting speeches that he could have put together to humiliate and intimidate an unprotected and innocent citizenry. Among other things he said, "A great crime has been done by destroying the Expositor press and placing the city under martial law, and a severe atonement must be made, so prepare your minds for the emergency. Another cause of excitement is the fact of your having so many firearms. The public are afraid that you are going to use them against government." - 11b

To the surprise of most and as it turned out, Joseph was not even charged with the professed crime of destroying a public newspaper press. Instead he was accused of the trumped-up charge of "Treason" for supposedly committing the treasonous act of calling out the Nauvoo Legion against the Illinois government troops. In reality he most certainly did not do that, nor did he ever have any intentions of the Nauvoo Legion confronting the Illinois government militia in battle. He judiciously and most reasonably too, just merely deployed the Legion to suppress the unrest in the city, which as the city mayor was his duty to try to keep the peace in the city of Nauvoo. – 12

The jail at Carthage was built of solid rock with most of the main floor used as a residence for the jailer and his family. The upper floor contained a long room called "the dungeon" that contained individual cells with thick steel bars, which were normally used for the more serious incarcerated criminals. However, the rest of the upper floor consisted of a large bedroom, which the kindly jailer had offered to his prisoners. Apparently, Joseph, Hyrum, Willard Richards, and John Taylor didn't appear to the jailer to be much of an escape risk.

On the hot humid afternoon of June 27th 1844, the mood among the prisoners was understandably quite melancholy as they were forced to listen to the Carthage Greys' filthy language as the soldiers profanely bragged about what they were going to do to Old Joe Smith. John Taylor felt he could bear no more, and suddenly began to sing in his low mournful English accent one of Joseph's favorite songs, "A Poor Wayfaring Man." Even though the song was very melancholy, it seemed to somehow shut out the obscene and abusive language from outside, while the last verse lifted their spirits as he sang, "The Savior stood before my eyes."

Apparently some of the Mormon haters in Warsaw thought that even the Carthage Greys were not vile enough to thoroughly take care of "Old Joe Smith." It was then that a Mormon-hating mob from Warsaw appeared on the scene to add their own profane, disgusting, and abusive clamor to the crazy Carthage circus. There is some speculation that Thomas Sharp, the editor of the "Warsaw Signal," was most likely the premier leader of these 150 men from Warsaw who showed up in Carthage. All of them had their faces blackened by a mixture of gunpowder and mud looking like evil itself embodied in the bodies of irrational men. Although Thomas Sharp was later indicted by a grand jury for his participation in the killing of the Smith brothers, he was never found guilty or punished in any way, just as no other villain of that crime ever was.

As all the noisy ruckus and the unsettling commotion went on and on at length outside the jail and continued through out most of the afternoon for a period of several hours, suddenly the prisoners realized that it was unusually quite outside. Something was in the air, something not good. When they looked out the window, to their shock they found that most of the Carthage Greys who were suppose to be protecting them, had all disappeared except for just a handful of guards. This posed the ominous question, "Why?"

At 5 p.m. the kindly jailor came to the brethren and suggested that they would probably be safer if they were locked in the dungeon cells where they would be protected by the steel bars. The Prophet said that they would do just that after supper. Then Joseph turned to Willard Richards and said, "If we go into the cell, will you go in with us?" Doctor Richards replied, "Brother Joseph, you did not ask me to cross the river with you; you did not ask me to come to jail with you; and do you think I would forsake you now? But I will tell you what I will do; if you are condemned to be hung for treason, I will be hung in your stead, and you shall go free." Joseph said, "You cannot," prompting the Doctor to say, "I will." - 13

Soon after the jailer had left the prisoners alone, they heard running feet, loud shouting, and even some gunshots coming from the mob outside. Meanwhile, the small contingency of Carthage Greys' guards appeared to just quietly step aside to get out of the way of the determined rabble. Being that the guards were highly prejudiced and complicit in very unprofessionally standing back and laughing, they then just hooted their heads off while the attacking blackened faced mob broke into the jail.

Suddenly without any warning and out of nowhere, there were gunshots being fired through the windows knocking the plaster off the ceiling of the prisoner's bedroom. When the Mormon prisoners heard the front door downstairs crashing in and then the sound of loud pounding footsteps coming up the stairs, they rushed to hold the inner door against the murderous mob. As bullets continued to fly through the window, there was the unmistaken sound of bodies slamming against the bedroom door accompanied by spine-chilling yelling and a whole lot of profanity.

Suddenly, a loud bang from a musket blew the latch off the door, and several gun barrels were shoved through the narrow opening all firing at the same time. John Taylor and Elder Richards struck wildly at the gun barrels with their "rascal beater" walking sticks, but to no avail. Meanwhile, the mob on the other side of the door was just too strong for Joseph and Hyrum to hold them out any longer and to keep them from bursting into the room. As the mob began to fire more musket balls through the door, the besieged prisoners fearfully began to back away from it. One of the musket balls hit Hyrum full in the face causing him to yell out; "I am a dead man!" Seconds later, a second ball from outside came through the window and hit him in the back, while a third ball coming from the doorway hit him fatally in the head. Joseph in anguished panic, rushed to Hyrum's side, but quickly realized that his dear Hyrum was beyond any help coming from this mortal world.

In a fit of rage, Joseph ran to the door and stuck the six-barreled "Pepperbox" pistol around the edge of the doorframe and fired all six barrels at the evil beasts on the other side of the door. Three of the barrels failed to fire, but the other three musket balls hit their mark causing screams of pain from the villainous scoundrels on the other side, and then there was the unmistakable thudding sound of at least one body falling.

Under the barrage of deadly fire, John Taylor attempted to reach the window, but a ball coming from the doorway entered his thigh, while another from outside the window struck him in the chest. Ordinarily this would have been fatal, except the ball was a direct hit on his finely made watch causing it to be destroyed, but it miraculously saved his life as it knocked him to the floor. The permanently ruined watch was stopped at exactly sixteen minutes after 5 p.m. This very watch is still displayed today in the Church History Museum just west of Temple Square still telling its violent story.

The musket ball hitting Brother Taylor's watch turned out to be a definite miracle, but then a second miracle occurred even as the guns belched long flames of fire with musket balls flying around the room like mad bees. Most miraculously, Brother Willard Richards through this storm of musket balls was untouched except for an insignificant graze on his left ear. In a remarkable prophecy just a year before this, the Prophet had told his friend, "Willard, the time will come when the balls shall fly around you like hail, and you shall see your friends fall on the right and on the left, but there shall not even be a hole in your garments." As one reads about the actual fulfillment of this amazing prophecy, once again there is the realization that here is further evidence that Joseph Smith was a true prophet and seer. - 14

At this point in the wild melee, Joseph now could see that there was little chance of staying alive inside the besieged room, so he attempted to leave by the same window as the wounded John Taylor had tried to earlier. As the Prophet's form showed in the window, one of the mob, possibly a guard of the Carthage Greys, shot from below and up through the window at the hated Old Joe Smith. The ball hit him in the front torso almost knocking him backwards, and would have except nearly simultaneously, two balls fired from the muskets coming through the doorway hit him in his back sending him out through the window to fall to the ground two stories below, as he exclaimed, "Oh Lord, My God." The force of the projectiles caused him to land hard out side near the stone water well. There was no movement coming from his bullet ridden body.

Ironically, the sight of the Prophet falling out the window to the ground would unintentionally save the lives of Joseph's two apostle companions who were left behind in the previously embattled bedroom. As soon as Joseph fell from the window, the murdering fiends who were painted up like wild Indians, immediately ran down the stairs thinking that Old Joe Smith had intentionally jumped out the window as someone yelled out, "He's leaped the window" and "is escaping at this very moment." This completely changed the mob's focus, and they quickly left the room leaving behind the other two prisoners still alive. While the mob was being distracted and chasing down the stairs to the outside and pursuing after

Old Joe Smith, Dr. Willard Richards took the brief opportunity to drag the wounded Elder John Taylor into one of the cells to hide him under an old filthy mattress.

As brother Richards anxiously waited for the mob to return to the upper rooms, he was thinking all the time that he and Brother Taylor most assuredly would sooner or later be found and so he reluctantly resigned himself to the fact that the two of them would soon be searched out and killed. However, that was not in the Lord's plan and then came the third miracle, which would save both their lives.

Suddenly from out of nowhere, someone yelled, "The Mormons are coming! The Mormons are coming! Let's get out of here!" Almost immediately, the murdering cowards who were deathly afraid of the 5,000 men of the Nauvoo Legion scattered like frightened quail, leaving behind two Mormon prisoners alive. This illustrated a case in point if not a humorous reminder of what the Prophet had once quoted; "The wicked flee when no man pursueth." - See Proverbs 28:1

Even though the large numbers of men in the very highly capable Nauvoo Legion were very intimidating and very loyal to the Prophet, they were not really coming; in fact, they were nowhere near Carthage. Never the less, the quickly scattering frightened mob soon left behind the bloody scene that testified to their diabolical deed, a deed that was nothing less than the unjustified assassination of a Prophet of God. The existing evil in the world had just executed a giant among men and brutally ended the life of the only true spokesman of the Lord on the earth at that time. In the much bigger picture of worldly events, these guilty assassins absolutely hadn't the faintest idea of what they had just done. – 15

The miracle that saved the lives of John Taylor and Dr. Richards would become significantly important to the Saints in the immediate future as well as to the entire Church in the time to come. Immediately after the martyrdom, it was the apostle Dr. Richards who became the leader of the Church by default, as he was now the senior apostle in Nauvoo. Brigham Young and the other apostles, who were at a conference in Boston, would not even hear of the devastating news of the death of the Prophet until nearly two weeks later. Then even after hearing the traumatic news, it would take them more than a month to all return to Nauvoo to take over the leadership of the Church, which left Dr. Willard Richards in that important leadership role during the interim.

The other important and very significant life that was saved by the miracle of the fleeing cowardly mob was that of Brother John Taylor. Yes, it was Elder John Taylor who was saved from the vicious mobs at the time of the martyrdom of Joseph Smith, and who would come to have a very important destiny in the beautiful mountains of Zion located in Utah. In the future, it was he that would be chosen as the third President of the Church and the third Prophet in line of the Prophets in the Church of Jesus Christ of Latter Day Saints when he became the successor to President Brigham Young in the year 1880.

Perhaps a few final thoughts would be appropriate and hopefully even somewhat of a comfort to those who feel in some strange way a burdening despondency after reading about the Prophet Joseph Smith's brutal death. Though it may be very disturbing and even emotionally unsettling for some people to ponder upon Joseph's bloody brutal martyrdom, there may be some consolation found in the understanding that this very traumatic and heartbreaking event was something that was meant to be. The New Testament verse found in Hebrews 9:16 states that a prophet's testimony must be sealed with his own death. "For where a testament is, there must also of necessity be the death of the testator."

In addition to the above enlightening scripture in the New Testament, Brigham Young also received a profound and insightful revelation of his own regarding Joseph's martyrdom. It was given to him at Winter Quarters, Iowa January 14th, 1847. It is now recorded in D&C 136:37-39. It also speaks of the sacrificial act of a prophet sealing his testimony and his work with his own blood. And so it was again affirmed that this very sad tragedy was meant to be. The Good Lord had taken the Prophet Joseph Smith to Himself and so did finally bring him home to a well-deserved rest.

The Lord said; "...from Abraham to Moses, from Moses to Jesus and his apostles to Joseph Smith, whom I did call upon by mine angels, my ministering servants, and by mine own voice out of heavens, to bring forth my work." - D&C 136:37 "Which foundation he did lay, and was faithful; and I took him to myself." - 136:38

"Many have marveled because of his death; but it was needful that he should seal his testimony with his blood, that he might be honored and the wicked might be condemned." - 136:39

*   *   *

1. See John Taylor's Biography, "Life of John Taylor" 1989 also History of the Church 6:542-545.

2. See Teachings of the Prophet Joseph Smith, Section Six 1843-44 p.376-377

3. See Teachings of the Prophet Joseph Smith, Section Six 1843-44 p.377 - Also History of the Church 6:549

4. See Teachings of the Prophet Joseph Smith, Section Six 1843-44 p.379

5. See D&C 135:4, see also Andrus and Andrus, "They Knew The Prophet", p.97

6. See Teachings of the Prophet Joseph Smith, Section Six 1843-44 p.380

7. See History of the Church, Vol.7, Ch.8, p.88

8. See DHC 6:597-598. - See also "Teachings of the Prophet Joseph Smith", Section Six 1843-44 pp. 382-383

9. See John Taylor, "The Gospel Kingdom", p.358-359

10. Joseph - See History of the Church, 6:587-590

11a. See History of the Church, Vol.6, Ch.31, p.586

11b. See History of the Church, 6:587-590

12. See History of the Church, Vol.6, Ch.35, p.623.

13. See "Teachings of the Prophet Joseph Smith", Section Six 1843-44 p.395

14. See History of the Church 6:619.

15. See History of the Church 6:616-621- Also "life of John Taylor", by B.H. Roberts, pp. 137-140.

*   *   *

Chapter Twenty-One

THE PROPHET IS GONE-WHAT NOW?

*   *   *

The morning after the assassinations of the Prophet Joseph Smith and his brother Hyrum, the streets of Carthage were found unusually quite and deserted. The disorderly and guilt ridden citizens of night before had retreated to their homes. Meanwhile the murderous rabble from out of town didn't waste any time getting out of the city and on the road and did so in a very big hurry. These "out-of-towners" fully expected some kind of retaliation coming from the formidable Nauvoo Legion and so they scurried away like startled rats after their murdering melee of the Mormon prophet during the wild and rowdy vigilante circus during the day before. The dirty deed they had committed had virtually been an illegal execution in the middle of town and had been witnessed by the majority of Carthage's citizens. So most of the locals in Carthage were afraid of repercussions now and hiding in a state of uneasy fearfulness. They too were fully anticipating the 5,000 men of the Nauvoo Legion to ride into Carthage and level it to the ground. The possibility was down right unnerving, and even very scary to the frightened citizens of Carthage.

Thus it was that Carthage had become almost like a ghost town with silent streets and pulled down curtains that hid the restless apprehensive souls who were fearfully anticipating a vengeance from Hell. They all knew the 5,000 dedicated men of the Nauvoo Legion were perfectly capable of bringing down devastating havoc upon the town to take justified revenge for their beloved leader. No one doubted that the Legion could have easily protected the Prophet from the bloodthirsty vigilantes if he had so ordered it. Yet the Prophet had not ordered it because he knew before hand that his fate was set and so it was that he had stayed the powerful hand of the faithful Nauvoo Legion. Never the less, the citizens of Carthage still had good reason to be anxious for it was still in the realm of possibility for the Nauvoo Legion in retribution for Joseph's brutal murder to come and level Carthage to the ground. And if the truth be known, there was not a militia in Illinois that had the numbers or the grit to have stopped them, but providence and the greater wisdom presided over the day and thus had declared it to not be so.

Meanwhile in another nearby city, the streets were also quite, but for a different reason. When the news from Carthage came to the citizens of Nauvoo announcing the unjustified bloody murders of Hyrum and the Prophet Joseph Smith, there seem to spread over the entire city an overwhelming atmosphere of despair that overshadowed every heart and mind. This dark mood and depression seemed almost tangible as it swept throughout the city like a fiendish fog. Strangely enough, it was accompanied by a very odd and most mystifying occurrence on that particular day. Even before the official word had actually reached the citizens of Nauvoo, Bathsheba Smith, the wife of the Apostle George A. Smith, remarked that she had never experienced or heard, "Such a barking and howling of dogs and bellowing of cattle all over the city of Nauvoo. I never heard before nor since." - 1

It was reported that when the bitter news came to Emma at the Mansion house, she exclaimed; "No! Oh dear God, please No!" And then she began rocking back and forth with her head in her hands repeating over and over; "No! No! No!" Hyrum's wife, Mary, was not quite as emotionally undone by the shocking news, as she was already somewhat mentally prepared for the bad news. She had had a very strong premonition during that entire day that something terrible was about to happen long before she had officially heard the reports. When the reports finally did come in, she received the news with an air of distressed control as she gathered her children around her while they all shed tears and attempted to console each other. – 2

On June 28th, the day after the martyrdom, the apostle Dr. Willard Richards, who had been in the cell with the Prophet during the murderous assault on Carthage jail, and whom the hand of providence had miraculously saved, returned to Carthage to find the town in a very subdued mood. The locals stayed out of sight, as they were still very apprehensive about what they thought would be an inevitable reprisal from the troops of the Nauvoo Legion.

Quiet early that morning, Dr. Richards had rode into town, made arrangements for picking up the bodies of the two fallen martyrs, and then proceeded to head out for Nauvoo with the two wagons that were carrying Hyrum and Joseph's last remains. Joseph and Hyrum's own brother, Samuel Smith, along with a Mr. Hamilton accompanied Brother Richards on this glum endeavor to transport the bodies back to Nauvoo. The bodies of the two martyred brothers had been gently covered and shaded from the hot sun with cut tree branches as they departed Carthage, and so now they were leaving the little town with out harassment or any kind of fanfare.

Traveling along with Dr. Richards and the wagons was General Deming of the Hancock County Militia who was leading an additional eight-man guard to serve as an escort to Brother Richards and his little procession. They had been sent along to see that the troublesome vigilantes would not bother the small wagon train carrying the hated Smith brothers. On their arrival in Nauvoo, the wagons were met in the mid afternoon by thousands of mourning Saints, many of whom were still nursing a mood of heartbroken and shocked disbelief. The bodies were then taken to the Mansion house and prepared to lie in state beginning the next morning at 8 a.m.

With the majority of the apostles still in the East, and while the apostle John Taylor was still recovering from his serious gunshot wounds, Dr. Willard Richards was the senior apostle by default. Therefore he took the lead and asked the Saints for a sustaining vote to agree that they would not take the law into their own hands or attempt to retaliate in any way for the death of their beloved Prophet and his dear brother. Any sort of a vengeful response or retaliatory attack by the Saints could easily have started a small war between the Mormons and the locals, and that might have possibly escalated into the surrounding towns, and eventually even brought on a show of force by the State's Militia.

So the Saints reluctantly sustained Elder Richard's proposal as they capitulated quietly and then humbly returned to their homes. Still, the proposal to do nothing about the murder of their Prophet and his brother was a very difficult thing to accept for some of the more able-bodied men among the Saints who couldn't help feel like they needed to do something, anything. At the very least, they thought they should seek out some kind of legal justice for their murdered Prophet. – 3

After the bodies were prepared for burial, Emma and her children, along with Mary Fielding Smith and her children, and the Prophet's own mother, all entered the room where Hyrum and Joseph were laid to rest. The scene was almost more than any of them could bear, and Emma nearly fainted and had to be taken out of the room. Mother Smith looked up to the ceiling and sorrowfully asked, "My God, my God, why hast thou forsaken this family?"

It was at this point that something extraordinary happened in the mind and soul of Lucy Mack Smith. Somewhere inside Lucy's consciousness, a very clear and distinct voice gently declared, "I have taken them to myself that they might have rest." Mother Smith's countenance suddenly changed and for a long time she stood and looked at the serene faces of her two sons, but now without the pervading deep sorrow that she had felt on her arrival. It was instead with an underlying peace and a comforting knowledge that though she was now looking upon her sons in mortality for the last time, she realized that it was only their physical bodies that she would be missing. Their superb spirits and the essence of what they were and stood for, and the good that they had accomplished would continue way beyond their violent deaths and far beyond their all too short lives, and she knew she would see them again someday. The greatness of their souls and their magnificent spirits were dwelling in a better place now, finally at rest and at peace with the world. – 4

A short time later back at the house while they were still in mourning, a welcomed visitor came to Mother Smith's home to express her condolences and to give of her support. Jane Manning was a freeborn black girl from Connecticut who had come to Nauvoo with a missionary group. She had been taken in and given a job by Joseph and Emma and so had been working at the Mansion House as a hired maid. As Jane was a hard working and pleasant person to be around, Emma and Mother Smith had grown quite fond of her and she had become a trusted companion in the Smith household. After the Prophet's death, there was no need for Jane's services at the Mansion House, and so after visiting and comforting Lucy and Emma, their young friend returned to live with her own mother. Later she would marry and she and her husband would eventually immigrate to Utah during the next fall after the first of the pioneers had arrived in Salt Lake valley in July of 1847.

It goes without saying that not everyone in Illinois felt saddened by the deaths of the two Smith brothers. In fact, there were more than a few of the enemies of Joseph Smith that were actually celebrating his murder. As Joseph's brother Samuel made haste towards Nauvoo after hearing the terrible news, some mob members who were still celebrating their great feat, took "pot shots" at Sam. They were trying to finish the job of taking care of the Smith brothers and they hoped to put him in the grave along with his hated siblings. However, he escaped their deliberate attempt to commit another murder, and he somehow made his way back home safely.

The many bitter enemies of Joseph Smith, even those living some distance away in other parts of the state, felt triumphant, and proceeded to celebrate the deaths of the Smith Brothers, as one apostle found out on his way back home. While traveling back to Nauvoo after hearing the news, Parley P. Pratt reported that there was great jubilation in Chicago over "Old Joe Smith's" death. The Chicago press had even expressed it as the "triumph" of the people over the fallen Smith brothers. – 5

The dedicated enemies of the Church were now thinking that surely the Mormons were all finished. They thought the Mormons must surely be a very confused flock of lost sheep without anybody to lead them, and therefore they must be feeling totally beaten into the ground, very much lost, and virtually crushed. There was little question in the thinking of the Mormon-haters now; the loathsome Mormon Church would surely just presumably fall apart and disband into a bunch of leaderless wandering vagabonds being that their very leadership was in serious question and in utter chaos. How could the Mormons even possibly continue on, now that their precious Prophet was dead and unable to hold them together?

Meanwhile, some of Joseph's worst enemies, they being steeped in their abhorrent and most gruesome desires, literally sought to obtain the actual head of "Old Joe Smith." This depraved collection of Joe Smith-haters who wanted his actual head included the violent "vigilantes," a variety of greedy bounty hunters, and the most vindictive apostates of the Church. However, it was the Missourian politicians who most seriously wanted the physical head of Joe Smith as they deemed it absolutely necessary to validate his death, and they were willing to pay handsomely for it. This they claimed was essential in order to make certain that Old Joe Smith was really dead and not just in hiding as it had been rumored. And apparently there were a number of greedy men that actually believed those rumors of the Mormon prophet being alive in a secret hiding place. Therefore there came to the Nauvoo area plenty of bounty hunters, just snooping around seeking after the great prize of the physical head of Joseph Smith as they dreamed of that substantial bounty offered for it by the Missourians.

Sadly, it wasn't just Joseph Smith's enemies that were thinking that the Church could not survive without their revered leader. Many of the Saints themselves were wondering just how the Church could possibly go on without the Prophet Joseph Smith. Those who doubted the survival of the Church, had apparently forgotten or didn't understand what Joseph had once said; "The works, and the designs, and the purposes of God cannot be frustrated, neither can they come to naught....Remember, remember, that it is not the work of God that is frustrated, but the works of men." Another one of Joseph's quotes expressing a similar theme stated; "....As well might man stretch forth his puny arm to stop the Missouri river in its decreed course, or to turn it up stream, as to hinder the Almighty...." - 6

Little did any of these doubters fully understand the eternal nature of what the Prophet Joseph Smith had begun here on earth or the full implications of his fated blood sacrifice, and neither did they appreciate the true strength and power of what the Prophet had restored upon the earth nor did they even come close to comprehending what God was about to bring forth in His establishing of Zion. These grim doubters and skeptics would soon be weeded out and their ill-founded assumptions and bad predictions, based in hopelessness, despair, and influenced by the negative chaff of their thinking, would soon be blown and scattered in the wind.

On the third day after the martyrdom and after some 10,000 mourners had publicly viewed the remains of Hyrum and Joseph at the Mansion House, the doors were closed and locked. A few especially chosen brethren then carried out a plan where they proceeded to secretly fill empty matching wooden pine boxes with just the right amount of sand to simulate the weight of a man's body. And then they carried the sand filled pine boxes to the temple site where they publicly buried them at the temple grounds where they held a very convincing mock funeral. At midnight, the real caskets with the actual bodies of Hyrum and Joseph were taken and covertly buried in the basement of the Nauvoo house on Main Street, with the exact spot being carefully disguised by what would appear to be no more than mere construction dirt and debris in the basement.

The Smith family, their friends, and the admirers of the Prophet Joseph Smith had a very real and legitimate concern that the villainous enemies of the Prophet might actually attempt to desecrate the bodies of Joseph and Hyrum. The bodies of the Smith brothers remained there in the Nauvoo house basement until that next fall when Emma requested that they be moved to the old Homestead. It was there that they were secretly buried under the "Springhouse." – 7

The Prophet's sudden death left an obvious and great vacuum in the Church's leadership. Being that it was especially self-evident to certain unscrupulous and misguided men, there were many opportunists now ready to step in and fill that important vacancy. John C. Bennett, Sidney Rigdon, William Marks, James Strang, Lyman Wight, and the Prophet's own brother, William Smith, all had their own personal ideas of just who should step into the shoes of the Prophet Joseph Smith now and preside over the Church. In many cases, the various fates of these unscrupulous men would be interwoven, but all of them would eventually come to suffer from being completely ostracized from the Church and they would obtain little for all their trouble except an inglorious and unavailing end. In their arrogance, they would reap nothing but the fruits of humiliation and failure as they attempted selfishly and unsuccessfully to sell themselves as the one and only true chosen leader of the Church.

It had only been two years since John C. Bennett had previously left Nauvoo in disgrace and shame. Having departed with extreme bitterness towards the Prophet and the Church, no one ever thought that they would ever see him again in Nauvoo. However, after spending two years on the road doing as much damage as he could contrive against the Church, and making money by selling his lies about the Church leaders, he unexpectedly showed up in the city again just before the rest of the Twelve Apostles arrived, and only a day ahead of Sidney Rigdon.

He had not come to Nauvoo to express his condolences, but to bring to the Saints a revelation from the Prophet Joseph Smith that he alone possessed, and it all had to do with just who should take the Prophet's place. Thus John C. Bennett claimed it was while he was filling in for Sidney Rigdon in the First Presidency that he had been given this particular revelation from the Prophet, and he had been sworn by oath to deliver it to the Church upon Joseph's death. The secretive revelation declared that his good friend, "Sidney Rigdon was to be appointed the prophet, seer, and revelator for the Church."

However, Brigham Young, along with the others who were acquainted with Bennett's handwriting, recognized it as a forgery and nothing more than another cheap blatant fraud perpetrated by Bennett. So once again, John C. Bennett left Nauvoo in disgrace and in bitter disappointment after he finally came to the realization that Sidney Rigdon would never be accepted and crowned as the Church's "Guardian." And therefore, Bennett himself would never be able to take advantage of his friend Sydney's high position to be appointed to some important leadership position that he had had his eye on and very much desired for whatever questionable reasons.

When Joseph and Hyrum were murdered in Carthage, most of the Twelve Apostles were in Boston at a Church Conference and they didn't hear the news of the assassination until nearly two weeks later on July 9th. Shortly thereafter, they all split up to make their separate ways back to Nauvoo at which time Brigham, Heber, and Wilford Woodruff along with Lyman Wight and Orson Pratt made the decision to travel back home together as a group.

After their little group left Chicago, they headed west to Galena Illinois on the upper Mississippi where they would be able to catch a riverboat going south to Nauvoo. On the way there, their stage was delayed by a heavily loaded freight wagon, which was stubbornly stuck in a muddy bog in the middle of the road and there was just no way to drive the stage around it.

The Norwegian handlers were cruelly striking the backs of their oxen with their whips while swearing a blue streak of profanities to no avail. Brigham not liking the situation, especially the treatment of the beasts, took off his boots and waded through the bog up towards the lead handler, greeted him, and then took hold of the whip from the driver and motioned for the Norwegians to all step back.

At this point and somewhat surprisingly, instead of using the whip on the backs of the oxen, Brigham reached down and began to scratch the neck of the lead beast as he spoke to it calmly and very softly. All six animals began to listen to his kind gentle voice and stopped their nervous stomping and the fidgeting of their tails, while the onlookers tried in vain to figure out just what strange language it was that Brigham was speaking to the animals. All of a sudden, Brigham stood up and cracked the whip over the heads of the muddy beasts of burden as he pulled on the lead yoke with his other hand and then yelled out "Hee yaw!"

Miraculously all the oxen began to pull as one powerfully straining team and they broke loose from the thick mud as Brigham continued to encourage them forward in a mysterious language known only to the beasts. When they were finally free of the bog and on the dry ground, Brigham walked over to the shocked handlers and handed them back their whip where he received an incredulous look along with somewhat of a reserved thank you. After he returned to the stage to put on his boots, Brigham's companions were still wide eyed in awe, along with the stage drivers, and they repeatedly asked him just how he was able to accomplish such an amazing feat and so skillfully handle those beast the way he did. – 8

Finally after many days of travel, the apostles arrived in Nauvoo on August the 6th 1844. So had Sidney Rigdon, who seemed to have forgotten all about his inauspicious departure from Nauvoo when Joseph had asked for him to be removed from the First Presidency just a year earlier. Now he returned unashamed and overbearingly confident. He had arrived in Nauvoo from Pittsburg Pennsylvania two or three days before the apostles arrived. On Sunday August the 4th, President William Marks of the Nauvoo Stake asked Sidney Rigdon to speak to the Saints in the grove of trees near the temple as part of a quickly put together agenda for their worship service that day. It was obvious that President Marks and Sidney had colluded to put together an orchestrated leadership agenda for Brother Rigdon to speak at this meeting and it appeared to be intentionally arranged rather quickly before the Twelve could arrive.

Sidney opened his speech by pointing out how close he and the Prophet had been, and what a very sad occasion it was for him to have to hear of the Prophet's death. And then to the "ahs and ohs" from his audience, he claimed to have had a vision from the Lord indicating that he was to be the new "Guardian" of the Church. He backed up his claim with Joseph's revelation found in D&C 100:9-11, "And it is expedient in me that you, my servant Sidney, should be a spokesman unto this people; yea verily I will ordain you unto this calling, even to be a spokesman unto my servant Joseph."

It should be pointed out that Sidney's use of the word "Guardian" is not found anywhere in this revelation nor is it used anywhere else in the Doctrine and Covenants, and so it appears to have come strictly from out of Sidney's personal interpretation and imagination. In this revelation to Sidney Rigdon, the word "spokesman" is used specifically by the Lord, and not the word "guardian", which has an entirely different connotation than "spokesman." A "guardian" is supposed to defend, protect, and look after, while a "spokesman" merely speaks on behalf of another person or a group.

Sidney went on in his haranguing speech to proclaim he would fight the battles of the Lord including even those against the forces of Queen Victoria. He bragged and pontificated that he would march up to her palace and demand a part of her riches and dominions. The verbally assaulted and overwhelmed audience was left stunned. – 9

By August the 7th, most of the Twelve had finally arrived in Nauvoo, if not by luck, then by the hand of providence in order that they would be able to thwart the contrived plans of Sidney and President Marks. At this point in time, it was President Marks that went ahead and called for a meeting at the home of the recovering John Taylor where it was attended by eight of the Twelve Apostles. As head of the Twelve, Brigham stood up and commented that in as much as the apostles had not heard Sidney's celebrated speech on the previous Sunday, he thought it would be appropriate for them to all hear it now. Sidney then happily stood up to repeat his speech and announce once again that he had had a vision the very day of the Prophet's death. He asserted once again that he personally was consecrated to be a spokesman for Joseph and to be the "Guardian" of the Saints, and then he went on to emphasize again that his calling was legitimate, even though some people might not think so, or that some might have a different opinion about him being a "Guardian" for the Church; but he assured them never the less, that it was what the Lord really wanted.

Then it was Brigham's turn to speak. He slowly arose and then very powerfully stated that the Twelve had previously been given all the keys and powers they needed to lead the Church and it had been conferred upon their heads by Joseph, a Prophet of God, and no man can come between the Twelve and Joseph upon which shoulders the Kingdom rests. Although the rest of the apostle's heads nodded in agreement, President Marks and Sidney were left somewhat disgruntled and very unsatisfied with the way things had turned out at this meeting. – 10

The next day on August the 8th 1844, there were two meetings held to decide the fate of the Church, one in the morning and another one at two p.m. In the morning session, Sidney Rigdon, being in full form with his exuberant pontificating, spoke for an hour and a half reiterating the revelation that supposedly charged him with being the "Guardian" of the Church. It was quite obvious to everyone that he was once again indisputably claiming the leadership of the Church. After he finally ended his lengthy monologue, he left the audience numb from his long haranguing sermon.

It was then that Brigham Young stood up before the large crowd. After already having been a little late for the morning meeting, Brigham took the podium and only after a few short words, dismissed the congregation until the afternoon session, but in closing, he requested that the Saints should be reassembled later in the afternoon with all the priesthood quorums seated in their proper places. It was obvious that he was not going to wait until a later time for a solemn assembly to decide the fate of the Church.

In that afternoon meeting, after the conclusion of the song and prayer, Brigham Young came to the podium once again. After mentioning a few minor points of information to the congregation, he quite unexpectedly and without beating around the bush, called for an audience-wide vote by the raised right hand. He then petitioned the congregation as to what it was that they wanted? Brigham asked; "Inasmuch as our Prophet and Patriarch are taken from our midst, do you want someone to guard, to guide and lead you through this world into the kingdom of God, or not? All who want some person to be a guardian or a prophet, a spokesman, or something else, signify it by raising the right hand."

Not a single hand voted for the guardian spokesman choice. He then firmly declared, "You cannot fill the office of a prophet, seer, and revelator. God must do this. Now, if you want Sidney Rigdon or William Law to lead you, or anybody else, you are welcome to them; but I tell you, in the name of the Lord that no man can put another between the Twelve and the Prophet Joseph. The Quorum of the Twelve has had the keys of the Kingdom of God conferred upon them by a Prophet of God and THEY ARE THE HEAD OF THIS CHURCH!"

Then Brigham called for the Members of the Church to sustain the brethren in the Quorum of the Twelve to be the head of the Church so that they could properly stand and take their place as the chosen leaders of the Church. Thousands of hands went up to sustain the Twelve Apostles as head of the Church of Jesus Christ of Latter Day Saints and thus it was that the members of the Church made it quite clear to every one present that the Twelve had their support and approval to be the leaders of the Church.

It was at this very significant juncture in Church history that the Lord effectively chose to show the faithful among the Saints just who He had chosen to lead His Church. Miraculously and stunningly, while Brigham was in the very act of speaking, the mantle of the Prophet Joseph Smith fell upon Brigham Young's countenance and dozens of people testified to hearing Joseph's voice coming from Brigham's mouth. And many said even his form and mannerisms were transformed into the personage of Joseph Smith the Prophet. George Q. Cannon who was only seventeen at the time testified, "If Joseph had risen from the dead and again spoken in their hearing, the effect could not have been more startling than it was to many present at that meeting, it was the voice of Joseph himself;....The Lord gave His people a testimony that left no room for doubt as to who was the man chosen to lead them...."

Wilford Woodruff then gave his testimony, which was very similar to George Q. Cannon's, as well as the many others that witnessed the miraculous transformation in that meeting. Benjamin F. Johnson, 26 at the time, said: "As soon as he spoke I jumped upon my feet, for in every possible degree it was Joseph's voice, and his person, in look, attitude, dress and appearance was Joseph himself, personified; and I knew in a moment the spirit and mantle of Joseph was upon him." - 11

Sidney Rigdon was then asked to speak but declined in the face of such a powerful moment. However, W.W. Phelps, Amasa Lyman, and Parley P. Pratt all did speak and they simply reaffirmed the obviously popular call for the Twelve Apostles to head the Church. And so it was that in spite of the many dubious claims by a number of imposters asserting they were chosen to be Joseph's replacement, the leadership of the Church by the Twelve had now been definitively decided overriding all other assertions and their suspect claims.

And so it was then settled that the Quorum of the Twelve Apostles would now proceed to lead the Church as they were presided over by the President of the Twelve, Brigham Young. Of course, all this left those other would-be prophets out in the cold without a valid argument or any outstanding claims to the Church's leadership, and so they slipped away into apostasy and to their own disappointing fate of abject failure and anonymity.

However, there was at least one of them who did not give up so easily. Even after Sidney Rigdon had been overwhelmingly rejected by the congregation following the powerful vote for the Twelve to lead the Church, he stubbornly continued to insist that his sacred and powerful calling was without question to be the "Guardian" of the Church. And therefore his righteous and divine calling should have priority even over the Twelve Apostles.

However, about a month after that decisive meeting in the grove where the Twelve Apostles were positively sustained by the Saints to be the head of the Church, Sidney Rigdon finally saw his stubborn bid for Church leadership come to an irrefutable and most convincing end. And so it was at that time that the leaders of the Church thus summarily and justifiably excommunicated him in September of 1844.

Ultimately, and after eventually accepting the fact that it was truly a lost cause, Sidney moved back to Pittsburgh where he started a "Church of

Christ" and it was there that he stoically presided over a small following of believers. He would later on start a newspaper, and finally, in the end, he passed away sadly in somewhat of an unbalanced mental state as he passed into historical obscurity somewhere in the state of New York.

There were others who failed too in their desire to be the premier leader of the Church. Among them was the enigmatic James Strang, another one of those fraudulent would-be prophets claiming to be the only true prophet of the Church. He was a rather unusual character in Church history and had only been a baptized member of the Church for a few months before the martyrdom of the Prophet. However, in a very short time with his charm and persuasive personality, he somehow was able to beguile some of the former apostles among the Twelve including William E. McLellin, John Page, and the Prophet's own brother, William Smith. These were not the only misguided Saints who he convinced to join with him in his ill-fated Strangite religion. This conniving and very persuasive fake then falsely claimed to have a letter from Joseph Smith appointing him to be Joseph's successor. Naturally, it too turned out to be fraudulent. In 1849, James Strang set up a religious colony in the northern U.S. on Beaver Island located in Lake Michigan where he pronounced himself as King. However, six years later after that pompous declaration, a disgruntled member murdered him and the ill-fated Strangite movement died with him and he disappeared into the files of history with the other forgotten failed religious zealots.

In another vastly wasted effort bound in futility, Stake President William Marks stubbornly continued to support Sidney Rigdon for a while and consequently lost the trust of the members of his Stake who refused to sustain him thereafter as the Nauvoo Stake President. He was subsequently released from that position. After following Sidney Rigdon for a short time, Brother Marks eventually ended up joining the ill-fated Strangite group under the questionable sanity of James Strang. However, it wasn't long before Marks became disillusioned by the ranting of James Strang, switched churches once again, and finally died as an unimportant member of the Reorganized Church of Jesus Christ of Latter Day Saints.

After Joseph and Hyrum Smith's death, William Smith, the quick-tempered brother of the Prophet and Hyrum was selected to be the new Church Patriarch, but he just simply could not accept the new leadership of the Twelve Apostles. He therefore was excommunicated in October of 1845 for adamantly claiming that he himself had the right to be the chosen leader of the Church in that he was Joseph's brother. After his claim was summarily rejected, he joined the Strangites for a brief period, but then decided to come back and present to the Church leadership with what turned out to be an unwelcome proposal. He proposed that he should be chosen as the interim rightful guardian of the Church until Joseph's own son, Joseph Smith III, by right of succession, that is, the father to son line of authority, could be carried out when the young Joseph Smith III was old enough to take over. His proposal was firmly rejected by the Twelve and he became very disgruntled and annoyed with the Church leadership in their lack of understanding and their inability to see what he thought was the obvious and the only rightful solution to Church leadership.

After he was excommunicated from the Strangite religion, William Smith started his own church using the title of the Church of Jesus Christ of Latter Day Saints, but later renamed it as the Reorganized Church of Jesus Christ of Latter Day Saints, which was organized in 1846. William and his followers were stubbornly insistent that succession in the presidency of the Church must be passed down in a line from father to son, and they drew into that belief a number of other former members of the Church who came to believe strongly in the same order of succession. A group of them met in Wisconsin on June 12th 1852 to organize a church, and then in 1859, the younger Joseph Smith III formally accepted the call to become the new president and prophet of that church. Finally in April of 1860, the group formally incorporated under the name of the Reorganized Church of Jesus Christ of Latter Day Saints, at which time, the majority of the Prophet Joseph Smith's own immediate family joined the RLDS Church during the early 1860s. William Smith, the hot-tempered brother of the Prophet Joseph, remained a significant energy force in influencing the RLDS Church. He was also often credited with being the main instigator in initiating a major falling out between the Prophet's immediate family and Hyrum Smith's family. His quarrel with Mary Fielding Smith was over her refusal to abandon the main body of the Church and join his RLDS Church, and that was what was said to have been at the heart of the bitter feud. – 12

Another unique individual seeking the leadership of the Church during that time period was Lyman Wight. He had been associated with the Prophet Joseph since the Zion's Camp mission to Missouri in the 1830's and at that time was known as General Lyman Wight. He was a civil war veteran and was chosen as the military leader over Zion's Camp under the direction of Joseph Smith. After the Prophet was murdered, Lyman Wight stated: "The only man who can handle me is dead." And he seemed to try to prove it by becoming conspicuously rebellious and uncooperative after Joseph Smith was gone, and he ended up just simply refusing to follow the leadership of Brigham Young and the Twelve insisting they should be following him.

As Wight followed up on an idea previously suggested by Joseph Smith, he led a group of his followers all the way down to Texas insisting that the rest of the Church should come to Texas and follow his leadership. Later on when the Twelve invited him and his group to rejoin the main body of the Saints, he refused, and was eventually excommunicated in 1848. He finally passed away there in Texas and thus faded away as all those other would-be prophets had, into that quite anonymity found in the obscure annals of Church history. – 13

All of these would-be leaders of the Church, who presented their claims at the time of Joseph Smith's death, appeared to have had an aggressive personal agenda supported by their own selfish motives to take Joseph's place in the Church leadership. Not a single one of them had a genuine divine appointment to back up their claims to lead the Church.

It was quite obvious to the majority of the Church members that the Twelve Apostles had been given the Priesthood keys by the laying on of hands by a Prophet and they had been properly chosen by Joseph Smith's inspiration to lead the Church. And it was just as obvious that not a one of these would-be prophets had been sanctioned by the Lord to follow through in the pursuit of their own ambitious agenda. Rather sadly, most if not all of them ended up dying in obscurity, after having been rebuffed by the main body of the faithful Saints and rejected by the Lord. None of them ever seemed to really quite understand that the Lord Himself chooses whom He will to lead his people, and it is only He who makes the final choice.

*   *   *

1. See "Restoration", p 621.

2. See "Mary Fielding Smith", Corbett – pp. 171-172

3. See History of the Church, Vol.6, Ch.35, p.626

4. See Lucy Mack Smith, "history of Joseph Smith by His Mother" Bookcraft, 1954, pp. 324-325.

5. See "Autobiography of Parley P. Pratt" pp. 292-294.

6. See D&C 3:1 & 3:3. See also D&C 121:33.

7. See History of the Church, Vol.6, Ch.35, p.628-29.

8. See History of the Church 7:224

9. See History of the Church 7:224-225

10. See History of the Church 7:225-230.

11. See "Church in the Fullness of Times" p. 291, also Kate B. Carter, "Heart throbs of the West" Daughters of the Pioneers 1943, 4:420. And History of the Church 7:236-239. Also volume 7, chapter 19

12. See "Church History in the Fullness of Times", pp. 292-296, also Encyclopedia of Mormonism, Vol.3, SCHISMATIC GROUPS

13. See Henry D. Taylor, Conference Report, April 1967, p.39 – and also see "Church History in the Fullness of Time" p. 305

*   *   *

Chapter Twenty-Two

PERSECUTION REPRISED

*   *   *

As they labored to deal with the loss of the Prophet Joseph Smith, the Twelve Apostles of the Church of Jesus Christ of Latter Day Saints moved forward under the very capable leadership of the senior Apostle Brigham Young. And they soon were involved in the important work at hand of governing the affairs of the Church beginning with each member of the Twelve being given an especially assigned individual responsibility. The still recovering John Taylor who had been shot by the mob at Carthage, the same man who would eventually become the third President of the Church, was made editor of the "Times and Seasons" newspaper and shortly thereafter, put in charge of the "Nauvoo Neighbor."

In addition to their individual assignments, the Twelve reorganized the Priesthood Quorums with seven new presidents over the Seventies, and established two new Church districts in Canada and the United States. And so it would seem that the loss of the Prophet Joseph Smith did not cause the Church to crumble into shambles, to just wither away, or fall into pieces of disarray, nor did it keep the Kingdom of God from rolling forth. Much to the dismay and bitter disappointment of the Church's dedicated enemies, the Mormon Church was not only going to survive, but was going to grow into a significant religious organization and would increase in numbers despite its ongoing trials, and it would eventually evolve into an even more strengthened and influential religion than before the Prophet's death.

Meanwhile though, within the confines of the Church itself, there was an obvious and inevitable clash brewing and about to boil over due to the tempestuous relationship between two of the strongest willed personalities in the Church, Emma Smith and Brigham Young. Even though both of them loved the Prophet Joseph dearly, as a matter of record the two were involved in a spirited debate regarding many personal issues. And they certainly had some serious differences of opinion concerning what belonged to whom. These were such things as their personal judgments of which of the Prophet's writings belonged to Emma and which to the Church, and then there was their very different thinking as to the ownership of certain real-estate properties, which properties Brigham was determined actually belonged to the Church. They especially had their differences of opinion concerning the practice of plural wives. All of these things generated a great amount of friction between the two and it grew into a real churlish argument and a right down bitter battle between them.

To begin with, given her personal dislike of Brigham, it was of no surprise to anybody that Emma also had a definite attitude about whether Brigham Young should even truly be the legitimate leader of the Church. It was said that she personally supported her good friend William Marks, the Nauvoo Stake President, to be the new Church President, but he showed little interest in the position and instead strongly supported the overly confident and very pushy Sidney Rigdon as the next Church President. Emma just could not seem to bring herself to support Brigham Young as a Church leader even though the vast majority of the Church members had already sustained him along with the Twelve Apostles as the new leaders of the Church.

Another very serious issue between the two was the distribution of the effects and property of Joseph's estate. They strongly disagreed on just who should be the inheritors of certain personal writings of the Prophet, which became a major source of conflict between the two. The Prophet Joseph had left many writings beyond the Book of Mormon scripture translations that were still in Emma's possession. Brigham most definitely had a whole different view from Emma's as to their ownership and he was particularly insistent that Joseph's translation of the Holy Bible belonged to the Church. However, Emma flatly stated that she was the one that had carried the manuscripts across the frozen Mississippi River beneath her skirts while dragging four children over the dangerous and icy waters in order to preserve the precious manuscripts, not Brigham. Thus she kept the manuscripts without any further argument.

Meanwhile, Brigham Young adamantly supported the revelation on "Plural Wives" seeing it as being the will of God that was instituted by the Prophet Joseph Smith himself. Yet, Emma hated every thing about polygamy and publicly made an unbending stand against it as she tried to convince the other women of the Church of its despicable nature. To counteract Emma's campaign against polygamy, Brigham Young officially suspended all Relief Society meetings as of March 9th 1845, due to what was widely reported as Emma using the Relief Society as her personal platform to defy the plural marriage revelation.

Perhaps their most volatile disagreements were over which of Joseph's properties belonged to Emma and her children and which properties were now being claimed as Church property. Brigham argued ardently that except for Joseph's personal living quarters, Joseph's other properties were to all be inherited by the Church.

Perhaps Emma Smith would have really made a good lawyer. In her rebuttal, Emma adamantly declared that she was the one that had worked side by side with Joseph to build the Homestead, the Red Brick Store, and the Mansion House, and then in addition to all that, she had been the one who had taken in boarders and washed and cooked for them all, to pay the family's household bills. In the end, she made an excellent argument for having earned the ownership of these valuable and soon to be revered historical buildings. Thus she did take ownership of the Homestead, the Red Brick Store, the Mansion House, and even the Nauvoo House.

Though Brigham Young was a formidable and very tenacious adversary, Emma somehow won the majority of the battles over the real-estate property, the distribution of Joseph's writings, and ownership of his personal effects. Her only loss to Brigham was on the issue of plural marriage. Unfortunately, most of the conflicts between Emma and Brigham would never be resolved to Brigham's satisfaction during Emma's and Brigham's lifetime. As it all turned out, there were just simply no easy solutions to resolve the differences between these two very strong willed personalities.

Beyond her personal battles with Brigham Young, Emma was also very critical of what she saw as a noticeable lack of attention and sympathy from the Church's Twelve Apostles after her husband's tragic death. Just where was the expected compassion that should have come from the Twelve for her and her children after her husband's brutal martyrdom? She truly felt the Twelve had been deliberately ignoring her. Perhaps there may have even been a bit of truth in that accusation since some of the Twelve actually did have some unkind feelings towards Emma as some did blame her in part for Joseph's untimely death. They felt it was her personal and selfish request that persuaded the Prophet to give himself up and come back across the river that led to his inevitable execution. Under these contentious circumstances, it was certainly not a surprise that Emma would simply refuse to follow the Church leaders on their long trek to the Rocky Mountains and settle among the rest of the Church members in their new home in Utah.

Joseph's manuscript of the Bible translation would eventually pass from Emma's hands into the hands of the Joseph Smith III and then into the possession of the Reorganized Church. The Homestead, the Red Brick Store, the Mansion House, and the Nauvoo House all passed from Emma to her family and then became the property of the Reorganized Church. The RLDS Church, which is presently called The Church of Christ, offers tours of these fine old historical buildings for the convenience, interest, and curiosity of the many tourists visiting Nauvoo.

It should be noted that there are several restored properties in Nauvoo, which do belong to and are maintained by the Church of Jesus Christ of Latter Day Saints, presently. These include both the Brigham Young home and Heber C. Kimball's home. And the Church does provide tours through these fine historic old homes.

After Joseph Smith's death, there seemed to arise for whatever unexplained reason, many unnecessary and petty little disagreements just popping up here and there, all over the place among the Church members. This general discord among some of the active Saints only added to the negative atmosphere already stirred up by the despicable and unrelenting actions of the rebellious apostates. The dissonance that came with this darkness of faultfinding and its negative atmosphere only contributed further to the gloomy clouds hanging over the unity of the Saints. Thus it greatly hindered the unifying spirit that most certainly should have existed through out the Church community. Ultimately, it would impede all the attempts to keep the general peace and the unity in the city of Nauvoo. Yet, this very serious internal disunity was only a part of the troubles that were about to come upon the Saints in "Nauvoo the Beautiful." Added to this very unsettled atmosphere of contention was another factor, the increasing hostility of the Mormon hating outsiders.

Thomas Sharp, along with the rest of his group of Mormon haters in Warsaw, was simply not satisfied with merely having the hated leader of the Mormons being assassinated; he wanted every last Mormon completely gone from out of the state. Even though the Mormon-haters were elated about the death of the scoundrel, Joseph Smith, they were still not content as long as so many of Old Joe Smith's followers remained in the area. And they weren't going to be completely satisfied until they reached their ultimate goal of getting rid of all the Mormons permanently, and so it was that they pursued that particular end aggressively.

Meanwhile, in the hostile rival town of Warsaw, business had become nearly stagnant and instead of seeing any growth, the city was actually loosing much of its population, where as Nauvoo was surprisingly thriving even after the murders at Carthage. This state of affairs created considerable jealousy over Nauvoo's thriving businesses and its further development surrounding its valuable property.

Thomas Sharp and his cohorts insisted that it was somehow the Mormon's fault that Warsaw's economy was shrinking and petering out, and he and his associates consequently made many trips to the state legislature to demand the repeal of the Nauvoo charter. A correspondent from Fair Haven Connecticut wrote an article, which was published in part in the "Nauvoo Neighbor" in August of 1844, that summed up the situation surrounding the city of Nauvoo after the Prophet was murdered.

"It is now known here that the lazy speculators of Warsaw, and the still lazier office drones at Carthage, cared nothing for Joseph Smith personally, or for his tenets either; but the prosperity of Nauvoo increasing as it did, beyond any former parallel even in the western world, excited in their bosoms envy, hatred and all ungodliness. This is the true secret of all their barbarous movements against Mormonism--and they supposed by destroying the Smiths they should extinguish their religion, disperse the Mormons--depopulating and desolating Nauvoo." – 1

In response to the mounting complaints against the Mormons, the insufferable Governor Thomas Ford wrote a letter demonstrating more of his arrogant and unmitigated gall, and so once again he showed his condescending and unsympathetic attitude towards the leaders of the Church. In the letter, he politely but patronizingly invited the Mormons to leave the State of Illinois and to seek their fortunes in California saying that it would be a very good place for them to find a place free from harassment and "you would be in no danger of being interfered with," to practice your unusual religion. - 2

By January of 1845, there was considerable political pressure on the Illinois State's politicians to repeal the Nauvoo charter and so the Illinois legislature feeling the mounting pressure, succumbed to the political agenda of their constituents and they did proceed to legally repeal Nauvoo's charter. Ordinarily this very constraining development would have been utterly disastrous to most cities.

The repeal of the charter effectively left the city of Nauvoo not only without the safety and protection previously provided by the Nauvoo Legion's militia, but it also left them even without a city police force to protect the local citizens from theft and crimes of violence committed within the city limits. Naturally this would leave the town in a perilous and insecure position as its citizens were exposed to many unscrupulous opportunists, and it literally left Nauvoo wide open to nefarious characters and any would-be-thieves to plunder the city without any fear of being arrested by the now defunct Nauvoo police force.

However, Brigham Young was not about to let the city be ravished by the scum getting off the riverboats and setting a loose foot on the wharf at the Nauvoo landing. Brigham Young and the former Chief of Police, brother Hosea Stout, organized what they called the "Quorums of

Deacons" where individual deacons were placed on every street corner both day and night to report any mischief that might be about. Although these deacons had no legal power to stop or arrest anyone, they kept Brigham apprised of any strangers wandering around town that might possibly be up to no good.

In his further practical and creative wisdom, Brigham also established the ingenious "Whistling and Whittling Brigades" which were well organized and very effective in deterring criminal behavior. They were composed of a large group of fifteen to twenty boys who would completely surround any suspicious characters who might have nefarious intentions. Encircling the suspicious character without getting too close to the suspect, they would never instigate any kind of physical contact with them, but remain close by enough to be intimidating and thus unnerve their quarry. The boys carried long hickory sticks and jackknives and would subtly intimidate the would-be thief by standing around a short distance away, while whistling and whittling on their long sticks. All the while they would be menacingly slicing away pieces of wood with their ominous looking jackknives. It wasn't long before the suspected opportunist was made to feel like a weakened caribou being encircled by a pack of hungry wolves. Following the potential thieves wherever they went, the boys were persistent, and after a while the mounting suspense and the relentless stalking by the boys would grate on the nerves of the unscrupulous stranger and he soon would become only too glad to jump back on the riverboat and "get the 'hect' out of Dodge." – 3

Meanwhile, the Temple construction was continuing with great energy in Nauvoo. However, the Saints in Great Britain were feeling somewhat left out of this important and worthy project. With this concern on their minds, the British Saints wrote letters inquiring as to what they could possibly do for their part in helping the efforts towards the construction of the sacred temple. In response, Brigham suggested that the Temple could really use a nice bell to be placed in the top of its majestic steeple. The British Saints responded enthusiastically by generously contributing a beautiful well-crafted 1500-pound bell and then sent it to Nauvoo to be placed in the steeple of the sacred edifice. This bell became very prized by the Saints and was eventually carried in the bed of a wagon by the pioneers all the way to Utah to become the well-known and historical "Nauvoo

Bell," which to this very day is heard on KSL radio every hour on the hour in Salt Lake City.

Brigham Young knew without a shadow of a doubt, that it would not be too long before the Saints would be forced to leave the state of Illinois, and he thought a lot about the words of the Prophet Joseph speaking of a refuge in the Rocky Mountains. Yet even knowing that they would have to leave Nauvoo soon, he still felt compelled by a strong impression; that they must finish the temple before they left Nauvoo so that the Saints could leave for the wilderness having first been endowed.

He put it this way; "If we should go to the wilderness and ask the Lord to give us an endowment, he might ask us, saying, 'Did I not give you rock in Nauvoo to build the temple with? Did I not through my providence furnish men to quarry and cut stone and prepare it for the building? Did I not give you means to build the Temple there?… Such may go away but I want to have the faithful stay here to build the Temple and settle the city." - 4

The goal of receiving their sacred temple endowments before they left for the wilderness became a genuine priority for the Saints, and so they became very determined to finish the Temple in order that as many as possible of the Saints could partake of this special endowment blessing. Eventually nearly 6,000 ordinances were completed there.

Meanwhile, the unjustified contempt that the Mormon-haters felt for the Mormon's beliefs along with the unfounded angst they felt about the potential of Mormon political power overtaking the state, was beginning to build up once more in the minds of the disgruntled non-Mormon locals. It resulted in further ridiculous accusations, deplorable rumors, and exaggerated lies about the Saint's intentions. Then in order to exacerbate these adverse feelings towards the Mormons and to keep the local population's loathing of the Saints full of vim and vigor, certain Mormon-hating individuals contrived a plan to incite further unrest and hatred towards the Saints.

Among the very worst of the lot in the anti-Mormon faction, were the unscrupulous leaders, Thomas Sharp, Colonel Levi Williams, and Frank Worrell. All three of these men had participated in the attack on Carthage jail and in the murders of Joseph and Hyrum Smith, and meanwhile they certainly had not improved any in their respect and love for the Mormons.

On September 9th 1845, a meeting was held in the Green Plains settlement about six miles out of Warsaw. It was ostensibly held to discuss how the Mormons were encroaching upon the local population's property and what should be done about it. The meeting quickly became a rowdy anti-Mormon rally, but in the middle of the frenzy, and without warning, several gunshots rang out and broke the glass windows of the meeting room. The conniving agitators who had sponsored the meeting then immediately yelled out that it was the Mormons who were shooting at them and endangering their lives. However, in all reality, it wasn't the Mormons at all, but a carefully and secretly planned staged attack by the devious Mormon-hating leaders who had deliberately contrived the incident to stir up the crowd enough to make them want to take up arms against the hated Mormons.

A staged false witness said he saw two riders riding hard south towards the Morley settlement, which was a local Mormon settlement. A member of the Church named Isaac Morley had originally started the settlement, but it was now called Yelrome, the name coming from the spelling of the name Morley backwards.

The lead instigator of the devious agitators, Levi Williams, very convincingly persuaded the angry crowd that it would be morally wrong to let this attack on their peaceful meeting go unpunished, therefore justice demanded that they attack the small settlement of Yelrome to teach the threatening and thieving Mormons a lesson. This rowdy mob led by the conniving agitators then proceeded to Father Morley's settlement to terrorize the inhabitants by burning barns, houses, and crops.

A letter to Brigham Young described it as such; "By letter from Solomon Hancock, Yelrome, we learn that the mob have burned all the houses on the south side of the branch [brook], and left last evening for Lima, said they would return this morning as soon as light, and swear they will sweep through and burn everything to Nauvoo. Colonel Levi Williams is at the head of the mob."

A somewhat revealing disclosure of the actual truth about the incident came from the Governor himself. Speaking about the contrived setup of the shooting at the Green plains meeting, the unsympathetic Governor Ford wrote in his own history of Illinois that; "Some persons of their own number" had perpetrated the shooting, meaning that it was actually members of the vigilante mob that had staged the fake attack on the supposedly "peaceful" meeting in Green Plains. – 5

Father Morley's settlement was now on alert. Anticipating the return of the mob to Yelrome as the mob had threatened they would, the Church Council sent all their available men with teams and wagons to Father Morley's settlement to move all the members and their belongings out of Yelrome into Nauvoo. Meanwhile the leaders in the settlement made a written offer to the mob leaders saying in part; "We wish to sell our deeded lands as well as our improvements as low as it could be reasonably expected, reserving to ourselves the crops now on the premises; and will take in exchange, working cattle, beef cattle, cows, sheep, horses, wagons, harness, store goods, and any available property and give possession as soon as our crops can be taken care of and we receive pay for the same; the whole of which may be purchased from the undersigned acting as committee or from owners." - 6

As one might expect, this offer was completely ignored by these hateful vigilantes who had no intention of cooperating with any Mormons about anything. The hatred for the Mormons went beyond reason, especially when you consider that the Saints had neither attacked nor hurt anyone, and had simply done nothing more in their peaceful communities than to try to live their religion while peaceably laboring to provide for their families.

The next morning after the attack on Yelrome, the violent mob returned again to burn nearly forty homes, barns, and out buildings. From there the raids continued for two more days resulting in over one hundred Mormon homes being burnt and destroyed. Brigham Young requested that designated scribes should record the full details of every house burning, including the names of witnesses and the times that the crimes occurred. He also encouraged all the families of the outlying communities to bring their belongings and all their foodstuffs, including grains, potatoes, and corn, and move in to Nauvoo. One hundred and thirty four wagons from the members were pledged to bring in the besieged Mormon refugees from the surrounding communities. - 7

Meanwhile in another town, Sheriff Jacob Backenstos, who had been elected as the Sheriff of Hancock County in August of 1845, soon became despised by the anti-Mormon faction, mostly because he showed an outward fairness in dealing with the Saints and of course, in return he was receiving their obvious voting support. Therefore he was dubbed as a "Jack Mormon," even though he was a non-Mormon and had no interest in joining their church. Nonetheless, it was a fact that the very important support of the Mormon voters had been instrumental in giving him the winning votes in the election, which caused a great deal of resentment towards him among the non-Mormons.

Unfortunately, it would be Porter Rockwell that would soon become an involuntary participant in the feud between the non-Mormons and Sheriff Backenstos. Just by chance and under some unusual circumstances, Porter was forced to help defend the Sheriff against the Mormon haters, who wanted to shoot down the law officer in cold blood just because he was friendly and fair with the Mormons.

This of course, was not Porter's first encounter with Mormon haters. Porter Rockwell had known Joseph Smith since they were children, and he had experienced some of the most trying of trials at the side of the Prophet while acting as his personal bodyguard. He had even been arrested for the attempted assassination of Governor Boggs and had suffered horribly for months in a Missouri jail after being falsely accused of doing that deed at the bidding of his old friend Joe Smith. He would now come face to face with the ugly hatred for Mormons once again in merely trying to protect Sheriff Backenstos from being murdered by some local and ruthless vigilantes.

After the martyrdom, and due to the episodes of raiding and burning by the Mormon-hating mobs at Yelrome, many of the Saints became a bit "jumpy" whenever they heard fast running horses coming their way. So when Porter Rockwell and three of his companions, on one particular occasion, heard a hard running horse coming down the road, they stopped their wagon and jumped down behind it with their rifles ready as a precautionary measure. The running horse turned out to be the horse and buggy of Sheriff Backentos trying to escape with his very life. He was at the moment fleeing from a mob of eight or ten men from Warsaw who were bent on killing what they called, that "Mormon loving Sheriff." This unjustified hatred had come about from nothing more than the Sheriff just trying to carry out the duties of his job, as he attempted to raise a posse to stop the raiders from burning Mormon homes.

The terrorized and unnerved Backentos brought his buggy to a sliding stop just in front of the defending Mormon's wagon. When he recognized Rockwell, he asked the Mormon men for help in the name of the law. At this point, the pursuers were close enough that the Mormons were able to identify some of the riders as being the very raiders that had attacked and burned the Saint's homes, and so the Mormon men didn't hesitate to help out the Sheriff.

The mob's riders rode up closer and then pulled their horses up short not knowing exactly what to do next in the face of these new and well armed defenders who were holding up behind a wagon with the Sheriff. The marauders then yelled out to the Mormons that if they would turn over the Sheriff, they would not be harmed, but otherwise they too would be killed. The Sheriff yelled back that he had just deputized these men that were with him, and therefore the riders had better be on their way and return to their homes if they didn't want to be arrested and hauled off to jail.

The warning fell upon deaf ears, and instead the very determined pursuers raised their guns and proceeded menacingly towards the defenders. Porter Rockwell was mostly a quite man who didn't say much, but beyond that, he was a dead shot. When it was obvious that the riders were not going to stop, the Sheriff ordered Rockwell to fire his rifle. Rockwell's musket ball hit the belt buckle of the leader, Frank Worrell, right where Rockwell had aimed, and it blew Frank out of the saddle and up and over the rump of his horse and he hit the ground hard. That caught the full attention of the rest of the "mob" creating a bit of a panic. The remainder of the Warsaw mob couldn't get away fast enough withdrawing in a very big hurry and leaving behind a big cloud of dust and profanity. After yelling curses at the hated Mormons and the Mormon loving sheriff, they later returned to pick up the body of good old Frank.

Church's history described it this way: "Sheriff Backenstos then turned to the mob and commanded them to stop, and as they continued to advance raising their guns, he ordered Rockwell to fire; he did so aiming at the clasp of the belt on one of the mob, which proved to be Frank Worrell, who fell from his horse and the rest turned back and soon brought up a wagon and put his body into it."

As an interesting side note, it should be noted that Sheriff Backentos himself was later tried for the murder of Frank Worrell, but was acquitted by a fair-minded judge who ruled it self-defense and handed out the same verdict for Rockwell. In addition, the Judge also charged two of the mob members, who had been witnesses during the trial, with perjury, and then sent them to jail for lying about the incident. Once in awhile, justice does prevail. – 8

Sometime after Hyrum and Joseph Smith were murdered, the state of Illinois made a halfhearted attempt to bring the guilty to justice. The state militia was sent to Hancock County to keep the peace while nine men accused of the brutal murders of the Smith brothers were indicted. To no one's surprise, the very biased local juries quickly acquitted all nine men.

The locals however, had a whole different idea of what real justice should look like in regards to the shooting of Frank Worrell by Rockwell in self defense as compared to the murder of the unarmed Joseph and Hyrum Smith. Even though the Frank Worrell shooting had already been declared as self-defense, the locals stubbornly saw it as a great miscarriage of justice and were infuriated that the Judge let Rockwell off the hook. Thus the Frank Worrell's shooting stirred up the locals to even a greater degree of seeking retaliation than before, and the incident only served to heighten their contempt and strengthen their unreasonable resolve to rid themselves of all Mormons.

Ironically, even the open-minded citizens of Quincy Illinois, who had been very sympathetic to the Saints in the past, eventually became increasingly anxious and concerned about all the violence besetting the Mormons. Even though the citizens of Quincy had been the very first to welcome the Mormons in the beginning and had been very Christian in helping the Saints back when the desperate Mormon refugees first came from Missouri, they now were feeling a great deal of anxiety about the violence spilling over. They now felt for everybody's best interest, the Mormons should just pick up and leave the state due to the possible collateral damage to their own citizenry.

In September 22 of 1845, the town of Quincy Illinois held a meeting that came up with a petition aimed at the very presence of the Saints, and delivered it to the Church leaders. The committee's letter basically said that since the Mormons had already talked about leaving the state, and now in the face of so much trouble brewing around the Mormons, they wondered how soon the Mormons would be able to leave? Two days later Brigham Young responded to the Quincy committee telling them that his people's only desire was to live in peace with all men, however his people would be prepared to leave in the coming spring. – 9

Then came Governor Thomas Ford's latest decree regarding the unrest between the Mormons and the locals. He basically said he was unable to provide any help to the Saints or give them any kind of protection from the law. He insinuated his hands were tied in the matter. The Governor subsequently sent a dispatch to the Mormon leaders summing up in his political double talk the reasons that he was simply unable to protect them from the violent mobs.

Governor Ford declared that though he was sorry that the Mormons were in conflict with their neighbors, he was powerless to fix the situation and insinuated that the Mormons were now on their own. He concluded his excuses by saying; he was simply unable to provide any full time protection from the State Militias to deter the local violence being perpetrated against the Mormon people and he thus washed his hands of the whole matter. Therefore he indicated, because the local long time residents were entirely set against the Mormon people living there "abouts," and they obviously were opposed to any Mormons living anywhere in Illinois, it would be best for everybody, if the Mormons just left the state. He emphasized once again that because he personally could not guarantee their safety, and he did not have any way of preventing the violence that would soon come against the Mormons, the best way to defend themselves, was by their leaving the State of Illinois.

The Governor's "Pontius Pilate" like excuses simply delighted Thomas Sharp and his cohort Levi Williams. This new unsympathetic and very ominous announcement from the Governor of the state amounted to nothing short of open season on the Saints, and there would now be virtually no legal repercussions coming from the state against any perpetrators of violence against the Mormons. Meanwhile an anti-Mormon rally was held in Carthage involving the Mormon-haters from nine different counties who were just licking their chops when they heard about the Governor's statement disavowing any responsibility for the protection of the Mormon people. As a result of the Governor's statement, the extreme rhetoric of the vigilantes reached a new heightened state and there arose wide-open talk calling for actual violent criminal acts against the Mormons. They now wanted to do much more than just rough up a few of them; this time they wanted blood. Consequently, schemes were made by the enemies of the Church to completely run any and all Mormons out of state and if that required extreme bloody violence, so be it.

Around this time, on October 5 & 6th of 1845, the Church leaders held their General Conference on which occasion Brigham dedicated the baptismal font in the unfinished temple vowing that they would finish it before they left Nauvoo. It is also believed that at this same conference, or at least shortly afterwards, Parley P. Pratt presented to the Saints his list of required travel preparations that would be necessary for the long trek west to their new home. It included a list of foodstuffs and all the other supplies and necessities for making the long arduous trip. Shortly thereafter, Nauvoo became a giant workshop turning black smith's shops, lumber mills, and brick kilns, into wheelwright shops, canvas cover shops, harness shops, and other wagon equipment making facilities. This concerted emergency effort was all being done in order to make ready for the long difficult journey and to get the Saints prepared for their anticipated demanding trek to the Rocky Mountains.

Any attempts of the Saints to get fair and reasonable prices out of their property from the non-Mormon local buyers were laughable. Pioneer John D. Lee later wrote that his large home that cost him $8000 was bid for only $800; a ridiculous offer which he refused. He then left his large home in the hands of the selected committee brethren who had been designated to stay behind in Nauvoo to sell Mormon property. Out of desperation, the committee eventually sold John D. Lee's valued $8,000 property for the insulting and paltry price of $12.50. – 10

At that same October conference, Brigham Young invited Lucy Mack Smith, the matriarch of the Smith family, to speak to the Saints. Even though she supported Brigham Young and the Twelve as the new leaders of the Church, and stated that their decision to journey West was the right decision, by that spring her health had deteriorated to the point that she elected to stay in Nauvoo with her daughter Lucy. She spent her final years living with Emma and died shortly before she turned 81 years old on May 14th 1856. – 11

Eventually, maybe out of guilt, the Governor finally got around to sending the state militia out to supposedly keep the peace in that part of the state. Some of the Saints felt safe enough to return to their homes in the outlying areas to salvage what they could. One such farmer was a long time faithful member of the church by the name of Edmund Durfee. Along with some members of his family, he returned to his farm to dig some potatoes and salvage some grain. After their wagon was all loaded, they left their burned out farm behind to go and stay at their neighbor's home for the night. However, in the middle of the night, a mob set fire to the neighbor's grain fields and barn. While Durfee and his neighbor were getting the livestock out of the burning barn, a shot was fired which barely missed the neighbor. All of a sudden, as if on cue, nearly twenty men who had been hiding behind a log fence started shooting at the two running men and Edmund Durfee was shot in the neck and killed instantly on the 15th of November 1845.

This made him one of the first martyrs since the deaths of Joseph, Hyrum, and their brother Samuel. Sam had died about a month after his brother's murders. Mother Smith said it was from the ill effects caused by being chased by the mob. – 12

In November of 1845, the Twelve and other priesthood leaders dedicated the attic story of the Nauvoo temple so that it could be used for performing the sacred endowments. The women helped decorate the attic room with plants, paintings, mirrors, and nice furniture that would be appropriate for such a hallowed place. Finally in December of 1845, the veil that had been sewn by the sisters was hung in the new endowment room in the temple attic for the special ordinances of the endowment. After those first sacred ordinances were performed, there seemed to come over the rest of the Saints a great desire and urgency to do as many endowments as possible before they had to make the long trek west. Between the 10th of December and the twentieth, in just ten days, a total of 561 Saints received their long awaited endowments. Before his untimely death, Joseph Smith had already sealed a few selected couples for time and eternity on the occasion when the ordinance had first been revealed as found in D&C sections 131 and 132. However, the sealing ordinance was not officially available to the general population of the Saints until January 7th of 1846. – 13

Needless to say, at this time in Nauvoo there was a great deal of anxiety concerning the recent incidents and a general uneasiness coming by way of the continuing anti-Mormon talk and the increased harassment involving further acts of violence perpetrated by their relentless persecutors. Under these circumstances, there was certainly not a whole lot of joy or humor to be found among the Saints as their enemies continued to doggedly attempt to drive them from their own homes. However, there is one true story called the "Bogus Brigham" story that did provide a few smiles for the Saints even in the midst of their oppression.

At around five P.M. one evening at the Nauvoo Temple, Almon W. Babbitt came into the Temple and reported that federal officers from Springfield accompanied by several state troopers were at the door of the Temple fully intending to search it for the purpose of arresting some of the Twelve, but most especially Amasa Lyman and Brigham Young. On hearing this, Brigham was somewhat unsettled for a moment, and then fell into deep thought. Suddenly a light bulb switched on in Brigham's head. Brigham told his coachman, George Grant, to go down to the front of the Temple and pull Brigham's carriage up to the temple door as if he was waiting for Brigham to come down the stairs and leave the premises in his coach.

Brigham then asked William Miller, who was about the same size and built, to put on Brigham's hat along with Brother Kimball's cloak and proceed downstairs where he was to attempt to get into Brigham's carriage. The Federal Marshal and his assistants were waiting at the door and just as Brother Miller was about to step into the carriage, the Marshal assuming that this was Brigham Young, stopped him and put him under arrest on a writ from the United States court charging him with counterfeiting the coin of the United States. Brother Miller pretended to mildly resist and proceeded to tell the Marshal that there must be some mistake as he was not guilty of anything, however the Marshal insisted that he was under arrest any way.

At this point, Brother Miller asked the Marshal if they could go down to the Mansion house so that he could get counsel and ascertain if the proceedings were all legal. After Esq. Edmonds examined the writ and pronounced it to be legal, the Marshall then insisted that they must be on their way to Carthage. Brother Miller continued to protest that there was some mistake about it all, for he certainly was not guilty of any of the things that had been charged in the writ, but he went along with the Marshal anyway. As they approached the town of Carthage, the troops escorting the procession began to whoop and holler, as they enthusiastically yelled to a gathering crowd that they had captured Old Brigham Young himself, as they all rode into the town.

The Marshal then proceeded to put up his infamous prisoner at the local pub and the rumor soon spread through out the town that it was Brigham Young in the custody of the Marshal at Hamilton's Tavern. It just so happened that a Mormon apostate named George W. Thatcher, who was now the county commissioner's clerk, was actually well acquainted with both Brother Miller and Brigham Young. So when he came into the tavern to see the notorious Brigham Young, he was quite shocked to discover that the famous prisoner was not Brigham at all, but in all reality Brother William Miller. He then gave a loud hoot and loudly announced, "That's not Brigham Young. It's William Miller." The Marshal then walked over to Brother Miller and then marched him into a private room. After a little bit of conversation, the Marshal said to Mr. Miller, "I am informed you are not Mr. Young."

Ah!" exclaimed Brother Miller, "then if I should prove not to be Mr. Young, it would be a worse joke on you than the Turley affair," he replied, "I'll be damned if it won't." The reference to the Turley affair was probably due to the false earlier arrest of Theodore Turley for making bogus money. The Marshal then asked Miller, if his name was Brigham Young or not, and Miller answered, "I never told you my name was Young, did I?"

"No," replied the Marshal, "but one of my men professed to be acquainted with Mr. Young, and pointed you out to me to be him."

It was then that Sheriff William Backenstos, who also happened to be in town, was called in and he also verified that the man in custody was not Brigham Young. Another man approached and said he would also swear that the prisoner was not Brigham Young. The Marshal apologized and said he was sorry, and asked Brother Miller just what the "hect" was his name. Brother Miller replied, "It is William Miller." The poor disgusted and embarrassed Marshal left the establishment accompanied by a great roar of laughter coming from the tavern's patrons, and left the Saints with a hilarious tale to tell their children's children. - 14

*   *   *

1. See History of the Church, Vol.6, Introduction, p.25

2. See History of the Church, Vol.6, Introduction, p. 25

3. See "Church History in the Fullness of Time" pp. 299-300 and also "American Moses", pp 122-123.

4. See History of the Church 7:256-257.

5. See History of the Church, Vol.7, Ch.32, p. 441. And also "History of Illinois" 1854 by Thomas Ford 2:293-294

6. See History of the Church, Vol.7, Ch.32, p.442

7. See History of the Church, Vol.7, Ch.32, p.439-443

8. See History of the Church, Vol.7, Ch.32, and p.446.

9. See History of the Church, Vol.7, Ch.32, p.447-453.

10. See History of the Church, Vol.7, p.535-536 Also "Erastus Snow" Larsen, p. 102

11. See "Encyclopedia of Mormonism", "Smith, Lucky Mack"

12. See History of the Church, 7:523, 528. Also Wikipedia SAMUEL H. SMITH

13. See History of the Church, 7:542-548 And also History of the Church, 7:566

14. See History of the Church, Vol.7, Ch.37, p.549-551

*   *   *

Chapter Twenty-Three

LEAVING NAUVOO

*　　*　　*

At the beginning of 1846, the January cold and dealing with the apostate traitors weren't the only things on the minds of the Saints that were creating trials for them. The anti-Mormon faction in Illinois wanted the Mormons gone for good and they certainly weren't going to patiently wait for the Saints to take their time to leave the premises, or for that matter, to even get out of the entire state by yesterday. Under the mounting pressure from their enemies to leave the state, along with the rumors that federal troops in St. Louis might be marching upon the Saints at any time, Brigham Young announced to the rest of the Church leaders that they would probably not be able to hold off the demands of their enemies much longer.

Even though he had petitioned local and state officials to let them wait until the spring grasses appeared on the plains before they left Nauvoo, the officials warned the Saints that they would almost certainly just be asking for further violence if they stayed any longer. Thus with the situation deteriorating by the day, Brigham organized the Church leaders into companies to be led by captains of hundreds, captains of fifties, and captains of tens, and he then informed and urged these Captains and the other Saints under their leadership to be ready to leave for the "West" at any time after the first part of February.

And so it was that during first week of February, the first of the Saints left Nauvoo, but without Brigham Young leading them. This first group on their own headed for the wide-open plains in their wagons as they anticipated a long haul to the untamed wilds of the "West" to ultimately find a new safer home in the Rocky Mountains. The first day out found them camping only 8 miles west of Nauvoo at Sugar Creek Iowa, which was located just on the other side of the Mississippi River near the settlement of Montrose, Iowa, and that's where they would wait for Brigham another couple of weeks.

At this same time another group of Saints led by Elder Samuel Brannan left from the East coast aboard a three masted sailing ship, which was headed for South America. Their ultimate destination was the Pacific shores of California where at that point they anticipated a trek overland to settle in the Rocky Mountains with the rest of the Saints. The good ship "Brooklyn" just happened to leave New York harbor on the exact same day as the first wagons left Nauvoo, which was February 4th 1846.

The "Brooklyn" would arrive in California six long months later after a 24,000-mile voyage. Meanwhile the Mormon pioneers, after a 1300 mile trek would not arrive in the Salt Lake Valley until a year and a half later after their hurried departure from Nauvoo. The by-land Saints were obviously much slower due to their many unanticipated delays along the trail, and those rest stops at Garden Grove, Mount Pisgah, and Council Bluffs, plus their extended wintering at Winter Quarters Nebraska. Their plodding 1300-mile journey was a slow endeavor, and sometimes felt so sluggish that it reached a point of being very discouraging to the weary pioneers. It was obviously a considerably slower and a much more difficult means of travel compared to the much faster, less physically demanding alternative, by ocean voyage to California.

Samuel Brannan, who in many ways was similar in nature to John C. Bennett, in that both men were more interested in promoting their own agendas than in any serious religious aspirations. However, Brannan after being counseled by Church leaders to find a way for the poorer New York Saints to make their way by ship to the new Zion would voluntarily become the leader who would eventually shepherd those "by-the-ship Saints" to California.

As a young man, Sam Brannan had joined the Church while living with his sister near Kirtland. Only later did he become active in the Church when he could see opportunities to advance his own personal ambitions, and so he then became an editor for a Church newspaper in New York where he would become acquainted with Elder Orson Pratt.

When Brigham Young was made aware that the poor Saints in New York didn't even have the means or equipment to even make it as far as Nauvoo, let alone make it across the western wilderness, he came up with a "by-the-sea" alternative. Yes, it was true that Brigham Young had assigned Samuel Brannan to investigate the possibilities of taking some of the Saints around the Cape Horn of South America by ship to reach California and from there, proceed overland to the Rocky Mountains. Never the less, Brannan had not received any authority to make any sort of binding agreements on behalf of the Church, especially with those slimy schemers in Washington D.C. There is little information on exactly who it was that sent Brannan to Washington D.C. to speak to government officials, if anyone actually had.

On January 29th 1846, Brigham received a letter from Samuel Brannan saying that the federal government had plans to not let the Mormons leave Illinois, which was rather ironic or maybe just a little suspicious since every other government official they had dealt with had been quite enthusiastic in inviting them to leave, even insinuating good riddance. Elder Brannan was a relatively new comer to the Church and often came off as being something of a "wheeler-dealer," a characteristic that prompted him into making some unauthorized deals of his own initiative in Washington D.C. and in New York.

Brigham Young recorded in the record: "At eight a. m., we assembled for prayer, Elder John E. Page was the mouth. After which I called the Twelve and bishops together and informed them that I had received a letter from Brother Samuel Brannan stating that he had been at Washington and had learned that the secretary of war and other members of the cabinet were laying plans and were determined to prevent our moving west: alleging that it is against the law for an armed body of men to go from the United States to any other government." - 1

While Brannan was in Washington D.C. there were reports that he had made a somewhat questionable deal with some scheming con men and thus fell foolishly for the flimflam scam of the former Postmaster General, one Amos Kendall and his partner A.G. Benson. These two Washington based schemers personally promised that they would persuade the Feds to let the Mormons leave for the West unhindered, providing that the Church leaders would sign a contract stipulating that where ever the Mormons settled, they would deed every other unit of land to Kendall and his partner. This deal was being portrayed as having been made with the confirmed approval of the President of the United States, the President supposedly being their silent partner. Otherwise, they insinuated that the President would be forced to commandeer all the arms from the Mormons to prevent the Saints from becoming an aide to a foreign enemy. Upon hearing the very suspicious details of this very questionable deal by Kendall and Benson, Brigham Young and the council of the Twelve Apostles perceived the contract to be nothing less than a contrived shakedown using fear tactics and was in all reality outright extortion, and so they forthwith rejected it completely. - 2a

Never the less, whatever kind of dealings were almost made with Kendall and his partner, Brannan came to realize the Church Council was never going to buy in to it, and so he was going to have to proceed on his own if things were ever going to come all together for his ambitious plans. Although Brigham Young wrote in his own manuscript that he had appointed Samuel Brannan to take the New York Saints by sea to California, some historical records say it was Elder Orson Pratt of the Twelve, the ranking Church Official in New York, who authorized Sam Brannan to organize the expedition to take the poorest of the New York Saints by sea to California and then on to their new home in the Rocky Mountains. Proceeding by whoever's authority, Brannan was able to secure a three masted sailing ship and its crew for a lease of $1200 per month to sail around the Cape Horn of South America and then up to the west coast of the Americas to California.

Thus the "Brooklyn" left New York harbor on February 4th 1846 with 238 people aboard, 175 of them being of the poorer members of the New York Saints. They followed the wind on a course that carried them along with the north-east trade winds towards the Cape Verde Islands just off the coast of Africa and then from there, they sailed upon another trade wind route that took them in the complete opposite direction. On this new course, they sailed in a southwesterly direction on a somewhat dangerous route that would take them around the "Cape Horn" at the very stormy and dangerous southern tip of the South American Continent. From that point, they sailed past the Magellan Strait and around the south end of the Chilean island of Tierra del Fuego and then they plotted a new course north by northwest towards the Juan Fernandez Islands that sat 400 miles off the very long and extended coast of Chile. At this spot, they took a more westerly course sailing all the way out to the middle of the Pacific Ocean to the Sandwich Islands, which the explorer Captain Cook had originally named after a British Lord and sandwich inventor, the Earl of Sandwich. The Sandwich Islands would later be renamed Hawaii after a chief named Hawaii-loa, who had allegedly led the Polynesians to these very islands. There in the balmy tropical isles, around the 20th of June 1846, the "Brooklyn" dropped off some cargo upon the local shores and re-supplied their own ship. Soon thereafter they set a new and more easterly course leaving Hawaii behind to resume their voyage towards their real destination of the U.S. mainland and their journey's end in California. – 2b

As they made the final leg of their journey eastward across the Pacific, they continued courageously on as they sailed towards the rising sun and finally arrived at the focus of their long ocean journey coming ashore on the mainland coast of California in July of 1846. They had just completed an amazing 24,000-mile voyage, roughly equivalent to the sum total of miles that make up the circumference of the entire earth. So after eventually reaching their long sought-after destination, they breathed a sigh of relief having made a very long and round about extended ocean pilgrimage, a journey by which the crow's route would have only been about three thousand miles.

In summary, this additional 21,000 miles constituting a much longer journey had started out by taking them in the opposite direction as they followed the Atlantic trade winds to the African Cape Verde Islands, then turning southwest they caught the southerly trade winds and sailed all the way down toward the tip of the South American continent, around the "Horn." Proceeding on they sailed North up along the Pacific coast with a several thousand mile side-trip to Hawaii and then on to California, all the while enduring considerable tribulation en route.

They had barely survived several menacing storms, had two new babies born, lost two milk cows overboard, and lost at least eleven passengers including some children to scarlet fever, scurvy, and other maladies. At one point, they ran into a terrifying storm that nearly brought the risky voyage to a very violent end, which had endangered their very lives and left them nearly drained of energy and hope. Yet, because they were still a far distance from any land and there was just nothing else to do but just keep sailing, they sailed on to California.

The strong-willed Sam Brannan and his weary passengers finally came ashore at San Francisco Bay in July of 1846 after six long months at sea, at which time they had completed one of the longest voyages ever made by a religious group. They had arrived just barely a month after the U.S. Portsmouth under Commander John B. Montgomery and his stalwart sailors had raised the American flag there and claimed the area from Mexico. If the "Brooklyn" had not made the cargo detour to the Hawaiian Islands, they would have arrived in San Francisco bay while it was still under the authority of the Mexican government, which might have resulted in an entirely different outcome in California's history.

However as it was, Samuel Brannan was able to establish a Mormon colony in the new land at a settlement that was originally called Yerba Buena. It had initially been settled by a mix of early Mexican and white mercenary adventurers, however, under Brannan's ambitious leadership it became the first civilian and family settled American colony in California. The settlement prospered greatly under the warm Californian sun through the labors of the hard working industrious Mormons who built their homes and businesses there. Sam Brannan also prospered greatly as he accumulated a number of flourishing financial holdings and several businesses, all of which would help him to become California's first millionaire. His personal fortunes were soon substantial and built up significantly through his own shrewd business dealings that were further added to by the many sundry needs of the "Forty Niners" and the quickly growing U.S. California territory.

A year after coming ashore in California, Sam Brannan and a small contingency of Saints from San Francisco would journey all the way to

Wyoming to meet with Brigham Young and his Mormon pioneer company at the site of the Green River crossing in Western Wyoming. It was there that Brannan enthusiastically tried to do all he could to persuade Brigham to bring the rest of the Saints to California to live in "the land of milk and honey." Brigham with the foresight of a prophet refused. Wilford Woodruff reported that the Prophet's words to Brannan were; "No, sir; I am going to stop right here. I am going to build a city here. I am going to build a temple here, and I am going to build a country here." – 3

Samuel Brannan the man was a very ambitious soul and seemed to have had a special knack for making fortunes. However, even though Sam Brannan did become a millionaire, an influential newspaperman, a prominent mercantile business owner, and a highly respected Church and community leader there in his home community of San Francisco, it would come to pass that it would all most regrettably be lost. His many good fortunes and his highly respected reputation would all eventually vanish by way of a surfeit of poor choices, which caused all his fortunes to sadly pass the way of the blowing wind.

His Church membership was lost when he was excommunicated for not being able to account for the tithing money he collected from the "Brooklyn Saints" and the California Mormon miners. This blow to his ego had followed a previous disciplinary action of having been disfellowshipped at an earlier time when he supported Joseph's own brother, William Smith, as the next leader of the Church. Late in life, after a bitter and very expensive divorce and a few other devastating economic misfortunes, he lost his businesses, drank heavily, was left penniless, and died with little respect from anyone he ever knew. And so it was that he passed away in the extreme poverty and shadow of his own bad choices. Yes, it was a very sad ending indeed for Sam Brannan, but it was not an unusual scenario for a man whose priorities and primary focus was on accumulating as many riches as he could possibly gather to himself, rather than keeping in mind where life's real priorities should be focused. – 4

Meanwhile back in Illinois along the Mississippi River in Nauvoo, the rest of the Saints were getting ready to abandon the state in droves as they faced increasing persecution. When the first Saints left Nauvoo, Brigham Young had originally planned on leading the first wagons himself as sort of a flagship for his people to follow as they crossed the mighty river by ferryboat. However, what he had not planned on was the large crowds of determined Saints waiting for him at the temple to receive their sacred covenants and endowments. Out of compassion for them and being unable to politely disperse them, he spent the next two weeks, day and night, inside the temple performing temple ordinances. Even though the Saints knew they would have to leave their beloved temple behind soon, they were very zealous in getting the most use out of it while they could. "Nor did their zeal and sacrifices go unrewarded; for from December 10th, 1845, when the first endowments were given, to the 7th of February, 1846, when the Temple was closed for ordinance work, 5,669 ordinances had been performed." – 5

Though the Temple was heavily used during the winter of 1846, it wouldn't be until April 30th of that year, while Brigham Young's group was already on the trail headed west, that the Temple received its official dedication after its completion. Certain parts of it had previously been dedicated for special use, but not the entire temple. Now Brigham's brother, Joseph Young, gave the dedicatory prayer for the completed temple in a private ceremony. The next day Elder Orson Hyde performed a second dedicatory prayer in a public ceremony, and stated that in the face of all their adversaries who said the building would never be finished or dedicated, "We have done both." – 5

Before the Saints left Nauvoo there was a fire in the temple caused by drying temple clothes too close to a stove. There was some damage to the roof but it was repaired. However, it would only be a couple of years later when the temple would be completely destroyed by an arsonist's fire, which was credited to the anti-Mormon faction in the area. Brigham Young made some interesting comments about the fate of the Nauvoo Temple.

"Previous to crossing the Mississippi river, we had met in that temple and handed it over to the Lord God of Israel; and when I saw the flames, I said, 'Good, Father, if you want it to be burned up.' I hoped to see it burned before I left, but I did not. I was glad when I heard of its being destroyed by fire, and of the walls having fallen in, and said, 'Hell, you cannot now occupy it." - 6

Two years later after the vast majority of the Saints had already left Nauvoo, the temple was totally destroyed by an arsonist on the 19th of November 1848; "…our citizens were awakened by the alarm of fire, which, when first discovered, was bursting out through the spire of the Temple,…seen first about three o'clock in the morning,…Although the morning was tolerably dark, still, when the flames shot upwards, the spire, the streets, and the houses for nearly a mile distant were lighted up, so as to render even the smallest objects discernible. The glare of the vast torch, pointing skyward, …men looked on with faces sad as if the crumbling ruins below were consuming all their hopes." - 7

It was Lewis A. Bidamon, Emma Smith's second husband and "the landlord of the Nauvoo Mansion, Illinois, who stated to Elders George A. Smith and Erastus Snow, that the inhabitants of Warsaw, Carthage, Pontusac and surrounding settlements in consequence of jealousy that Nauvoo would still retain its superior importance as a town and might induce the Mormons to return, contributed a purse of five hundred dollars which they gave to Joseph Agnew in consideration of his burning the Temple: and that said Agnew was the person who set the building on fire." - 7

The Nauvoo temple represented years of hard labor and the very best that the Saints had to offer to the Lord and it had become the symbol of their most heartfelt and fullest commitment to their God. Its loss was heartbreaking to the Saints, but never the less this holy edifice had fulfilled its divine purposes for its designated limited time in history and thus it had served and completed its earthly journey through its own finite season for the needs of the Lord and His people.

Unfortunately, it seems to be with human nature in general that the best of leaders will be criticized and second-guessed by someone or another for any decisions they make, in one way or another. While Brigham was very busy performing the sacred work at the temple, the Saints waiting on the other side of the river in Montrose and Sugar Creek were complaining because he wasn't there to lead them west. Meanwhile back in the city of Nauvoo, there were other Saints who were criticizing him because Brigham had not yet led them out of Nauvoo and across the river to start their long journey, and all this delay was forcing them to just sit around idly wasting time, waiting for their leader to get them on the road. As one recognizes the typical human nature being illustrated here, one must remember that not even Jesus Christ was able to please everybody.

Finally on February 15th 1846, Brigham left Nauvoo with his twenty something wives and children among a larger company of about fifty souls, and they proceeded to meet up with the Sugar Creek Camp Saints about nine miles into the Iowa territory. Unfortunately, when many of the other Saints saw Brigham leave Nauvoo, they got themselves into too big of a hurry to leave with him and consequently a great many of the Saints left unprepared with inadequate supplies, no more than a week's worth in many cases. On the westward side of the river, there were other generous brethren who had kindly let their horses be borrowed so that their stranded neighbors could now pull the waiting wagons on the other side that were still left in Nauvoo, but this left the lenders themselves without their draft animals to go onward. Many of the Saints were not only ill supplied and lacking enough horses, but they were definitely not prepared for the bitter winter weather that was about to come upon them with a vengeance.

In the last week of February, when there had still only been a few hundred Saints that had actually left Nauvoo in spite of the increased persecution by the mobs, there was a record breaking cold that descended upon the mid-west. It was twelve degrees below zero weather and 8 inches of snow that hit the plains and the city of Nauvoo like a blast of Artic vengeance. This was a highly unusual weather occurrence, which saw the grand old Mississippi River freeze solid all the way across from bank to bank. However, in a case of reverse fortunes, it turned out to be a miracle from the Lord as hundreds of Saints in their wagon groups were able to simultaneously cross the mighty river over the solidly frozen ice, rather than to wait for and go singly by the considerably slower ferry, which couldn't have operated anyway considering the solidly frozen river. – 8

The next day after leaving Nauvoo, President Young spent February 16, 1846, in organizing the camp. After two weeks of further delays, even though Brigham wasn't feeling well, he decided they could wait no longer. The first of March finally saw the break up of the encampment at Sugar Creek where some of the Saints had been camping for several weeks as they waited on Brigham Young's leadership. March weather brought cold windy storminess with thawing muddy trails that were sometimes virtually impassable. Several members of the camp died from exposure to the weather, and many of the wagons were still without a sufficient amount of horses to pull them. After three more days of travel, they pulled up for rest and repairs, but were still less than thirty miles out of Nauvoo.

Drudging onward, April finally saw the initial great body of the departing Saints on their way to the West. Somewhere near the Chariton River of southeastern Iowa, the pioneers were then at last organized into companies and the individual apostles were appointed to take charge of the leadership duties in their separately organized divisions. – 9

Contrary to the popular pioneer lore of there being just one big exodus from out of Nauvoo, the Saints actually left Nauvoo in three entirely separate waves during the year of 1846. Brigham's initial group of about 50 souls finally left Nauvoo on the 15th of February and camped at Sugar Creek where they met up the vanguard group who had already began their trek back on February 4th 1846. After joining with the first bunch that had been waiting for them, the now much bigger group was finally on their way. Traveling an average of only about two miles per day during the spring thaw, the two joined groups found themselves barely 116 miles out of Nauvoo after two months. Brigham Young then seeing that there was going to have to be some real adjustments if they were to make any headway, made some needed changes that sped up their journey west. After many trials and bitter hardships, and a year and half later, Brigham would eventually lead 147 Saints all the way to the Salt Lake Valley arriving in July of 1847. His very confident and strong leadership, his solid planning and guidance, and his divinely inspired wisdom, would later cause some historians to call him the "American Moses."

Meanwhile, after that first wave of Saints left in February 1846, the second wave left Nauvoo three months later in the late spring. At that time it was Wilford Woodruff who spoke to some three thousand Saints at the Nauvoo temple site on the 10th of May extolling the idea that there is "a time and a season for everything," and he thus initiated the second wave of migration. It was by far the largest group consisting eventually of more than 11,000 Saints all departing during the celebrated "Spring Exodus," and continuing their massive departure through all of the month of May and extending it into June of 1846.

And then there was the third wave of Saints, consisting of around 1,000 Mormon refugees, who had been forced to leave Nauvoo at gunpoint as they fled the besieged city sometime in the fall of that year. They camped at the "Poor Camp" in Montrose Iowa with little or no provisions and thus had been unable to make but very few preparations for the long trip.

They soon found themselves on the verge of starvation and in a state of true desperation trying to survive under very dire circumstances. So they knelt to very humbly pray before the Lord their God to give them some kind of help. Suddenly a huge dark cloud coming out of the west blacked the sky. In a miraculous answer to those prayers, the Lord sent a form of "manna from heaven" to save their lives at this hallowed site of the famous "Miracle of the Quails." Thousands of birds tumbled out of the sky and dropped at their feet. At this very special place, the starving pioneers were inundated by massive numbers of flocks of easily caught quails, which saved them from sure starvation. It was a miraculous rescue that staved off what could have been a very tragic and disastrous fate, but instead they were saved by their sincere and humble prayers. Divine providence had surely kept them from a very tragic and catastrophic outcome during that October of 1846. -10a

Meanwhile, Brigham Young's advanced company of pioneers was trekking onward through the unpredictable spring weather of the random and uncertain April showers of 1846. By this time the pioneer company had grown to some 400 wagons. They were able to finally make it as far as the Grand River area in Iowa on April 24th, after many weeks of having to deal with rough rutted trails, prairie fires, and even rattlesnakes. They settled in an encampment on the Locust River 150 miles from Nauvoo. Here extensive crops were planted. It was there among many acres of wild onions that they decided to establish a temporary settlement that they called Garden Grove where 359 men cut trees, built fences, dug wells, built bridges, and constructed 48 homes. In addition, there was a significant acreage of land prepared for growing crops for the use of those Saints who would be coming later.

Parley P Pratt had gone ahead of the main body to search for the Grand River. Twenty-seven miles farther west in southern Iowa, a short time later on May 18th, Parley P. Pratt established Mount Pisgah on a fork of the Grand River that was 191 miles west of Nauvoo. These temporary settlements turned out to be a blessing and a very beneficial idea of well-planned inspired thinking for the welfare of the many Saints that were still coming up behind them. Brigham and the other leaders wisely instituted these temporary settlements or "stop-overs" for the main purpose of raising food crops and to provide provisions to help those members of the Church that were following in the rear guard on their westward journey. - 10b

Brigham Young, who was the divinely chosen leader of the LDS Church at this juncture of Church history, was visionary man in more ways than one. In addition to his seemingly many inspired leadership decisions, he apparently experienced more than one vision concerning the Church's destiny in the Rocky Mountains. The first was in Nauvoo, as recounted by George A. Smith, where Brigham saw the Prophet Joseph in a vision, and the Prophet Joseph Smith showed Brigham Young the inspirational landmark called Ensign Peak just north of the site of the future downtown Salt Lake City. The second vision happened somewhere on the plains of Iowa as reported by John R. Young in which Brigham saw the Salt Lake Valley so clearly that he would later recognize it the instant he saw it saying: "This is the right Place." – 11

By June 14 1846, President Brigham Young, along with the help of Heber C. Kimball, Parley P. Pratt, and the other church leaders had finally led the advanced company of the Mormon Pioneers all the way across Iowa to the east bank of the Missouri River to a spot that was soon to be called Council Bluffs. The next day a council meeting was held where the leaders decided to move back onto the bluffs where there was spring water and some protection from the Indians. However, the brethren found that the Pottawattami Indians were quite friendly after all and the chief showed the Saints his desire to interact with them peaceably. The Omaha Indians on the other side of the river were not quite as friendly, never the less, the Mormons developed a reputation for treating the Indians fairly and consequently they had very little trouble with them along the way to the Salt Lake Valley.

The east side of Missouri River at the site of Council Bluffs Iowa would in future times become an important site for the pioneers. For the thousands of Latter-day Saints who would later be unable to find any available space in the camp at Winter Quarters Nebraska, they would find this alternate camp site at Council Bluffs on the east side of the Missouri River to be quite adequate. Between 1846 and 1852, Western Iowa would become the headquarters for a substantial Mormon population. It soon became known as Kanesville. Not too surprisingly, there were a number of the pioneers who finally decided to not gamble their lives and fortunes by proceeding any farther west, and they found Western Iowa to be a perfectly suitable place to settle their families and make their permanent homes and farms on the east side of the Missouri river. Much of the growth there came a little later after the Winter Quarters site on the Nebraska side of the river was abandoned in early 1848 in response to pressure from the U.S. governmental to vacate the Indian lands. – 12

Just two weeks after arriving at Council Bluffs, on June 29th, the pioneers finished building a ferryboat on the east bank of the Missouri river under the skilled supervision of Frederick Kesler. The next day Brigham Young and others crossed to the west side of the river looking for a site where they could locate the camps of Israel to settle in for the winter. Finally, after three months of delay, during early September of 1846, a site was chosen on the west side of the Missouri in Nebraska, which they would call Winter Quarters. This would be the site that would become the final jumping off point for the pioneers to continue their long journey to the Great Basin and the Salt Lake Valley. – 13

Most certainly just dealing with the elements and the hardships of the trail would have been plenty to deal with, without any petty criticisms or stiff-necked uncooperativeness from certain members of the pioneer group stirring up trouble. Some people just have a difficult time following leadership because in their own mind, they are convinced that their thinking is better, more logical, and more suited for the task at hand than the designated chosen leader.

Such was the case with Brother George Miller. After Bishop Partridge had passed away, Elder Miller was made the "Presiding Bishop" of the Church. However, after the Saints left Nauvoo, Bishop Miller, who had been a steadfast supporter of Joseph Smith, became increasingly insubordinate and showed an increasing reluctance to follow Brigham Young as they crossed Iowa. In an act of pure stubborn defiance, he ended up leaving the main body of Saints and led his own small group of Saints 150 miles north of Council Bluffs to stay near the Ponca Indian Village. After he sent a message to Brigham who refused to follow Bishop Miller and his group to Oregon, George Miller requested that his name be removed from the Church records. Soon thereafter, he left the Church to follow Lyman Wight in Texas for a while, and then eventually joined the Strangites in Michigan. Unfortunately, being hopelessly bogged down in his own stubbornness and his vacillating allegiances, he passed away without ever having returned to the Church. – 14

Meanwhile, the U.S. government showing its typical inclinations and proclivities in their dealing with civilians came into the bigger picture of the plodding pioneer odyssey to Utah. Apparently the U.S. government, as its history has shown in so many cases, seems to have a very short memory and very little if any conscience regarding their own complicity in any type of unfairness in their government dealings with real people. In 1846, the U.S. Government seemed to have forgotten all about the atrocities committed against the Mormon people in Missouri and Illinois and their own flagrant indifference and lack of concern regarding this abusive treatment. Their own accountability in regards to the redressing of those wrongs should have already been taken care of and at least looked into by any number of government officials, officials who should have been obligated to uphold the constitutional rights of its own unfairly persecuted citizens. Yet, it had never happened.

On the 13th of May 1846, President Polk declared war on Mexico and shortly thereafter, he unapologetically drafted Mormons to serve in the U.S. Army in June of that year. This seemed rather ironical given the fact that the government had routinely ignored the plight of the persecuted Mormons for years, and now in their own audacity was asking for the help of the Mormon people to fight for the U.S. against Mexico. Still, as things turned out, the deal was beneficial for the Saints and so it ended up being of mutual benefit to the Mormons and to the government.

At that time, Brigham Young had sent a letter to Brother Jesse C. Little as President of the Eastern States Mission instructing him to deal and bargain with President Polk for any government assistance that they could get to help the Saints immigrate to the West. Brother Little with the help of Amos Kendall, former Post Master General, was able to gain an audience with President Polk on June third 1846. As it turned out, President Polk was somewhat more sympathetic towards the Mormon's grievances as compared to any previous administrations, and he genuinely seemed dismayed by the aggressions that had been committed against the Saints. However, President Polk didn't dither in his request and pointedly asked the Mormon representative for 500 Mormon men to volunteer to serve under a U.S. Army officer in the war against Mexico and in return he offered the Church some $70,000 in government favors.

Soon thereafter, Colonel Stephen W. Kerney was assigned to be the commanding officer over enlisting the Mormon Battalion. However, the official notice and request for the 500 Mormon troops coming from Washington D.C. and from Elder Little, did not arrive at Mt. Pisgah Iowa before the Saints had inadvertently found out from another source what they had already been committed to do. It was an army officer who informed them that they were going to be recruited into the U.S. army to fight against Mexico. So it was Captain James Allen that first recruited the Battalion at Mount Pisgah on June 26th of that year. He was then referred to Brigham Young who was residing at Council Bluffs at the time, which was where the main Mormon Battalion would leave from on July 21st, 1846. The Battalion would finally form up at Fort Leavenworth Kansas a short time later. - 15

The long trek to California was full of trials, dangers, and hardships for the Mormon Battalion. Even so, the army allowed 34 women and forty-four children to accompany the Battalion to act as laundresses, cooks, and seamstresses, and supporting families. If the trek itself wasn't difficult enough, they also had to endure the "by-the-book" strictness of a Regular Army Lieutenant, as well as an incompetent army doctor, a Doctor George Sanderson.

Whether it was out of incompetence, callous uncaring, or even just plain stupidity, the Doctor was systematically and essentially poisoning the members of the Battalion with his prescribed drug of a strange powder mixed with molasses and arsenic, all of which was gradually weakening the Mormon troops and making some of them sick. And even though they all were very leery of his remedies and suspected that it was making some of them feel ill, they were militarily obliged by orders from the Lieutenant to submit to the so-called officer doctor's questionable treatments.

However, when it became apparent that some of the soldiers were becoming very weak, and would probably not be able to endure the expected hardships in making the very demanding forced march crossing the desert to San Diego to comply with General Kearny's timeline, a new plan was initiated. It was finally decided that it would be best to separate into two different detachments for the most practical efficiency of their deployment. So in addition to weeding out the already weakened soldiers, the troop's families were also assigned to this second so-called "sick group." On October 3rd, the Mormon Battalion was split up into two distinct groups with two totally different destinations. The infamous Dr. Sanderson mercifully continued on with the advanced group going to San Diego. And so it was that the weakened troops would not have to further endure the Doctor's dubious treatments on their way to the considerably closer destination at the army Fort in Colorado.

The "sick detachment" along with the women and children were then ordered to proceed to Fort Pueblo, Colorado. This was where the weakened soldiers and the women and children would find that more than forty southern Latter-day Saints had already settled at the fort and were now making it their temporary home. Unknown to the main pioneer group, these southern Saints from out of Mississippi had previously proceeded farther west than the main body of the Saints who had been traveling on the northern route in Iowa. Meanwhile, these combined Mormon groups of the Battalion members with their families and the Southern Saints with their families were all now residing at Fort Pueblo making up a large group of some 275 Latter-day Saints. This was where they all spent an unusually mild and pleasant winter under the command of the Mormon Battalion Captain, James Brown. After the battalion reached Santa Fe, it was discovered that there were more members of the Battalion, which were becoming very weak and not up to a forced march. So a second "sick detachment" was then formed and sent back for recuperation.

The next spring, part of the Mississippian Saints and some of the Battalion members journeyed north to Fort Laramie to meet up with Brigham Young's advanced group so that they could travel with them to Utah. Brigham then assigned the Apostle Amasa Lyman to go back down to Pueblo Colorado to organize and lead the rest of those remaining Pueblo Saints to the Salt Lake Valley. This same group would arrive in Utah on July 29, 1847, only five days after Brigham Young's own group had arrived. Four years later Amasa Lyman, who had been a loyal and trustworthy supporter of Brigham for many years, would be called to establish a self-sustaining unit of the Church in San Bernardino, California.

Meantime, the Mormon Battalion was still trekking through the desert unopposed by the Mexican army. Somewhat surprisingly, the only real violence that the Mormon Battalion ever engaged in happened to be a battle against some ferocious wild bulls in the desolate Sonoran desert. On December 3rd 1846, the Battalion reached Rancho San Bernardino California on the border of present day Mexico. A few days later on December 11th, without any provocation or warning at all, dozens of rogue wild bulls fiercely attacked the marching Battalion. They savagely charged at the men and their draft animals and in their very aggressive fury, they even damaged some of the wagons and the livestock. As many as twenty wild bulls were eventually killed, two mules were gored to death, and three of the Mormon Battalion men were wounded. This was an unprecedented and an extremely mystifying incident. One can only speculate as to any beneficial purposes or any necessary tests of faith that the good Lord may have had in mind with this particular trial of faith at "The Battle of the Bulls." – 16

There are some critics who thought that this severely demanding assignment from the U.S. government, that had been placed upon the backs of the Mormon Battalion, had overall been a failed venture from the beginning and simply a waste of time being that they never did engage in any military action against Mexico. The small numbers of Mexican soldiers that they encountered chose to run rather than confront the rather intimidating numbers in the Battalion. Never the less, in the overall historical view, the Mormon Battalion actually did make some very significant accomplishments in their long unprecedented and historical journey.

They made the history books by making an epoch-making 2,000-mile heroic march, which has been touted as one of the longest infantry marches in history. It stretched from Fort Leavenworth Kansas on the Missouri River, down through Oklahoma, Texas, New Mexico, Arizona, and finally all the way out to San Diego California located just north of the Baja California Peninsula on the Pacific coast. During this long long march, they cleared a much needed wagon road from Santa Fe New Mexico all the way to San Diego California securing real estate for California and the Southwest at the same time. The 630-mile wagon road they built running along the Gila River all the way to the Colorado River in Yuma Arizona influenced the U.S. government to make the 1853 Gadsden Purchase from Mexico. This agreement would establish the southern boundary between Mexico and the U.S. This now historic boundary still runs along the southern boundaries of Arizona and New Mexico today dividing The United States from Mexico.

Although the Mexican authorities were aware of the Battalion's presence, they chose not to engage the Mormon Battalion. The little Mormon army clearly deterred the Mexican government from getting a stronger foothold in the new United States territory. And in addition to all this, they actually helped to preserve an unsteady peace in that territory before the signing of the Treaty of Guadalupe Hidalgo that would eventually end the hostilities between the U.S. and Mexico.

Furthermore, if one takes a good look at the broader view of the history making Mormon Battalion, some of the former members of the Battalion would turn out to be rather important players in America's western history. Some of them were directly associated with the gold discovery at Sutter's Mill where six of the Battalion members were involved in the initial discovery of gold made on the American River on January 24, 1848. This epoch-making economic discovery would significantly help stimulate the development of California and played a most important part in civilizing the entire Western United States.

Some of the Battalion men chose to stay in California to find their fortune; eighty-one reenlisted in the U.S. army; others stayed to live and work there contributing to the building up of that state. Many stayed, built homes, and raised families there. Yes without question, these hearty stalwart Mormon men did indeed help civilize the West.

In summary, the history making Mormon Battalion saw some 340 men out of the 500 initial Mormon Battalion troops make a record breaking 2,000-mile march while securing new territory for the United States. In addition, they built needed roads in an isolated area, aided in the deterring of Mexican aggression into the future state of California, and established a much stronger U.S. foothold. They most certainly contributed to aiding in more fully civilizing the entire Territory, and overall, achieved a great many accomplishments during their historical military trek. They would finally march into southern California to end their long journey in January of 1847.

In the end, despite their critics, their very physically demanding foot soldier odyssey was worthy of the praise they would receive, and their dedication and contributions to their Church and their fellow Saints in a time of great need were immensely helpful in bringing in government payments to aid the Saint's move to the Rockies. Overall, they had made a significant contribution to their country, their Church, and to the building up of God's Kingdom. – 17

*   *   *

1. See History of the Church, Vol.7, Ch.37, p.544

2a. See History of the Church, Vol.7, Ch.37, p.587-591

2b. See "Voyage of the Brooklyn" by Lorin K. Hansen 1971 pp 53-60

3. See History of the Church, Vol.7, Ch.39, p.589 - Also Discourses of Brigham Young, p.475

4. See Wikipedia.com – Brannan, Samuel, and History of the Church, Vol.7, Introduction, p.25.

5. See "Church History in the Fulness of Times" p. 317

6. See Discourses of Brigham Young, p.412.

7. See History of the Church, Vol.7, p.617, Footnotes and the L.D.S. Biographical Encyclopedia, Jenson, vol. i. p. 692

8. See History of the Church, Vol.7, p.589-598 - & "American Moses" - 121, 127 & Joseph Fielding Smith Jr., Doctrines of Salvation, Vol.3, p.337 - p.338

9. See Joseph Fielding Smith Jr., Doctrines of Salvation, Vol.3, p.337 - p.338

10a – See "Saints In The Wilderness" by David Crockett, pp 213-214

10b. See Joseph Fielding Smith Jr., Doctrines of Salvation, Vol.3, p.338

11. See Journal of Discourses 13:85-86

12. See ENCYCLOPEDIA OF MORMONISM, Council Bluffs (Kanesville), Iowa

13. See Joseph Fielding Smith Jr., Doctrines of Salvation, Vol.3, p.339

14. See "Who in the Doctrine and Covenants" Susan Easton Black, pp. 196-197 and "Ensign" January 1997 "On the Trail in January"

15. See History of the Church, Vol.7, p.614, also Encyclopedia of Mormonism, Vol.4, Appendix 2

16. See Encyclopedia of Mormonism, Vol. 2.

17. See Encyclopedia of Mormonism, Vol.1, CALIFORNIA, PIONEER SETTLEMENTS, and also EOM, Vol. 2. MORMON BATTALION.

*   *   *

Chapter Twenty-Four

———⊶∾⊷⊙⊶⊷⊙⊶∾⊶———

THE FINAL JOURNEY

*　　*　　*

As people today read about the Mormon pioneers' hardships and how they trekked by horse and wagon for five long months across the plains from the mighty Mississippi all the way to the Missouri River to reach their campsite at Council Bluffs Iowa, most people don't realize that the journey was only over in a small part at this point. Even after all those months of travel, the pioneers were still less than a fourth of the way to their destination in the valley of the Great Salt Lake in the Utah territory. It was on June 14th 1846 that the Saints finally arrived on the east bank of the Missouri River and they most certainly had earned a good rest. Yet, they were still only about 300 miles out of Nauvoo and they still had another 1,000 miles left to go to reach their destination in the Utah desert. Having left Nauvoo back in February and having journeyed for many months at a snails pace of only 2 miles per day average, they felt quite exhausted now, and yes, discouragingly inefficient as they were reminded that this was all the headway they had made after a journey of five long months.

If that wasn't demoralizing enough, even after having endured those long difficult months of torturously sluggish progress, it would now seem like they were just squandering away another three months of valuable trail time in just moving to the other side of the river to set up a more permanent camp on the west side of the Missouri, only a few yards away. As they labored to get ready for the right time to make the big move to the other side of the river, they made use of the previously built ferry, which they had constructed back in June. They finally crossed to the west bank of the Missouri River on September 11th 1846 to set up a more permanent camp for their long winter stay. The Winter Quarters Nebraska campsite was thus finally established and it would be at this site that they would make their temporary home for the next eight months through the Nebraskan winter of 1846-47.

Their Winter Quarters camp was just a little bit northwest of the Alpheus Cutler's Park site, which had been initially selected back in June when Frederick Kesler supervised the building of that first ferry. This new campsite was farther up on the bluff and would be safer from the spring flooding. The camp covered a rather large area of approximately one mile long and a half-mile wide with several creeks that provided fresh water, which alleviated the need of having to make frequent trips to the river.

Soon after their arrival, Brigham had ordered the construction of a gristmill to be built on the creek that ran through what is today the suburb of Florence Nebraska in present day Omaha. Even though Brigham knew his own advanced party would get very limited use out of the mill, his foresight would soon be evident to the Saints that were following behind him who found good use for it. This old Mormon pioneer mill still exists and is currently operated as a museum for interested tourist.

By the end of September 1846, Winter Quarters had already begun to look like a real city, even though the cabins were rather small and crudely built. Eventually there would be some 4,000 Saints occupying Winter Quarters in a well-planned city of thirty-eight blocks, with twenty lots to each block, along with 800 cabins, huts, and other makeshift shelters built of logs or blocks of sod. Besides the large log octagonal council house they had built for their meetings, there was in addition a sizable stockade to protect and corral the large number of cattle they possessed. Later on, because of the crowded conditions on the Winter Quarters side, many of the Saints had to necessarily remain on the east side of the river at

Council Bluffs site where there were another 3,000 pioneers waiting and anticipating the journey westward to the Salt Lake Valley.

Amazingly enough, during 1846-47 there were nearly 16,000 Saints stretched out across the plains of the Iowan prairie, all the way from Nauvoo sitting on the mighty Mississippi River clear to the far western banks of the muddy Missouri in Western Iowa. No wonder the pioneer exodus is sometimes likened to the Exodus of the Children of Israel leaving Egypt. – 1

Winter Quarters turned out to be more than just a resting place on the way to Utah. It became a place of implementing new Church practices and government. It was there that plural marriage was first openly practiced, even though the principle had been first taught in Nauvoo in a more selective and confidential manner. Winter Quarters was also where Brigham Young and the Quorum of the Twelve Apostles finally considered seriously the general aspects of the properly organized leadership in Church government. It was here that they conferred with each other and agreed upon the need to choose and put in place a new First Presidency, whereas now they were wholly led by the Quorum of the Twelve under Brigham's leadership as senior apostle. The role of bishops in the Church was also refined and Winter Quarters became the first community to be divided into small wards of a few hundred people each with a bishop responsible for each of the 22 wards, thus setting a pattern for future church organization. – 2

When word came to Winter Quarters through Daniel Wells and William Cutler that the Saint's beloved Nauvoo had surrendered after a short battle and then had been plundered and ravaged by mobs of greedy scavengers, Brigham was appalled by the reports. Even though a treaty had been signed to let the Mormons leave peaceably, roaming "posses" shot some Saints from ambush; others mockingly baptized an old man until he nearly drowned, and the rest severely harassed every Mormon they came to who hadn't left yet.

Brigham became highly concerned over the destitute state of the refugee Saints that remained in distressed circumstances at Montrose Iowa just across the river from Nauvoo. Even though the pioneers were somewhat short of manpower at Winter Quarters, especially after the departure of the Mormon Battalion, Brigham compassionately called for a rescue mission to return to Montrose to aid the poor, the sick, the suffering, and the badly brutalized. Their mission was to help the refugees to leave the poor camp there in Montrose and facilitate their journey to come out West and join the rest of the Saints on their way to Utah. He called for ten volunteers to be led by Orville M. Allen to go all the way back to east Iowa and get the refugees out of there and on their way west.

Winter Quarters provided community life, safety, provisions, shelter, and a jumping off place for the Saints during the winter of 1846-47. Never the less, it is estimated that some 2,000 Saints, many of them children, died at Winter Quarters from June 1846 to Oct 1848. Most of the deaths came from the complications caused from acute fatigue, unsanitary conditions, vermin, and mal-nutrition, all of which contributed to a lowered resistance to disease, which jeopardized their overall health and made them susceptible to a variety of maladies including malaria and the dreaded "Black Leg" scurvy.

Finally spring arrived on the plains and the advanced party was ready to leave for the Rocky Mountains. Brigham Young set out for the West with an advance group of 143 men, 3 women, and 2 children on April 5, 1847. The general plan was for the individual groups of the advanced party to all meet at the Elkhorn River some twenty miles west of the Winter Quarters site and form up their wagon train there. After Brigham arrived at the Elkhorn River for the initial gathering, he unexpectedly ended up having to return to Winter Quarters twice to meet and confer with certain important brethren.

The first return trip was to meet with Parley P. Pratt who had just arrived at the camp from his mission to England. Sometime between May of 1846 when Parley helped establish the Mt. Pisgah settlement in southern Iowa and April of 1847 when Parley arrived at Winter Quarters Nebraska, he had served a short mission to England on Church business and brought back some very much-appreciated tithing money.

Shortly after conferring with Parley, Brigham returned to the Elkhorn River to continue the journey west. However, he no sooner arrived there than he received a letter saying that John Taylor was also coming home from his English mission. He too was bringing much needed cash donations from the British Saints, and several hundred dollars worth of scientific instruments, surveying equipment, and other supplies that would prove to be very valuable to the pioneers later on. Thus Brigham and seven other apostles went back to Winter Quarters the second time to have a joyous reuniting with Brother John Taylor.

After a delightful reunion, Brigham left John Taylor and Parley P. Pratt behind at Winter Quarters to organize and lead the remaining pioneer companies west who were still waiting to head out. Parley and John Taylor were to bring along that large group as soon as they could get them ready to go, which somewhat surprisingly turned out to be only a month later. Brigham and the other apostles then rode on ahead catching up with the advanced Pioneer Company at the Platte River on April 15th 1847, and then they prepared to move out the next day to cross Nebraska heading for the Rocky Mountains.

During the pioneer's journey across Nebraskan plains, on May 29th just a few miles past Chimney Rock at Scotts Bluff, Brigham interrupted the normal routine of camp, gathered them all together, and severely chastised the men of the priesthood saying he would go no further with them unless, "a different spirit changed the course of their conduct." Apparently a spirit of laziness, quarrelling, profane language, card playing, and loud improper laughter and unnecessary merriment had taken over the camp. After Brigham spoke frankly and firmly to the group, an entirely new and more humble atmosphere came over the entire company as they followed the North Platte to Fort Laramie. – 3a

The route for the advanced Pioneer Company had been partly laid out for them by the maps of the famous explorer John C. Fremont. Following Fremont's maps they would travel west from Winter Quarters forty-six miles to the Platte River and then maintain a westerly direction along the Platte River until they met the Platte's North Fork near the modern day city of North Platte, Nebraska, at which point they would turn to the northwest and proceed along the North Platte River to Fort Laramie Wyoming. From there they would continue following the Oregon Trail going up and over South Pass and on to the "Parting of the Ways" in Western Wyoming where they would leave the Oregon Trail and turn south and cross the Green River to Fort Bridger. From Fort Bridger they would cross into Utah territory at which point they would trek down Echo Canyon and then determinedly ascend the Wasatch Mountains and finally drop down through one of the canyons of the Wasatch for their last leg to their final destination in the Valley of the Great Salt Lake.

It all sounded simple enough, but as the pioneers dealt with the unpredictable aspects of nature, bad weather, swollen rivers, steep mountains, mountain sickness, break downs, and a hundred and one other little aggravations, it often became discouragingly difficult for them and even disheartening enough to make them wonder about the wisdom of what they were doing. Yet they relentlessly trekked on to find that dreamed of place of "all their own" and the hoped for peace to practice their religion as they saw fit.

On arriving at Fort Laramie, they were somewhat surprised to find the so-called "sick" detachment from the Mormon Battalion there, who was accompanied by some of the Mississippian Saints from Pueblo Colorado. When the advanced pioneer company finally lumbered into the Fort on June 1st, the two groups from Pueblo had already been at Fort Laramie waiting for Brigham's group for about two weeks. Now the recovering Battalion members along with some of the anxious Mississippi Saints would be able to join up with Brigham's advanced party as they all headed west.

As this motley crew of pioneer nomads became more diverse, it is interesting to note that there were a few blacks traveling with the Mormon Pioneers, although that is not widely known. The Brigham Young party of 1847 brought 3 slaves with them to Utah that included Green Flake, Oscar Crosby, and Hark Lay. These three slaves actually belonged to some Mormon converts from the southern states who had sent their servants on ahead with Brigham's party to prepare things for the southern owners' later arrival in the Salt lake Valley. Many of the earlier converted southern Mormon slave owners had compassionately freed their slaves previously, just as soon as they joined the Church. Others had not. However, for diplomacy reasons and to maintain harmony among the Saints, Brigham somewhat tolerated, to a certain extent, the other Saints who were still holding slaves or indentured servants. Never the less, he had a very unfavorable attitude towards holding slaves and only tolerated the practice of indentured servitude because it at least stipulated the giving of freedom to the indentured servant after a set time of service. Brigham had a deep-seated belief that every human being ought to have the right to make their own life's decisions based on their own free choice and will. Regarding the question of slavery in their new wilderness home, Brigham's personal feeling was a desire to completely discourage slaveholding in the Salt Lake Valley and throughout the new Utah territory.

The Mormon's anti-slavery views were a major reason that the Missourians had pushed the Mormons "just plumb out" of Missouri because they feared that the Mormon influence would encourage the "anti-slavery" abolitionist to sway the voters in Missouri to actually free the slaves and make Missouri a non-slave state. Brigham's original policy was that black servants brought into Utah had to come of their own free will and they could not be sold or be removed from the territory without their personal consent. However in 1863, one of the most significant and major political announcements in history was made; it was the very divisive Federal declaration called the "Emancipation Proclamation." It effectively ended the touchy slavery and servitude issue for the pioneers in the Utah territory, and eventually, across all of America thanks to President Lincoln.

"Though few in number, blacks have been attracted to the Church since its organization. Early converts such as Elijah Abel joined during the 1830s; others such as Jane Manning James joined after the Saints moved to Illinois where she became a trusted companion to Emma and Lucy. Among those who came to Utah with the Pioneers was "Green Flake, who reportedly drove Brigham Young's wagon into the Salt Lake Valley." Another highly respected black Mormon was Samuel D. Chambers, a freed slave, who was converted in Mississippi in 1844 before the Saints left Nauvoo and came to Utah with his wife Amanda Leggroan in 1870 after the Civil War. He proved himself to be a dedicated and loyal member of the Church and contributed faithfully for eighty-five years in the Church as he joyfully served the Lord along side his fellow members. He was highly respected member of the Church by all that knew him. – 3b

Leaving Fort Laramie behind, the pioneers continued to follow the North Platte River to a spot that would become known as the "Last Crossing" near present day Casper Wyoming. The pioneer company had an extremely difficult time getting the wagons over to the western side of the river due to the fast high water and spring flooding. It took six long hard days to get everybody across. They had already built a special wagon that had been covered with hides and then waterproofed, which they dubbed

"The Revenue Cutter." It had been specifically designed to carry their unloaded supplies from the wagons across the practically unmanageable river while it kept their goods dry and safe. The swollen river was however, still a challenge even for an empty wagon to cross, and so several rafts were then built to aid the crossings.

The Pioneers ended up putting together and constructing "The Mormon Ferry" to assist in the deceivingly difficult task of crossing the North Platte at high water, and to accommodate the rest of the Saints that were coming up behind them in making that "Last Crossing." After constructing the ferry and the necessary docks, they left nine men behind to operate the ferry. It would thereafter become a major crossing place on the pioneer trail, not only for the continuing parade of Mormon Pioneers who had to cross the river, but also for a great many non-Mormon emigrant trains that would also find the famed "Mormon Ferry" a great help in crossing the unruly river, as well as being considerably more convenient for everybody. A few years later, the legendary Mormon Ferry crossing would become the site of Fort Casper.

Back at Winter Quarters, there were now nine different companies coming together, which became known as "The Big Company," consisting of over 1500 Saints and 575 wagons. Brigham had earlier assigned Parley P. Pratt and John Taylor to lead the large group west. They left Winter Quarters about the 13th of June to form up into their wagon companies at the Elkhorn River. Following in the tracks of Brigham's advanced company, they would arrive in the Salt Lake Valley only three months after they left, and just two months after Brigham Young's arrival. The lead wagons of "The Big Company" started to roll into the Salt Lake Valley during the last week of September with the trailing wagons continuing to roll into the valley until the last wagon arrived during first part of October of 1847.

Meanwhile, getting back to Brigham's original pioneer company, after having left the North Platte River at the "Last Crossing," this Advanced Company under Brigham Young would then follow the Sweetwater River as they passed by Independence Rock, the Devil's Gate, Muddy Gap, and the future site of the infamous Mormon Handcart tragedy at Martin's Cove. Their next obstacle was to cross over what was the somewhat deceiving altitude of Wyoming's South Pass, which was higher than it appeared as one viewed its broad rounded expanse. Though it was over 7000 feet, it was still a comparatively lower pass than any alternatives as it spanned a much broader and more gentle Continental Divide compared to the much higher, steeper, and rougher elevations of the Colorado Rockies.

It just happened to be on the anniversary of Joseph and Hyrum's martyrdom that Orson Pratt used barometric readings to calculate at the top that South Pass was about 7085 feet high, while William Clayton used his wooden wagon wheel odometer to calculate that it was 822 miles from their departure point at Winter Quarters Nebraska. From there, they headed in a southwesterly direction to cross the relatively shallow "Little Sandy River."

Just past the "Little Sandy" crossing in Western Wyoming, George A. Smith, who had been doing some scouting, came back to the wagon train accompanied by a rough looking scruffy mountain man. It was none other than the famous Mountain Man, Jim Bridger, who was on his way to Fort Laramie to do some trading. After quizzing him extensively about the route to the Salt Lake Valley and what the valley itself was like, he basically painted a picture of it not being a good place for any permanent settlements or for growing any crops. The story goes that the skeptical Jim Bridger offered Brigham Young a thousand dollars for the first bushel of corn that they raised in the Salt Lake Valley. There is no record of Bridger ever paying up on that bet although the bushel was raised. Despite Jim Bridger's skepticism, the Mormon pioneers would develop a highly efficient irrigation system and thus were able to turn large sections of the barren desert into a rich and fruitful land that would as Isaiah had prophesized, "Blossom as the Rose."

Two days after Jim Bridger's visit, as previously mentioned, the enterprising and very bold Samuel Brannan coming up from California with two companions, met up with Brigham's advanced company at Wyoming's Green River. Although Brigham was delighted to see his brethren from California, Brannan's very persuasive arguments regarding the riches and beautiful climate of California did not deter Brigham's determination to settle in the Salt Lake Valley, which he had so vividly seen in his vision while traveling on the plains of Iowa. Disappointed in Brigham's resoluteness to settle in Utah, Brannan returned home by a route that branched off from the Oregon Trail and followed the California Trail through Nevada to San Francisco.

In addition to Brannan's surprise visit, another nice surprise came on the fourth of July 1847. While the pioneer company was camped and celebrating Independence Day at the Green River, where once again they had to ferry across, thirteen men from the Mormon Battalion walked into camp for a very happy reunion with their families and friends.

When the Mormon Battalion was discharged from the U.S. Army in California in January of 1847, they broke up into various groups with different plans and arrangements in their various itineraries. Some reenlisted in the U.S. Army; others stayed in California to work. Many headed for Utah going over Donner's pass in company with Levi Hancock to meet up with Samuel Brannan and Captain James Brown at the Truckee Lake in the Sierra Nevadas. One of the groups returned to California with Captain Brown to collect $5,000 dollars in gold from the Army for the Battalion's back pay.

Some of the Battalion members, as has been previously noted, stayed in Northern California and went to work for John Sutter who was building a sawmill on the American River. These particular battalion members would help to make western history as a part of the men who discovered California gold at Sutter's mill on January 24th 1848. This discovery brought about one of the biggest gold rushes in American history and attracted a virtual stampede of "Forty-Niners" to northern California seeking their fortunes, which boosted California's population to 100,000 by the end of 1849. Later on during 1849 and 1850, Brigham called certain small groups of Saints on missions to go to California to mine gold for the Church. It is estimated that they brought back up to $30,000 in gold to help boost the budding Utah economy. – 4

Most of the way after leaving Winter Quarters, the Mormon Pioneer Company had basically followed the famous Oregon Trail all the way across Nebraska and through most of Wyoming. However, at a place called "The Parting of the Ways" near the Little Sandy River in Western Wyoming, they would leave the Oregon Trail and head south to Fort Bridger where they would pickup and follow the famed "Hastings Cut Off," which had been blazed in 1845 to aid emigrants in finding a shortcut to California. When the Advanced Party reached the Green River in southwest Wyoming, they once again had to build rafts to ferry across one more wide fast river before they trekked on to Fort Bridger. It has been said that the entire West passed by the gates of Fort Bridger at one time or another. This parade of western travelers included mountain men, trappers, prospectors, explorers, many emigrant trains, soldiers, and of course, Mormon pioneers, and allegedly, even some Indians trading for whiskey and guns.

The Mormon pioneers stopped at Fort Bridger only for a day to get much needed information and secure a few supplies. They found Jim Bridger's prices to be a little on the high side. Unfortunately the dealings between Jim Bridger and the Mormons would become a very volatile relationship, and in the future, it would result in accusations, take-overs, disputed claims, and arguments over property rights. There was even a confrontation between Bridger and the territorial Governor, Brigham Young, over Bridger allegedly selling illegal trading items, such as ammunition and whiskey to the Indians.

Later on, after 8 years in the Salt Lake Valley, the Church finally purchased Fort Bridger from Louis Vasquez, Jim Bridger's partner. This was in 1855 when the Church leaders decided that it would be wise to purchase the fort due to its strategic location. When the Mormon men who were sent to occupy Fort Bridger encountered armed mountain men that stubbornly refused to vacate the premises, the Mormons decided to avoid a violent confrontation and instead established "Fort Supply" twelve miles to the southwest. Eventually the Mormons took possession of Fort Bridger, but when the Federal Troops came in 1857 to deal with the so-called Mormon problem during the "Utah War," the Mormon pioneers would abandon and burn both Fort Bridger and Fort Supply as a part of their "scorched earth" strategy of leaving nothing behind for the invading soldiers to use. – 5

Meanwhile, getting back to the original Pioneer Company of 1847, they continued on from Fort Bridger and followed the shortcut to California called the Hastings Cutoff, and that's where they started their descent down through the beautiful red rocks of Echo Canyon. Just as they crossed over the future border of Wyoming and Utah, Brigham Young came down with tick fever or more commonly called "Mountain Fever" and became so ill that he was unable to continue traveling. The decision was made to leave behind the sick group to rest and recover, while the main company went on to the mouth of Echo Canyon and stopped near present day Henefer Utah. This is where some of the Twelve and other priesthood brethren, out of concern for their beloved leader, climbed to a private place among the rocks of the canyon near the unique Hoo Doos rock formations, sometimes called the "Witches," just east of the famous "Devil's Slide" formation in Weber Canyon, and fervently prayed for Brigham's quick recovery and the health of the other ill Saints in his group.

At this point, the Pioneer Company, for practical reasons and under Brigham's direction, split up into three different companies. The first group was designated as the advanced scouting party consisting of 42 men and 25 wagons placed under the leadership of Elder Orson Pratt. The second company, which was the main body, camped along the Weber River in Weber Canyon near what is today the community of Henefer Utah. They waited there until the third smaller group, which was dubbed as the "sick detachment," could recover and catch up. Unfortunately, Brigham had a relapse of Mountain fever after they caught up and so his sick group spent some additional time camped at the crossing of the Weber River about a half-mile from the future town of Henefer.

This was around the 19th of July, the very same day that Orson Pratt's scouting party sighted their first magnificent view of the Salt lake Valley from the top of Big Mountain. They then would descend down the mountain and entered the valley three days before Brigham Young's party. The main body of the Saint's advanced group then left Weber Canyon and continued through Main Canyon to East Canyon and up and over the top of Big Mountain and then over Little Mountain following the old Donner-Reed trail as they tracked just behind Elder Pratt's scouting party.

The legendary Donner-Reed Party had made some improvements to the Hastings Cutoff just a year before on their way to California, but found going down Emigration Canyon to be a little too laborious. So they made their way up and over an alternate route, which was later dubbed Donner's Hill, and then from there, they trekked on to their ignoble and disastrous fate in the High Sierras of Nevada and California.

Some historians have called the infamous Mr. Lansford Hastings an overzealous promoter and blame him for creating the situation that caused the Donner tragedy of trying to cross the high passes in the early winter.

The ill-fated travelers experienced a truly horrifying calamity, becoming snowbound and buried under three feet of snow, and then succumbing to exposure; they suffered severe starvation and were forced to eat their own shoe leather. Finally in horrid desperation, they resorted to eating their own dead. Only forty-eight out of 87 immigrants survived the ordeal.

The Saints themselves found Donner's Hill to be an unsatisfactory option and thus pushed, chopped, and cut their way down through Emigration Canyon through all the thick under brush, abundant willows and trees, around the canyon boulders, and made several forced crossings across the fast running creek. After a substantial amount of toil, they worked their way downward through the rough canyon with considerable effort pushing their horses and wagons to the limit as they traversed the nearly impossible canyon route. And it was then that the "Mormon Pioneers" finally emerged at the mouth of today's Emigration Canyon. This famed canyon mouth would be very near the site of what would someday become the very popular Hogel's Zoo, and also the site of what is presently the very famous tourist spot, "This Is The Place" monument. – 6

In summary, after finally making their way out of Emigration Canyon, the Mormon Scouts, Orson Pratt and Erastus Snow, actually entered the Salt Lake Valley on July 21st, three days before Brigham Young's party. Returning to the Main group, Orson Pratt and his companions led the Main Body to the mouth of Emigration Canyon and entered the valley the next day in the late afternoon where they built a dam, made irrigation ditches, and plowed ground for a potato field. Meanwhile, Brigham Young who was still in the wagons of the "sick attachment," came a day or two later after that, arriving on the highly celebrated historic scene on the 24th of July 1847.

As the sick wagons came to the point where they could see the valley opening up before their eyes, Wilford Woodruff turned Brigham's wagon to the side so that President Young could raise up off his sick bed and take in the sight. Wilford reported that Brigham was then "enwrapped in a vision for several minutes" wherein he saw the glorious future of the valley and the mighty growth and glory of Zion as it was to become. Brigham immediately recognized this place that he had been shown by the Prophet Joseph Smith in an earlier vision back on the plains of Iowa. Wilford wrote that Brigham then said, "It is enough. This is the right place, drive on." - 7

Brigham describes their arrival in the Salt Lake Valley: "...myself, with others, came out of what we named Emigration Canyon; we crossed the Big and Little mountains, and came down the valley about three quarters of a mile south of this. We located, and we looked about, and finally we came and camped between the two forks of City Creek, one of which ran southwest and the other west. Here we planted our standard on this temple block and the one above it; here we pitched our camps and determined that here we would settle and stop." – 8

Summing up their long odyssey, the Saints had trekked out of Nauvoo in February of 1846 and then plodded at a snails pace across some 300 miles of plains from the Mississippi River to the banks of the Missouri River in Western Iowa finally arriving at the mid-western river in the middle of June. By September they had built a ferry and crossed over to the other side of the river and set up camp on the west bank of the Missouri in eastern Nebraska. This became a major stop over of some eight months at Winter Quarters while they spent the 1846-47 winter preparing for a spring departure as they rested up on the banks of the Missouri. This particular location on the Missouri River would someday become the future site of the two highly populated sister communities of the mid-west called Council Bluffs Iowa and Omaha Nebraska.

On the second leg of their journey after a long cold winter, Brigham's advanced party finally left Winter Quarters Nebraska on April 5th 1847. Leaving Nebraska behind, they trekked approximately 1,032 miles while courageously overcoming extreme fatigue, various sicknesses, time consuming repairs, dangerous trails, the crossing of swollen rivers, negotiating impossible canyons, climbing steep rough mountains, and even dealing with the occasional rattlesnake. Surprisingly, and for reasons not clearly explained, that much rougher 1000 mile second leg took less time to traverse than the first 300 miles over the flat plains. After leaving Winter Quarters they arrived 111 days later in the Salt Lake Valley on July 24th 1847. All total, they had covered 1,300 miles from Nauvoo to the Salt Lake Valley; a valley they found delightfully peaceful nestled in the Great Basin of the Western United States, and their final destination. It took about a year and a half to complete the historic trek from Nauvoo to the Utah territory.

In spite of all of the trials encountered on their determined journey west, for the most part, the greater part of them arrived safely. However, the ill-fated and luckless Donner party did not arrive safely at their own destination, but never the less, their back-breaking and determined efforts in the Utah Mountains were much appreciated by the Mormon Pioneers who followed their trail. The Donners had taken sixteen days to cut their road from Henefer to the head of Emigration Canyon, while the Mormon Pioneers were able to make it in four days thanks to the Donner's earlier trail blazing feats the year before. – 9

On the 26th of July 1847, Brigham was taken to the top of Ensign Peak. He had seen this landmark in a vision that the Prophet Joseph Smith had shown him, and it was there that the brethren and Brigham raised up a banner to symbolize the fulfillment of the words of Isaiah:

"THE wilderness and the solitary place shall be glad for them; and the desert shall rejoice, and blossom as the rose." – See Isaiah 35:1 - Also see Wilford Woodruff Journal 3:236

Very soon after arriving in the valley, Brigham Young began to lay out a well thought out plan for the city with extra wide streets of 132 feet in width running straight north and south, and straight east and west in an easy to navigate grid system. There would be 8 home lots to a block with houses set back 20 feet from the street. Many lots were designated as mini-farms with animals, barns, and lush green gardens. Even today, Salt Lake City is considered as one of the better laid out and well planned cities in the U.S.

Brigham has been touted as a great visionary as well as an extensive and acclaimed colonizer as he sent many groups of Saints out to colonize all parts of Utah, as well as in Idaho, Wyoming, Nevada, California, and Canada, and even a few border towns in Mexico. Having the distinction of establishing more than 200 settlements, his Mormon colonies were spread all over the Western United States from Canada to Mexico. One source even estimated that there were as many as 400 different colonies encouraged and influenced by the Mormon leader, including Las Vegas which was finally turned over to the gentiles in 1857. Brigham Young has been called by many the greatest colonizer in American history. He is also widely known as "The Great American Moses," as he courageously led with dogged determination some 16,000 Saints through the wilderness some 1300 miles across the great expanses of the Wild West. – 10

Two days after their arrival in the Salt Lake Valley, Brigham Young picked out the site for the Salt Lake Temple as he marked it in the dirt with his cane, and proclaimed, "Here we will build the temple of our God." Even though the temple took some forty-six years to build and wasn't finished until after the St. George, Logan, and Manti temples had been completed, and was still not finished at the time of Brigham Young's passing in 1877, the magnificent and historic Salt Lake Temple was finally dedicated in 1893. And even today, it stands as a worldwide iconic and beautiful tribute to the Mormon pioneers and their unfailing dedication to the Lord.

After having been settled in the Salt lake Valley for awhile, Brigham Young spoke of the circumstances: "We wish strangers to understand that we did not come here out of choice, but because we were obliged to go somewhere, and this was the best place we could find. It was impossible for any person to live here unless he labored hard and battled and fought against the elements, but it was a first-rate place to raise Latter-day Saints, and we shall be blessed in living here, and shall yet make it like the Garden of Eden; and the Lord Almighty will hedge about his Saints and will defend and preserve them if they will do his will. The only fear I have is that we will not do right; if we do we will be like a city set on a hill, our light will not be hid." - 11

Six months after their arrival in the Salt lake Valley, in that December of 1847, Brigham Young and the Apostles left Utah temporarily and made a return trip to Council Bluffs, Iowa, where the majority of the Saints were still waiting to come to Utah and settle into their permanent new home. The Church leaders' traveled to Council Bluffs with the intention to take care of some important Church business at the place where the majority of the Saints were now residing, an area known as Kanesville. The Mormon population in Pottawattamie County, Iowa, including Kanesville, may have reached as many as 8,000 people across forty settlements at the height of their population growth, which at the time was far more than in Utah. However, after a few more years of development in the Salt Lake Valley, a large scope effort was made in 1852 by the Church leadership to move the Saints out of Iowa and into Utah, which greatly reduced the population that had once been a part of the Mormon settlements in Iowa.

Since the majority of the Saints had not yet arrived in Utah during that first year of the settling of the Salt lake Valley, it was back in Council Bluffs in December of 1847 that the Twelve Apostles took up the business of sustaining the first new First Presidency of the Church since the martyrdom of Joseph Smith. At that time, Brigham Young, the Senior Apostle, was sustained as the President of the LDS Church with Heber C. Kimball and Willard Richards as his counselors. The following year, the Saints in Utah gave their own approval and unanimously voted to sustain Brigham Young and the new First Presidency of the Church at a conference in Salt Lake City. – 12

And so it was right there in the high desert among the rugged mountains of the Utah wilderness that the Saints finally found their final resting place and their first real permanent home after having been driven out of four different states and virtually out of the Union itself. Finally, they were now nestled comfortably and permanently in the Valley of the Great Salt Lake in a place where they were quite sure that nobody else wanted. At last, it felt like they really were once and for all in a place that seemed safe and secure and was truly theirs so they could live their religion and their lives as they saw fit and proper. However, even though they had finally arrived at their coveted Zion and were settled into a seemingly safe place where they could worship as they pleased, all their trials were not over, which is an understatement in so many different ways. - 13.

*   *   *

1. See Encyclopedia of Mormonism, Vol.4, WINTER QUARTERS

2. See Encyclopedia of Mormonism, Vol.4, WINTER QUARTERS also YOUNG, BRIGHAM

3a. Journal of William Clayton May 29th 1847

3b. See Encyclopedia of Mormonism, Vol.1, BLACKS, - HISTORY and also "111 Days to Zion" by Hal Knight & Stanley B. Kimball, p. 127

4. See "The Mormon Battalion" p. 140, also – See also Encyclopedia of Mormonism, Vol.4, CALIFORNIA, PIONEER SETTLEMENTS

5. See Encyclopedia of Mormonism, Vol.4, WYOMING, PIONEER SETTLEMENTS and also Vol.2, HISTORY OF THE CHURCH

6. See State of Utah History

7. See "A Comprehensive History of the Church of Jesus Christ of Latter Day Saints", Century !, 6 vol. 3:224 also "The Ensign" July 1997 Pioneer History

8. See Discourses of Brigham Young, p.473 - p.475

9. See //history.lds.org – Winter Quarters, and also www.lds.org/ensign/1997

10. See Encyclopedia of Mormonism, Vol.1, CITY PLANNING – Also see BRIGHAM YOUNG - Encyclopedia of Mormonism article

11. See Discourses of Brigham Young, p.474

12. See Encyclopedia of Mormonism, Vol.2, HISTORY OF THE CHURCH

13. See State of Utah History – THE MORMON PIONEERS

*　　*　　*

Chapter Twenty-Five

——⁓⁓⦿⦿⦿⦿⦿⁓⁓——

EPILOGUE: STATEHOOD

*   *   *

Yes, the Saints were now safe from the violence of the marauding mobs and the brutal militias of the Illinois and Missouri eras, but there would come new trials to test the true strength of their faith. In the coming years, there would be bitter cold winters, wide spread sickness, tick fever, droughts, flooding, countless ravenous Mormon crickets and hordes of huge grasshoppers that seemed determined to devour their crops. Only a miracle made up of hungry white beautiful seagulls would save those crops. On occasion, there were even some violent Indian raids that interrupted their peace during the 1853 Chief Walker war, and then again during the 1865 Black Hawk Indian war. And that wasn't all.

The year 1857 was a bleak and inauspicious year for the Mormon settlers; a year plagued by a series of unfortunate events. President Buchanan had just been inaugurated and was determined to make good on his promise to get rid of two evils, slavery and polygamy. Biased politicians and newspaper articles spewed out the anti-Mormon rhetoric that spread false and highly exaggerated rumors portraying the Mormons as being in open rebellion against the Federal government and practicing a type of gross immorality. The inflated and inflammatory reports persuaded President Buchanan, who was politically motivated to show his toughness towards the wayward Saints, and to declare the Mormons to be in a state of rebellion. And therefore, he became intent on replacing Brigham Young as the Territorial Governor. Brigham had held that position for seven years, ever since 1850 when President Fillmore had appointed him to that office, and so Brigham wasn't exactly pleased about being replaced by a political imbecile.

Adding to this already highly charged state of anxiety among the Saints, in May of 1857, Parley P. Pratt was returning to Utah from another one of his missions, this time from the eastern states. As he was passing through Van Buren Arkansas on his way to Salt Lake, a disgruntled alcoholic wife-beater accused Brother Pratt of trying to steal his wife and children to haul them off to Utah, and he consequently violently attacked and murdered poor Parley having stabbed him 3 times in the vital parts of his body. A biased judge and jury exonerated this murderer Hector McClean. They found him justified in the killing of Parley P. Pratt in that he was just trying to protect his family, and therefore not guilty of murder. They completely ignored the fact that McClean's recently baptized wife, Eleanor, had actually and inarguably already left McClean, and she had already decided in her mind to follow Parley back to Utah to be with the Saints. However, the local very biased Arkansas jury could only see that a "Damned" Mormon gigolo was guilty of trying to break up a peaceful Arkansas family and so deserved what he got.

This news of poor Parley's death hit the Saints hard, particularly as they were already being stressed by the rumors of President Buchanan sending Federal Troops to Utah. They were furthered troubled by a great deal of anti-Mormon news coming out of the eastern states. The untrue stories were saying the Mormons were in rebellion and living in sin and so many citizens were calling for the Mormons to be dealt with harshly.

On June 29th 1857, President Buchanan mobilized a complement of 2500 Federal troops to escort the new Governor, Alfred Cummings, to the Utah Territory to put the Mormons under control, establish order, and enforce the law. When Brigham Young got wind of Buchanan's plans and his intentions to replace him, and making the unnecessarily move to send Federal troops to Utah, he adamantly stated, "We will never be driven again," and asked the Saints to prepare for and resist any such military takeover. - 1

In late summer of that year, a Captain Van Vliet was sent as an emissary to Utah to ask the Mormons to prepare accommodations and provide supplies for the coming Federal troops. He had already been warned that the Mormons were in a state of rebellion and might be very hostile. However, these negative rumors were found to be totally false by the Gentleman officer. This Captain being a somewhat reasonable man and more or less sympathetic to the situation, was treated well by the Saints and he left Salt Lake City as a friend of the Mormons and would later become an advocate on behalf of the Mormon people. - 2

The worrisome news concerning Johnston's army coming to Utah along with the very sad news of the well-beloved Parley P. Pratt being murdered in Arkansas only heightened the Saint's state of nervousness, especially when they heard the very disturbing reports of a large group of Arkansas immigrants passing through southern Utah. The unsettling news only served to renew their worries all over again of being run out of their homes and being persecuted for their religious beliefs. The juxtaposition of all these events at this particular time resulted in an extremely appalling and tragic event that took place only a month after Captain Van Vliet left Salt Lake City.

This horrible and a most regrettable incident was called the "Mountain Meadows Massacre." It was perpetrated on September 11, 1857 and ended up placing an abominable stigma upon the heads of the Saints for many decades, even though the responsibility for the loathsome deed lay solely at the feet of just a few paranoid individuals. These few overly suspicious and very irrational individuals completely lost their heads during some highly volatile and emotional circumstances that came all together at a very unfortunate time. Regrettably it all erupted into a horribly violent incident that was exasperated by bad timing and fueled by exceptionally unreasonable assumptions.

As the wagon train of the harmless Arkansas immigrants passed through the countryside 50 miles west of Cedar City in September of

1857, a small group of Mormon militiamen steeped in a state of uneasiness, suspicion, and unwarranted fearfulness took it upon themselves to "nip in the bud" any type of anti-Mormon persecution that might possibly be perpetrated by the Arkansas group. These Arkansas immigrants had not given any indication at all that they wanted to do the Mormons any harm, although there were some so-called "Missourian Wildcats" traveling with them, who had made some vulgar and sinister threats.

The Missourians had joined up with the Arkansas wagon train sometime before reaching Utah. These Mormon hating Missourians, though they were few, had been loudly voicing through their crude vulgar bragging just what it was that they had delightedly done to the Mormon women back in Missouri and then boasted about what they were going to do to them in the near future. This kind of inflammatory rhetoric, not surprisingly, soon spread throughout the surrounding communities, and of course, it only served to inflame the fearfulness and resolve among the local settlers. These local Saints, a normally a good people, became profoundly stirred up by the inflammatory rumors, and the very concerning threatening prospects, as well as the highly provoking vulgar rhetoric of the "Missourian Wildcats." And then their own exaggerated and disastrous false assumptions would even further spur on their fears. And so at this point their very hostile thinking developed quite rapidly into an unbelievably paranoid state of mob mentality and thus eventually resulted in an inconceivably heinous act of an extremely hellish nature.

A day or two before the attack took place, the overly apprehensive Church brethren in Cedar City engaged in a heated debate as to what they should do and then decided to send a rider and messenger to Salt Lake City to ask Brigham Young what should be done about the Arkansas immigrants passing through Utah. Unfortunately, the ten-day, 600 mile round trip ride to Salt lake took way too long for the edgy mob minded settlers and their restless Piute accomplices to wait it out until the worn-out rider could make it back. The exhausted messenger, a Brother Haslam, was simply unable to return in time with Brigham's vital message, which said; "…we must not interfere with them until they are first notified to keep away. You must not meddle with them." So as it turned out, the order from President Brigham Young to let the immigrants pass unharmed and without interference was not received until at least two days after the heinous deed had already taken place. If the very impatient locals had only waited a few more days, the Arkansas wagon train would have moved on headed for their original destination without incident.

And so it was that the Mormon militia's dangerous and unpredictable impatience combined with their out of control paranoia incited them to carry out a bloody massacre and the unholy unjustified brutal slaughter of up to 140 Arkansas immigrants made up of men, women, and children. And yes, it did include the vulgar talking "Missouri Wildcats." This most regrettable and infamous incident was forever dubbed the "Mountain Meadows Massacre" and was perpetrated by a small group of local Saints with the aid of a small band of somewhat perturbed Piute Indians who had been persuaded to join with the angry Mormon settlers. The Piutes had been led to believe that the Missourian white men had poisoned a waterhole killing some of their tribe, which may have not been true. It was at this volatile point of critical timing that these two highly emotionally charged hot-blooded groups decided to slaughter the men, women, and children of what they deemed to be an invading enemy, and it resulted in a most horrifying scene of totally unjustified executions.

After a mild skirmish, the Arkansas men were somehow persuaded to give up their arms based on the proposal that everybody concerned in this matter, including the Mormon militia, very much desired the situation should come to a peaceful solution, being that no one on either side desired for anyone to come to any harm. This ruse was not only completely deceitful and purely evil in its intent, but seemingly totally without any conscience. So after the Arkansas men gave up their rifles and pistols, then without any warning, the mob-minded Mormon men carried out their dirty deed. All of the unarmed Arkansas men were brutally and summarily shot ambush style. Meanwhile the women and the older children were marched a little farther to the north across the meadow and then they too were also mercilessly executed, except for the small children.

In the light of today's thinking, it seems almost impossible to believe, if not absolutely incomprehensible that four or five-dozen religious and "God Fearing" members of the Church could even come anywhere near the thinking of doing such a heinous deed. It doesn't even seem conceivable that they would actually become so crazy paranoid and so mob minded that without any conscience they would mercilessly slaughter men, women, and children during an unreasoning mindless "state of hysteria." One historian, Author Juanita Brooks, put it this way; "they were led to do what none singly would have done under normal conditions, and for which none singly can be held responsible…" – 3a

The brutal massacre of the Arkansas immigrants cannot be justified in any way, shape, or form, and most certainly shouldn't have ever happened and wouldn't have happened if this small group of hysterical Mormon settlers had only taken the time to patiently wait a few more days for the "…we must not interfere with them…" message from the President of the Church, Brigham Young. There were only 17 of the smaller children that were spared from the executions who were then taken in to live with local Mormon families. Two years later, with the help of the U.S. Army they were returned to their relatives in Arkansas. – 3b

There were some Church members excommunicated for the dreadful deed and nine other Saints indicted for the crime, but even those nine would later be questionably pardoned by the non-Mormon Governor Cummings as part of an amnesty agreement. As it all turned out, the only perpetrator that was ever punished was the pioneer John D. Lee, famed for constructing "Lee's Ferry" across the Colorado River in Arizona. It would be John D. Lee who would be formally charged as the ascribed leader and thus the only perpetrator who would in due course be executed for that crime. This halfhearted attempt to attain some kind of justice for the victims of the inexcusable murders at "Mountain Meadows" was eventually carried out by a firing squad of the U.S. Army, but only after two decades had come and gone. And it was only then that John D. Lee, the accused massacre leader, who some have called nothing less than a "designated fall guy," was finally stood up and ceremoniously executed by the U.S. Army at the very site of the "Mountain Meadow Massacre" in March of 1877. - 4

After the massacre, relations between the U.S. government and the Mormons continued to deteriorate, especially after President Buchanan unfairly and unnecessarily replaced Brigham Young with the incompetent Alfred Cummings as the Governor of the Utah territory in 1858. This act of unmerited humiliation of the Saints seemed as though it was meant to deliberately demean and shame them into "buckling under" to his authoritative directives. The Mormon pioneers naturally resisted this purely political appointment of the new incompetent governor and so further conflicts and antagonisms would come from this particular appointment.

Most certainly Government relations with the Mormons didn't improve from the time of the Mountain Meadow massacre forward as that incident only seemed to legitimize the rumors of the rebellious nature of the Mormons to the public. To further exasperate relations between the Saints and the U.S. government, the government's official opposition against polygamy and its harsh handling of the controversial issue only intensified the Saint's worrisome fears, especially when they heard that a large detachment of Federal Troops was being sent to Utah to put the Mormons under control.

After Johnston's Army spent a miserable cold winter at the burnt out site of Fort Bridger, they found the hit and run tactics of the Mormon militia to be most effective in impeding their progress as Brigham Young implemented them in March of 1858. The Mormon militias had previously burnt Fort Bridger and Fort Supply to the ground so that the invading soldiers could not use them, as well as having burned the grass feed along the trail. In addition, they made some fake cannon fortifications using black painted logs that appeared to be jutting out menacingly from the cliffs of Echo Canyon to make it look as though they were totally prepared to do some serious artillery warfare against the Federal troops.

Finally on June 26th of 1858, General Albert Sydney Johnston led his 2500-man army through a completely deserted Salt Lake City. Brigham Young had already ordered the city abandoned, and even burned if need be, if and when the army tried to occupy it. No usable supplies whatsoever were left behind in the city and even the temple foundations were buried under the dirt. When General Johnston saw that the city was completely deserted, he cussed and swore at the Mormons, but never the less chose to not occupy the city itself, and instead went on to establish Camp Floyd forty miles farther out in a desert valley southwest of Salt Lake City. The Troop complement there would eventually grow to 3500 men. Never the less, Camp Floyd was deserted a couple of years later at the beginning of the Civil War in 1861 as the troops were badly needed in the east. The temporary occupation and the completely ludicrous notion of bringing about a humbler and more compliant Mormon population, while at the same time propping up an inept Governor, and the botching of the infamous "Utah Mormon War," would all come to be known as "Buchanan's Blunder." - 5

In 1862 Congress passed a law prohibiting polygamy in all states and in all territories, and the Army proceeded to establish Fort Douglas at the very edge of the upper part of the city in downtown Salt Lake, ostensibly to protect the Overland Mail Route, but the real reason was well known. Soon after this, an anti-Mormon Commanding officer, one Colonel Patrick Edward Connor, took command and was determined that the Mormons were not going to run Utah just how ever they pleased. He became noted for strongly encouraging a steady influx of non-Mormons into the Utah territory and was intent on making sure the Mormons had as little political influence and power as possible.

The very next year Colonel Connor would become infamous for his cruelty at the "Bear River Massacre" where he commanded the slaughter of a large encampment of the Shoshone Indians located on the Bear River along the Utah-Idaho border. The unmerciful Colonel Connor ordered his men to summarily shoot the poorly armed braves as they tried to swim across the frozen waters of the Bear River to escape, and then to top it off, he heartlessly confiscated the food from the women and children that the Mormons had previously given the starving Indians. The Shoshone had been mercilessly pushed out of their hunting grounds and were half-starved when Brigham Young compassionately instructed the Saints to have pity on them and feed the Indians rather than fight with them.

As the Commanding officer of Fort Douglas, Connor was exerting great energy into encouraging non-Mormon miners and other non-Mormon workers to come to Utah to curb and dilute the political influence of the local Mormons. These actions along with additional non-Mormon railroad workers coming to Utah to construct the transcontinental railroad in 1869, gave the Saints a great deal of cause for concern about being overrun by an unrefined gentile population. And so it came to pass that many of these outsiders coming to Utah with their "Gentile" habits and their "heathen ways" insisted on settling right among the Mormon families bringing a certain amount of consternation and emotional distress to the Saints in the Utah territory.

Brigham Young became greatly concerned over these rapidly increasing numbers of outsiders. He was worried that they might become the majority and eventually try to take over and run the Saints out of their own homes as they had in the past. He was also worried that the influence of these outsiders would dilute the Saint's morals and values and play an unwanted, if not a negative and significant part, in the future direction of Utah's politics. As it turned out, this wasn't the only concern; there came into the territory certain non-Mormon civilian political groups that were supported by the anti-Mormon opposition newspapers that rose up in Salt Lake City. They blatantly attempted to counteract any political influence of the "Mormon Church" in the new territory. However, the outsiders disappointingly found out that their political tactics worked somewhat poorly given the ingrained moral fiber and the dedication to the religion of the community at large.

In any large population area, the most desirable situation is a circumstance where the local political policies reflect the views and values of the majority of the citizens who live there. That is usually most beneficial in general to the majority and community at large and throughout the region. And it is most often a circumstance that is agreeable among most of the citizens, as long as there isn't any unfair abuse of any minorities. On the other side of this social justice coin, it is a very undesirable thing when certain unscrupulous politicians and manipulating political party minorities try to dictate and force their political agenda on to the majority of the population that doesn't agree with them.

Twenty years after the first polygamy laws were passed; Congress passed the Edmunds Act in 1882, which declared polygamy to be a felony. The wide spread political opposition and the new laws against the practice of polygamy would then culminate in an exasperating and a very controversial bitter dispute over the Mormon's Constitutional First Amendment right's to practice their "Freedom of Religion" entitlement as it pertained to their plural wives practice.

Never-the-less, as time passed, the government's very adamant opposition to plural marriage combined with the wide spread and generally negative feelings of the great majority of American's across the country against the idea of polygamy, would win out and prevail over the strictly Mormon practice of polygamy. The government then made a dedicated push to eliminate polygamy and as a result there were several Church leaders who were imprisoned for their crimes of polygamy and quite a few other prominent Church leaders that were forced into hiding. To add to the Church's mounting problems of their leadership being decimated, there were also a number of confiscations of Church property due to the government's new laws against polygamy. – 6a

And so it was inevitable, just like the first warm day after a cold winter, spring weather would eventually come, and so would the great unavoidable new day of the polygamy free era of the Church, which finally came in 1890. Church President Wilford Woodruff was inspired to put a permanent and an official end to the practice of polygamy among the Saints and among all those belonging to the Church of Jesus Christ of Latter Day Saints forthwith and henceforth. In his edict, the Saints were ordered to "refrain from contracting any marriage forbidden by the law of the land." - 6b

Naturally, some polygamist groups defied the idea of having their large families broken up, and so they refused to obey the new edict. Therefore many of them went into hiding in the more sparsely populated and isolated areas of the southwest Utah and Arizona to avoid the law. A few of these small Fundamentalist polygamist groups remain today living on the Utah-Arizona border and persist in practicing their Fundamentalist beliefs while continuing to ignore the mandate of the law and the official position of the Church of Jesus Christ of Latter Day Saints.

However, they have generally been left alone and are most often ignored by the law officials of Utah and Arizona. Anyone with any kind of true compassion must feel some kind of empathy for these polygamist families that were to be broken up and separated. For practical reasons, attempting to completely eradicate polygamy would be a monumental and a very awkward task to carry out. Sticking completely to the letter of the law would be most difficult for many reasons, and so the Attorney Generals of Utah and Arizona have mostly left them alone. Strict adherence to the law would mean breaking up families, leaving women children without fathers and husbands, and creating an absolute disaster for Family Services, which would border on cruelty for those polygamy families involved. Enforcing the laws against polygamy would also bring about an enormous and overwhelming economic burden on the government and a social services nightmare for the many bureaucratic agencies involved. Any attempt to deal with the needs of these large broken up families would be extremely complicated, and it just might possibly create a public relations fiasco.

Although the Church had completely abandoned the practice of Polygamy in 1890, and even though the great majority of the Saints had never practiced polygamy, all of the previous bad PR, the awkward misunderstandings, and the adverse public relations, would continue to politically hinder the Utah territory in gaining its Statehood right up until the landmark year of 1896. It was in that year that Congress finally made Utah officially a state of the Union.

In spite of the various dedicated efforts of the non-Mormon outsiders over the years to attempt to negate in a somewhat calculated shrewd way the political sway of the Mormons in the state, the prevailing moral impact of the Saint's family oriented lifestyle has had a much bigger influence on the overall character of the territory and State. The Saint's community-wide high standards would continue to foster a significant and beneficial influence upon the different communities in the territory and throughout the state for many years to come. It would also contribute greatly to creating family friendly and upstanding moral communities, with fewer divorces, less street crime, fewer acts of violence, and fewer health problems related to alcohol and tobacco, as compared to most of America. However, Salt Lake itself is certainly becoming more secular all the time. Never the less, Utah is a pleasant place to live for the majority of its citizens. So, in spite of all the trials and the growing pains of finally becoming a respected state of the United States, the Saints had finally found their safe, secure, and permanent home in the beautiful mountains of Utah.

In the future, Utah would become somewhat famous as the State of "The Industrious Mormons" as symbolized by its iconic State logo, a bustling energetic beehive. The state would also come to be highly esteemed for its admirable attributes of Praiseworthy Moral Lifestyles, Admirable Family Values, Low Crime Rates, Meritorious State Management, Noteworthy University of Utah Medical Advances, Moneymaking Commercial Investments, Profitable Mining and Smelting, above average rate of Matriculating College Students, and having a Well Qualified Work Force for the employers in Big Business and Tech companies. Utah would also gain fame with its World Records at the Bonneville Salt Flats International Speedway, for having the World's Greatest Snow and Skiing, sporting World Class Boating and Fishing at

Flaming Gorge Reservoir and Lake Powell, and famous for those unsinkable bobbing swimmers floating in the extremely salty waters of the Great Salt Lake. However, today's Utah may be best known for being the State of the Five Most Magnificent and Spectacular National Parks in the U.S. that are visited by many millions of tourist each year. Zion's Natl. Park alone totally mesmerizes five million visitors each year.

In the next one hundred and seventy years after the pioneers first entered the Salt lake valley, Zion would grow exponentially to the vast number of nearly 17 million followers worldwide. Though The Church of Jesus Christ of Latter Day Saints would become a global church, it would always significantly, permanently, and magnificently be headquartered amongst the snow-capped mountains in the valley of the Great Salt Lake.

"And it shall come to pass in the last days, that the mountain of the LORD'S house shall be established in the top of the mountains, and shall be exalted above the hills; and all nations shall flow unto it." - Isaiah 2:2

*   *   *

1. See Utah War, WIKIPEDIA.com

2. See Utah War, WIKIPEDIA.com

3a. See Brooks, Juanita. "The Mountain Meadows Massacre," p. 218.

3b. See "Voices from the Mountain Meadow Massacre" – www.thespectrum.com

4. See Encyclopedia of Mormonism, Vol.2, HISTORY OF THE CHURCH

5. See Utah War, WIKIPEDIA.com

6a. See Encyclopedia of Mormonism, Vol.3, PLURAL MARRIAGE

6b. See Official Declaration -1 at the end of the Doctrine & Covenants

*   *   *

Printed in the United States
by Baker & Taylor Publisher Services